Pound/Cummings

Pound/Cummings

The Correspondence of
Ezra Pound and E. E. Cummings

Edited by Barry Ahearn

Ann Arbor
THE UNIVERSITY OF MICHIGAN PRESS

1999   1998   1997   1996   4   3   2   1

A CIP catalog record for this book is available from the British Library.

Library of Congress Cataloging-in-Publication Data

Pound/Cummings : the correspondence of Ezra Pound and E. E. Cummings /
    edited by Barry Ahearn.
        p.   cm.
    Includes bibliographical references and index.
    ISBN 0-472-10298-2 (hardcover : acid-free paper)
    1. Pound, Ezra, 1885–1972—Correspondence.   2. Cummings, E. E.
(Edward Estlin), 1894–1962—Correspondence.   3. Poets,
American—20th century—Correspondence.   I. Ahearn, Barry.
PS3531.O82Z4827   1996
811'.52—dc20
    [B]   96-19031
                                                                CIP

Within the right of fair usage, the editor includes the books and articles cited.

1298 -38

Contents

Abbreviations

Carpenter   Humphrey Carpenter. *A Serious Character: The Life of Ezra Pound*. Boston: Houghton Mifflin, 1988.

Complete Poems   E. E. Cummings. *Complete Poems, 1904–1962*. Ed. George J. Firmage. New York: Liveright, 1991.

Doob   *"Ezra Pound Speaking": Radio Speeches of World War II*. Ed. Leonard W. Doob. Westport, Conn.: Greenwood Press, 1978.

Eimi   E. E. Cummings. *Eimi*. New York: Covici-Friede, 1933.

EPPP   *Ezra Pound's Poetry and Prose: Contributions to Periodicals*. Ed. Lea Baechler, A. Walton Litz, and James Longenbach. 10 vols. New York: Garland, 1991.

Firmage   George J. Firmage. *E. E. Cummings: A Bibliography*. Middletown, Conn.: Wesleyan University Press, 1960.

Gallup   Donald Gallup. *Ezra Pound: A Bibliography*. Charlottesville: University Press of Virginia, 1983.

Gordon   *Ezra Pound and James Laughlin: Selected Letters*. Ed. David Gordon. New York: Norton, 1994.

Kennedy   Richard S. Kennedy. *Dreams in the Mirror: A Biography of E. E. Cummings*. New York: Liveright, 1980.

Mariani   Paul Mariani. *William Carlos Williams: A New World Naked*. New York: McGraw-Hill, 1981.

Materer   *Pound/Lewis: The Letters of Ezra Pound and Wyndham Lewis*. Ed. Timothy Materer. New York: New Directions, 1985.

Norman   Charles Norman. *Ezra Pound*. New York: Macmillan, 1960.

Paige   *The Letters of Ezra Pound, 1907–1941*. Ed. D. D. Paige. New York: Harcourt, Brace and Company, 1950.

Selected Letters   *Selected Letters of E. E. Cummings*. Ed. F. W. Dupee and George Stade. New York: Harcourt, Brace and World, 1969.

Selected Prose   Ezra Pound. *Selected Prose, 1909–1965*. Ed. William Cookson. New York: New Directions, 1973.

Terrell   Carroll F. Terrell. *A Companion to the Cantos of Ezra Pound*. 2 vols. Berkeley and Los Angeles: University of California Press, 1980–84.

Editorial Practice
and Acknowledgments

Pound/Cummings contains the surviving correspondence between Ezra Pound (1885–1972) and E. E. Cummings (1894–1962). It consists of 221 letters and cards from Pound to Cummings, 181 letters, cards, and telegrams from Cummings to Pound, 4 letters from Pound to Marion Morehouse Cummings, 1 letter from Pound to David Diamond, 3 letters from Dorothy Pound to E. E. Cummings, 1 letter from Omar Pound to E. E. Cummings, 8 letters from E. E. Cummings to Dorothy Pound, 3 letters from Marion Morehouse Cummings to Ezra Pound, 2 letters from Marion Morehouse Cummings to Dorothy Pound, a portion of a letter from E. E. Cummings to James Sibley Watson Jr., and 1 letter from David Diamond to Ezra Pound. Also included is an hitherto unpublished memorandum by Max Eastman concerning a dinner he had with Pound and Cummings. There are other letters that passed between the Pounds and the Cummingses (many more, for example, between Marion Morehouse Cummings and Ezra Pound), but I have tried to keep the focus on the exchange of letters between Ezra Pound and E. E. Cummings. Letters written to or from them by other people have been included only for the sake of clarification. I have not been able to find all the letters they exchanged. There are occasional references in both Pound's and Cummings's letters that indicate they are responding to something in the other poet's previous (but now lost) letter.

Pound's letters to Cummings are in the Cummings papers at the Houghton Library. Cummings's letters to Pound are divided in two. Most of the prewar letters are at the Beinecke Library; most of the postwar letters are at the Lilly Library. Several letters are to be found elsewhere: in the Charles Olson papers at the University of Connecticut, in the Wyndham Lewis papers at Cornell University, and in the Max Eastman papers at the Lilly Library.

I have not found the original copies of two of Cummings's letters (21 March 1942 and 24 June 1954), which were previously published in F. W. Dupee and George Stade's *Selected Letters of E. E. Cummings* (New York: Harcourt, Brace and World, 1969). I have found the originals of the twenty-two other Cummings letters to Pound published there, as well as the original of one letter to Pound published first in Noel Stock's *Ezra Pound Perspectives: Essays in Honor of His Eightieth Birthday* (Chicago: Henry Regnery, 1965). (Someone, however, abridged the letter and normalized Cummings's eccentric spacing. Furthermore, Cummings's salutation, "Share Thunderer," was changed to "Dear Thunderer.") The originals of the six letters from Pound to Cummings printed in D. D. Paige's *The Letters of Ezra Pound* (New York: Harcourt, Brace and Company, 1950) are at the Houghton Library. In a few cases Pound's original letters to Cummings do not survive, but exist in the form of carbon copies. These are so designated at the top of each letter.

When D. D. Paige was preparing his edition of Pound's letters, Wyndham Lewis wrote, "E.P.'s letters tidied up would no longer be E.P.'s letters. The 'old hickory' flavour is essential" (W. K. Rose, ed., *The Letters of Wyndham Lewis* [Norfolk, Conn.: New Directions, 1963], 466). The same can be said of Cummings's letters. To "clean them up" would be to destroy the very effects for which Cummings strove. My intention is to present—as closely as possible—a faithful version of the letters as they were received by the two poets. Spacing, spelling, punctuation, and other physical characteristics of the words in the letters have been reproduced as they appear in the originals. Where the editor has felt it necessary to intrude with an explanation or amplification, such intrusions are placed between square brackets. Pound's and Cummings's own afterthoughts and additions are placed within angle brackets. There are no omissions or deletions. All ellipses are reproduced as in the originals.

The form and number of pages of the letters are indicated at the head of each. For example, TLS-2 indicates a typed letter signed by the author, consisting of two pages. Other abbreviations used are ALS—autograph letter signed; ACS—autograph card signed; TCS—typed card signed; TL—typed letter unsigned; AL—autograph letter unsigned; AC—autograph card unsigned; TC—typed card unsigned. Signatures are located on the pages as closely as possible to the same position in the originals. Cummings and Pound often did not provide the date or the place at which they were writing. But it has often been possible to assign a probable date and place. Where the editor has done so, such data are inside square brackets.

Wherever possible, notations at the end of each letter inform the reader about people, books (including Pound's and Cummings's own works), journals, organizations, and the like that Pound and Cummings refer to. In a few cases the references remain unidentified. Readers wanting further information about some of the people named should refer to the Biographical Notes.

I am indebted to authors who have gone before me. In Pound's case, I made extensive use of biographies by Charles Norman, Noel Stock, James Wilhelm, and Humphrey Carpenter. Without the existence of Richard S. Kennedy's *Dreams in the Mirror: A Biography of E. E. Cummings* (New York: Liveright, 1980), I would not have been able to undertake this project. Donald Gallup's *Ezra Pound: A Bibliography* (Charlottesville: University Press of Virginia, 1983) and George J. Firmage's *E. E. Cummings: A Bibliography* (Middletown, Conn.: Wesleyan University Press, 1960) were also indispensable guides. Often in use were Guy Rotella's *E. E. Cummings: A Reference Guide* (Boston: G. K. Hall, 1979) and Volker Bischoff's *Ezra Pound Criticism: 1905–1985* (Marburg: Universitätsbibliothek Marburg, 1991). Previous volumes of Pound letters, edited by D. D. Paige, Timothy Materer, and David M. Gordon proved essential sources.

I am deeply grateful to all the research librarians who helped me. Special thanks go to Patricia Willis, Curator of the Collection of American Literature at the Beinecke Rare Book and Manuscript Library (Yale University); Saundra Taylor, Curator of Manuscripts, the Lilly Library (Indiana University); Rodney G. Dennis, Curator of Manuscripts, the Houghton Library (Harvard University). For their generous assistance I also thank Pamela Gray Ahearn, Massimo Bacigalupo, Henri Behar, Adriana Bonfield, Paul Bowles, Joseph Bray, George L. Bernstein, Linda Carroll, Anne Chisholm, Cathy Davidson, Guy Davenport, David Diamond, William di Canzio, Yvette Eastman, Valerie Eliot, Richard Finneran, Simonne Fischer, Richard M. Frazer Jr., Norman Friedman, Donald Gallup, Marie Goodwin, David Gordon, James A. Gray, Leo Hershkowitz, Eva Hesse, Anthony Hobson, Richard S. Kennedy, Hugh Kenner, Michael Kuczynski, James Laughlin, Jackson Mac Low, Ellen Mankoff, Julie Martin, Charles Norman, William H. O'Donnell, Omar Shakespear Pound, Zhao-ming Qian, Mary de Rachewiltz, Alastair Reid, Virginia Stallman, Mary Helen Thuente, and James J. Wilhelm. Joyce Harrison of the University of Michigan Press was the first editor there to take up this project. Susan B. Whitlock, her successor, has seen it through to its conclusion.

The Tulane Committee on Research provided funds for summer research. So did the National Endowment for the Humanities. To both I am deeply grateful.

Grateful acknowledgment is made to the following individuals, organizations, and estates for permission to use the following previously published or archival material:

The Beinecke Library, Yale University, for a drawing by Cummings showing Pound at sea (YCAL MSS 43, Box 9, letter of Jan. 29, 1936 [misfiled as 1935]); a drawing by Cummings of Coney Island "Loopoplane" (YCAL MSS 43, Box 9, letter of 9 June 1936); and a drawing by Cummings of hands (YCAL MSS 43, Box 9, letter of Dec. 1936). Reprinted by permission of the Yale Collection of American Literature, Beinecke Rare Book and Manuscript Library, Yale University.

The E. E. Cummings Trust for E. E. Cummings's correspondence with Ezra Pound and for selected lines from Cummings's published and unpublished prose and poetry.

David Diamond for his unpublished letter to Ezra Pound. Copyright © David Diamond.

Yvette Eastman for Max Eastman's memorandum about a dinner with Ezra Pound and E. E. Cummings. Copyright © Yvette Eastman.

Valerie Eliot for quotations from Thomas Stearns Eliot.

Eric Glass Ltd. for a sentence from Ronald Duncan's letter to E. E. Cummings.

The Houghton Library, Harvard University, for a portion of Theodora Bosanquet's diary, bMS Eng 1213.2. Reprinted by permission of the Houghton Library, Harvard University.

James Laughlin for quotations from his letters.

The Wyndham Lewis Memorial Trust for sentences from *The Letters of Wyndham Lewis*, ed. W. K. Rose (New York: New Directions, 1964). Copyright © Wyndham Lewis Memorial Trust.

The Estate of Archibald MacLeish for two sentences from an unpublished letter by Archibald MacLeish to Ezra Pound, November 13, 1939. Quoted by permission of the Estate of Archibald MacLeish.

New Directions Publishing Corporation for selected lines from Ezra Pound's published poetry and prose. Reprinted by permission of New Directions Publishing Corporation.

The Ezra Pound Literary Property Trust for Ezra Pound's correspondence with E. E. Cummings.

Omar S. Pound for unpublished letters by Dorothy Pound and Omar S. Pound to E. E. Cummings. Copyright © Omar S. Pound.

Introduction

This edition had a number of beginnings. As David Gordon reveals in *Ezra Pound and James Laughlin: Selected Letters,* Laughlin wrote to Dorothy Pound on 26 January 1971 that he was discussing with Ezra the possibility of bringing out an edition of the correspondence between Pound and Cummings. Nothing came of the suggestion at the time, but in the mid-1980s Laughlin began again to think seriously about such a project. Eventually New Directions asked me to look into the poets' letters and assess whether they should be published. Although New Directions decided not to proceed with the volume, credit is due to them and to James Laughlin for providing the initial impetus, which has finally resulted in the publication of *Pound/Cummings*.

The true genesis of this book may be located in 1921, when Pound and Cummings first met. They were introduced on a Paris street by Scofield Thayer, editor of the *Dial*. The *Dial* was then the most influential of the avant-garde little magazines in the United States. Cummings's poems, prose, and drawings had already been prominently featured in the *Dial* in 1920. Pound and he shared space in the June 1920 issue, where Pound's "The Fourth Canto" and Cummings's review of T. S. Eliot's *Poems* (1919) appeared. Pound was the older (by nine years) of the two and much more experienced in the art of literary politics. He had begun making his reputation in London when Cummings was still a student at the Cambridge Latin School. But Pound's name had carried back across the Atlantic by 1915, when Cummings was introduced to his work by S. Foster Damon. This first acquaintance with such early works as *Canzoni, Ripostes,* and *Cathay* marked the beginning of Cummings's deep and lifelong respect for Pound.

Cummings recorded the first Paris encounter in a letter he wrote to his parents on 23 July 1921. "The other night,as we were walking back from the Rip revue 'Ca Va' Pound disengaged himself from a pillar and bowed. Thayer had previously threatened to allow me to meet the great one,I had demurred. 'Sooner than might have been expected' was P's remark:leaving the editor at that person's hotel I began an evening with the poet. Which lasted until the croissement of the Boulevard S Germain with the rue des Saints Pères, where I tentatively promised to visit the great one and disappeared. If it would amuse you:Mr. Ezra Pound is a man of my own height,reddish goatee and ear whiskers,heavier built,moves nicely,temperament very similar to J. Sibley Watson Jr.(as remarked by Thayer)—same timidity and subtlety,not nearly so inhibited. Altogether,for me,a gymnastic personality. Or in other words somebody,and intricate" (*Selected Letters,* 79). For the next two decades Paris would be the rendezvous for Cummings and Pound, and Cummings's happiest recollections of the older poet would be associated with the City of Light.

Contact between Pound and Cummings in the years when Cummings was living in Paris (1921–23) seems, however, to have been quite limited. A letter Cummings wrote to his mother on 24 October 1923 suggests that he was infrequently in Pound's company. "In fact Kantor took me around the Pound's studio(I had been once introduced by Thayer,in Paris)where we had much and excellent tea. (Note: Pound liked the pomes.and is taking [for the first number of Ford Madox Ford's *Transatlantic Review*] 4 out of 5(the 5th being too rough for the Hinglish Sensor). As you may know,I have for some years been an admirer of Pound's poetry:personally,he sometimes gives me a FatherComplex)" (*Selected Letters,* 104). The remark about the "FatherComplex" jokingly indicates why Cummings may have limited his personal encounters with Pound. The dynamic, energetic Pound seems to have awed and intimidated Cummings. Traces of that awe were still evident in 1957, when Cummings wrote to Charles Norman, "& please let me make something onceforall clear:from my standpoint,not EEC but EP is the authentic 'innovator';the true trailblazer of an epoch;'this selfstyled world's greatest and most generous literary figure'—nor shall I ever forget the thrill I experienced on first reading 'The Return'" (*Selected Letters,* 254).

The first letter of the surviving correspondence dates from November 1926. In it Pound appeals to Cummings for his assistance with Pound's planned periodical, the *Exile.* The beginning of the letter indicates that Pound thinks of it primarily as a literary journal. But at its close he remarks that he would prefer to see a contribution from Cummings somewhat like "bits of the E[normous]. Room that were good and not in the least bit clever." In other words, Pound asks for prose, not the poems that were making Cummings a reputation as a radical, daring experimenter with the English language. Pound's dissatisfaction with governments had aroused his interest in economic and political issues. This first letter to Cummings is balanced between Pound's former interests in literary production and his more recent concern with circumstances that repress or prevent human achievement in the arts and in other fields. In the future, Pound would most value Cummings for those poems and prose works—in particular, *Eimi*—which denounced political and ideological bullying. Hence the preference Pound expresses for the "bits" of *The Enormous Room* that most lucidly describe the injustices visited on Cummings and the other inmates of the French detention compound.

The correspondence between Pound and Cummings in the years 1926–33 might best be described as spasmodic. Pound wrote to Cummings when he had something specific to request, such as help in gathering material for the projected "American" issue of the Brussels journal *Variétés.* On two occasions Pound asks permission from Cummings to include poems in anthologies he is editing. Clearly

Pound thought of Cummings as one of the livelier contemporary poets—but only *one* of them. In 1933, however, Pound read *Eimi*. Thereafter his typewriter went into high gear and he wrote Cummings quite frequently. *Eimi* proved that Cummings—so far as Pound was concerned—was the man who could and would plumb the depths of twentieth-century political folly and knavery. In short, Pound saw in Cummings someone who had the talent to join him in his crusade for a better world.

Pound was correct in his assessment of Cummings, up to a point. Cummings had a settled dislike for big, intrusive government and any school of thought that hampered individual freedom in the name of a greater good. After all, Cummings had quoted approvingly a remark made to him in Russia about the nature of communism as simply "everyone ecstatically minding everyone else's business" (*Eimi*, 126). Furthermore, he saw totalitarian tendencies dominating the world in his lifetime. As he notes in "Is Something Wrong?" (*Harper's*, April 1945): "all over a socalled world, hundreds of millions of servile and insolent inhuman unbeings are busily rolling and unrolling in the enlightenment of propaganda. So what? There are still a few erect human beings in the socalled world." Where Cummings parted company with Pound was over the question of the role of the artist in such a world. Pound thought the artist should take sides with those who wanted to make the world safe for individual liberty, even if some of those allies were political leaders—such as Mussolini. Cummings had no use for direct political action beyond entering a voting booth, because he thought grand schemes to improve mankind were at best ridiculous. One of his comments on human fallibility suggests that such projects were bound to fail: "For life is mercilessly not what anyone believes, and mercifully is life not what a hundred times a thousand times a million anyones believe they believe" (*Eimi*, 88).

Of course Cummings, like Pound, considered his art an appropriate medium for expressing some degree of political truth. Cummings felt moved to sketch individuals beset by oppression, such as Olaf, in his poem, "i sing of Olaf glad and big." Olaf, a conscientious objector, is mercilessly persecuted by fellow soldiers of the U.S. Army, but heroically refuses to conform to their "patriotic" principles. "I will not kiss your fucking flag," he says. Cummings himself was a pacifist. The first two words of this poem, glancing at Virgil's "Arma virumque cano," suggest it is high time that we celebrate those who decline to bear arms. Pound was delighted by the poem.

Another of Cummings's poems that Pound frequently mentioned was the antiwar "plato told." One reason he liked the poem was because he too hated war (except wars against the power of international bankers). As Pound notes in the brief chronology that precedes his *Selected Poems,* he in "1918 began investigation of causes of war, to oppose same." One of the causes, Pound believed, was the greed of armaments manufacturers and other war profiteers. Cummings's poem specifies that the shell that kills an American soldier was once part of the Sixth Avenue El. Big business, in other words, has been trading with the Japanese empire. Scrap metal has been sold overseas and returned as weapons of war. In the process someone has gotten rich. At least this is what Pound would have stressed about the poem. One might, however, emphasize other aspects of the poem, such as its indication that people do not learn from history. This rather negative dimension of the poem, though, would not sit well with Pound. He had faith that if people were shown the truth they would rise up in righteous anger.

Therefore Pound kept urging Cummings to produce a book about life in the United States that would do for the country what *Eimi* had done for Soviet Russia. That is, it would show the sorry state of the nation. As he wrote on 11 November 1934, "Since the victory at the pollparrots, the COUNTRY needs (hell yes) an historian. than which none other than the late Kumrad Kcz/ is an any way qualified." Pound nominated Cummings for the task and found him "qualified" not only because Cummings had the requisite opinions and literary skills, but because Cummings resided in the United States. Pound himself had not visited his native land since before the Great War; he no longer enjoyed an intimate knowledge of current American culture. Twenty years later, nevertheless, when Pound had been back in the United States for almost a decade, he was still calling on Cummings to join the campaign for a renovated civilization. In January 1955, he complained about Americans' ignorance of decent standards and lamented (with a nod to Robert Burns) Cummings's silence about them.

> wd/ some power to Ez shd/ giv it
> to make the Estlin's feelinkz livid
> and lead the noblest native to
>   curse the swine as Ez might do

Pound never doubted that Cummings thought as he did, nor did he question Cummings's capabilities. He assumed that only laziness kept Cummings from publishing scathing indictments of American ineptitude and corruption.

Yet Cummings told Pound plainly enough that he saw little point in such exercises. His response to Pound's summons to "curse the swine" was typical Cummings. Replying on 22 January 1955, Cummings referred him to a passage in *i: six nonlectures:* "hatred bounces." In the same letter Cummings speaks of "Joy." Cummings had little time for hatred that, if persisted in, consumes the hater. He preferred to attribute his differing reaction to cultural and political crimes to a difference in temperaments. Pound would have none of this. He continued to believe that if only Cummings were better informed, he would be roused to action. So in the 1940s and 1950s Pound hoped to overcome what he regarded as Cummings's handicap (a Harvard education) with recent books that told the truth about how the Western world has been run in the twentieth century. Thus, in March 1951, "Yr l'il friend Eva sure IZ one brright y. llady. Eddikatin the rising by quotin' 'em yr/ Sixth Av/ L, en retour via Nippon. (theme as mumbled by Ambruster in 'Treason's Peace".. and I take it it wd/ be otiose to assume that you hv evr/ heerd tell of Ambruster. AND he dunt git down to bed rok, or as near as Veith 'Citadels of Chaos.' (which the kumrad prob/ aint read.)" Eva Hesse had translated

Cummings's "plato told" into German, and Pound took this as a sign that in Germany at least there lived someone interested in alerting the citizenry to the causes of war. In the hope that Cummings would once again take up the "theme" of war profiteering, he directs Cummings to two obscure books that see conspiracy at the root of modern wars. Cummings's reaction to such recommended reading was polite but cool. At no time did he indicate to Pound that such works had opened his eyes, that he was irate, and that he was about to produce a devastating poem or book. It was not Ezra Pound, but events in Hungary, that produced his most notable political statement of the 1950s, the poem "THANKS-GIVING (1956)," which expresses his disgust with the failure of the United States to aid the rebels in Hungary.

Pound's wish that Cummings would follow *Eimi* with a similar analysis of the United States, and his insistence on thinking of *Eimi* as one of the century's prose masterpieces, is reflected in his nickname for Cummings: "The Kumrad." He begins addressing Cummings in this fashion after having read *Eimi*, where Cummings describes the Russians he meets greeting him as "comrade Kem-min-kz." Pound's use of "kumrad" is an indication of how fixedly he associates Cummings with *Eimi*; it is also an ironic reminder to Cummings during the 1930s that Cummings is most certainly *not* a comrade. In some letters Pound also refers to Cummings as "Kez" or "Kz," again recalling the Russian pronunciation of his name. Perhaps Pound kept addressing his friend in that manner in the hope that Cummings would once again produce an indictment of those aspects of contemporary life involved in being a comrade: regimentation, suppression of spontaneity, the centralization of authority, the loss of individual independence, and so forth.

One can reasonably ask why Pound did not see precisely these phenomena present in Germany and Italy, rather than in the Soviet Union and the United States. Max Eastman wondered about that too. In a memorandum (published in this volume for the first time) that Eastman made in the summer of 1939 after dining with Cummings and Pound, he recalls questioning Pound about life in Mussolini's Italy.

> "Don't you as an alien escape the regimentation wh. is the essence of it [Italian Fascism]?" I asked. "I wouldn't say you would greatly enjoy being regimented yourself."
>
> "Fascism only regiments those who can't do anything without it," he said. "If a man knows how to do anything it's the essence of fascism to leave him alone."

By 1939 Pound was firmly convinced that the ruling cliques of the western liberal democracies and the Soviet Union thwarted men who knew "how to do anything." The money power in the democracies and the communist dictatorship in the Soviet Union were alike in their determination to keep talented, benevolent men out of power. Cummings certainly agreed with Pound about the Soviets, and may have agreed to some extent in the case of the democracies, but he still refrained from springing into action. It was not in his nature to beat the drum for reform or revolution in politics. To oust one form of government and replace it with another would be futile. As he wrote to his sister on 27 March 1953, "With every serious anarchist who ever lived,I assume that 'all governments are founded on force'" (*Selected Letters,* 223).

Cummings's persistent reluctance to join Pound's crusade may also explain his curious absence of comment on Pound's poetry. Any reader of Cummings's letters might well come to the conclusion that Cummings had not read any of the poems Pound wrote after 1920. The letter Cummings wrote to James Laughlin on 23 September 1949 in support of Pound says nothing of the value of the *Cantos,* the work that Pound valued most. "Dear Laughlin—there's one poet you pub-lish;and he's very young—the youngest(am certain,rereading Personae)alive." Cummings was always quick to congratulate Pound on honors and awards that came Pound's way, and he would thank Pound for volumes of the *Cantos* as they were published, but Cummings did not mention the value (or lack of value) and pleasure he had gotten from reading them. There may have been too much of what Cummings remarked in another letter (to Pound), that is, a tendency on Pound's part to see people as expressions of principles.

Cummings may also have been hurt by Pound's ranking of other authors as more significant than Cummings. As Pound notes in a letter of 29 May 1947, Cummings did not quite rank with the "quadrumvirate" of Ezra Pound, James Joyce, Wyndham Lewis, and T. S. Eliot, the presiding geniuses of modernism. Cummings even had to ask the identity of the Irish member of the quadrumvirate, assuming at first it was Yeats. Pound had a tendency to write in code despite the fact that he was quite obsessed with exact definition in language. On 31 January 1935, he recommended Charles K. Ogden's BASIC language experiment to Cum-mings. Although Pound did not wholeheartedly approve of the approach, he praised it as an "a/tempt to clean up the brit/ muck." He was no doubt heartened that others were working for greater verbal exactitude. At times he called Cum-mings on the carpet for not doing so. On 21 March 1938 he summed up his response to Cummings's *Collected Poems* (1938). Some were "bullseyes," but some "you WUZ in to much of a hurry to write." Pound scolded Cummings for not following his advice: "ef you hadda listened to papa you wd NOT have written better poetry / BUT some of youh poetry would have been BETTER WRITTEN."

Cummings chose not to dispute Pound about who could write better poetry. He was content to point out, repeatedly, that he was a different human being and therefore wrote differently. When he wrote to Pound on 30 September 1937, thanking him for a copy of Pound's recent translation, *Confucius: Digest of the Analects,* Cummings noted that "was it Ramakrishna who . . . did discover that everyone may,via the very limits of his or her own religion,attain God?" It was a plea from Cummings that Pound recognize that individuals should be allowed to pursue their own paths to salvation, rather than being herded into a Confucian state—or into particular literary modes. In other letters Cummings subtly indicated that politics and public debate required a tougher skin than he possessed. He wrote on 9 June 1936 that the publication of *Eimi* "seems to have started ye Spank Kumains movement." He treats the subject lightly, but in fact the reaction it provoked troubled him deeply. Here, perhaps, was the true reason Cummings never again attempted something similar: not laziness (as Pound kept assuming in his letters) but a determination to avoid further personal turmoil.

Each poet gave the other advice that the other could not follow. Cummings hoped in a letter of 10 September 1945 that his old friend would now "appear not quite as conscientiously as possible concerned with the shallwesay wellfare of quote mankind unquote." Pound, of course, was constitutionally incapable of giving up the fight for political and economic reform. Furthermore, as we have already seen, no amount of badgering by Pound was going to move Cummings to write a sequel to *Eimi*. Compounding their disinclination to attend to their mutually well-intentioned admonitions, they expressed themselves enigmatically. One suspects that on Cummings's side he was puzzled more often than he would admit, especially by handwritten letters from Pound, where obscurity of reference is often compounded with puzzling penmanship as well as untamed orthography. (See Cummings's letter of 27 May 1947, where he reports to Pound that he and Marion have just "microtelescopically explored the hypereinsuperstein expanding-&or-contracting universe of finitebutunbounded chinoiserie which only our illimitable contempt for soi-disant fact impells us playfully to misnicname your handwriting.") Not that Cummings felt too proud to ask what Pound meant. One suspects he simply wanted to avoid being berated for his ignorance. The following exchange would probably have happened a good deal more often than it did, if Cummings had been so unwise as to ask for frequent clarification.

McN/ trying to get a statement out of Pine[.] (Pound, 30 June 1955)

& who *is* "Pine"? (Cummings, 15 July 1955)

YU LOUSSY litteraRRRatti, yu write a poem about Olaf large
                                               large
and big   (proof reader . . . . heah, heah.)

and then yu go off Throvianly and let a sowbellied ape bitch
the consterooshun, (NOT asking why conscription is NOW.
        and when some ole buzzard kicks the swine in
belly and stops the avalance yu say:
                              OO iz Pine? (Pound, 20 July 1955)

Of course Cummings himself was not always crystal clear, a fact Pound sometimes brought to his attention. On Cummings's side, it was not a case of retaliation. As his *Selected Letters* show, he habitually composed perplexing letters to his family and close friends.

Perhaps Pound's tendency to grow short-tempered when the "Kumrad" did not follow the drift of his letters had something to do with the tendency after the war for Cummings to write short letters and notes to Pound. The letters written by Cummings between 1926 and 1941 are generally longer than those written after 1945. Cummings may have wanted to avoid such comments as those made by Pound in a letter of July 1950.

> O.K. wot <u>are</u> you talkin about? This one (yrs 4th inst.) beats me, unless yu putt the <u>wrong</u> le'r in the envlp. addressed to S Liz
>
> ---
>
> no use tg spekkg me to git refs to JJ's opus mag. as read it fer las' time in 1922 & have other more active etc animals to conserve[.]

Pound tended to grow impatient with what he regarded as Cummings's indolence. That impatience was often expressed sharply.

Another factor besides the determination to avoid exasperating Pound may have contributed to Cummings's reduction in the length of his letters after 1945. Now that Pound was back in the United States after a residence of thirty-five years abroad, he could gauge the nation's temper and the concerns of its citizens at first hand. To put it simply, Pound no longer needed Cummings and his other American correspondents to fill him in on what he was missing in his absence. That he had been missing developments on the American scene is evident not only in the length and subject matter of Cummings's prewar letters, which served Pound as a substitute for American residence; it is also evident in those moments when Pound misses a reference that Cummings assumed he would understand. When Cummings, in a letter of 3 April 1937, mentions Al Jolson, Pound's next letter shows he thinks Cummings once again has been writing in code.

> The term Al Jolson is a bit vague to me/ that shows how far out of touch I am with my comPathriots. I reely dunno WOT iz a Al J.
>
> youah mean the fecetious touch/ the as it were un Johnsonian (Saml) phrase now and again in the midst of seereeyus an huplifting or puplifiting discourse ??

After Pound's involuntary return to his native land, however, he had ready access to magazines, journals, and newspapers. He also enjoyed as many visitors as he could stand. There were limits to the extent to which Pound could keep his finger on the national pulse from Saint Elizabeths, but he was unquestionably much better informed than before about what his countrymen were saying and thinking. In the letters after the war we find Cummings and him considering such phenomena as flying saucers, Ethel Merman, Danny Kaye, and Elvis Presley. And neither has to ask the other what he is talking about.

Pound's occasional impatience with Cummings, as expressed in the letters after 1945, rose out of a respect for Cummings's talent. Here, Pound thought, was someone with a rare capacity to do good by exposing the threats to civilization. Yet this talented artist refused to turn his ideas into action. One must be aware, in reading Pound's letters, that he considered Cummings and himself as two of the handful of survivors of the great literary generation that had come to prominence in the 1920s. Hemingway and Eliot, the best-known figures of the group, were not about to campaign for Pound's causes, as he well knew. But Pound saw in Cummings someone who had the same values and who had in his younger days been moved to brilliant expression of those values. Why, he kept asking, was Cummings so torpid when it came to the important issues? So Pound kept advising Cummings on the importance of reading the works of economists such as Alexander Del Mar, the revelations of Pound's young disciples (such as Eustace Mullins's book on the Federal Reserve), and the little journals published by other disciples: Noel Stock *(Edge)*, David Gordon *(Academia Bulletin)*, and William McNaughton *(Strike)*. At times Pound resorted to doggerel to express his frustration with his reluctant pupil: "we assert that at the time of his fall / the said kumrad / wuz more in'erested in Sally Rand / than in Tallyrand /" (letter of 17 September 1952). The rhyme borrowed from Ogden Nash reinforces Pound's charge that Cummings was content to let his muse dally with only trivial subjects.

It is understandable that Pound thought Cummings might be roused to Poundian interests and action. Both were of old Anglo-Saxon stock, both were conservative politically (but artistically daring), both were extraordinarily intelligent, and both shared a number of American middle-class prejudices. One of these appeared when Cummings wrote Pound to explain who Al Jolson was: "Al Jolson was the first kike to make a Big Racket out of singing mammy songs in blackface" (April 1937). This is not the only suggestion of anti-Semitism in his letters. Cummings sends an anti-Semitic joke to Pound in a letter a few months later (7 July 1936), and in another letter from the same year presents a parodic advertisement for a play by "an unattractive Jewish lad who failed to lay the boss's daughter despite a Christian nom de plume." Cummings, like Pound, was prepared to make individual exceptions in his relations with people not of his ethnic type. Just as Zukofsky and a few other Jews found favor with Pound, David Diamond did with Cummings. It is only fair to point out that Cummings's anti-Semitic expressions were no worse than those commonly found in the United States in the first half of this century; they were in fact much milder than comments by some other people. (I find the statements in letters from the young James Angleton to Pound more shocking than anything Cummings ever wrote.) But it is also fair to add that not every middle-class, well-educated American Gentile would use the word "kike" so casually. Artists are alleged to be sensitive, but in the case of Cummings and Pound we find a curious lack of awareness of the pain such words can cause.

This blind spot coexisted with their remarkable generosity. Pound's willingness to help others is well documented, and it appears in these letters as well. In the 1930s he would inform Cummings about magazines—such as *Esquire* and the short-lived *Globe*—willing to pay for poems and articles. Furthermore, Pound would bombard the editors of magazines and literary journals with the names of those he considered worthy contributors. Cummings was always on the short list in these letters. After 1950 Cummings was on a sounder financial footing and less in need of tips about placing his work. Pound continued to "help" Cummings, however, by directing talented young men and women to 4 Patchin Place. So many of them descended on Cummings that one can detect a certain reluctance to entertain them in Cummings's reply to Pound's insistence that Louis Dudek was worth having to tea: "sorry we received the news of your-latest-human-discovery a trifle late; but,if he's real, he'll endure till autumn(& we assume he *is* real)" (9 June 1950). Cummings too was generous. Joe Gould stopped by daily for a fifty-cent handout. A more substantial gift—to Pound—was made at a crucial moment in his career. When Pound was brought to the United States and Julien Cornell was retained as his lawyer, Cornell went to New York to see if Pound's friends could be of assistance. Cummings promptly turned over to Cornell a check for one thousand dollars. Not only was that quite a large sum in 1945, it was also money that Cummings himself badly needed. Cummings and Marion Morehouse Cummings also visited Pound at Saint Elizabeths at least half a dozen times. And Pound knew he could rely on the Cummingses to be hospitable to the young men and women he sent their way. As he wrote to Marion Cummings about Marcella Spann and Pansy Pinkston in 1957, "IF they send me their N.Y. address can I send 'em to YOU fer to tell 'em how heaven will protect the workin goil in J.York? . . . If yu kno of a job fer Marcella, spill it" (6 September 1957, letter not included here).

Despite the occasional fits of ill temper, frustration, and petulance evident on both sides, the fundamental friendship and respect they had for each other pervades the letters. They happily share anecdotes, jokes, odd newspaper clippings, news of their great contemporaries, family gossip, and recollections. On Pound's side we find little of the condescending tone that could appear when he wrote to younger authors. He writes as if to someone who, though not quite his equal, is at least in the same league. For his part, Cummings might sometimes be irritated by Pound's demands, but he always considered Pound a genuine artist. In one of a number of undated drafts of notes about his friend, Cummings had this to say.

> Ezra Pound is a damned fool,according to those who know their economics. He is a great poet,according to those who know their literatures.
> I don't know anything. Quite the contrary.
> According to my way of feeling,there's no such thing as a great poet. There's only a true poet;that is to say,a poet. This poet might very well be a fool. And he might be not merely a fool; he might be a fool who is damned. But he might be not merely a fool who is merely damned:he might be a noble fool who is God damned . . . I take off my hat to the sole and singular Ezra Pound.
> May God bless him.

The bond of friendship between Pound and Cummings extended to other members of both families. Marion Morehouse Cummings corresponded with Pound and with Dorothy Pound. She and Cummings often had Omar Pound as a guest at Patchin Place or at Joy Farm. There was also a warm and extensive correspondence between Marion and Mary de Rachewiltz, the daughter of Pound and Olga Rudge. It turned out that shared values, interests, and affection brought together not only the two poets, but their loved ones as well.

The Letters

1. Pound to Cummings

TLS-2.

10 Nov. 1926   Rapallo

Dear Cummings:
                Three week's of bad weather, driving one off the tennis court;
and the general spread of Vinalism thru the "field of murkn licherture";
possibly resurgence of early and preneecious habit, have driven me to consider
a infinitessimal review as "outlet".
                I suppose you ought to be consulted about it. I shd. like to
have you at hand to parody my editorials before they ⟨get⟩ into print; the
difficulty of getting any simple fact or idea into terms simple enough for
transmission even to the smallest conceivable number of subscribers . . . . . etc
. . .
                It will not, need we say, pay. I shall probably offer head
money, but no rates. Spectamur agendo; or rather, not by the act but the effect
shd. etc. the value be judged.
                In your case I shd. incline to overlook your early misfortunes.
                I wonder if Bishop and his scholastic friends have done any more
provençal philology (a little of it might be useful to annoy my more modern
collaborators . . . . if I get any.)
                In fact any measures that wd. save the proposed affair from the
monumental pomposity of both our generations.
                (Parenthesis. can't afford suppresion or stopage by customs house,
at the outset.)
However the natural functions are probably known by now to the majority of
our possible readers.
                Is there anyone whom one ought to have, that all of our honoured,
perhaps too highly, contemporaries absolootly refuse to print at any price?
                I don't want anything people can sell, or that they wd. find useful
⟨to them⟩ in keeping the wolverine from the portals.
                (neither do I want slabs of "work in progress" unless there is some
vurryspeshul reason for it),

Can't announce publication till I get at least three items of interest.

                yours sincerely

                                Ezra Pound

No objection to perfectly serious articles IF the authors thereof have anything to say.

In yr. own case, you neednt feel obliged to keep up to your godawful reputation for cleverness (perhaps you find it rather constricting at moments
. . . .

like, let us say Possum's rep. for decorum and subtlety.) There were bits of the E.Room that were good and not in the least bit clever.

Vinalism: A term Pound derived from the name of Harold Vinal (1892–1965), American poet. Founder and editor of the poetry magazine *Voices*. Vinal's editorial taste tended to favor poets who wrote in traditional meter and rhymes, though *Voices* permitted some free verse. The May 1926 issue of *Voices* was devoted to sonnets by such poets as Clement Wood, Benjamin Hall, Elizabeth Coatsworth, and Stanton A. Coblentz. Among the book titles published by Vinal in the fall of 1926 were *Amy Lowell: A Critical Study,* by Clement Wood; *Star Gatherer,* by Jamie Sexton Holme; *Moon Shadows,* by Sherman Ripley; *Flesh and Spirit,* by Kate L. Dickinson. Reviewing John G. Neihardt's *Songs of the Indian War* in the issue for November 1926, George Sterling praised some lines and asked the reader to "compare such with *The Waste Land.* It is the difference between a gladiator and a diabetic." In the issue for May 1926, Emanuel Eisenberg evaluated the poetry of H.D.: "Her poetry is as disembodied and unworldly as a winter star. By virtue of its lack of humanism, it has no comprehensiveness, no universality, and remains always the individual work of a single person." In another review (June 1926), Clement Wood disparaged poets who were guilty of "Eliotic ravings," calling them "Eliot-apes." Pound had no doubt also read Cummings's 1923 poem, "POEM,OR BEAUTY HURTS MR.VINAL" (*Complete Poems,* 228).

review: The *Exile,* edited by Pound. Its first number appeared in spring 1927 in Paris.

Bishop: John Peale Bishop (1892–1944), American poet. Edmund Wilson notes in his introduction to *The Collected Essays of John Peale Bishop* (New York: Scribner's, 1948) that during Bishop's residence in Europe (1922–24), he "studied ancient Provençal and took to translating the troubadours" (x). A few of Bishop's translations appear in *The Collected Poems of John Peale Bishop,* ed. Allen Tate (New York: Scribner's, 1948).

Possum's: T. S. Eliot.

2. Pound to Cummings

TLS-2.

17 Feb. 1930   Rapallo

Dear Cummings
            Van Hecke is asking me to help him make up an American
number of Variétés. I don't know whether you know the review. It has weak
numbers; but four or five together keep up a more lively average with less
chapelle than anything else I see hereabouts. He seems willing to take my word
for certain lit. values.
            I am expecting a set of yr. books, that I ordered some
weeks ago. I hope (praps vain optimism) to find an intelligent translator. In the
mean time I want yr. photo. and any suggestions you have to offer re/ what bits
of yr. work you wd. prefer to have translated into french. i;e; if there is
anything you think more representative than anything else or wd. prefer to see
transd. before anything else. OR inedit that won't pass censor in N.Y. and that
needs european imprint. (mag. is pubd. Bruxelles)
            You might mention any one (or thing) you think ought
to go in and whom or which I am likely to omit. AND a bibliography of yr.
woiks.
Photos ⟨illustrating the number⟩ to be mainly machinery etc. plus the noble
and rep. viri murkhani. Of course if you have any really funny photos.
representing the habits of the american peepul they cd. be used with
advantage. I shd. like the number to be as good as my French number of the
Lit. Rev (1918) but the photos. need not maintain the level of high seriousness
demanded by our late friend the Dial.
            Van H. has already printed photos of Voronoff
operation; the Streets of Marseilles; etc. Bandagistes' windows also a favorite
subject.
            IF you have a photo of a Cigar Store Indian or can get one it wd.
be deeply appreciated. Our autochthonous sculpture is comparatively unknown
in yourup though I suspect the c.(or segar) s. i. was possibly of Brit. or
colonial origin. Van H. has got a lot of Bernice's photos. of N.Y. I don't know
just what. Still he hasnt mentioned an indian and B's is prob. too young to
remember 'em.
                        yrs.
                        E.P.

Van Hecke: P.-G. Van Hecke, editor of *Variétés: Revue mensuele illustrée de l'esprit
    contemporain* (Brussels). Despite Pound's efforts to round up American mate-
    rial for *Variétés*, the magazine ceased publication in 1930 before it could be put
    to use.

French number: *Little Review,* vol. 4, no. 10 (February 1918). Pound's "A Study in French Poets" appeared in this issue (Gallup C327).

Voronoff: Serge Voronoff, a French surgeon who tried to rejuvenate elderly men by transplanting the sexual glands of monkeys into their testicular sacs. There are two photographs of an operation in progress in *Variétés,* vol. 2, no. 9 (15 January 1930), 666–67.

Bandagistes': *Variétés,* vol. 2, no. 9 (15 January 1930), has one photograph (by Eugene Atget) of a shop window displaying girdles, elastic bandages, and hernial trusses.

Bernice's: Berenice Abbott (1898–1991), American photographer. In the 1920s, Abbott had worked as a portrait photographer in Paris, where Pound most likely met her.

3. Cummings to Pound

TLS-1.

[1 March 1930]   [4 Patchin Place]

when through who-the-unotherish twilight updrops but his niblicks Sir Oral Né Ferdinand Joegesq(disarmed to the nonteeth by loseable scripture befisto -zr- P——nd subjesting etsemina our lightwrittens)and him as mightily distant from a fit of the incheerfuls as am our hero but naturally encore when the ittorian extroverts Well why not send your portrait of you and your portrait of me? J,says sprouts,itch'll be pigged,if only in the name of Adver the Tisement;but will they immaculate it on t'other conception(meaning Brussels)which being respondfully preanswered we thusforth are proceeding.— Play in Regress meanwhile(sub rosa s.v.p.)am trying to untangle from Carpy D.M.(alias Kid)Liveright;with a view to otherwhere(post quite the usual literally decades of shushment)pub- among whispers of Too bad & Say foo & Every Lawrence Has A stalling & What We Need Is More welfare to legs or the importance of being arnnest & A William Bleats Is A Johnnycake But Achilles Is Only A heel -lish a picturebook called CIOPW among whose Os occur likenesses of the unlikenesses beforementioned:but Ye Kid is hitting in the clinches and ruffurree Brandt&Brandt's one glasseye had an attack of sic unleashing pandemonium until the audience was on my feet to a manhole(What Comma Indeed comma Is civileyesehshun)?—Tears Lyut

I hope Variétés won't feel unitied,under the waistland or viceversa . . . For the rest,I am proud to be "translated" as you select

A recent cable from interrogation point reads:Masser Zorach maybe own one piece nicotine redman stop have dispatched angel with suitable prayers for

closeup stop no doubt Western Electric will have them talking soon but
however(signed)the enormous room stop tulips & chimneys stop xli poems
stop & stop is 5 stop him stop

it is a pleasure to hear from you, Sir!

e.e.c.

one three thirty

Sir Oral: Joseph Ferdinand Gould (1889–1957), American author and Greenwich
   Village Bohemian. The subject of Cummings's poem, "little joe gould has lost
   his teeth and doesn't know where" (*Complete Poems*, 410).
Play: *Him,* produced by the Provincetown Players in 1928.
Liveright: Horace Liveright (1886–1933), American publisher. The firm of Boni
   and Liveright had published *The Enormous Room* (1922; Firmage A2), *Is 5*
   (1926; Firmage A6), and *Him* (1927; Firmage A7). Its successor, Horace Live-
   right, Inc., brought out *ViVa* (Firmage A11) in 1931.
CIOPW: *CIOPW* (Firmage A10) was published by Covici-Friede in 1931.
among whose Os: The "Os" are black-and-white reproductions of oil paintings by
   Cummings, including a portrait of Joe Gould (61) and two self-portraits by
   Cummings (63, 64).
Brandt&Brandt's: Cummings was represented by the literary agency Brandt and
   Brandt.
Tears Lyut: T. S. Eliot.
Zorach: William Zorach (1887–1966), Lithuanian-born American sculptor.

4. Pound to Cummings

TLS-1.

25 Marze [March] 1930   Rapallo

Yr Eimminence
            One piece nicotine refined woodlady 2 views ⟨recd.⟩. re/
regress priority claimed. Expressed thanks già Sacher Zorach. Ever a pleasure to
have something to decipher that AINT dear Jim or oedipous Gertie.
Bibliography duly registered. Competition of soviet number Variétés
demanding all poss. pathriotic zeal. Mr Rus. Wright appreciated.
            HELLass have llost the llovelly pixture (helas only nzp cut) of nat.
com. of largeladies visiting blanchehouse.
            Wots the belgium fer "Yale"?

tears of nostalgic inwit welling at name of Patchin youth returns aged thorax.
Cd. use yet again more seegar injuns.

N.Y.Herald Paris has beat us on Coolidge, one of Cal. with parrot that in onconscious humour defies concurrence. Besides one might find something of more topical interest.

agreez, etc.

E

Does a venerable figure called Dahler still live at No. 7. Pat. Pl.?

Jim: James Joyce.
Gertie: Gertrude Stein.
soviet number : *Variétés,* vol. 2, no. 11 (15 March 1930), included an anthology of writing by young Russians, including Isaac Babel, Ilya Ehrenburg, Serge Eisenine, Vladimir Mayakovsky, and Boris Pasternak.
Wright: Russel Wright (1904–1976), American designer.
Dahler: Warren Dahler, a painter Pound met during his stay in New York in 1910–11. Pound refers to him in Canto 80, *The Cantos of Ezra Pound* (New York: New Directions, 1970), 508.

5. Pound to Cummings

TLS-2.

24 Jan. [1931]   Rapallo

My Dear Estlin
            A noble but eXcentric character here has asked me to introduce our national minstrelsy to renewed and rising Ytaly. He always loses a little money on every book he prints (pays for same by clerking in Hoepli's // very noble character // however it seems to give him pleasure//
            Only trouble is that there is no remuneration save a couple of nicely printed (not de luxe) copies. He don't want to print more than 200 including the gifts to the authors.

The only advantage is laurel conferred by my worthy hands and the chance of the anthology more or less orienting a few of the younger wops//
            might at 500 to 1 ⟨chance⟩ act as feeler to see if ANY chance of doing continental edtns. of something better than that goddamnddd Tauchnitz will stand for (I mean without waiting ten or twenty years till the bloody hun knows (absolootly) that he can make money by selling the aged pelt.

My copy of IS 5 is in Venice at the moment. This incoherent appeal is to know whether I have yr/ permission to include 3 or 4 poems.

I don't really by law need the permish as I am adding a few lines of commentary re/ the respective nobility of the included, but I don't want to pick any man's pocket without asking him first.

I dont expect Scheiwiller (the nob. ch.) to sell out to n.r.f. like that bloody belgum bastud that occasioned my last correspondence. If Putnam don't die of ameobas first I trust he will use the remains of that former argosy sometime in the course of the year present.

Salute, we pray thee, the eminent Gould.

If you think my selection of immortals is likely to do flagrant injustice to anyone, do flag me, I shd. hate to omit all the rising Poes and Whitman's of 1931"s Manhattan.

Please onnerstan that it will not be a LARGE book. I aim at something under 100 pages.

> and remain yr/ obt. svt. as the phrase was

> E.P.

character: Giovanni Scheiwiller (1889–1965). The book in question is *Profile: An Anthology Collected in MCMXXXI* (Milan: Giovanni Scheiwiller, 1932) (Gallup B28). Pound included five poems by Cummings.
Hoepli's: A Milan publishing house founded in 1848, with a bookstore in Milan.
n.r.f.: The *Nouvelle Revue Français.*
bastud: P.-G. Van Hecke.
Putnam: Samuel Putnam (1892–1950), editor of the *New Review* (1930–32), of which Pound was an associate editor.

6. Cummings to Pound

TELEGRAM.

18 February 1931   Paris

Greetings present address American express paris include poems by all means. Cummings

7. Cummings to Pound

ALS-1.

[April 1931]   32 bis rue du Cotentin
                                                                    Paris

Dear Pound—
            your invitation received: salutations!*
            I always have to seem a Russian lesson at 2 sauf Sunday; so how
about Sunday next (19th)? Perhaps with Putnam (my circumstances not having
been shiny lately, thanks to dewteas etc)? At the Régence? I hope! if not before
                                                                    #
                            C'gs
Здравствуите, как Вы поживаете? ['Hello, how are you?']

e.g. terrace of Coupole
  Friday (17th) betw.
  7 & 7:30, to meet
  M. et Mme. C for dinner

Putnam: Samuel Putnam.
Regence: The Café de la Régence, at 161 Rue Saint-Honore.
Coupole: A café on the Boulevard du Montparnasse near the Boulevard Raspail
    (close to the Café du Dome, Café Rotonde, and Le Select).

8. Pound to Cummings

TLS-1.

23 Feb. [1933]   Rapallo

Dear Cummings
            Faber has just sent me a letter - which I take to mean he is going
to let me edit a vol. of new poetry to be printed in ⟨the⟩ fog/smothered isles of
Britain.
            I want to include yr/ trans/ of Aragons bolcheviko poEM. ⟨(from
Contempo⟩
            Am dividing the procedes among the colly/bore/eaters. I dunno what
OTHER chance the Aragon has of getting by the blasted British frontier.

As you will have frequently heard from gents. in similar purrDikkyments, the
funds at dispojal are limited. But any suggestions re/ what I shd. include, either

by E.E.C. or rising auroras of the occident will be committed to my deepest attention.

If you have time to send on, say about 8 pages of anything ⟨of yours⟩ you think the Brits. ought to have between book=covers . . . etc///

I dunno what vols. of yours they have already ????????
Other considerations being equal
Shd. be stuff that hasn't been in other books, but author shd. have got his magazine rake off wherever possible.

> yrs
>   EP

Faber: Geoffrey Faber (1889–1961), British publisher. Chairman of Faber and Faber, Ltd.

a vol.: *Active Anthology* (London: Faber and Faber, 1933) (Gallup B32).

yr/ trans/: "Red Front," *Complete Poems*, 880–97. Louis Aragon's "Front Rouge," translated by Cummings as "Red Front." *The Red Front* (Chapel Hill, N.C.: Contempo Publishers, 1933) (Firmage A12). Richard S. Kennedy notes that "the translation had been done as a gesture of thanks to Aragon, who had written a letter of introduction for him to his sister-in-law in Moscow in 1931" (Kennedy, 507n). Pound said that "Aragon has written probably the best lyric poem in favour of a political movement that has appeared since Burns's 'A Man's a Man for a' That.'" "Personalia," *New English Weekly,* vol. 2, No. 19 (23 February 1933) (Gallup C926). Reprinted in *EPPP.* Pound included "Red Front" in his *Active Anthology* (see the note to letter 14).

9. Pound to Cummings

TLS-4.

6 April [1933]   Rapallo

Dear Cummings
          Somewhere or other there is a l'er ov mine saying I want to include yr/ trans of Aragon's Red Front in a nanthology Faber is bringing out in London.
Share out and small proportional advance to contributors / Bill/ Wms/ Marianne etc.

1. Because I want it.
          also want a few poems of yrs/ not already known in England, preferably poems that have not been included in published vols. (mag. printing dont

matter), or in my Profile (if I repeat from Profile it will look as if there lacked abundance of prudukk).

2. Because I think it may be the only way to get the Red Front printed in Eng. (tho' that may be error)
    or at any rate as good a way as any immediately available.

3. I want to ram a cert. amount matterial into that sodden mass of half stewed oatmeal that passer fer the Brit. mind. or or at any rate . . . . . .

Thank either you or Covici for EIMI.
I dunno whether I rank as them wot finds it painful to read . . . . and if I said anything about obscurity it wd. far ridere polli, in view of my recent pubctns.

Also I don't think EIMI is obscure, or not very

BUT, the longer a work is the more and longer shd. be the passages that are perfectly clear and simple to read.

            matter of scale, matter of how long you can cause the reader to stay immobile or nearly so on a given number of pages.
           (obviously NOT to the Edgar Wallace virtue (?) of the opposite hurry scurry.
           ///
Also despite the wreathes upon the Jacobian brow . . .

a page two, or three, or two and one half centimetres narrower, at least a column of type that much narrower might solve all the difficulties.
         //
           That has I think been tested optically etc. the normal or average eye sees a certain width without heaving from side to side.
           May be hygenic for it to exercise its wobble . . . . but I dunno that the orfer shd. sacrifice himself on that altar.
at any rate I can see

           he adds, unhatting and becombing his raven mane. ==

but I don't see the rest of the line until I look specially at it. multiply that 40 times per page for 400 pages. . . .
         ///
           Mebbe there IZ wide=angle eyes. But chew gotter count on a cert. no. ov yr. readers bein at least as dumb as I am.

Even in the Bitch and Bugle I found it difficult to read the stuff consecutively.

which prob. annoys me a lot more than it will you.

At any rate damn glad to have the book and shall presumably continue
taken er chaw now here n naow there.

I suppose you've got a Brit. pubr/ for it or possibly Cov. has a Lunnon orfice
by naow?

Otherwise . . . yr/ opinyum re/ advisability of putting a few into anth/ as horse
d'overs or whetters.
as fer XMPL P; 338.

OH w ell Whell hell itza great woik. Me complimenks.

yrs

E

Please try to reply suddenly re/ anthol/ as Faber is weepin' fer the copy and I
want to finish the fatigue before I go up to Parigi. (address Chase Bank there
After May 5th.) but please answer this note to this Rapallo address.

EIMI: Cummings's account of his trip to Russia, published by Covici-Friede on 28
  March 1933 (Firmage A13).
Edgar Wallace: (1875–1932), a popular and prolific British mystery novelist and
  thriller writer.
Jacobian: The colophon of *EIMI* stated that "the author joins with the publishers
  in congratulating S. A. Jacobs; who designed the format of EIMI, solved all
  technical problems connected with the typesetting and printing, and from start
  to finish personally supervised the book's production."
Bitch and Bugle: *The Hound and Horn,* edited by Lincoln Kirstein, 1927–34.
P; 338: On page 338 of *EIMI*, Cummings records an encounter with "a very black
  nigger a real coon not stuffed not a ghost he might have stepped out of Small's
  Paradise."

10. Cummings to Pound

TLS-1.

Saturday 15th [April 1933]   4PatchinPlace

Dear Pound

thanks for the just received epistle!

By all means include "my" "translation" of A's Choo-choo— since
opinion of both finds itself in am;shall forbear further silence.

"Pat" alias Pascal did send you a copy of latter at author's suggestion—
probably not a numbered copy,however. However . . . ()

Re few poems of mine not already known in England,humbly-suggest-
proudly

page	line	to	page	line	inclu
240	11thfrombottom		244	8th from top	
	wouldn't this go well with puff-Puff would it				
259	last	to	261	9thfromtop	
264	12thfromtop	to	266	last	
303	4thfrombottom	to	307	4thfromtop	
351	10thfrombottom	to	353	16thfromtop	
376	19thfromtop	to	377	26thfromtop	
387	first	to	388	10thfromtop	
	(correction:9th line;-some- should be,-some-))				

sette 417   4thfrombottom   to   419   6thfrombottom
rosa   (Xaipete)

expect to leave ny for Paris,Judgement of on Saturday(? 22nd)next. What I
actually wish is a lovenest with a bathandkitchenette without too rent or one
aesthete* . . . svp let fall a mot c/oAmerican Express should any such occur to
eyes which,I hope,shall morethansurvive imperfectly-unclear-nonsimplicities-
preoptipostcal &

> here's hoping to see you well—
>   C'gs

         *comradeyorotherwise

A's Choo-choo: "Red Front."
Pascal: Pascal Covici (1888–1964), American editor and publisher.
poems of mine: Selections from *EIMI*. The numbers refer to pages, and hold true
   for the second edition (William Sloane Associates, 1949) and the third edition
   (Grove Press, 1958). See the note to letter 14.

11. Pound to Cummings

TC.

25 April anno XI [1933]   Rapallo
The pellucidity ov yr/ style poss/ apparent to yr/ own genrtn/ however if you
mean you are leavin N.Y. on last saturday: le'z ope to meet in Paree whither I
(bar obstaculation) on Thursday (prox)

Lóͳͼ ᴴͼͪͳ at 1000 a month offered by Mrs Wm. Nell
71 bis Rue de la Tombe Issoire XIV
(or potential ditto)
3 rooms in all/ bath bang an kitchenett from [app]rox May 15. unless someone
has b[lacuna in manuscript] I xpect to remain in Paris [le]ss than one month.
yrs E.P.

yrn just to hand / and am about to consider chopments from Blimi.

Address after May 5
Chase Bank/ 42 r. Cambon

Blimi: That is, editorial excisions from Faber and Faber.

12. Cummings to Pound

ALS-1.

[May 1933]   [Paris]

Dear Pound—
many thanks allthesame for info re nid l'amour &
am sub rosa writing from one "Neagoe" ⟨apparently in America at present⟩ 's
poipil pallis, perhaps known to yourself (bob 17.16) anyhow, come incog see a
sunset if otherwise unoccupied (days, we quiver among carpenters, masons
bruits etc.)
& salutation!
Cgs

Wednesday (?)

"Neagoe": Peter Neagoe (1882–1960), Rumanian-born American novelist and
short-story writer. He lived in Paris from 1926 to 1933 and returned to the
United States that May. Pound contributed to his 1932 anthology, *Americans
Abroad* (Gallup B30). According to Brian N. Morton's *Americans in Paris* (Ann
Arbor, Mich.: Olivia and Hill Press, 1984), Neagoe's apartment was "some-
where" on the Rue du Douanier.

13. Pound to Cummings

ALS-2.

[September?] 1934   [Venice]

Venice as from v. Marsala, Rapallo.

The Kumrad's reply if transmitted to Treas. Dept. will have sustained
reputation ⟨his⟩ for noted "umorismo"

———————

Nevertheless, the said Dept. does write solemnly to say "Administration iz
considerin' etc".

———————

The econ. system so god DAMN idiotic that it could be improved. Enclosure
(worn state of grandad's paper money shows it FUNCTIONED.

———————

& the thing to burn into Sec. Wallace walloci's backside or whencever his
motor reflexes emerge iz that if govt. own that thaar projuice or pigs enough
to order destruction they own it or them enuff to issue orders for delivery.
                  (OR I.E. money against the commodity.)
Granpop's money worked in Wiskonsin before the banks got the strangle hold.
Morgytau sez ⟨in reply to me⟩ "interestin' exampl of private money"—missin
the point that it was valid money against goods ⟨no matter whether privik or
pubk.⟩ without any professional logarithms. The boards were an inch thick
after planeing.
                                                    yrz. Ez. P.
with devotions to the fair Kummradess

Wallace: Henry A. Wallace (1888–1965), secretary of agriculture (1933–1941) in
   the Roosevelt administration.
Granpop's money: Thaddeus Coleman Pound (1832–1914). He issued paper
   money to the employees of his Union Lumbering Company of Chippewa Falls,
   Wisconsin. The legend on the money stated that it would "pay to the bearer on
   demand . . . in merchandise or lumber."
Morgytau: Henry Morgenthau Jr. (1891–1967), secretary of the Treasury in the
   Roosevelt administration from 1934 to 1945. On 18 June 1934, Herbert A.
   Gastons, an assistant to Morgenthau, wrote Pound, "The Secretary asked me to
   thank you for the unusual postcard [depicting Thaddeus Pound's paper money]
   which you have recently sent him. This is, as you say, an interesting 'exhibit' in
   the way of local currency." Pound wrote to Morgenthau on 7 August 1934,
   noting that "The point of my grandfather's money against lumber IS NOT, for
   immediate application, that it was private money, but that it was VALID
   MONEY ISSUED AGAINST GOODS."

14. Pound to Cummings

TLS-2.

25 Oct[ober] XII [1934]   Rapallo

Deah Kummiknkzz

My legitime is again greatly enjoying EIMI now that the copy borrowed by the woplomat's wife has been replaced, by same, who had spent years in belief that she had returned etc//

Legit/ even goes so far as to say: "It makes SENSE if you read it carefully enough" (this in disparagus of Jhames Jheezus' hiz later flounderings.) and thass thaat.

I don't suppose the sales are overwhelming/ no British edtn yet??

Is there anything I cd/ do to shake it up a bit? There are practically NO magazines / Eliot takes 9 months and a forcepps / ETC.

The Act/ Anth/ very much disliked in England/ so far so good/ wonder if copy ever reached you in Morocco or wherever?

Gimme luv to the Fair Comrad if she is still in residence.

I dare say Farrar wd/ provide you with a 'review copy' of 31/41 . . . NOT to review . . . , if he won't, I will.

Now that Bitch and Bugl/ and Chimpanzeeum are extinct/ etc. do you see, feel, or adumbrate, ANY nucleus or non=resistence to a monthly, for 1935, that shd/ at least consider the possibility of doing now something more or less nearly as active as the Little Review was yr/ infancy, back in 1917/19

Aza bruvver murkn/ I feel the country ought not to recede uninterruptedly into the state of Sigwik/Canby/Col/Harvery & the pre McKinley era etc.

Ole Doc/ Willyams iza holdin up the proletaires/ and New Democ/ every 15 days murmurs Douglas legal tender an true/
but that don't seem to me quite enough food for even an etiolated hemihebraic continent.
HELL !!!!

Are there ANY inhabitants?

I cd/ do with a monthly bulletin of Frobenius (young Fox now with him and capable of dishing it out in legible doses) Cocteau, Crevel, our selves, Doc. Willyums, I spose Joe's oral history continues . . . strictly non=proletarian . . . Five or six y/m wd/ read it if they got free copies and expected to contribute mss/ sooner or later.
I don't spose there is any nooz service in them mountings/ or that you will have noticed that Muss/ went out on Oct. 6. and buried scarcity econ/ and

damn well confirmed nearly everything I wrote in Feb. 1933 and can't bloody well get printed. requests from various that I send "literary material" LITERARY mat/ee/ree/ial.

Wal/ anyhow/ EIMI was worth writin' . . . I'll tell the trade if you think it is the least damn use my saying so.

It strikes me at this momeng/ 8.22 a.m. unless the clock's wrong that you might do a noo Deal vollum/

wot I hear about some of them koomittees iz nearly as wunnerful as MossKOW..

I don't quite know how your're to get in/ but you might save Bill Woodward's life, if you wd/ consent to make his acquaintance .. are you evuh in Noo Yok/ city. (W.E.W. 340 East 57th.)

yrz

Ez P'o

Did anything ever become of that limp but not offensive Watson, after S.T's collapse?

Jhames Jheezus': James Joyce.

Act/ Anth/: Pound's *Active Anthology,* published by Faber on 12 October 1933 (Gallup B32). It contained Cummings's translation, "Red Front," 157–69 and two "Fragments from EIMI," 173–81. The first, beginning "soon rain" and ending "smile)—I like everything" is from *Eimi,* 303–7. The second, beginning "O have you seen a prophylactic station?" and ending "I mean I've seen it and I know" is from *Eimi, 351–53.*

31/41: Pound's *Eleven New Cantos: XXXI–XLI* (New York: Farrar and Rinehart) (Gallup A37). Published 8 October 1934.

Bitch and Bugl/: *The Hound and Horn.*

Chimpanzeeum: *The Symposium,* edited by James Burnham and Philip E. Wheelwright, 1930–33.

Sigwik/Canby/Col/Harvery: Ellery Sedgwick (1872–1960), American editor. He was the owner and editor of the *Atlantic Monthly* from 1908 to 1938. In the *New English Weekly* of 21 June 1934, Pound, writing as "B. H. Dias" remarked that "The anile 'Sidge-' or 'Sedge-which' still pirouettes in the Boston jazz hall: a frowsty atmosphere; and in every number is something that had once been called modern" ("Murkn Magzeens," Gallup C1079). Henry Seidel Canby (1878–1961), American editor and literary critic, who edited the *Saturday Review of Literature* from 1924 to 1936. George Brinton McClellan Harvey (1864–1928), American editor and publisher. He edited *Harper's Weekly* and the *North American Review.* President of Harper and Brothers, 1900–1915.

New Democ/: *New Democracy,* the Social Credit journal in New York edited by Gorham Munson.

Frobenius: Leo Frobenius (1873–1938), German ethnologist.

Fox: Douglas C. Fox, an assistant to Frobenius.

Cocteau: Jean Cocteau (1897–1963), French poet, dramatist, and film director. Pound met him in Paris in the early 1920s and considered him a great poet. See Pound's "Jean Cocteau, Sociologist," *Selected Prose,* 433–36.

Crevel: René Crevel (1900–1935), French novelist and essayist. See Pound's "René Crevel," *Criterion,* January 1939.

Joe's oral history: Joe Gould's "Oral History of the World." See the Biographical Note on Gould.

Muss/: In a speech at Milan on 6 October 1934, Benito Mussolini declared that the problems of economic production had been solved and that the next step was to solve the problems of distribution.

Bill Woodward's: William E. Woodward (1874–1950), American historian who corresponded with Pound. See "Letters to Woodward," *Paideuma,* vol. 15, no. 1 (spring 1986), 105–20 and James Generoso's "I Reckon You Pass, Mr. Wudd-wudd," *Paideuma,* vol. 22, nos. 1–2 (spring–fall 1993), 35–55.

Watson: James Sibley Watson Jr., co-owner (with Scofield Thayer) of the *Dial* from 1919 to 1929. Watson had met Cummings when both were students at Harvard University; Watson became Cummings's "closest friend throughout his lifetime" (Kennedy, 81).

S.T's collapse: Scofield Thayer suffered a nervous breakdown in 1926, after which he retired to private life. Cummings had a daughter by Thayer's wife, Elaine, in 1920. Elaine divorced Thayer in 1921, married Cummings in 1924, and was divorced from Cummings in the same year.

15. Pound to Cummings

TLS-2. Enclosures.

11 Nov. anno XIII [1934]   Rapallo

Right yew air, bruvver Kumrad
             an I stuck thet francobolus not in vain. I don't see what we can DO with it save print it privately in Rapallo fer membrz ov th eeeLIGHT social register. but keep it going/ them IZ the line . . .
             ZA matr/ of act wouldn't "Blast" print most of it/ leaving Rapallo only necessity of supplying missing passages/ listed
             A.
             B.
             C. etc. where omitted.
       The rubber dollar and the man from Cape Horn/ yes/ yes/ a z artstootle sez/ swift perception of relations/   thanks for arousing that one.
Will pay to bearer in condoms or rubber goods/

[in margin] ⟨This is <u>not</u> a dignified letter⟩

Unfortunately/ for antisemites and others/ the capitalist whale HASN't an a/h /
an perhaps more is the pitty.
                    Apart from this contradiction in mere matter of doctrine/
YES/ by all means
Since the victory at the pollparrots, the COUNTRY needs (hell yes) an
historian.
                    than which none other than the late Kumrad Kcz/ is an any
way qualified. Any bits for the Noo Deal anthology. To be shown un a new deal
door under the stairs.
[Page 2. Pound's "Volitionist economics" questions printed on the left side of
the sheet.]
Just to put it on a clean peice of paper/
Caress thrice <u>de ma parte</u> the fair Kumrad/ in fact go as far as she likes,
            de ma parte (strictly de ma parte)
                yrz,
                    EZ P'o
                    out at of Patchin Pl.

Nooz item/ the Boss here rewrote the Decl/ of Indep/ on 6th. Oct I dont spoe
the murkn press haz bin TOLD yet.

Enclosures: (1) Brochure on Rapallo. (2) Pound's printed advertisement in Italian
    for concerts in Rapallo featuring Gerhart Münch, Tibor Serly, and Olga Rudge.
francobolus: "Postage stamp" in Italian is *francobollo.*
it: Enclosure lacking. Subsequent references in the letter to "rubber dollar" and
    "the man from Cape Horn" seem to be taken from this document by
    Cummings.
"Blast": *Blast: A Magazine of Proletarian Short Stories* (New York: 1933–34).
    William Carlos Williams was listed as an advisory editor.
artstootle: *Poetics* 1459a 5-7. "But the greatest thing by far is to be a master of
    metaphor. It is the one thing that cannot be learnt from others; and it is also a
    sign of genius, since a good metaphor implies an intuitive perception of the
    similarities in dissimilarities." Richard McKeon, ed., *The Basic Works of Aristotle*
    (New York: Random House, 1941), 1479.
Kumrad Kcz: Cummings.
"Volitionist economics": "Volitionist economics. Which of the following state-
    ments do you agree with? 1. It is an outrage that the state shd. run into debt to
    individuals by the act and in the act of creating real wealth. 2. Several nations
    recognize the necessity of distributing purchasing power. They do actually
    distribute it. The question is whether it shd. be distributed as a favour to
    corporations; as a reward for not having a job; or impartially and per capita.
    3. A country CAN have one currency for internal use, and another good both

for home and foreign use. 4. If money is regarded as certificate of work done, taxes are no longer necessary. 5. It is possible to concentrate all taxation onto the actual paper money of a country (or onto one sort of its money). 6. You can issue valid paper money against any commodity UP TO the amount of that commodity that people WANT. 7. Some of the commonest failures of clarity among economists are due to using one word to signify two or more different concepts: such as, DEMAND, meaning sometimes WANT and sometimes power to buy; authoritative, meaning also responsible. 8. It is an outrage that the owner of one commodity can not exchange it with someone possessing another, without being impeded or taxed by a third party holding a monopoly over some third substance or controlling some convention, regardless of what it be called.

> Answer to E. Pound
> Via Marsala, 12/5. Rapallo.
>
> > Italy."

16. Cummings to Pound

TLS-1.

December 6 1934   4 Patchin Place   New York City

Dear Pound—
I don't often wish I had a dollar and should have thereby sent you 1 "modern library" edition of The E R,not to edify but for its preface re Am per me. Possibly legitime will encounter same:my meanwhile salutations,wherein daybyday fairer comrade joins!

FLASH—New York:upon morning immediately following electionnight,the postman arrived like a swallow halfblown to the wall chez my tomorrow-75-years-old mother
                "well" he remarked <u>sympathetically</u> "we're in the soup".
And they talked of the "natural disintegration of capitalism"

FLASH—New York:Lewis Galantiere,now with Federal Reserve Bank and formerly of Chambre de Commerce Internationale when he found JJ the room & JJ wrote the book,reports(dessous la rose)
                                1st Businessman:I see Yale
licked Harvard. 2nd Businessman:So what. 1st:Well that must give the White House Jeezus a swift pain. 2nd:Listen,you got The Great White Father wrong. 1st:Owe ye-yea-uh? 2nd:If some punk fucked his alma mater that cuntlapper would hug himself.
                And the shepherdess meeting

FLASH—New York:yestreen Marion and myself visited the 2bit "newsreel theatre",watching wigglies of a small man who'd invented a concussionofthebrainproof footballhelmet vainly dashing against a large wall;then along came "F.D.R." (con Eleanor)aturkeying for lots of little Thanksgiving-orphan-CHILDREN

"first we take off the spinach" he said,meaning parsley & suiting the action to the word "which you like to eat so much;then we do" sharpening carvingknife "this:then" dumbclumbsily hackattacking corpse "we" loudening "COMMIT MURDER". Tic-ing sick-pasteboard glue-askew unfaceness . . . et les putains

FLASH—Universal City,California:a recently abouttoreturn ex-Hollywoodist says that this valley registered 125 degrees F;whereas Mr Carl Laemmle's airconditioned office,containing only ye magnate (for he feared lest the prescence of anyoneelse might cause a rise in temperature) registered 60 degrees F. One day he absentmindedly stepped out on the sidewalk and fainted

I've naught more to report,save que generally your letters gave great pleasure and especially la latest's musical addendum. Last Spring Watson was flying a hired airplane,his earthly address being Prince Street Rochester NY. If social,will take a peep at WEW;if not,he may comprehend

seeming to recall that ΠΡΟΜΗΘΕΓΣ [Prometheus] heartily inquired copiously wherewith refuting government Of the foetus By the foetus and For the foetus

τί δ' ἂν φοβοίμην ᾧ θανεῖν οὐ μόρσιμον

["Why should I fear whose fate is not to die?" The quotation is from Aeschylus's *Prometheus Bound*. See *Aeschylus*, vol. 1, trans. Herbert Weir Smyth (Cambridge, Mass., and London: Harvard University Press and William Heinemann, Ltd., 1963), 298–99.]

,I am

eec

The E R: *The Enormous Room* (New York: Modern Library, [1934]). Cummings's "Introduction" (dated 1932) is on pages vii–x, and is a conversation between Cummings and an interlocutor. Part of the conversation concerns *EIMI*.

"And have only just finished your second novel?
Socalled.
Entitled ee-eye-em-eye?
Right.
And pronounced?
'A' as in a, 'me' as in me; accent on the 'me'.
Signifying?
Am."

they talked: Perhaps an echo of lines from Pound's poem "The Encounter": "All the while they were talking the new morality."

Galantiere: Lewis Galantière (1895–1977), American playwright and translator.

Laemmle: Carl Laemmle (1867–1939), German-born American motion picture producer. Head of Universal Pictures from its founding in 1912 until 1936.

17. Pound to Cummings

TLS-1. On "Volitionist economics" stationery.

17 Dec. [1934]   [Rapallo]

My Dear Estlin/ my pious tribute to yr/ glories and pubk/ soivissis shd/ appear in nex issue of New English Weekly (obtainable at 55 Fift Ave. (Noo Democracy, office). N.E.Wkly fer 20 Dec.) G/K/ has printed Uncle HIRAM/ and so forth.

What about yr/ annoying peopl by introducing the herewithenstamped enquiries into perlike conversation in N.Y ? I know yr/ speciality is picking up the negative and oh hell more plenTiful data/

What about the rarities?

What about cohesion among the half doz or 12/ not utterly god damn idiots /

as saving of postal expenses/

perhpas the printed page is a demnition bore if you are N/Y and hearing too bloody MUCH..

mebbe only the isolated etc/

still I did read 32 pages a month even when in London.

As against what Canby lets thru/ to the perpetual and unceasing STULTific of Am Pubk/

with whom yr/ old age may be spent.

Frobenius, Cocteau (yes , still on the map) Crevel, ole bill Wms/ a few technical writers, Marianne, what a wumman/

a half dozen young who are NOT (oh hell NOT , in the least satisfied with what is printed by the week).

No NOT , a nuthr/ muggyseen for the pubk/ but of stuff you and I can read/ or the pt/ view we might conceivably ex/squeeze in private correspondence//

An there is allus ole Joe [Gould]/ unavailable//

he ought to look at these queeries.

I think, u pussnly/ (being on record as having approved yr/ entry into Rhooshy/ that you ought to investigate the Douglas movement/ New

Democracy gang ay 55 Fifth Ave/ (not perhaps mundane or Parisian ??? but still some horse sense HAS been printed in that wyper.

I file yr/ contemporary history/ I dont demand reports of what is NOT i:e: intelligence ? unless it is. and you do keep my focus or whatever rectified..
                                    ad interim.
                                        yrz
                                      B'so o

pious tribute: "E. E. Cummings Alive," *New English Weekly,* vol. 6, no. 10 (20 December 1934), 210–11 (Gallup C1128). Pound praises *Eimi.* "Does any man wish to know about Russia? 'EIMI!' Does any man wish to read an American author whom the present harassed critic has read and can re-read with pleasure?" Reprinted in *EPPP.*

G/K/: "Hiram, My Uncle," *G. K.'s Weekly,* vol. 20, no. 508 (17 December 1934), 222.

Hiram, My Uncle

My ole great uncle had a wooden leg,
Went stumpin' 'round after Gettysburg,
Ole Uncle Dot-an-carry-One!
Every gun was a golden egg
     For the bankers in New York, O . . . ooo

Here sat the bloke wot sold the guns,
A little here and a little there,
Fer to build him a palace with a golden stair
And a record-breaking lib-aireee
     To mark the fallen of Dixee.

GOLD! My Gold! Let her fluctuate!
Got ter have TAR on the Ship ov State!
We made five bones on every barrel
That was sold to calk the nation's quarrel.

Another version of the poem, with minor variations, was printed in *Poetry,* vol. 45, no. 4 (January 1935), 234 (Gallup C1132). Reprinted in *EPPP.*

enquiries: Pound's "Volitionist Economics" questions.

Canby: Henry Seidel Canby.

Cocteau: Jean Cocteau.

Crevel: René Crevel.

18. Pound to Cummings

TL-1. On a letter from Stanley Nott.

12/22/34   Rapallo

Ezra Pound Esq   December
Rapallo   Nineteenth
Via Marsala   1934
Italy

Dear Ezra Pound:
        I am interested in your article on "EIMI" appearing in this weeks "New English Weekly"
Can you let me have some particulars about it? Would it cost much to publish?
                        Yours sincerely
                        Stanley Nott

respected Kumrad/
                        here at least izza nibble/ As Nott is pubing Orage, me,
Alf Venison and the Dean of Canterbury, I dont want him not go bust (even
on EIMI), am suggesting the best thing wd/ be to photostat it/
                        brit printer will never git thru yr/lang.bdy. widge.. not
fer 400 pages.

I dont know that Nott will stand for the EIMI once he has seen it, the idea of
"plain British common sense" etc. is still deeply rooted.
                        And/or, if he takes, or if he don't take it/ I think he wd/
undoubtedly do a brief book on the noo de/ul. either in the pamphlet series/
⟨say⟩ 20 pages / or whatever came out on the brush.
                        After all fer the slow of mind, 20 pages by the agile E.E. will keep the flag
flyin.
                        Personally wd/ rather have a brief NOO vollum.
yr/ two emissions on the subject (with a few asterisks to slide 'em thru.. the
brit. censors// etc. wd/ soive ter interjuice yeh to the Nott or N.E.Weekly pubk.
⟨P.S.⟩ N/E/Weekly nacherly in crisis due to Orage's death/ cant pay/ but wd/
appreciate any Cummin/ication you cared to send it. And might even print
some JOE. Has Joe any NewDealings. If so I will suggestum to N.E.W. better
send 'em to me. a few pages to try.

Nott: Stanley Nott, British publisher. Nott published a series of "Pamphlets on the
    New Economics," including *The B.B.C. Speech and the Fear of Leisure,* by A. R.
    Orage; *Social Credit: An Impact,* by Ezra Pound (Gallup A40); *Alfred Venison's
    Poems* (Gallup A39); *Social Credit and the War on Poverty,* by The Very Reverend
    Hewlett Johnson, D.D., Dean of Canterbury.
Orage's death: Orage had died in London on 6 December 1934.
JOE: Joe Gould.

19. Pound to Cummings

TC.

[30 December 1934]   Rapallo

Deer Kumrad/ git Gesell's Natural Econ. Order or at least the money part/
from brother H. Fack. 309 Madison St. San Antonio. TexAS, and then get
round an havva good laff specially long about P. 164. just browse round till you
strike the tender meat.
                    / re the Introd to E.room/ sombuddy gimme a nenglish edtn/
wiff Graves and Tommy Lawrence . . . that wotcher mean? or some peculiarly
yankerican hoola ??
                    New Eng/ Weekly may go left wing literchoor/ no pay, but chanct
ter meet th bhoys/ got any typefodder?

greetins to the fair.
                              yrz E P'O
30 Dec. anno Xiii

one wayter keep th wolf from th door

Gesell's: Silvio Gesell (1862–1930), German economist. See Tyrus Miller,
    "Pound's Economic Ideal: Silvio Gesell and *The Cantos*," *Paideuma,* vol. 19, nos.
    1 and 2 (spring–fall 1990), 169–80.
Fack: Hugo Fack. German-born American publisher and editor of *The Way Out:*
    Devoted to Showing the Nation the Basic Causes of Our Economic Problems and
    Their Adequate Correction, and to Furthering the Realization of Our National and
    Humanitarian Ideals (published monthly). His Free-Economy Publishing
    Company, in San Antonio, Texas, published a two-volume translation of
    Gesell's *The Natural Economic Order: A Plan to Secure an Uninterrupted Ex-*
    change of the Products of Labor, Free from Bureaucratic Interference, Usury and
    Exploitation in 1934 and 1936. The first volume (1934) was the "Money Part" of
    Gesell's work. The second volume (1936) was the "Land Part." Gesell's remedy
    for economic problems was "Free-Money" (also called *Schwundgeld*), a cur-
    rency which would depreciate by a certain percentage every month. Fack wrote
    to Pound on 18 January 1940, "The Finnish Russian war would have been
    avoided, had it not been for the old meddler Britain with her Continental
    politique. I hope they will soon accept reason, make peace, neutralize the
    Africanian Colonies—all—get the Jews out of France, England and the rest of
    Europe, ship them over here so that the re-action may be intensified. As soon as
    peace is restored, and Hitler is victor, economic development will pace ahead in
    Germany on a big scale."
P. 164: Here Gesell describes the reaction of the financial speculator when faced
    with Free-Money. "Duping the public has become a difficult business. My

working capital, moreover, is invested in this carrion money and rots away in my safe. To carry out my stroke at the right moment I am forced to keep a reserve of money. If I count this reserve after a lapse of time, I find that it has already suffered a considerable depreciation. A regular and certain loss in return for a very uncertain chance of profit!"

nenglish edtn/: *The Enormous Room,* with an introduction by Robert Graves (London: Jonathan Cape, 1928, 1930) (Firmage A2b and A2c). Graves's introduction reprints part of a letter to him from T. E. Lawrence about *The Enormous Room.*

20. Cummings to Pound

TLS-3.

1/2/35   [4 Patchin Place]

Dear Pound—
                        may I insult my intelligence by reminding me that you are intrinsically what ye knights & ladies of ye slippery pasteboards have nicnamed A Trump,while extrinsically you ressemble what those selfappointed stewards of a heavenly realm or "spiritual roofgarden"(as my leaning from his unitarian pulpit with his economicosociologico background where backgrounds belong i.e. in front of you mightily father entitled it)call The Last ditto?

there is a miracle in NYCity. this miracle is worth your traveling to NYCity. This miracle is a "natural" history museum. As one(if not two)would expect,nothing in this museum is natural. All the animals are not alive(this would be natural)or dead(this would be not unnatural)but stuffed. Natural history museums are made by fools unlike me But only God can stuff a tree;hence the trees are not stuffed, they are merely sectioned. I ardently recommend the tree room,in which is a sectioned tree,cross may I add,conclusively proving that it began growing 500 A.D.. that is a very big thing for a tree to prove,Mr P;but that tree is a very big tree. The "rings", which are how a tree grows,have been counted and grouped and marked in groups and the groups have been labelled with flags bearing dates,Mr P, from the centre or birth of that tree to its circumference or murder. Of course if that tree hadn't been murdered,& murdered crosswise,that tree would have remained a mute inglorious milton. Naturally this milton would have been alive,but science doesn't care for this. Science never did care for what is alive,you know; hence mitrailleuses. What is alive has no sections,either transverse longitudinal or sagittal. Besides,what is alive has a strictly unscientific habit of growing. Corpses(if properly prepared)do not grow, hence anatomy. Close the window, Mr Manship,I feel a draghtsmanship. Science,as we both know,cares for what my father(towering like a doge through unpunctual air cluttered with wishless refractions from fragments of a prettily coloured infratransparency)thunderingly described as A Spiritual Roofgarden. ¶ Donnez-moi un arbre,SVP.

But to return to the unnatural itstory ponderum:having heard the old tree's story,we thank the old tree and proceed(for we are proceeders). We are now in the evolution room. A tree is just a tree but now we have left tree on our right and we have attained to a hollow rectangle pardon me cube full of evolution;evolution meaning all about animals. So now,I take it,we are at last among all about animals. And what do we find in this all about animals room? Why,a tree! Yessir. And not a sectioned tree either. Not an alive tree,of course. Naturally not a dead tree. Know. This tree is even more unnatural than even you and I could believe—for it is a manufactured tree. I mean that somebody made it in his spare time out of the ingredient of a discarded musicbox and a pair of old bicycletires. But mark you:every inch,naye centimeter,of this multifariously manufactured & ceremoniously synthetic phenomenon or tree is labelled;just like the real tree but not th phenomenon we just came from. That is confusing at first,Mr P,until I read you a few of the labels. Scientists are of course pederasts,as we neither know nor care;& unnaturally enough this natural history museum is a temple or cathedral of the scientific spirit,so let us get a little scientific spirit for ourselves. Standing beside this strictly scientific and not alive and not dead and not even stuffed tree,Mr P,let us pretend(P is for pretend)that we are pederasts(no offence)comma too. I reiterate:to put the whole thing in a nutshell—let us start at the bottom. What is the bottom of this tree? The bottom is PROTISTA. What is the beginning of the trunk, just above the bottom? PROTOZOA. Welwel. What happens then? A branch, bedad. The name of which branch is which? Wel it seems to be two branches. I mean that there seems to be a fork, with two whichs,one which being ENTEROCOELE and the other which being MESOBLAST. Pardon me,I have skipped a jellyfish. Not forgetting COELOMATA but of course they don't really count. Let us return to the fork,please. it is something to hang to,if you don't mind;and I do. On the first branch are hanging starfish,seacucumbers, fishes,frogs, birds,an opossum(how did he escape the NRA?)apes,and merely what men call men. On the second branch are hanging spiders,crabs(not what you think)bees,earthworms,clams,snails,and a squid. I am sure I have forgotten something. Never mind. And you don't. Whatatree whatatree.

"Owe loog" a scientifically spirited descendant of the seasquirt,aetas 9 in its last shortpants,gulped(entirely jumping before my at the moment merely cephalopodic self & totally—for an unnatural nonce—Owening not only the dendronous mechanism in question but All Evolution Personified. "Disis" our eventual concatenation of rotiferous animalcules triumphantly continued "howe LOIF biggun!"

"Ugh-huh" its oledur bruddur almost fatally hazarded

—that sir,is the Miracle Spirit for you:and well worth the uprooting of a foliate
& doubtless immemorial phobia re H2O plus x(And How)alias seawater.

But if anything else were required,My Consort will be on the dock to greet you
in case The Offical Committee OF Welcome am asleep

yours

eec

gertrude steinie
let down her heinie
all on a summer's day
as it fell out
they all fell in
the rest they ran away

"natural" history museum: The New York Museum of Natural History.
NRA: The National Recovery Administration. A New Deal program that sought to
regulate working conditions, wages, and hours in industry. The law by which it
was created, the National Industrial Recovery Act, was declared unconstitu-
tional by the U.S. Supreme Court in May 1935.

21. Cummings to Pound

TL-1.

January 7 [1935]   [4 Patchin Place]

superruthianX transoceanic swat fabulously incinerates pilule pink As Cowards
Sheer and blushful beholder's bereft borsalino bounds proudly from soi-disant
brains(item who in serene glee suddenly stood on my head)paragraph

& so let's all begin next year all over again & let's all wake up on the wrong
side of the right & turn on the raddyoh & so let's all get down on all fours &
let's all become one big mitotic family & all grow together like two little cells or
something & so let's all of us shut both our eyes wide and tight counting 1935
until I say BOOdle when you drop another five billion conundrums into Big
Jim Farley's chaise percée because didn't Polyanna The Glad cry "doles are
degrading" or something or what?

item now the Murrikun pippils are a Patient pippils so long as there's a Doctor
in the house particularly when one of his feet happens to be all the way down

their Alimentary Canal while his other hand is affectionately groping their Rectum Hesperorum. We-wee,I didn't raise my P.W.A. to be a C.C.C. is ein chic diastole if you've mastered the Longfellow or can step six rounds with a Thanatopsis,poisonally ah pif furs dat unmitigated monotony which is aptly occasioned by belatedly breathing on red combs through green toiletpaper(& they shot McKinley). Item the now one of two Broadway hits—"Thumbs Up" by John Murray Anderson—harbours an excellent frankly-antikikeanticommunist skit which frightens your welldressed audience almost to laughter(Did We Not Recognise Russia?Then Why Allow Such Travesties On The Stage?);you'd like even more however the even however less hoipolloi tapdancing of a very certain Paul Draper whose mere accent grave(not Ruth,Muriel)recently I am informed informed(via picturepostcard from Moscow)some succulent aspi&perspi-irrational crony It Won't Be Long Now before Wussia Wuns The Wurld

owe,the petty of it paragraph. Jimmy(James)Light directed the then unknown O'Neil at MacdougalStreet's Provincetown Theatre which smelt like its formerly horses. Eleanor F.(Fitzie)Fitsgerald,a hothearted Irish nolongeryounggirl(who had nurtured her god Emma Goldman's A. Berkman & cordially outkicked the equally h.h. & I. police who arrived at her diggings to snatch him for anarchy during Ye War)insisted that Him be produced. Jimmy,I think he had vetoed same,said oke & directed. Sibley the Watson put up le cash. It turned in that Him ran 45 minutes too long,horrifying all O'Neilists—whose idol had meantime moved uptown & was pouring thousands of $ into Ye Theatre Guild per Seerious Drahma beginning the afternoon before and ending the evening after;one ate,it is said,in the middle thereof. Jimmie took the book of Him to me;said:you cut what you think you can cut & I'll tell these pricks that's final. All NY "theatrecritics" puked except John Anderson(Hearst's Journal);Gilbert Seldes stood up on his toes & took a poke for art;crowds gathered;Him began "making money"—so Fitzie began paying the longdue backrent of the theatre so Watson put up de l'argent again. (Erin O'Brien Moore as Me #). Paragraph. Years past. Light sweated(sic)over monneyworries by night;his wife wrung sheets & painted a few but good pictures which almostnobody almostbought. Finally Hollywood. Two yirs passed. He returns,poor & a ghost;but a good ghost & Madame looks better than formerly even. "Gene"(O'N)now divorced,then married "Carlotta" hay hactress;inhabited France,hay shatch;ordered on dit Moxie By The Case & on sait rit cosmick crab(Lizzierus Luffed). Time,present—James struggles with punks called "The Theatre Union" which produce Proletarian Melodramas at Eva(l'Aiglon)Legalliene's 14th Street Pippil's Tearter. (She moved ⟨back⟩ uptown). Fitzie is Unioning & a lot of exmacdougals & Jimmie is trying to sell them the idea of doing Cariolanus by making the crowd a Red Mob. Yes & do they like it? "Nothing" he said to me wistfully "is so conservative as a radical".

My own father being perhaps America's earliest exponent of a(then preexisting)"science" called Economicosociologico,very am naturally ignorant;wherefore cordially second your timeless suggestion that condoms become currency. A nightwatchman in a floristshop encouraged my hope of snow;adding—just as your correspondent was sailing forth to destroy all comfortstations & join the nearest Red Corner under mistaken Und Wie impression that Taste is not the root of Aristocracy & vv—"IDDUD GIFFUH LODDUH GOYS WOIK"(meaning "iddud costtuh siddy $15,000"). Croyez-le ou non,cette neige n'est tombe qu'une fois et ça c'est pendant la nuit de '34-'35 while self was exploring Big Bad Bushwaws At Play meanwhile noting good friend Max Eastman("art is communication")'s alsoTrotsky son Dannie(whom Marion & I'd brought because his father highly approved and the kid seemed sort of kind of lonesome etc.)steer straight for the only woman in the room who inherited thirteen millions . . . dada. Ich glaube nel instinct

> Air For Muted Dumbbells
> 　　by Kumrad Nyez Neyeoo
> (author of Lenin's Lullaby or
> 　　day soitinly uhvengt Kirov
> 　　　§§§§§§§§
> 　　　here lies a national hero
> 　　　(who goverened by fits and by starts)
> 　　　framed(it was well below zero)
> 　　　in a garland of petrified farts

> 　　　　　"but my good man—how can I knock you down
> 　　　　　if you don't stand up?"

[postscript in Cummings's hand]
I should be honored to meet the enclosed somewhere,
correctly printed; for these are "the worst"
of a new family of 70: & nobody loves them and
their hands are not cold

Farley's: James Aloysius Farley (1888–1976), Democratic Party leader and U.S. postmaster general (1933–40).

P.W.A. . . . C.C.C.: The Works Progress Administration and the Civilian Conservation Corps. These New Deal programs were intended to provide jobs for the unemployed.

"Thumbs Up": A musical-comedy review. It opened on 27 December 1934 and ran for 156 performances. I have not been able to locate a copy of the play, and the original typescript of *Thumbs Up* is missing from the New York Public Library's Library of the Performing Arts.

Paul Draper: American dancer (b. 1909). Cummings had been a friend and lover of his mother, Muriel Draper (Kennedy, 273). Poem 48 of *No Thanks* is an appreciation of Draper's dancing (*Complete Poems,* 431).

Jimmy(James)Light: American director (1894–1964). He joined the Provincetown Players in 1917 and directed many plays until 1930. He directed *Him.*

(Fitzie)Fitzgerald: M. Eleanor Fitzgerald (1877–1955). She began her career as an assistant editor of the anarchist magazines *Mother Earth* and the *Blast* (not to be confused with Wyndham Lewis's *Blast*). Her activities in radical leftist politics ended with the deportation of her mentors, Emma Goldman and Alexander Berkman. She became the business manager of the Provincetown Players in 1918 and later directed plays.

Him: Provincetown Playhouse produced *Him* on 18 April 1928.

John Anderson: American theater critic (1896–1943). His review of *Him* appeared in the *New York Journal* for 19 April 1928. Though Anderson thought the play flawed, he pointed out certain merits: "The middle section of 'Him' consists of some rowdy and often hilarious burlesques of the current dramas. Mr. O'Neill, a director of the Provincetown, is kidded cruelly in a sketch on 'The Great God Brown,' the Theatre Guild and the New Playwrights for their negro folk plays, and the Messrs. Shaw and Sherwood for their up-to-the-minute versions of ancient history." Anderson concluded, "Though it can have little popular interest, 'Him' is a provocative event in the theatre, and if these notes have disobeyed orders and tried to understand the author, I hope he will do them a reciprocal courtesy."

Seldes: Gilbert Seldes (1893–1970), American editor and journalist. Seldes was managing editor of the *Dial* in the 1920s. He also had a monthly column in which he reviewed the field of the theater and the popular arts. Seldes contributed an introduction to *Him and the Critics* (New York: Provincetown Playhouse, 1928); here he noted that "There is very little obscurity about the essence of *Him*" (Kennedy, 296). He also wrote on *Him* in the *Dial* (July 1928), 77–81.

Erin O'Brien Moore: The actress who played ME in *Him.*

"Gene" . . . "Carlotta": Eugene O'Neill married Carlotta Monterey (1888–1970) in Paris on 22 July 1928. Carlotta Monterey was her stage name; she was born Hazel Neilsen Tharsing. This was her fourth marriage, the third having been to Ralph Barton. Anne Barton, Cummings's second wife, had been married to Ralph Barton before he married Carlotta.

"Theatre Union": The Theater Union was organized in 1933. It presented such plays as *Peace on Earth* (by George Sklar and Albert Maltz), an indictment of war profiteering, and *Stevedore* (by Paul Peters and George Sklar), which advocated racial unity in the labor movement.

Legalliene's: Eva Le Gallienne (1899–1991), Anglo-American actress. Le Gallienne organized the Civic Repertory Theater in New York City in 1932. The company's productions took place at the Fourteenth Street Theater. In the fall, winter, and spring of 1934–35, however, Le Gallienne was appearing in a production of Rostand's *L'Aiglon* at the Broadhurst Theater and on a national tour. During that time she sublet the Fourteenth Street Theater to the Theater Union.

Dannie: Daniel Eastman (1912–69), Max Eastman's only son.

22. Cummings to Pound

AL-1. On verso of letter of 10 January 1935 from Merton S. Yewdale, editor, E. P. Dutton and Co., declining the opportunity to publish poems by Cummings. The letter is addressed to S. A. Jacobs.

[After 10 January 1935]   [4 Patchin Place]

"Jacobs" being the Persian who setsup all my poems in his spare time (they "suggest Hafiz" so it's easy) & my mother drew out 1/2 her savingsbankaccount ∴ 70 poems (including those I sent you, [illegible]) will be printed by "Jacobs" himself in the course of 6 months or so—I'll forward a copy!

"Jacobs": S. A. Jacobs, Cummings's typesetter.
70 poems: *No Thanks* (New York: Golden Eagle Press, 1935) (Firmage A14). Published 15 April 1935.

23. Pound to Cummings

TLS-1.

25 Jan[uary 1935]   Rapallo

Waal; m ydeah Estlin an consort
                You coitunly are a comfork inna woild thet is so likely to go aphonik.
                an wot with this bootshaped pennyinsula sufferin from premature bureaucracy ANDhow !! an we allus were having such a nice quiet revolution (continua) all but the local hill=habitators who are all out and bigod they wont have any more COWS if they aint got FREEDUMB to leave tubercules in the MILK.

and soforth/ anyhow, the old line, is beginin to notice the new boys in 40 lire neckties and a forrinoffice manner, a nd I hope it busts somewhere else, so'z the boys can git on WIFF it. Anyhow/ the poEMS iz sent to Lunnon espresso with a prayer to print all that can print without pinching/ English printer's libilty/tea law being az iz.

and yes the Kikeson Trotsk IZZ real one/ gheez the semite problem blew in
here INcarnate/ ⟨broke of course⟩ and has now got a hired wop to cut the
stone, while the kike sets round being a SCULTPure.

Speakin of Ogden/ impertinent queery do I think th Kumrad's style is basic
slag/ but she admitz thet is slander and don't do it justice. [Marginal note: ⟨? so
omitted⟩] I wuz horrorfried at her levity myself. Anyhow I hope Mairet will
have the guts to print it with only such assterisks as the law requires/ tho' I
don't kno if Hem'z reppretashun reely reaches from Bowree to th Bowbellz . . .
and haow thet Beowuerry excen will penetrate Mairet's cockney EAR
                    godsinhisheavenalone can TELL.

I blush to say that Mr Eliot's later verse descends to a personal level; or rather
more exactly, starting at level refers to personal rising and isthereforequite
useless for purpose of RAISING the level of the Noo Englush Wealky.

I am afraid both yr/ eldercessors have taken a turn for the bawdy toasitwere
greet the coming yeAH.
            well thats as may bee. I am glad Watson has again decided to
soive his cuntry. Thass a good thing. I wuuzza fraid th boy had gone sour on
life. He nevvur did much approve of ole Ez/ but thassall rite so long as he aint
a dead loss.
            and I nevuh did thenk much of deh teeyater. Tho I approve of
teeyaters feeding you/ and have even cashed in 10 or 12 quid brittanic (fer
Fenollosa's ghost.)

Well an ow granpop runs on/ AT LAST a pubr/ haz askd me to write on Econ/
instead of tryin to bribe me to NOT.
Morning Post edtr/ (second in cowmand) has gone on 3 months vac// I dunno
if it was fer printin' 14 of my letters on how to save England.
            The lass thing he sez wuz/ "we can't attack the banks" (???? which
in view of what I had SHOT precedin was a touching air.)
            Well a lottuv Brit/ choinilists izza goin to Africa, som mebbe that
aint why he iz gawn.
an the Yuksheer Post has took it up where the Lonnon Mourning P/ layed
down to deeeeee. and so on.
Anni see the NooYORK ur hazza professed to differ with Lippmann. wall naow
whoda thort it.. any how, and the N.Y.Post (circ. I hear iz 1500, which is LOW
fer a daily wyper, sez Frankie musss looka th currency.
            (which iz true, even if it is inna noozwyper)

If you ever write anything you dont want me to TRY to make 'em print in the
N/eg/WkLY. please encoicl it witta red pencil.

England needs you. I am afraid my popular style is rhetorical
    just broad. not very pointed.

To Ramsay   (McDonald to
                        England)

Ye ha' ca'd canny on food and drink
The bairns can no eat your blather,
You'd buggar a horse for saxpence
Or sell up your dyin' father.

simple old fashioned songs/ I can no other. and anyhow, they wd/ pass over the
head of the pub/ulace.
note "saxpence", lowland scots for "a tanner".

In any case remember I'm oldern you are.

As for new dollar substitutes / old tradition dies hard. I saw one yesterweek
hung on pine tree by the sea bord. Such is the Mediterranean spirit.

an so forf
        Ez P'o

thither sailors trophies of the sea
            in thanks for salvation from shipwrech
                or etc/

the poEMS: Three poems by Cummings were printed in the *New English Weekly*,
    vol. 7, no. 17 (7 February 1935): "conceive a man,should have have anything,"
    "Jehovah buried,Satan dead" and "what does little Ernest croon" (Firmage
    B112).
Trotsk: Leon Trotsky.
semite problem: Henghes (Heinz Winterfeld Klussmann) (1906–75), German
    sculptor. He came to Rapallo in 1934 to meet Pound. Pound put him up and
    arranged for him to acquire some stone. According to Massimo Bacigalupo,
    Henghes "slept on the Via Marsala terrace until he was taken on as a lover by a
    local Lady Valentine." "Pound Studies in Italy, 1991," *Paideuma,* vol. 22, nos. 1–
    2 (spring–fall 1993), 14.
Ogden: C. K. Ogden (1889–1957), British philosopher. Pound had recently re-
    ceived seven books on BASIC from Ogden. Pound wrote him on 21 January
    1935 that these were the "only *set* of books issued in Eng/ that show ANY
    interest in thought Whatsobloody ever." On 28 January, Pound added, "I pro-

pose startin a nice lively heresy, to effek, that gimme 50 more words, and I can make basic into a real /licherary and mule=drivin' language, capable of blowin freud to hell and gettin' a team from Soap Gulch over the Hogback. you watch ole Ez/ do a basic Canto." BASIC (British American Scientific International Commercial) was a language developed by Ogden that reduced English to 850 common words.

she admitz: Unidentified.

Hem'z: Ernest Hemingway, the subject of Cummings's poem, "what does little Ernest croon."

Watson: See letter 21.

a pubr/: Probably Stanley Nott, who published Pound's *Social Credit: An Impact* in May 1935 (Gallup A40).

Morning Post: Robert Hield, assistant editor of the *Morning Post* (London), wrote to Pound on 5 December 1934 that "surely I have shown myself well disposed to you and your ideas. We cannot go on campaigning against the Bankers, for reasons into which it is not necessary to enter." The newspaper had printed Pound's letters on politics and economics since March 1934.

the NooYORK ur: Disparaging reference to Walter Lippman unidentified.

Frankie muss: In "American Notes," *New English Weekly,* vol. 6, no. 17 (7 February 1935), Pound writes, "The 'New York Post' has printed the most enlightened editorial that I have yet encountered:—'The Two vital essentials of recovery are . . . (1) Monetary Reform to give the Federal Government emergency control of credit. (2) Increased purchasing power equitably distributed . . . We cannot have revival of purchasing power without reform of the monetary system to permit the Federal Government to create the purchasing power. Beside these fundamentals, all other problems facing Congress are secondary . . . to deal with these . . . and gloss over the fundamentals of purchasing power and monetary reform will be building a worthy structure upon a distorted and unstable foundation.'" Gallup C1149. Reprinted in *EPPP.*

McDonald: Ramsay MacDonald (1866–1937), British prime minister (1924, 1929–35).

substitutes: Pound may refer to the smaller paper currency introduced in 1929. Or he could be referring to the Federal Reserve Notes that were issued starting in 1934. After the passage of the Gold Reserve Act of 1933, Federal Reserve Notes could no longer be exchanged for gold. Prior to 1934, the currency indicated that "The United States of America will pay to the bearer on demand . . . Dollars . . . Redeemable in gold on demand at the United States Treasury, or in gold or lawful money at any Federal Reserve Bank." The new notes, however, said that "This note is legal tender for all debts, public and private, and is redeemable in lawful money at the United States Treasury, or at any Federal Reserve Bank." See Robert Friedberg, Ira S. Friedberg, and Arthur L. Friedberg, *Paper Money of the United States* (Clifton, N.J.: Coin and Currency Institute, [1986]).

24. Pound to Cummings

TLS-3.

31 Jan[uary] XIII [1935]   Rapallo

To the rev estlin or east lynn
                Thanks for Enormouse Rm/ recd/ with preface (American)
wich
                "compares favourably" (anglicé) with thet in the Eng/ edtn.
Whether it wd/ be advice/able to reprint same in N/E/W/ or be'r ter lemme
quote it, I dunno. Wd/ rather they, if, shd/ continue noo poEMS, an in nanny
kase I ain't penEtrated the dark forest of my coll/bore/ators, le'l lone the dark
backward abyssy/um of the supposed readers and purr/chasers ov th pyper.
                Also it razis keweschuntz. Not only about gk/ pronounci/ation,
wich I dunno nuff erbout to cover a farden . . . but /and/also/nevertheless//

re/ econ ghosts. There maynt BE forces. (printed harf an inch deep on her
backside, as the black wench said to the jedge) but there IZ mechanisms/ and a
causal sequence// sech AZ if the tee/yater management is too god damn silly
(sillier than even theatrical boneheads EVER have been) as not to print tickets
fer each seat in the house. They will not have the seats filled/ (unless they go
bolo/chevik, wich wd/ bee dee/plorabl).

What happens now/ 30% of tickets fer some parts/, and then handed to ticket
scalpers, to sell at premium/ and that they call SOUND finance.

Bro/ Gingrich, seems a remarkable character. Note Feb/ ESQUIRE. C'mon in
and help me lower the tone of the paper. Ging he don't answer letters, except
once about 14 pages/ Still it is so rare a thing to get "Enclosed chq/ Mr G/ (or
whoever) says he will shortly bee writing"
that I think you might take a chanct on it.

The only bks worf a damn that I have seen coming from Eng/ apart from
econ/ are Odgen's series (about one in four) Orthological, what the helluva
word fer a bloke sposed to interest in langwitch. Insichoot/ another peacherine.
                However a/tempt to clean up the brit/ muck.

apart ça.

                also / since yew git see/reeus in yr/ pref/ the molicule EG/ or EP or
EEC, yaaas, but existing in a gd/ saline solution that slowly pickles, peetrefies
or permits to, to it, have "happen".

         This here senescent concern (as of EP) with natr. of the
gordamn solution may arter all have somefink to do with the
keweschunn. . . . . .
                   wot happens to EZ/ EEC etc. it sure does to the
Yeatsian "asylum fer me affections" i.e four walls of room not too bloody
enormouse, our uncushioned.
                   Admitting that the Harmud de/faculty prob/ didn't connect
the two ideas durin' yr/ under/grad days. and that it taint the academic
approach to econ/
                                   The question were do we lie
without interference/ izza kneeconomic one.
To say nothin' ov the more altichoodinus reaches/ WHEN do we get printed or
get th buks we want without having Stunkum Kirsteins/ Kennel/lees, maniacs,
bastids/ punks/ the murkn weakly press, with shitson Villard/ and all that
bastardly old gang of pewked begbugs obstructin the traffik.
                             hence my interest in econ/ tho' NOT
in Upton Sinclair's epoch. or in all that old crap that was pissed off before
about 1917. Gesell, Douglas/

, until you get back to VanBuren or further to blokes that KNEW <u>something</u>, I
don't care a fht WHAT, but that at any rate knew <u>something or other</u>.

NOT in itself very interesting/ any more than one wants to substichoot a
pompe à merde for the Salon Carré; but to have the damn thing THERE
blockin the traffic, between me you and the front gate/ it too bloody SILLY. It
had orter be MOVED,
      so'z we can git on with livin'.

            ef yew git me/ and tender regards to th lady.
                with apostolic fury
                     ez ever
                       E

Gingrich: Arnold Gingrich (1903–76), editor of *Esquire.* The February issue con-
    tained Pound's article, "Mug's Game?" (Gallup C1147). On 30 January 1935,
    Pound had written to Gingrich, "to run the Noo Yokker gaga you need Kumrad
    Kumminkz/ vide my New Eng/ Weekly article. The Kumrad has 70 poEms thet
    nobuddy loves. and itZa shyme he has to send'em out of the country. Not that I
    am sure London will print 'em. But still, the cachet. To git the younger pubk/
    there is nuthink like Kumrad Kumminkz/."
Ogden's series: See the note to letter 23.
asylum: "Give me the world if Thou wilt, but grant me an asylum for my affec-
    tions," is an epigraph Yeats added to *The Wanderings of Oisin* for his 1895
    Poems. Yeats attributed the statement to the Czech painter Josef Tulka, but, as

Richard J. Finneran notes, Yeats may have invented it. See *W. B. Yeats: The Poems, a New Edition,* ed. Richard J. Finneran (New York: Macmillan, 1983), 680–81.

Kirsteins: Lincoln Kirstein.

Kennel/lees: Probably Mitchell Kennerley (1878–1950), British-born American publisher. Publisher of the *Forum* (1910–16) and the *Papyrus* (1910–12). One of the books he published was *The Lyric Year: One Hundred Poems,* ed. Ferdinand Earle (New York, 1912), which prompted William Carlos Williams's poem, "On First Opening *The Lyric Year.*" Kennerley also published Arthur Davison Ficke, Witter Bynner, D. H. Lawrence, Vachel Lindsay, Edna St. Vincent Millay, John G. Neihardt, and Edgar Saltus.

Villard: Oswald Garrison Villard (1872–1949), American editor. Editor of the *Nation* during the 1920s and 1930s.

Sinclair's epoch: Upton Sinclair (1878–1968), American author whose novel *The Jungle* (1906) exposed corruption in the meatpacking industry.

Salon Carré: A hall in the Louvre for Italian masters, containing works by da Vinci, Raphael, Titian, and Veronese.

25. Pound to Cummings

TLS-2.

1 Feb[ruary] XIII [1935]   Rapallo

dear eeeeee
                         Thus Mairet/ vide enc/
Wot about some of the rest of the septuagint?

Nott wd/ like to pub/ the EIMI, but all hiz keppertel is at work. New firm. Going good. I shd/ think he might be in position to do it later.
                         It is quite definitely a case of good will and insufficient cash to pay printer.
                         Whether it is worth trying to find anyone to invest in Nott I dunno. England is england/ Banks and bookstalls may try to "GET" him for printing advance economics but they aint as brash as they were.

At any rate this line up is the livest in ENG/ and means right.
                         I shd/ be personally glad to have 'em print anything you can spare.
                         AND, on the prakkikal side, of bustin into Eng/ and the ultimate reflux onto the Eu/S/AA . . . it might appeal to yr/ baser instinks. From my point of view, looks as if London was going to move faster than the U.S. during next five years.

You might send the poEms via me/ as I shd/ like in nanny case to see 'em.

Seems to me the PyRAMid Press of Paris might do the poEMS unXpurg'd.

I will havva try, when I get the lot. IF that meats wiff yr/ Kumradly pleasure a napproval.

Mrs A/R/O/ also expresses pleasure thet you shd/ be in th pyper.
  wot I mean IZ thet the mill/ieu iz favourabl.

EP

Mairet: Philip Mairet, who succeeded A. R. Orage as editor of the *New English Weekly*.
enc/: Enclosure lacking.
PyRAMid Press: Pound probably means the Obelisk Press, active in Paris from 1930 to 1939. It had published Henry Miller's *Tropic of Cancer* in 1934 and was known for its willingness to handle "some of the most controversial books of the past half century, many of them branded as pornographic and obscene or serious or all three." (Hugh Ford, *Published in Paris: American and British Writers, Printers, and Publishers in Paris, 1920–1939* [Yonkers, N.Y.: Pushcart Press, 1980], 345).
Mrs A/R/O/: A. R. Orage's widow.

26. Pound to Cummings

TLS-2.

13 Feb[ruary 1935]   Rapallo

Deerly Belovvd Kumrad
     Differing tho' yr/ style does from that of the late Thos/ Jeffrsn, I yet feel in this matter of the nacherl histry mooZEEum thet severl ov the early incumbents of W'ite 'Ouse wd hevv apprecierated yr/ views on thet subjekk.
  AZ to yer/ ma's bk/ account/ helas!! an anny how, wotz thet to do wiff a Nenglish edishun IF, Mr Nott; two TTs making a negative un/negd/ at least in prospekk.
    Remains to be seen if the solidity UNpromised by the first three letters, is too strong fer the last. WOT thet baby SEZ iz/ second series ⟨pamphlets⟩ etc/ "You (thet iz ME, E/P) as editor wd/ be O.K.", whereat postulates shortness on a/c printn/ costs.
    but whether I autonomize or merely snuggest, is not yet clear.

And when you think what his PARENTS had him baptozed, it does seem azif a
sense of HUMour wuz not omniversal.

JUST as nooz/ the Church Assembmy (of England, 7 bishups etc.) haz up'd an
SED "employment aint WORK, woik may be a moral discipline etc/ BUT
scripschoor don't say you gotter go out and SELL it."
    if that aint one up on the bloomsbuggars, I DUNKno. "sale of ones
energy under economic pressure" aint got old daddy slap'emwith slab, behind
it and the British banks any longer . . . do we root fer religion..the half time
religion or where do go for science?

Mebbe you better take over the poesy dept/ fer a bit, an lemme an yr/ ole pop
run Social Credit/?
Butchart apologizes fer printin yr/ name along with the rest of the versifiers/
found the form locked or something, next a/m/ etc. too late . . . but wont
occur again.

I see by the Reynolds. the Bunk of Eng/ employees have brung out a comic
paper, inside the building or zummat/ sayin it is time the monopoly bust . . .
            and so forth/

            yrz
            Ez P'o

second series: Pound had hoped that Nott would be able to publish a series of
    pamphlets to follow those on the "New Economics." He wrote to Nott on 23
    January 1935, proposing a series to be called "ESSENTIAL ENLIGHTEN-
    MENT," and listed William Carlos Williams, E. E. Cummings, and T. S. Eliot as
    potential authors. See the note to letter 31.
ma's bk/ account: Cummings's mother paid three hundred dollars to help subsi-
    dize the printing of *No Thanks* (Kennedy, 351).
Church Assembly: The Church Assembly of the Church of England had endorsed
    a report on unemployment by the Assembly's Social and Industrial
    Commission.
ole pop: Pound cannot mean Cummings's father, since he had died in 1926.
Butchart: Montgomery Butchart, assistant editor of the *New English Weekly.* The
    table of contents for the issue of 7 February 1935 lists Cummings, Mary Bar-
    nard, Rayner Heppenstall, and J. P. Angold as contributing poems that appear
    on page 354. Although the other three poets do have poems on that page,
    Cummings's poem appears on page 351.
Reynolds: *Reynolds's Illustrated News,* a London weekly newspaper.

27. Cummings to Pound

TL-1. Enclosure.

[14 February 1935]   [4 Patchin Place]

catter
Saint Valentine

Dear Pound—
I appreciate and approve of your reaction to the ER preface and am profoundly
glad this little pickanniny feels unworthy to convert any maneating
missionaries

as 1 castration complex to another:"fuck" has been changed to "trick" in n e w
today arriving with editor's compliments. This (said our hero with illdisguised
restraint) settles the ? of Angleterre

I hear that No Thanks will occur in three editions(simultaneously)

> (a)"holographic",modestly priced at $99.00 per copy; and consisting of 1
>   poem—"the boys i mean are not refined" but keep it under your
>   hat—by me written with pen and ink
> (b)&(c)successively less violently valued,and in which said poem is
>   represented by its number and by a note referring the reader to said
>   (a) and by much blank space
>   —also sub rosa—sub watch—sub ward

should a responsible(i.e.honest)European publisher wish to make shine while
the hay suns,let him or her(i.e.not it)so state in writing to S.A.Jacobs,48
Charles Street,New York City,U.S.A. who's prepared to furnish what are aptly
called sheets;thereby

> (1)saving the itless considerable time & money
> (2)insuring that both versions(native & foreign)are identical as to content
> (3)eliminating 1,356,249 socalled typographical errors—since J. sets up
>   every poem himself on his own machine & a cloud of witnesses not
>   excluding your humble proofread all

but speaking of tickets & theatres I'd rather plant potatoes in a blind man's
pocket than suffer a single trick,or even an asterisk, at the prehensile hands of
those lousy limeies who are just so good no milkfed moron would trust their
fifth cousins with a red hot stove he tactfully concluded,proving his opponent's
point avec ees

—yours

Enclosure: Carbon copy of letter from Cummings to Arnold Gingrich inquiring if he would be interested in selecting poems for *Esquire* from the forthcoming *No Thanks.*

n e w: See the note to letter 23. Philip Mairet, the editor of the *New English Weekly,* had changed one word of "Jehovah buried,Satan dead," in line 23. Cummings intended that the last word of that line be "fuck," but Mairet altered it to "trick."

28. Pound to Cummings

TLS-2.

24 [23] Feb[ruary] XIII [1935]   Rapallo

My dear Estlin

dont be more of a foooll than natur has made you.

Poor Mairet is doin' his damndest/ and cant risk suppression. England wd/ certainly stop the paper the minute it fuck'd. BUT

once past the initial difficulty / and once you get a real toe hold in that funny oh very country; I dont think you wd/ have difficulty in fuckin away to ye/ cocks content, IN between book covers; and in de lookx editions.

ref/ to the Rev/ Arnaut Daniel, on the value of fast movers who like 'em slow (male as opposed to Mae's view).

I am; concretely, and without hyperaesthesia, aimin at an eng/ edtn of EIMI.

and I think a delayed fuck is worth that. (and the poem as pore Mairet did it, still retained quite a good deal of pleasure to the reader . . .

May I say to the rev/ etc/ and so forth e:e:c: as has been said to me even thru years of greater etc/ so to speak gulf stream ⟨flour's in th arctic⟩ etc . . . YOU ARE NOT known in England / however bad for yr/ feelings, this means that you aint known either MUCH or enough.

Graves' bloomsbuggy AINT enough

Tho I admit the company of bro <u>hoff</u> will be more entertainin' than that of the prospective Ogden, and whatever other bloody brits/ one can scare together.

Still, it wd/ be even more entertainin to bring <u>hoff</u> and the Archbishop together

Not that his LeftReverence has yet N/E/Wd.

WHY don't them buzzards in Noo Yok/ play bro/ Tiborr Serly's muzik.

Stokowsky keeps PROMISING, and then Tiborr has to come here or go to Budapesth fer concerts (hand made) or orchestrated.

AT any rate buggar the castration complex/ Mairet, Nott, Newsome have NOT
got it/
                    It is a plain question of the cop/ on the corner and a
shut down of the works.

Whoa down yew skittish thoroughbred . . . and wait fer the steam roller to
pass.

If we had Doug/ divs/ we could print what we liked WHEN we got ready/
            this here in'erest in soshul credit / aint confined to pertatoes.
"I kno wot you thinkin' TDAMN yer vater, dats vot you thinkin.

yr. venerable Unkl EZ

Daniel: Arnaut Daniel, twelfth-century poet whom Pound greatly admired. Pound
    may be thinking of Daniel's poem "Doutz brais e critz," in which Daniel prays
    to be with his lady so "That we lie in some room communally / And seal that
    pact whereon such joys attend / There with embraces and low laughter blending
    / Until she give her body to my vision, / There with the glamour of the lamp
    reflected" (*Pound's Translations of Arnaut Daniel,* ed. Charlotte Ward [New York
    and London: Garland Publishing, 1991], 51).
Mae's: Mae West (1893–1980), American actress, film star, and playwright. In the
    film *She Done Him Wrong* (1933), she sings "A Guy What Takes His Time."
hoff: Syd Hoff, American cartoonist who worked for *Esquire.* He illustrated
    Pound's "Reflexshuns on Iggurunce" and "Mug's Game?" in *Esquire* for January
    and February 1935 (Gallup C1131 and C1147). In the first article, Pound noted,
    "He [Hoff] has the pluperfect grasp on the type of mind to which the great
    american public has for 40 years entrusted its diplomacy and economics."
Ogden: C. K. Ogden.
Archbishop: William Temple (1881–1944), archbishop of York from 1929 to
    1942. Temple was keenly interested in social justice and was a member of the
    Labour party from 1918 to 1925.
Serly's: Tibor Serly (1901–78), Hungarian-born American composer.
Stokowsky: Leopold Stokowski (1882–1977), British-born conductor. Conducted
    the Philadelphia Symphony Orchestra (1912–38).
Newsome: A. Newsome, a British writer associated with the *New English Weekly.*
Doug/ divs/: C. H. Douglas discusses the nature of the national dividend in *Social
    Credit.* He calls for "a country to be organised in such a way that the whole of its
    natural born inhabitants are interested in it in their capacity as shareholders,
    holding the ordinary stock, which is inalienable and unsaleable, and such ordi-
    nary stock carries with it a dividend which collectively will purchase the whole
    of its products in excess of those required for the maintenance of the 'produc-
    ing' population, and whose appreciation in capital value (or dividend-earning

capacity) is a direct function of the appreciation in the real credit of the community." *Social Credit* (London: Eyre and Spottiswoode, 1935), 185.

29. Pound to Cummings

TC.

[24 February 1935]   Rapallo

day after my letter/ prob/ misdated
                                this iz the 24 th.
Re/further/flecting on the luminous sentence that there are 70/ and unloved. I suggest you send on the lot/ and i will take it UP with the Rev. Eliot, who will I believe nnjoy the text. and be no longer as in case of some of yr/ earlier wersers, oppressed by the feelink thet yew air treadin on the tailof his shoe leather. If Faber wont/ I shall try a new pubr/ called Nott, with two TTs. and an all too luring pun initially. who seems rathe to tread where others tread not. Of course the asteriskial risk is higher in Eng/ than in Am/ but also the moral force is greater and N/Yuk needs dis/ci/pline / and OhYeah/ and we believe so. If you gotta contax wiff Fortune (th maggy/zeum) poke 'em up re/ Fox' note on Frobenius/ confound em it ought to bbeeee printed. T.S.E. Bloomsbgd on subjekk cause some aqq like Kaiserling has been spreaddin smoak SCREEN/ ohelllllll and a brit/ zsplorer differs my Xxxxt. and so on.

queery/ why does the Yale Univ/ Press respect the New Porker and think brother Gingrich's paper for men IZ L o w ?? I try to unnerstan my country . . . and I beeliev Ging/ pays a higher rate/ also wd/ provide a hoAM fer unloved poEMS . . if. . . . and then enters the unknowd CONponent wich I again fail to penEtrate. Of coarse (very coarse) theN/Pkr DOES 4 or 5 cols/ of ads fer one of next. and Ging hasn't that amount of underbush. I see THAT. but thought Condé invented it.

70: The seventy poems of *No Thanks.*
Fox' note: Probably a reference to Douglas C. Fox's article, "Culture in the Rocks," published in the May 1937 issue of *Globe*. See the note to letter 63.
Kaiserling: Hermann Alexander, Graf von Keyserling (1880–1946), German social philosopher.
Yale Univ/ Press: Pound was corresponding with Eugene Davidson of the Yale University Press about possible publication of a new work by Pound. On 24 February 1935, Pound wrote him, "Stanley Nott, is doing, I believe my Jefferson and/or Mussolini, do you want sheets?" Evidently Davidson demurred, since Pound wrote to Stanley Nott on "1 or 2" April 1935 that, "as the Yale University Press, New Haven. Conn. U.S.A., have written wanting 'a book' by E/P/ to go

with in the autumn, I have told'em they ought to do a MAKE IT NEW ECO-
NOMICS, like Faber Make it New (of literchoor)."

Gingrich's paper: *Esquire.*

Condé: Condé Nast (1873–1942), American magazine publisher, principally
known for three periodicals: *Vogue, Vanity Fair,* and *House and Garden.*

30. Cummings to Pound

TL-1.

[Early March 1935]   [4 Patchin Place]

snow,

March,

NY

O nuncle
this is a brave night to cool a courtezan unquote

if it would give you any sort of a kick to see Eimi published in Albion, go
ahead—provided there are no(sic)alterations. Otherwise,good nuncle, absent
thee from felicity unquote. Ditto re poems. Leer. Omelet.

I like very much your extremely flattering "thoroughbred"-"steamroller"
metaphor(one of the fool's favorite toys,when he too was young,happened to be
a "rollerengine" & at least two of his friends were Horses)

Marion having quote turned on her charm,Gingrich departed with an article
which he didn't seem to much care for & about 40 poems. Don't know
whether;but he said that if I'd holdup publication of No Thanks for 15 days
he'd kill unquote a page of Aiken,substituting for the corpse a selection from C
plus a drawing(by C);I arranged my quote end of it.

"I'm always interested ⟨O yesOyesOyesOyes⟩ in the mental coefficient" I
said(speaking of maladies)" and suspect that every disease has a large one; if we
could only understand it". That's the way we were goingon. "Well" G said "I
had anmalady for 7 years which didn't have any mental coefficient". We were
goingon like that;quite illiterately. "Really" I said:and then he told me . . . for 7
years his face swelledunrecognizablyup at the most unexpected moments—the
first seizure(italic mine)occured shortly after his wife's baby had been born—G
asked the doctor who'd delivered her what to do and the doc said put cold
water on it and forget it—things got worse;prodigious pain,partial
paralysis,etc.—final seizure on a train,with his wife playing nurse & G
practically non compos:she insists he see another doctor—he did—2nd doc

told G that the first doc's advice was "like telling a woman 'you're just a little pregnant;but don't pay any attention to it;nothing will happen' "(verbatim) so G had his tonsils out and is now "knocking on wood" & hoping for no more seizures. (His own words for what he said to doc one were these "I'm getting inflation—will I burst?")PS the pain had something to do with "sinus"

how would YOU like to edit a magazine unquote for 25 people with 4 ciphers always after them:see Freud;persecution,comma

more arrows to toi Sebastion mboi

v

s

SCIENCE

(just forwarded to me by a friend who is now in Hollywood)

"The encounter(of the earth with a comet)would probably not be harmless. A continent broken up,a kingdom crushed,Paris,London,New York or Pekin annihilated,would be one of the least effects of the celestial catastrophy. Such an encounter would evidently be of the highest interest to astronomers placed sufficiently far from the place of encounter . . . Such an encounter would then be eminently desirable from a purely scientific point of view;but we can scarcely hope for it,for we must admit,with Arago,that there are 280 millions to one against such an occurrence. However,although the probability against it is so great we need not entirely despair.

Popular Astronomy,by Camille Flammarion"

Gingrich: Arnold Gingrich, editor of *Esquire.* He published five poems by Cummings in the issue for May 1935: "that which we who're alive in spite of mirrors," "sh estiffl," "o// sure)but," "sonnet entitled how to run the world," and "IN)/all those who got" (Firmage B112). In addition, Cummings's essay "Exit the Boob" appeared in the June 1935 issue (Firmage B113).

Aiken: Conrad Aiken.

Popular Astronomy: Camille Flammarion, *Popular Astronomy: A General Description of the Heavens,* trans. J. Ellard Gore (New York, D. Appleton and Company, 1894). Cummings quotes from a footnote on page 529. "The encounter of these two lightning trains would probably not be harmless. A continent broken up, a kingdom crushed, Paris, London, New York, or Pekin annihilated, would be one of the least effects of the celestial catastrophe. Such an event would evidently be of the highest interest to astronomers placed sufficiently far from the point of encounter, especially if they could approach the fatal spot and examine the cometary remains left on the ground. The comet would bring, doubtless, neither gold nor silver, but mineralogical specimens, perhaps diamonds, and perhaps, also, certain vegetable *debris* or fossil animals, much more precious than an ingot of gold of the size of the earth. Such an encounter would, then, be eminently desirable from a purely scientific point of view; but we can scarcely hope for it, for we must admit, with Arago, that there are 280 millions to one against such an occurrence. However, although the probability against it is so great, we need not entirely despair."

31. Pound to Cummings

TLS-2.

24 March [1935]   Rapallo

e e c
        Remittance Advice/ a good thing, like death of Woodrow Wilson there ought to be MORE of it.
waaal, if you will send adwants copy of 'NO THANKS', I will try it on NOTT thanks, an niff he will stand it WHOLE I will not hole it/ butt tiff it is too stiff, I will then (assuming he in interim has concreted re/ pamphlett seereezzzz/ propose the alternative end of the WIDGE.

As to the oooo after the 25// ⟨scribers⟩ waaal, back seat drivin ever wuz mine/ an ni see no reazun to alter olde habits at my time of life an proliferation/
                                wot I'd like wd/ be a regular mensile delivery/ and possibly the substichooshun of e e c's views fer those of the protoplaxmousius verminous Rascoe/ butti spose in america all sorts of things have a licence to be kept/ 7⟨s.⟩6⟨d.⟩ for dawgs in england, and prob/ Rascoe is able to go round the block after dinner without its cutting into the butler's or housemaid's time.

at any rate, you, me and hoff wd/ make any paper super/eeelight as the Possum sez the register is called (social) in St Louis.

I wunne(r wot the Ging plays our li'l playmate Oinis// however if Oinis ttttrusts him / thass thaaat. And I spose Oinis got me in, and so you/ so let him catch tunny fish/ all I drore the line at iz lions/ I can't have him shootin lions. the lion izza sympathetic animal up to a certain age/ or with a bit of grill work in between us. and I don't think they shd/ be removed to make room for colonists/ Apart ça (the word pue will rise to readers of mr c's first extensive prose woik) apart Ça / I am glad Mr wilson's amph/ will have at least two readable pages/

sorry the T/C/W/ seems to be descending to the Jos/ Wd/ CRUTCH.
I dunno whether you can putt a skid under him and render him unCanbyable/ one NEEDS a bdy/ bureaucracy/ ⟨or BUT⟩ and it is a nuissance to have it go bad on ones shoes prematurely.

the jex M/ and the Jas iv. still show signs of adolescence. But apart ça !!
(feetnotes/ 2 rising citizens of Occidentalia) apart ça !!?5⟨delete⟩(?%

Wot/ I rote seereeyus to th GING wuz/ to gimme a few back pages fer to run
high/brow.. seems to me hoff wd/ carry most anything.
However / mebbe the resitrixshuns of the FORM (if Ging/
prints it) will nnnnable one to do as much "good" by a nockasional word, as
by a longDial'd BLEAT abaeowt ahwt.
A few close=ups of theodore jr/ Og/Mills og/REid or some viggi/nits of the
amurkn scene/ wd. come handy.

It is like awl prakkikal aXshun / IF one cd/ putt thru a sane econ/ system in
three years/ the rest of our long and upstanding lives might be Voronoffd
peacefully along the umbraggeous banks of whatever steam or plage/ etc.
Benito is beginin' to use his sense of humour/ got the goAT of the pewking
N.Y.Herald by tellin' em more infants, wd/ ⟨solve⟩ crisis, cause kids iz
destructive, and what they are yellin' for is consumers.
apparently it went to some frawg reporter. I am
trying to see what it goes like in french.
Lippman's Paris a/rag don't like it.
In the interim; did I say Wm/ Ebor expressed his thanks ⟨to me⟩ (which is one
UP on the Possum, tho if I hadn't seen the York postmark I wdn't have paid
the postage due on the letter. But knowing (of parenthesis) no one else in
them parts.
He ain't however gone on to answer my queeries as to
doctrine (? mebbe he dunno wot it IZ).

and so I must clothes
Ez P

P/S wot bekum ov all the uther brite lads in amurikuh ? all gone to seed⟨#⟩
from the cervix upward?
⟨# the N.Y. weakly writers couldn't.⟩

No Thanks: *No Thanks,* published 15 April 1935 in New York by the Golden Eagle
Press.
NOTT: Stanley Nott. The "seereezzzz" Pound refers to was the "Ideogramic Se-
ries" (so named by Pound). The series was intended to be include volumes by
Pound, Cummings, Eliot, Williams, and possibly others. Only two numbers of
the series, Pound's edition of Ernest Fenollosa's *The Chinese Written Character
as a Medium for Poetry* and Pound's translation *Ta Hio, the Great Learning,*
appeared before Nott stopped publishing altogether.
Rascoe: Burton Rascoe, American literary critic. At the time, *Esquire's* literary
critic. In 1932 there had been a sharp exchange between Rascoe and Pound. It
began when Rascoe asserted that he had been an early supporter of Hemingway

("A Bookman's Daybook," *New York Sun,* 16 April 1932). Pound charged that Rascoe lied ("Pound to Rascoe," *New York Sun,* 11 June 1932). Rascoe repeated his claim in "Rascoe's Riposte," *New York Sun,* 11 June 1932.

hoff: Syd Hoff, American cartoonist who contributed regularly to *Esquire.*

Possum: T. S. Eliot.

Ging: Arnold Gingrich.

Oinis: Ernest Hemingway. Pound's remarks about "fish" and "lions" refer to *Esquire* articles by Hemingway about his sporting activities. In one article, "a.d. in Africa," Hemingway notes, "In two weeks and three days in lion country we saw 84 lions and lionesses. Of these twenty were maned lions. We shot the twenty-third, the forty-seventh, the sixty-fourth and the seventy-ninth." *Esquire,* April 1934, 19.

wilson's amph: *Westminster* 24, no. 1 (spring–summer 1935), edited by Pound, John Drummond, and T. C. Wilson, with a brief foreword by Pound.

CRUTCH: Joseph Wood Krutch, American critic and essayist.

jex M: John Jex Martin, a young Chicagoan and admirer of Father Coughlin. He corresponded with Pound from 1932 to 1936.

Jas iv: James Laughlin. In 1936 he founded New Directions.

theodore jr: Theodore Roosevelt Jr. He became a vice president of Doubleday, Doran and Company in 1935.

Og/Mills: Ogden Livingston Mills, secretary of the Treasury from February 1932 to 4 March 1933. In his "American Notes" (*New English Weekly,* vol. 7, no. 9 [13 June 1935]), Pound wrote that "Og. Read and Og. Mills can't eternally prevent the American people from hearing what is said in the American legislature" (Gallup C1213). Reprinted in *EPPP.*

og/REID: Ogden Mills Reid, editor of the *Herald Tribune.*

Voronoffd: Serge Voronoff, a French surgeon. See the note to letter 2.

Benito: Benito Mussolini.

Lippman's Paris a/rag: The international edition of the *Herald Tribune.* Since 1931, Walter Lippmann had regularly contributed his column, "Today and Tomorrow" to the *Herald Tribune.*

Ebor: William Temple, archbishop of York. The archbishop of York signs with his Christian name and an abbreviated form of the Roman name for York, which was Eboracum.

32. Cummings to Pound

TLS-1. Enclosure.

April 4,1935   [4 Patchin Place]

Dear E.P.

yes,shall send you Merci hot off the Quoidonc. Respectfully prospectus hereby submitted(gratissimo).

Messer Gingrich bought,shortly after poems,a by moi versus-cranks article;at $150. (I only had to rewrite which & ain hoid uh woid sins). Re thy financial queery:Oinis is paid $450,on dit,for his monthly crap . . . pretty damn shitty— seeing as how another pugilist has just(on dit)been offered by your favorite perfidious Albion $250,000 plus 40% of any excess profit for one(1)go;which meer buggertail the latter(a hebe) is even rumored to be considering!!!NOW will you believe in the DEPRESSION?(ecco enclosure).

Paragraph

I met Strawinsky today---it is not a stone,thank God;he is a rock

be good

eec

Marion sends you her best

Merci: *No Thanks.*

prospectus: Announcement of the forthcoming publication (15 April 1935) of *No Thanks.* The prospectus included a note by Wallace Brockway: "BECAUSE of an early masterpiece, *The Enormous Room,* a war autobiography of vision and honesty, and obviously a poet's work, E. E. Cummings, by a ponderable section of his audience, was pigeonholed as a novelist, his poetry as a temporary makeshift. Even the development of a special notation—a new ideography, in fact—was imperfectly assessed.

    No Thanks may make no impact on those who stubbornly admire but one phase of Cummings' genius, and who merely want *The Enormous Room* re-peated. For *No Thanks* is not 'better' poetry—Cummings has always been dynamic and sure—though his metaphysical genius, never inhibited, is more than ever evident. For those who conceive of poetry as something more than an exercise in 'pretty words,' I recommend this new book by a master of poetic concentration." Below the information on the holograph edition, limited to nine copies, including "one entire poem not appearing in any other edition which will be written in the author's own hand," Cummings wrote, "Can't you see me writing in my own hand?"

article: "Exit the Boob," *Esquire,* vol. 3, no. 6 (June 1935), 33 and 155 (Firmage B113). Reprinted in *E. E. Cummings: A Miscellany,* ed. George J. Firmage (New York: Argophile Press, 1958) (Firmage A26).

Oinis: Ernest Hemingway.

another pugilist: Probably Max Baer (1909–59), heavyweight boxing champion of the world from June 1934 to June 1935. Baer wore a Star of David on his boxing trunks.

Strawinsky: Igor Stravinsky (1882–1971), Russian-born composer.

enclosure: Second enclosure lacking.

33. Pound to Cummings

TLS-3.

28 Ap/ [1935]   [Rapallo]

Deer Kumrad/
                    All I can is to turn backward Oh Time in thy to a scene in
Chelsea/ Mr H/J/ havin' been on bed presented by the ineffable Gosse with
gold medal signifyin the ORDER of Merit, havin ⟨gosse⟩ pinned same on
pillow as pyjam didn't afford etc
            or whatever/ and the god damn Gosse (this has nothing to do with
YOU) the goddam Gosse having exited, the nurse riz the window curtain so'z
H/J/ cd/ enjoy the vision of honour.
and H/J/ sez: Nurse spare my blushes.
                                            an died.
well that aint part of the answer ANYhow/ At least I am younger.
            an nervously open the watch to etc/etc/ how one is involved by
tradition.

AS the book is too handsum to send up to be messed by printer, I hope and
suppose (or viceversa) you have sent a copy to Stan
            (the Ltd. NOTT)
Letter yester said he was ready to go ahead with pamphlets.
As 'NO THANKS' is only 70 pages
it is up to him to decide whether he will (and/or) import sheets, or import a
few sheets and print 30 pages in Ideogramic series (pamphs)
incidentall have you anything ELSE for a pamph, IF he (NOTT) decides on
taking sheets?
USE of greek chastity onp/ page whatever ⟨54⟩ CHEERS/
            aint we got discretion
an on the hole more chick an refeenment/ in fakk the laught bursts louder.
And the british printer will nevvuh kno/ OH HO
            and Mr Wells (H /G hully gee) won't have to lock up the book in
the sherry cupboard with the vinegar cruet to keep his kid bastids frum readin
it.
                            HOW did he make 'em by phk? we suppose
so. by cock we suppose so.

        //
did I say a fair lady said send it to th kumrad/

            HEREDITY?
            High Bourgeois

The father a buggar, the mother a bitch,
Which of the children will turn out which?

waaal
        damn it all, 56 worth more than the prix nobel, from 17 non conformist
parsons⟨#⟩ but fer krize ache dont say so YET
                cause the li'l illegit needs the money fer schoolin.

(foot note. ⟨#⟩ SWEEDES)
an now to leave the pursunnul to which by handwriting in his own book
attracted/

it is more fun to be l'il Joe's false teeth than FrankieD Roosevelt's crutches.
                        WHAT and when and where IZ li'l Joe a doin/
and HAVE I got to elect bill Borah and REFORM th wholebloody econ/ system
in order to get Joes ORAL [History of the World] imprinted??

And adimttin that you can't move 'em with a cold thing like EKONomics/etc.
and that I bore the bastids to death/ if I don't they stop movin like Parson
Possum

can anyone spill it that Sir. Monty Webb is quotin me in free silver paper in
Karachi (Injy(s coral strand) and I am printed In old Madrid, in Olde Madrid,
where ⟨whoosis⟩ whooses made the kid, and that Odon Por is or sez he iz
quotin me at length in the next Cultura Fascista. (He zin charge of the
Instituto di Politica Internazionale. ⟨at ROMA⟩

CAN by christ anybody get my M/I/N Econ/ printed NOW
so"z bichrist we can get on with Kulchr an the amenities and not HAVE to stay
here writin about econ/ fer ANOTHER blasted ten years of crop restriction and
bums cadgin ha pence
and that bastardly shit Schacht out with a beggin box for Berlin Christmas??

DAMN if I don't want to be a ECONOMIST all the rest of my life. why dont
the bastids find out than I AM one, and then let me quit it.

I putt me aged limbs down on th tennis tournament/ and the god damn econ/
system is such that the internat/ champs aint GOT THE CARE fare to come
here and let me get defeated with honour. ⟨#⟩
                IN another ten year I wont be able to trot round the campo. AND
so on.
                        ⟨# meanin they aint no Turnymint.⟩
                        regards to th ledy,
                                yrs EZ

Mr H/J/: This anecdote about James first appeared in print in James S. Bain's *A Bookseller Looks Back: The Story of the Bains* (London: Macmillan, 1940), 221–22. "When Henry James was actually on his death-bed, in the early days of 1916, he received the Order of Merit, a richly deserved honour, though it came too late. Sir Edmund Gosse, one of his closest friends, himself told me this charming story about it. He had asked leave to tell Henry James of the award, but, on entering the sick-room, he found his friend lying with closed eyes, and the nurse told him she was afraid the patient was past hearing anything. Leaning over the bed, Gosse whispered, 'Henry, they've given you the O.M.' but not a sign of interest showed in the still face, and Gosse quietly left the room. Directly the door closed Henry James opened his eyes and said, 'Nurse, take away the candle and spare my blushes.' A few days later, on February 28th, 1916, he died." The transcription that Theodora Bosanquet made of her own diary notes, however, tells a different story. "*Saturday, January 1st.* H.J. in the New Year Honours list, awarded the Order of Merit. When I went to his flat I was told that he was 'much more himself' and had been immensely pleased by the news. He had told Kidd to 'turn off the light to spare my blushes' and when Mrs. James read him some congratulatory telegrams, he had remarked 'what curious manifestations such occasions call forth'" (Houghton Library, bms Eng 1213.2).

that: Pound drew an arrow from "that" to "died" in the previous line.

the book: *No Thanks.*

greek chastity: Page 54 of *No Thanks* contained the poem "Jehovah buried,Satan dead." Line 23, instead of ending with "fuck," ended with the Greek letters phi, upsilon, and kappa.

fair lady: Possibly Dorothy Pound.

illegit: Pound and Olga Rudge's daughter, Mary.

false teeth: Pound refers to poem 27 of *No Thanks,* "little joe gould has lost his teeth and doesn't know where."

Borah: William Edgar Borah (1865–1940), U.S. senator from Idaho (1907–40). See Daniel Pearlman, "Fighting the World: The Letters of Ezra Pound to Senator William E. Borah from Idaho," *Paideuma,* vol. 12, nos. 2–3 (fall–winter 1983), 419–26.

cant move 'em: In October 1921, Pound met the Irish nationalist Arthur Griffith (1872–1922) in London. He recalled Griffith as responding to his comments about economics by saying, "All you say is true. But I can't move 'em with a cold thing like economics." Pound cites this several times in the *Cantos.*

Possum: T. S. Eliot.

Webb: Sir Montagu de Pomeroy Webb (1869–1938), British businessman and publisher in India. Chairman of the Daily Gazette Press, Karachi. In a letter of July 1935 to the *National Citizen* (London), Pound noted that "Sir Montagu Webb's paper 'Better Money,' published in Karachi at the Daily Gazette Buildings, is one which no live economist will miss seeing" (Gallup C1219). Reprinted in *EPPP.*

old Madrid: Gallup's *Ezra Pound: A Bibliography* lists no Pound items published in Madrid for 1935.

Por: Odon Por (b. 1883), Italian journalist.

M/I/N Econ: *Make It New Economics. Make It New: Essays by Ezra Pound* (London: Faber and Faber) had been published the previous September. The essays were on literary subjects. Pound planned to write a companion volume on economics. In a letter of 23 September 1935 to James Laughlin, he mentioned, "the new econ. book . . . I was typing" (Carpenter, 539). Writing to Louis Zukofsky on 16 March 1936, however, Pound said, "If Eliot has had the jism to get OFF Faber's bed ⟨socks⟩ The second vol of MAKE it NEW wd/ have dealt with TIME/ Music, Mussolini/ etc/ Kung/ Jeff/ ACTION and vol III. wd/ have dealt with Gaudier, und alles was RAUMLICH ist."

Schacht: Hjalmar Horace Greeley Schacht (1877–1970), German financier. President of the Reichsbank 1933–39, as well as Reich minister of economics 1934–37.

34. Pound to Cummings

TLS-2.

28 April [1935]   Rapallo

Dear Kumrad
                    second effusion/ I cant remember everyfink/ but have just
writ/ GING to git you to git some of JOE[Gould]'s oral HISTORY fer Esquire/
                    an I spose joe cd/ use it, if he haint hatched a blue EAGLE?
                    or whatnot.
⟨Joe fer governor of Albany!⟩
Yes; yes, yr/ bardic burst brung it it to mind. an' ESQUIRE is the foist reel
muggerzeen thet cd/ c do it .
and thass that.

WHY shd/ we ALL our lives be governed and edited by piffling little
pustulents/
                    waaal, as I sez to someone
ESTLIN might take up with orthology/ and dissociation of idears that wdn't
commit him to crankisms. in fact it is fair delouser.

ANY bright ideas as to how to concentrate anything fit to read, either paid on
GING / or unpd/ on N/E/W

Am tellin NOTT he ought to do WHOLE No Thanks.

IF he won't,I think we might begin on those that I can understand/ and then on those that there is some chanct of London thinking it can.

I started makin list (not complete and merely first look over.
     all from 49 to 55, 57/58/65/67/69/71
devil to s chop up a book. I wasnt watching up to then.

whether to include next (probably best to do so) those already used in N/E/W/, or to try to print greatest number of those not in N/E/W/.
          anyhow, waste of time to worry until I hear from Stan/

This postage stamp affixed fer sake of ole JOE.

AN I will try to giv/ joe a boost in N/E/W/ when Mairet works off what he has on hand.

DAMNIT, nobody but Og/ has even tried to put on a show fit fer humans in Britain (not of course that the population clamours fer intellexschool pyrotechnics.

WILL take months fer Mairet to git round to it.

Have you an opinion re/ the other blokes in Active Anth?

          j'evver git yr/ copies ANYhow?

anybody except joe (and ?? ole Doc/ Williams) that you include in the murkn census?

apart from
the domestic companion   y
& decor   EZ
gloria
ἄγαλμα [glory, delight]

EAGLE: A blue eagle was the symbol of the National Recovery Administration. *No Thanks* was published by the Golden Eagle Press.
bardic burst: Possibly Cummings's poem, "little joe gould has lost his teeth and doesn't know where," the twenty-seventh poem of *No Thanks.*

35. Cummings to Pound

TLS-1.

[May 1935]   [4 Patchin Place]

there,Mr P" Mr C said,tightening his vagina femoris by a not to say skilful adumbration of the trochanter major dexter(& with almost unequal pomposity flicking a horsebun off his left eyebrow)"we perceive the crux or gene of the matter." I too was at Bennington College,The Higher Education,meaning que les demoiselles—of all dimensions and costumes—sit around eachother's rooms quaffing applejack neat;to read for 45 minutes,for 25 $. 1 girlinmate observed dreamily "we had a behaviour problem here . . . " "what" I suggested "is a behaviour problem?" "Williams" she answered "college is only 47 miles away. One night some of the boys—they had been drinking—climbed into several 2ndstorey windows and were found kneeling beside the girls' beds . . . " "anything happen" I inquire. "Well" she remembered dimly "the faculty"(whose function is to unexist except when a BP arises)"decided it had better install a nightwatchman . . . " "anything happen?" I almost whisper. Vaguely "well" she said,and almost hopelessly "he arrested the first man he found on the campus that night . . . " "Who was?" I venture. "The professor" she prettily murmured "of physics . . . " & as your correspondent entered ye lecture halls 200 maidens were chanting for the 3rd time a poem concerning Buffalo Bill—but what was the crux?something to do with one's deciding to appear in public before one's(nonpubic)hair had disappeared . . . —ah yes:vanity,sah!—there,Mr P" Mr C said, extracting a Woosevelt nickel from his armpit & carefully if not decorously laying same on the astonished herrober's tray plate or goingaway basket "is the chromosome of the crisis." And with that he farted so suddenly as to extinguish a Swedish match held at some distance by a Lett named Doomer Fees who was momentaneously sitting in his Chinese laundryman's garretwindow at the redolent crossing of Eggshit and Cowpiss Avenues,Leningrad,duh brongz . . .

Bravo JoeGould—Esquire!! where isn't Das Gingrich?wrote twice but sans riposte

we,I received Active Flowerword & it's the only "anthology" have liked(Profile excepted,if you wish);at Marion's suggestion I even intoned pp 179-181(at aforedit Kneeling Academy);only to find,muchmuchmuch later,that meine hostess vas a kumrad—however;"sombreros")and expecially enjoy pages
          45 185-6 189-209
even made a visitor read&understand 185-6,not long ago.
Paragraph. Your own poems which I most aime are absent. —Say isn't that a whale of a pp207-9 not that anything could top her

```
                    the lucid movements of the royal yacht upon the
(*)                         learned scenery of Egypt
        . . . . . . . . the shadows of the Alps
                    imprisoning in their folds,like flies in amber,the
                            rhythms of the skating rink
```

Thank you very much for both letters including the appreciated couplet &
muchissimo re Notty work at the crossroads. He & Jacobs seem already
intercommunicado. My greetings to George R et I

a lady te salue

eec

##

"Since there is so much sexual freedom,must there not be a great number of
children born out of wedlock? . . . it is very remarkable to note that
illegitimate children are rare. The girls seem to remain sterile throughout their
period of licence,which begins when they are small children and continues
until they marry;when they are married they conceive and breed,sometimes
quite prolifically . . . Why . . . ? . . . One thing I can say with complete
confidence:no preventitive means of any description are known,nor the
slightest idea of them entertained. This,of course,is quite natural. Since the
procreative power of seminal fluid is not known,since it is considered not only
innocuous but beneficent,there is no reason why the natives should interfere
with its free arrival in the parts which it is meant to lubricate. Indeed,any
suggestion of neo-Malthusian appliances makes them shudder or laugh
according to their mood or temperament. They never practice coitus
interruptus,and still less have any notion about chemical or mechanical
preventives."

pp 195-197,The Sexual Life of Savages,by Bronislaw
Malinowski, Harcourt Brace & Co.

Bennington: Cummings read at Bennington College on 24 April 1935 (see Kennedy, 361–62). Helen Stewart, a student who was instrumental in getting him invited, later worked as an editor with William Sloane Associates, where she assisted in the production of the reprint of *Eimi*. See also the note to letter 38.

Buffalo Bill: *Complete Poems*, 90.

Active Flowerword: *Active Anthology* (Gallup B32). Cummings refers to pages containing an excerpt from *Eimi* (179–81), William Carlos Williams's "The Red Wheelbarrow" (45); Ernest Hemingway's "They All Made Peace—What Is Peace?" (185–86); Marianne Moore's "Camellia Sabina," "The Jerboa," "The Plumet Basilisk," "No Swan So Fine," and "The Steeplejack" (189–209). "The Steeplejack" appears on pages 207–9.

George R et I: "George, Rex et Imperator." Probably a reference to George V, king of England. He celebrated his Silver Jubilee in 1935, having become king on the death of his father, Edward VII, in May 1910.

Malinowski: Bronislaw Malinowski (1884–1942), *The Sexual Life of Savages in North-Western Melanesia* (New York: Harcourt, Brace, 1929). Cummings condenses Malinowski's remarks, but makes no changes. On page 198, Malinowski admits he remains puzzled by the low rate of birth "when women begin their sexual life young, lead it indefatigably, and mix their lovers freely."

36. Pound to Cummings

TCS.

20 May [1935]   Rapallo

yrs of undated presumably inst/ recd/ omission of Beefalu Bull poEM regretted as can't recog/ as part of pre/1905 paideuma of them U.States. please remit if worthy of postage/ or in any case to tranquilize curiosity of omnicurious elderly lit/gent.

prublum of Activ Anth/ wuz to shoot in all that printed matter (unwanted in Eng/ or by pubrs/ and then nowBishoprunlikehell.

The Zukof/ still wondering WHY they ⟨them brits.⟩ dont want a hole book of him!!!

Waaal, econ, is driftin up from the kumtoJezus Y.M.C.A. level into the level of science an generl kulchur (in the be'r sense of the word) an with them soft woidz I pass.

further than that the Wilson sez the far South/ is worried by yr/ lang WIDG/ and that I WISH some local force wd/ the gifie gie MUNSON to see how I cd/ liven Noo Demrocracy MORE than is poss/ fer me to alleviate brit/ class/inf/ cx/ in N.E.Weakly

je salue th lydy.

E.

et TOI mong vieuXX
       note re Malinkowski
C/I/ not to be despised in present imperfect state of occidental societyi / at any rate it includes technical training.

Zukof: Louis Zukofsky.
Wilson: Theodore C. Wilson. Coeditor, with John Drummond and Pound, of the spring–summer 1935 issue of *Westminster Review* (Oglethorpe, Georgia).
MUNSON: Gorham Munson, editor of *New Democracy* (New York).
C/I/: Coitus interruptus.

37. Cummings to Pound

ALS-1.

[May 1935]   [4 Patchin Place]

never talk to me of "elders and dullers", you—after the prize place you copped
in May "Esquire" & I don't mean May Be & I do refer to page 30 or (more
precisely) la poule. What with that 30-31 spread, Uncl. Sam is going to be
proud of himself yet!

S.V.P., when you get your copy of No Thanks, correct as follows
        9 line 2 (o pr) should be one space rightward
            i.e. p over r and r over e
        69 line 12 should read
            "put on one not imaginable star"
these corrections should be made (in the type) by Jacobs, for the (if any)
English edition.

Have you heard what happened to Johnnie (Tarzan) Weismuller in Hollywood?
His body went to his head. Unquote

a mischievous friend landed la princesse et moi at Webster Hall, last night,
where the kumrads were having a feester—it looked like A Housemaiden's Idea
Of Paradise & it stunk like motor oitly and the princess let fly at a bunch of
truckdrivers (sic) with the observation that she was "a royalist." They cried
"enemy of the people" (sic) & made horrescent gastriflexions; but our aforesaid
hosts—happening to be Cleon Throckmorton—gave the highsign &, presto!
les bois became pleurs de real honesttogod scene-shifters, nyet tovariches . . .
that held the punks Et Comment

                                        Sois Sage
                                           eec

or (as they used to say in the metro)
    pilules pink pours personnes palis

May "Esquire": Pound's "A Matter of Modesty," *Esquire*, vol. 3, no. 5 (May 1935),
    31 (Gallup C1186). Reprinted in *EPPP*. Pound urges the adoption of a combina-
    tion of the economic reforms advised by Major Douglas and Silvio Gesell.
Weismuller: Johnny Weismuller (1904–84), Olympic swimming champion in
    1924 and 1928. Star of *Tarzan the Ape Man* (1932) and *Tarzan and His Mate*
    (1934).
Throckmorton: (1897–1965), American scenic designer. He was active with the

Provincetown Players, the Theatre Guild, the Group Theatre, and other New
York theatrical companies.

pilules: Cummings recalls Paris Metro advertisements for Pinkerton's Pills.

38. Cummings to Pound

TLS-1. Enclosure.

[May 1935]   [4 Patchin Place?]

Share Thunderer
many thanks for the Ezra Shrapnel!it arrived,avec excellent rabbitman's Honest
Obus,from Nott(positively). Of what I can understand—as you would say—
enjoyed peculiarly "god or no god" passage:and a sketch about her sloppin'
soul.

Met Joe [Gould] il y a quesques jours &,b jeezuz,never have I beheld a corpse
walking . . . said he was planning to go "on relief" as there seemed nothing
else for it. Told me he'd been previously deterred by fact that already "on
relief" are 2 classes—"the kind of people you wouldn't be found dead with and
the kind of people who need it so much more than we do"(sic). Alleged his
failure to comply with an ancient suggestion of mine and write yourself was
due to lack of a 5 cent postagestamp;but I wouldn't let the devil himself get
away with that,so am a nickel worthier. I mentioned Messer G "Esquire" to Joe
& he brightened. Then,taking the horns by the bull,I flew a 2nd article toward
Chicago:& this despite fact that my twain letters to aforesaid ridactur stay
unanswered,or in other words,nobody asked me to do nawthing els. As
postscript to missive accompanying the dit article I furnished Master Gould's
whereabouts,towit:Central Hotel, 149 East 14th Street

Elizabeth,my sister,works for the "COS"(Charity Organization Society). Her
business is to struggle with bums & plutocrats. She makes the latter turn on
people's gas when bills aren't properly paid at 10 below zero etc.. The former
sometimes try to convert her to communism,sometimes threaten her with
razors. But what I thought you'd like to hear is something else:the other day,
for the first time in her career,she was stopped cold—hitherto,whenever
somebody called up and wanted a handsome man to mind an airdale or a
mechanic familiar with the vertabrae of Zeppelins or a professor to teach
Esquimaux or a deserving pregnancy or whathaveyou,she's just dipped into the
unemployed and fished up a little bit of all right;but now comes a voice
demanding,on behalf of a huge radio-network-act "a whole family with
coughs,NOT CONTAGIOUS;to cough into the microphone" . . .

<blockquote>
"   words better left unsaid
Come back to grieve us when we think them dead"
</blockquote>

(James Boyle O'Reilly)on which I was brought up;but also on Plato's Republic fortunately comma My sister Elizabeth says that if Joe can only keep on relief for a few years he'll have a new set of somebody's teeth;I can't believe it. As a single man,she says,he ought to get $5 every two weeks for food(& something a month for rent):that I can believe.

Must remember to tune in on Italia via maternal radio!

My aunt is inheriting thousands,none of which we will get. She writes charmingly about nesting robins & bought a de luxe No Thanks. I am quite fond of her. But I don't like a pimply gent labelled "Mr. Mitchell" who,safely ensconced behind the bars of the "Corn Exchange Bank"(depositors will kindly remove their shoes to make it easier)observed that it must be nice to have a mama who gives you money . . . those were the Good Old Daze of chequebooks & speakeasies & 2 chickens in every garage and And. Hwel hwel,eat ease quiet unuzz air sing-hyes?

Apparently poverty is not doing what you want to whereas riches are doing what you don't

    .. yrs for whatever's at rightangles to both.

eec

        I know a fine fellow(professor,banker,etc)
        to whom please ask Nott to
        send your Impact with my compliments
            name Walter Stewart—(personal)
            address Case Pomeroy & Co. 120 Water Street

Greetings from
Madame

[Enclosure]

copy of letter sent with the enclosed) ⟨which am submitting to my "agents" e'er departing, I trust, for California via Mexico with la princesse in some friends' 8 cylinder Packard (recently purchased for 300 $). Never did like Cadillacs!

Be good—
EEC⟩

Dear Gingrich—

    if you don't think as much(which is considerable)of this as I do,will you please return same de suite so that I can try on some less deserving victim before pawning the proverbial shoestring?

    —Yours

PS)Pound writes me that he wrote you about Joe Gould,whom I ran into the other day and who looks more like a corpse than ever and whose address is Central Hotel,149 East 14th Street,NYC

Shrapnel: *Social Credit: An Impact* (London: Stanley Nott, 1935) (Gallup A40).
rabbitman's: *Alfred Venison's Poems: Social Credit Themes by the Poet of Tichfield Street* (London: Stanley Nott, 1935) (Gallup A39). "Venison" (Ezra Pound) purported to make his living by selling rabbits. Cummings refers to a line from "Ole Kate": "God rest her sloshin' soul."
Elizabeth: Elizabeth Cummings.
O'Reilly: John Boyle O'Reilly (1844–90), Irish-born American writer. I have not found this passage in O'Reilly's works. Cummings also attributes the passage to O'Reilly in *Eimi:* "words better left un-(said John Boyle)return to create ample sorrow when we consider them comfortably defunct" (31).
Italia: On 11 January 1935, Pound had spoken on the *American Hour,* a short-wave radio program broadcast from Rome.
aunt: Jane Cummings ("Aunt Jennie"), the unmarried sister of Cummings's father.
Stewart: Helen Stewart's father. She had been largely responsible for inviting Cummings to read at Bennington College. "She had also arranged for her father, who was on the board of trustees, to accompany him up on the train and to see that he was properly accommodated at the Bennington Inn" (Kennedy, 362).
enclosed: Poems Cummings had submitted to *Esquire.*

39. Pound to Cummings

TCS.

5 June [1935]   Rapallo

Seay / burthr, doan yuh KNOW Mr GinRicth doan LIKE tuh rite letters? Waal, I keep tellin him I READ some of Joe[Gould]'s hissory, thass awl I kin do. as to yr/ labouring POINT waaal/ to get metaphysics into 250 000 izza tecknikl prubmlum . . . Econ. is all I can concrete. . . . you didn't enc/ any inskrukshns with the mss.. I dunno anyone that will PAY.
        Learchus Guerra has just passed under the back window. (if that interests you . . . it is a popular subject. will try remember ask NOT T send Impact/ Stewart. I re/re/peet the rerequest fer text uv Buffaloo Bill.
                        Yrz/ bong voyage
an luv to deh lady
                E

Guerra: A celebrated Italian long-distance bicycle racer.

40. Cummings to Pound

TL-1.

[1935?]   [?]

Dear E/P—
                am rerisking your august july by enclosure of 1 second sample of
trivial tabloid titilation—this blurb being a blast against The Other Side of the
stalin-hitler coin. Now to descend from the vertical to the perpendicular:I read
each word of Saint Peter("hornsey" to his friends)Hargrave who is most
certainly Nott an unnice chap("man does not live by bread alone" saith Ye
Goode Booke extrinsidentally). Prof Chas Barbe announces war in Scribner's
"magazine",mentioning that the same democratics generously manage to
preceed same(Jeffersonians—W of 1812;Jacksonians—Civil W;Sistie &
Buzzie—W of ? . . . Wilson doesn't count;that was just the W to end Ws,if you
recall). Night before last,watched a friend trying to persuade himself he'd give
up the legit if raddyoh gave him down. But armor ribbil SAH ar believe that
waterclosets should fight the next war(provided you could get the punks out of
their own shit:for which succinct purpose have invented a large libidinous
hook with a small ecocentric handlemanufacturable complete con gasmask for
due bits nomoreno). Then comma too comma capital s herman said quote war
is hell unquote period. Personally,prefer the alltooillunknown psychological
axiom "take a SAD man to a FUNERAL"(not to a musicalcomedy). Anticipate
early visit from Esquire gingrich who sounds decievingly pliable?
Marion sends her best. so do I

here's to wee mamels
creatures of impulse
threading needles with camels
treating pimples with simpulse

                                    tinkling,at that

enclosure: Enclosure lacking.
Hargrave: John Hargrave was a British novelist, cartoonist, and Social Credit
    Advocate. Author of the novel *Summer Time Ends* (1933), a panoramic study of
    a year in the lives of the inhabitants of an English industrial town.
Barbe: My examination of *Scribner's Magazine* for the first two terms of the
    Roosevelt administration reveals no articles or letters by a Professor Barbe.
Sistie & Buzzie: Franklin Delano Roosevelt's grandchildren, Sistie and Buzzie Dall.
    They were the children of Anna Curtis Roosevelt Dall and Curtis B. Dall (a New
    York broker), who divorced in July 1934. The press frequently reported Sistie
    and Buzzie's White House activities.

41. Cummings to Pound

TLS-2.

[14 July 1935]   Santa Monica, California

wel welll
            here we are in Sunny californIA, having shot up from May He Ko
(a city) via (1)Ford trimotor,11 1/2 hours(2)Douglas bi-,5 hours. And never
have I less enjoyed migration than the former. Yes sir,that Ford fell&rose all
day,with a roar like the anus of Hell,with bags being sick into people,with
positively incredible heatednesses,with wastelands like nothing Tears ever
dreamed of,with versa & vice and et et al. The Douglas was mild by
compare;soundproofed & gadgetish:step into the controlroom some time when
you don't feel like reading H.G.Unwells. Proudly be it said that neither your
correspondent nor La Princesse parted with a morsel—though I occassionally
found myself corkscrewing toward the roof & snapping a lunch back into me.
O Don't see Naples and then:fly instead . . . besides,it's scarcely more expensive
than a high-class coon fooneral;& far far far orfooler.

the socalled Indians(Mexican)are the finest people I've met—so of course
everybody else is trying to bring them up to date. Altruism thy name is
Jealousy! They ⟨(Ind)⟩ work only because when or if they enjoy that.
Otherwise,no hay. Discovered what an "uncivilized" person is:a person who
won't do something he doesn't want very much to do,especially when offered
(as an inducement)everything which he doesn't actually need.
E.G.communism,money,security,education and close quotes((you should see
the Mex kumrads trying to close quotes on the (Mex)Indians!)))

the mountains of northern Mexico are superb: they dislike roads & shrug them
away every other moment. A Rotarian,Mex (there were merely 8000 Rotarians
of all nationalities in M City at the instant,but the Lions were next)told me
there was a rumor that during one of these shrugs two cars disappeared—to be
discovered later,10,000 feet down,with licenseplates practically
intertwined;'twere 2 pairs of honeymooners,1 American,1 greaser(PS,I am not
a RotarianPPS nor a Lion)paragraph. Item

?have you ever been to --------IA¿ it's never cold so it's never hot so it's full
with a great and little emptiness—the emptiness of sick people. If any sick
people aren't in IA,why not? "eyedeal" climate,too-many-
everythings,hungerizing & sleepizing. BUT 1 miraculous ocean!!! Did you ever
swim in the Pacific¿¿¿ snap out of that wop choint un catch a hulk of surf
pronto pardunur,as guys with black masks say in the westerns and apparently
nowhere else. —By night,the beaches are lousy with literally Zoroastrians

figuratively;whole and potential families(clad in swimmingrags)frolicing &
dreaming beside fires fires fires fires fires fires not a condom in a cartload
but I am not here to sell you anything. Not that if you can sell it etc. I haven't
Buffalo Bill,neither has the Santa Monica Library Poetry Am. shelf;but voila 3
of your volumes! To quote Kipling—If Gingrich was what Gingrich seems And
not the Gingrich of our dreams But only kaka shit & piss How quick we's
chuck him

but he iss!

With which words(being

en route to la peinture)I give you a catbird a mockingbird and what may or
may not be a nightingale

Salud,& from Marion

eec

849 Eleventh Street Santa Monica California
quatorze juillet

Almost forgot to mention that there is a place,near here,named
"Hollywood"(or something like that). It consists of factories(or something like
that)for the manufacture of american womanhoods,or so I am told;you never
can tell

PS) Excerpts from the preface by William Roscoe Thayer to "The Best
Elizabethan Plays"

"Few persons possess the fifteen or twenty large volumes in which the
Elizabethan drama is published, and fewer still have the time or the patience to
plod through many tedious or dirty pages in order to come upon the treasures
they contain. For, just as a traveler in an Oriental city is often obliged to turn
his eyes from some mosque or graceful minaret to the ground beneath his feet
so as to avoid ordure and garbage, so the reader of the Elizabethan plays has
his attention often distracted, and his sense of decency shocked by the vulgarity
in many passages of them. This coarseness was due in part to the habit of the
time, when men spoke openly to each other and even to women on subjects
about which we are, if not ignorant, at least reticent, and in part to the
deliberate effort of the playwright to please the vulgarist persons in the
audience. But as filth is always filth, though it be thrust upon us in a work of
art, or come to us along with much that is noble under the sanction of a great
name, and as each age has more than enough of its own obscenity to flounder
free from, without falling back into the sty of a former generation,I have
selected plays as little as possible tainted. Moreover, I have not scrupled to
strike out phrases or lines where it seemed proper, being guided by decency
and not by prudery; yet it will not be found that this purging interferes in the

least in the understanding of the following dramas,-a sufficient evidence, if evidence be needed, of the unnecessariness of obscenity from the artistic as well as the ethical standpoint."

"Among Ben Jonson's plays two have ranked, and deservedly ranked, foremost,—Volpone and The Alchemist. The former seemes to me to be the superior, but its ineradicable coarseness precluded its publication in this volume; whereas the Alchemist is both an admirable example of Jonson's skill in applying the rules of classic composition to an English subject, and a fair representative of his satire and erudition."

Concerning ⟨the plays of⟩ Beaumont and Fletcher—" These are The Maid's Tragedy, Valentinian and Philaster: the first two contain passages equal to the best their authors wrote, but they are besmirched with so much coarseness, and brutality is so hopelessly interwoven in their plots, that I was forced to reject them;"

published by Ginn, 1890
supplied by Santa Monica Library (to MM) 1935

Tears: T. S. Eliot.
Kipling: Rudyard Kipling (1865–1936), British poet and novelist. Cummings parodies lines from his poem "The Return." "If England was what England seems, / An' not the England of our dreams, / But only putty, brass, an' paint, / 'Ow quick we'd drop 'er! But she ain't!"
Thayer: William Roscoe Thayer, ed., *The Best Elizabethan Plays* (Boston: Ginn and Company, 1890). See the preface, pages 3–5.

42. Pound to Cummings

TL-2. Carbon.

29 Lug. [July 1935]　　　　　　　　　　310 San Gregorio, Venezia

Unclear as to who what is,or is which In yr. quatrain on the effulgent Gingrich; hesitate to contradict WHOM has seen on the hoof WHEREOF have no aural or occular proof

Save by letter outthrusted that by Ernest, the Hemingway, was "trusted"; not by that gent confirmed, nor for that matter contradicted,
Meaning perhaps that Hem thought he could HANDLE the case,
which we naturally are not up to doing.

waaal m I dunno. Zall right bei me, up to present. and the case of hoff, sub judice.

> or I dunno noddings.

some likes and some doesn't

resistence MUST be considerable, all the Rascoes and Seldeses constantly poiring OIL) hail oil onto the psycosis.

> Remarkable feat to git you, me, the egregious Fordie into so a

paper. Can/could it continue??

> and if not, show us a b'er pyper

or to paraphrase sweet Nell "faithful till given the gate. and anyhow we OUGHT to know MORE.

What the hell CAN one say that 250,000 or whatever will stand for//
> and HOW does one say it if one could?

Am goin SalzHolberglywood, not that I much care about it, but promised a bus ride back.

Why wont some ARYAN pay me, iss my fvirst nhame a pogrum?

Rascoes: Burton Rascoe.
Seldeses: George and Gilbert Seldes. George was the author of an unflattering book about Mussolini, *Sawdust Caesar* (1932).
SalzHolberglywood: Salzberg, Austria. The site of an annual summer music festival that Pound attended on several occasions.

43. Cummings to Pound

TLS-1.

August 18 [1935]   849 11th st. SantaMonica California

how do you do,signor
> sunny cally salutes you,not to mention what is called profusion
> which does the same(or so I assume). Hope

> to wangle enough jack out of somewhere else to get the Hell out of
> anywhere here pronto,e'er kike makes right since wrong is wrong
> and wrong etc

> any noose?

eec

44. Cummings to Pound

TLS-1.

Ocotber 3 '35   Silver Lake,New Hampshire

Dear Pound—
haven't heard from yer honor in a number of epochs & am naturally
suspicious:what with Roosevelt growing whichfully Boulder at Hoover dam &
Robinson Crusoe translated into Basic for the benefit of marinated moujiks &
social discredit goosing Father Coughlin in the Alberta & the Quintuplets still
taking nourishment & Lawrence puking postumously all over his Doubleday
Doran & Mussolini busily barking up the woebegone arsehole of Solomon!
Sure an' 'tis a fine hoblate horange yer cronie Joymes Jace has uprightly
decided to walk blindly upon. All the more cause,I'm thinkin', fer a couple
o'dizzily undelapidated & otherwise prematurely noncrepuscular
correspondents like our blessed selves to hark forwardly backward into the
pettifoggering salaami o' the ringstrakers & to cry oop fer a Mann named fer
instance Thomas

> "For distance in a straight line has no mystery. The mystery is in the
> sphere. But the sphere consists in correspondence"—what was I atellin'
> you—"and redintegration"—a translator's word,to be unsure—";it is a
> doubled half that becomes one, that is made by joining an upper and a
> lower half,a heavenly and an earthly hemisphere,which complement each
> other in a whole,in such a manner that what is above is also below;and
> what happens in the earthly repeats itself in the heavenly sphere and
> contrariwise. This complementary exchange of two halves which together
> form a closed sphere is equivalent to actual change—that is,revolution.
> The sphere rolls—that lies in the nature of spheres. Bottom is soon top
> and top bottom,in so far as one can speak of top and bottom in such a
> connection. Not only do the heavenly and the earthly recognise
> themselves in each other,but,thanks to the revolution of the sphere,the
> heavenly can turn into the earthly, the earthly into the heavenly,from
> which it is clear that gods can become men and on the other hand men
> can become gods again." (Joseph And His Brothers,page 205-6,Knopf
> publisher)

compare Gaudier.

Come come,me fine boyo⟨quoth the flyder to the spi⟩;haul up yer catgut
out o'the pretty pond o' putrid politics & bait a strong rope with all o' yourself
& jump you out right inwardly at the Isful ubiquitous wasless&shallbeless
quote scrotumtightening unquote omnivorously eternal thalassa pelagas or
Ocean

And just to prove there is nothing provable or I'm not joking,shall be sending you(in the was of an aeon or twain unless it's tomorrow-come-yesterday)one book of a ballet which nobody here will produce by the oozing artichoke of impassioned ishtar

—be good!

eec

Roosevelt: President Roosevelt spoke at the dedication ceremonies for the Boulder (now Hoover) Dam on 30 September 1935. In his remarks, Roosevelt empha-sized how this project and many others were contributing to economic recov-ery. "We have helped mankind by the works themselves and, at the same time, we have created the necessary purchasing power to throw in the clutch to start the wheels of what we call private industry."

Robinson Crusoe: *Robinson Crusoe, by Daniel Defoe; Put into Basic by T. Takata* (London: K. Paul, Trench, Trubner and Co., 1933).

Basic: British American Scientific International Commercial. A language developed by C. K. Ogden that is a reduction of English to 850 common words. Cummings's reference to *Robinson Crusoe* may have been inspired by a BASIC version of the beginning of the novel included in C. K. Ogden's *The System of Basic English* (New York: Harcourt, Brace and Company, 1934), 280–86.

social discredit: On 27 August 1935, the voters of Alberta, Canada, gave fifty-six of sixty-three seats in the province's legislative assembly to the Social Credit Party. For a full account of the campaign and the election, see John A. Irving, *The Social Credit Movement in Alberta* (Toronto: University of Toronto Press, 1959).

Coughlin: Father Charles E. Coughlin, whose radio speeches on economic reform earned him a large following in the first half of the 1930s. Coughlin's popularity was at its height in 1935.

Quintuplets: The celebrated Dionne quintuplets of Canada. See also letter 56.

Lawrence: T. E. Lawrence, author of *The Seven Pillars of Wisdom: A Triumph* (New York: Doubleday, Doran and Co., 1935).

Mussolini: Italian forces invaded Abyssinia on 2 October 1935.

Solomon: King Solomon is visited by the queen of Sheba in the tenth chapter of 1 Kings. One legend that grew up around their encounter was that they had a son who founded the Abyssinian dynasty.

Joymes Jace: In this sentence and the next, Cummings mimics the style of Joyce's *Work in Progress,* which was published in 1939 as *Finnegans Wake.* In the penultimate sentence of this letter, Cummings uses a word ("scrotumtighten-ing") coined by Joyce in the first chapter of *Ulysses.*

Mann: The quotation is from *Joseph and His Brothers:* trans. H. T. Lowe-Porter (New York: Knopf, 1934).

Gaudier: Henri Gaudier-Brzeska (1891–1915). Cummings probably has in mind the brief essay by Gaudier, "Gaudier-Brzeska Vortex," reprinted in the first chapter of Pound's *Gaudier-Brzeska: A Memoir* (Gallup A10). Mann's remarks seem to have reminded Cummings of some of Gaudier's observations, such as: "Religion pushed him to the use of the VERTICAL which inspires awe. His gods were self made, he built them in his image, and RETAINED AS MUCH OF THE SPHERE AS COULD ROUND THE SHARPNESS OF THE PARAL-LELOGRAM."

ballet: Cummings refers to *Tom* (New York: Arrow Editions, 1935) (Firmage A15).

45. Pound to Cummings

TLS-1.

15 Oct[ober 1935]   Hotel Italia, via Quattro Fontane
                                              ROMA

Deeuh estlin et uxor
                    Canchuh onnerstan ITZ me sportin sperrit

I like playin tennis, but it wd. givv me no sort ov pleasure to shot a pore subaqueous hipperpoTAmus with all odds on the powzder an shot.
          When you got some real big buzzard like the bloody Bank of Eng. it is fun trailin the varmints
                    WHAT else IS worth shootin?

and fer provin/ now Krizeferusalland hell be merciful to the hinmost WHEN in hell did I ever try to PROVE anything; aint I allus been content to TELL th bastids.
                              If they cant see it, as Sweedybug sez is what think the angels, If they cant SEE it, they wont when its proved.
          anyhow itza grreat life. and I been havin fun fer a fortnight. benedictions.
                    yrz EZ
                    an me luvv to th lady.

Sweedybug: Emanuel Swedenborg (1688–1772), Swedish mystic. In *Heaven and Its Wonders and Hell, from Things Heard and Seen* (New York: American Swedenborg Society, 1925), Swedenborg observes that the angels, being entirely spiritual, know things directly and unerringly. Pound's interest in Swedenborg is covered in Demetres Tryphonopoulos's "Ezra Pound and Emanuel Swedenborg" and Andrzej Sosnowski's "Pound's Imagism and Emanuel Swedenborg." Both articles are in *Paideuma*, vol. 20, no. 3 (winter 1991).

46. Cummings to Pound

TLS-1.

[November 1935]   [4 Patchin Place]

Seen your—
why take coronam in manu re someone who doesn't do idem¿ ?election lost 1
whole bottle of cognac;but haven't paid, unlike the hero that steered a peanut
with his nose through wasn't it Broadway at rushhour & wouldn't it be all
goodnights of the hammer and sickle who voted themselves clean out of their
ballot with what might be called their enthusiasm. Hereupon everything's so
much less worse you'd possibly feel ill natured chez nous for the première fois
since you never showed up Biggerandbessemer biece-niece has taken to raining
down extradividends but well Marion & me . . . some folks just don't seem to
be born for "relief." Give you my word we haven't even bothered to turn up
our collars —how's my favorite city Paris(France) or are you just playing
tennis in vennis

                HERE ONE SINGETH
          b is for business
          u is for i
          l is for liberty
          l is for lie
          s is for shoe &
          h is for hat
          i is for you &
          tit is for tat

                            —vive les nichons!
                                  c'gs

"You know that it is commonly said that Freud being an unmarried man and
an Austrian has gained most of his knowledge of women through prostitutes
and that he is by no means to be taken as a criterion on the psychology of
women of a different type."

                                  Amy Lowell

(so now we understand that notorious quarrel)

election: New York state elections were held on 5 November 1935. The Republican
    Party gained control of the State Assembly as well as a majority of up-state
    mayoral offices. In New York City there were two elections to the U.S. House of
    Representatives, both won by Democrats.

nichons: French slang for "breasts."

Lowell: Cummings cites a 1917 letter by her printed in S. Foster Damon's *Amy Lowell: A Chronicle* (Boston and New York: Houghton Mifflin, 1935), 431.

47. Pound to Cummings

TLS-1.

[23 November 1935]   Rap

                                                           alley

Estlin of East Lynn ben Patchin
comfort of my declinin' yeeurs

                                    allus by address takink me back to the night
I spent at the Brevoot givin my bed at Joe Britten's to choolia/ and she didn't
like it and tried to slip on a bundle of noozwypers either at yr/ joint or at No.
8 cause I fergit which way the numbers run in the ct/yd.

Vive les mamelons! in my chast' an bienpensant dizshunary there is no sech
woid as <u>nichons</u>.

                        so I cant tell if you use it is some other division. such is dics/
wot they givs us in kawledges.

                but it has a "summary of the alterations introduced by the french
academy".
The Amy is az ever sublime// and a paralel pendant to Freud's DAUGHTER ⟨#⟩
who gives psych anal to CHILDREN wiff Mr Tiffany's darter right there in Vi/
enner having the two young uns psychd.

        Now which unmarried ore did freud beget that one ⟨#⟩ on/ or was the
swan of Brooklyne and HiLow kennels misinformed?

                        sublime/ of course: allus sublime on Kimborazzo's summits.

                yrz

                        EZ P

& gimmy luv to the lady.

Brevoot: The Hotel Brevoort (since demolished) on lower Fifth Avenue at Eighth
Street. The cafes of the Brevoort and the Hotel Lafayette were gathering places
for Greenwich Village artists and intellectuals.

Joe Britten's: Charles H. Britting (ca. 1847–1914) owned what *Trow's Directory*
termed an "eatinghouse" at 124–26 Greenwich Avenue, an address close to
Patchin Place. Pound had lodgings there in October 1910. He describes Britting

in a letter to Margaret Cravens; see Omar Pound and Robert Spoo, eds., *Ezra Pound and Margaret Cravens: A Tragic Friendship, 1910–1912* (Durham, N.C.: Duke University Press, 1988), 52-53.

choolia: In the autumn and winter of 1910–11, Pound was living in New York. There he renewed acquaintance with Julia Wells, a "kindly old woman . . . who had fed Pound and given him some free lodging in Venice back in 1908" (James Wilhelm, *Ezra Pound in London and Paris, 1908–1925* [University Park: Pennsylvania State University Press, 1990], 58. Wells lived at 4 Patchin Place.

DAUGHTER: Anna Freud (1895–1982), a pioneer in the field of child psychoanalysis.

Tiffany's darter: Dorothy Tiffany Burlingham (1891–1979), the youngest child of Louis Comfort Tiffany. Her two eldest children, Robert and Mabbie, were analyzed by Anna Freud. See Michael John Burlingham's *The Last Tiffany* (New York: Atheneum, 1989).

Kimborazzo's: "On Chimborazo's summits treads sublime" is a line from Anna Letitia Barbauld's poem "Eighteen Hundred and Eleven." See the note to letter 243.

48. Pound to Cummings

TL-2. Carbon

26/ Dec[ember 1935]   [Rapallo]

Dear Estlin et uxor
                      DID the Gordian NOTT ever import them copies? or did he between the two bundles hesitate and still is??
        No use my happologizin fer hiz slowness. Have just had proofs of the Chinese Character, with my new notes . . . which wuz to lead off the series.
                              though I had a set up of Ta Hio months ago/
        lakk of Kappital. pore Stanny means well, and has at least got out Butchart's "Money"
                              50 copies sold to Japan.
        But 12/6 book prob/ tukk up all his REsources.

LATER

days nooz/ Tony Eden, the squit/ At A LAST identified.

In 1923 he married daughter of Westminster BANK, same year became an M/P/
                wet subject fer pooSEEEEE.
and THAT li'l deTECtiv story comes to a pause.

nothing iz without efficient caws
said the Crow
To hell with Poe.

      Wot I started to rite WUZ
is there any sense in my coming to the Eu S.A.
and where are you. If I did?

I am FED U P with sanctions/

England is a nuissance/ result of this shit is
restriction of consumption
rise in price of petrol
gun sales by Mitsui, for benefit of frog share holders.

Hope you will LOOK at Newd Eemocracy fer the 1st Dec.

I hadda piece in it. Laughlin wd/ cert like to print you in his segment. (I hadn't
thorter thaat when I started ritin)

WOT wd/ in DO in amurikuh fer a few weaks? God knoze
It is the WET weather that sets me fancy rovin.

ask the blind comrades WHY they collaborate with Mr Eden rather than with
those of us who
WANT to COMMUNIZE the PRODUCT and USE abundance

whereas the socialists want to communize the productive plant (or state
capitalize it) and PREVENT abundance.

      of course they won't SAY, but I allus think I am a better Leninist
than isss Trottszk.
      Lemme know if you meat any thinkin
FRAGMENTS.
Waal; that BLUE Max Ernst that I got when we wuz in Paris IZ still a comfort.
Wot else?

copies: Copies of Cummings's latest collection of poems, *No Thanks.*
proofs: Proofs of *The Chinese Written Character as a Medium for Poetry* (London:
    Stanley Nott, 1936) (Gallup B36). This was the initial work in the projected
    "Ideogramic Series, Edited by Ezra Pound."
"Money": Montgomery Butchart, ed., *To-Morrow's Money, by Seven of Today's
    Leading Monetary Heretics* (London: Stanley Nott, 1936). A collection of essays

by J. Stuart Barr, Arthur Kitson, Frederick Soddy, R. McNair Wilson, C. H. Douglas, G. D. H. Cole, and Jeffrey Mark.

Eden: Anthony Eden (1897–1977), who became British foreign secretary in December 1935. In 1923 he had married Beatrice Beckett, daughter of Sir Gervase Beckett (1866–1937), a partner in the banking firm of Beckett and Company, and later director of the Westminster Bank, Ltd.

sanctions/: In response to Italy's invasion of Abyssinia on 3 October 1935, almost all the members of the League of Nations imposed economic sanctions on Italy.

Mitsui: The House of Mitsui was the most powerful business enterprise in Japan in the 1920s and 1930s.

piece: "Who Gets It?" *New Democracy,* vol. 5, no. 7 (1 December 1935) (Gallup C1275).

Laughlin: James Laughlin regularly contributed to *New Democracy* in a column headed "New Directions."

Ernst: Pound refers to a seascape by Ernst, purchased by Dorothy Pound in the mid-1920s. In "The Coward Surrealists," *Contemporary Poetry and Prose,* no. 7 (November 1936), 136 (Gallup C1375), Pound says, "I can not believe that a knowledge of Pier della Francesca's researches into perspective dims my eye for the Ernst 'Blue' that now faces me." In "Method," *New English Weekly,* vol. 10, no. 23 (18 March 1937), 446 (Gallup C1397), he notes, "The effect of usury in the fine arts is weakening in some quarters. It was wearing thin when Wyndham Lewis did Timon, it is quite thin in Max Ernst's blue seascape." Both articles are reprinted in *EPPP.* The seascape is now at Schloss Brunnenburg, the home of Mary de Rachewiltz.

49. Pound to Cummings

TLS-1.

5 Jan[uary] 1936   Rapallo

Dear Estlin

   EF I shd/ git a cheap ticket ⟨to N.Y.⟩ and look into murka fer a few weeks WHERE and HOW?

   I heard the Brevoort is not. Are there any hotels where a guy with uncertain habits, and vague political views can stop fer 1.50 a night without getting gangstered? or held to ransom by Mike Gold's accomplices?

   I sent ⟨you⟩ me noo yrz greetins to the far westurn coast.

   Any close ups on the leading red lights? This guy Bob Miner fer ezampl ? any accessibility to idea of communizing product?

   Longer I much round with these alterers and re/changers more it seems they are ⟨aren't⟩ so WRONG as PARTIAL,

        each gang got a piece and NONE a whole machine.

Several violent oppositions cleared WHEN opponents find out what other op/ iz drivin at.

which, as they NONE of 'em read anything but themselves they ALLUS ignore.

I spose a fat man like Fordie stays in the Plaza for two nights and the Bowery fer the rest of it?

I shd/ have to see me own country first, I spose as far as Buffalo and Baltimore or zummat.

earlier epistle ⟨to you⟩ was longer but on other.

greetins to a lady.

yrz EZ

Gold's: Michael Gold (born Irwin Granich) (1893–1967), editor of *New Masses*.
Miner: Robert Minor (1884–1952), American Communist, cartoonist, essayist, and formerly executive editor of the *Liberator*. Communist candidate for mayor of New York City in 1933.
Fordie: Ford Madox Ford.

50. Cummings to Pound

TLS-1.

January 29 [1936]   4 Patchin [Place]

Dear Pound—
delighted to learn that you're casting your anchor and blowing newworldward!!!!!

as to hostelries:you'll probably have to pay more than you mentioned if you stop at,say,the Lafayette(or else be bathless):there are a few cheaper dumps in this vicinity but all somewhat dismal. Uptown,on the contrary,am told they're pleading for customers—whereof I know nothing.

It's been colder than socialism here. Maybe you'll bring us a real blizzard;so far we've enjoyed mere tempests. Dos Passos tells me that "Bob" Minor is (a)in New York and (b)irritable. The kumrads sound as if they'd folded. I recommend the Irving Place Burlesk(stripteasers in excelsis)& to hell with I.D.Ology

—as usual

eec

la signor(in)a sends congratulations to the seafarer. Let's know when

> Lily Langtry & O. Henry used to live at
> the Chelsea Hotel—that's supposed to be
> circa your price

NB)I pay $45 a month for 8 Patchin—two rooms,1 tub,1 washery,1 gasstove,1 electrolux (meaning gas refrigerator,better than frigidaire which is electric),i gas cookstove,1 closet,1 shower,1 toilet. This is better at the price than anything else I know of;but such "apartments" are rented unfurnished. If you need a hotel,that's çela—why not go to a supercolossal one(Edison or Lincoln,in the 40s)? Naturally if there's anything we can do we'll do it con(piacere)n

Lafayette: A hotel on lower Fifth Avenue at Ninth Street, since demolished.
Langtry: Lillie Langtry (born Emilie Charlotte Le Breton) (1853–1929), British actress.
O. Henry: The pen name of William Sidney Porter (1869–1910), American short-story writer.
Chelsea: A hotel on Twenty-third Street between Seventh and Eighth Avenues. Wallace Stevens lived there from 1909 to 1916.
Edison: Located at 228–48 West Forty-seventh Street, it had opened in 1929.
Lincoln: Located at Eighth Avenue and Forty-fourth Street.

51. Cummings to Pound

TLS-1.

June 9,1936   4 Patchin Place

Dear Pound—

not long ago,received a genuine and otherwise deeply more than pleasant postcard from Hiler,wishing me luck and mentioning you;later,glandmaster George nay Antheil let a toot with yourself in its friendly offing. What happened to E's American voyage I haven't(of course)heard;the P being silent. And should like to know!

one dizzily tilting cigar of prodigiously luminous emptiness grazed Greenwich Village's model Hotel de Putains of an evening:the eyes of our hero & heroine failed to discern a distinguished form descending per parachute. Deutchland having failed us,Britain builded bloody boat big enough for 1000 cantos;New York's pet fireskiff jetted while 96 varieties of heavier(than lust)craft noisomely capered—again no E.P. Are you wilfully waiting to ride an unwellsian moongun?or(as they ask at the Veterans' Administration desk around toitysumpn strit)Wut

if moan sewer the tone of above's peremptory warum pas? We,sah,is distinguished people. No wie? Bikus quite impractically everyone both of us ever knew has gone to most hypercolossal not to say superprodigious trouble re we. Wut trubl? Why,trouble enough to run out on us via 10,000,000 directions. Verily,suh,our combined experiences over the late few months ages or moments would convince nearly any less inelastic folk or folks that Stink(B.O.to the proletariat)were a kindly mot for our average mental soi-disant odor. Eimi—to speak singular—seems to have started ye Spank Kumains movement;No Thanks produced a bevy of vomits,Tom scored several impurely fantastic blurpz for the woodwinds or shall we perchance write arseholes?(We shall write arseholes). E PERICOLOSO SPORGERSE:if you've still got a slippery trace of a slightest toe on Patchin's pellucid platform,prepare for perpetual showers of punkdung on all your freethinking fronts simultaneously . . . talk about the prophet Ezra's "Hell and putridity"/owe boi

"we eat what we can and can what we can't"(old saw)

or to make a short story even longer:come va? Dancing a highland fling in union handcuffs with twenty trillion nitwits in your hair,I'll bet;and each of them bound in a different shade of Buchman,as befits all wugged inferiorlists of this prenatal ewa. But(sh)the funny whole of the sad part of it is that they can't get us down without our touching mother earth—something,seh,that hasn't even occurred to Adolphus Stalin Inc. whose knowledge of mythology is confined to the book of job. My own mother,on the other hand,is very fond of said metaphor and I wish I could remember the name of the lucky protagonist

my my your,how surprised they'll all be down in where was Moses when the light went out not Warsaw what the Watercloset somehow isn't exactly right O sure you got it Washington. D for dirty and C for cuntlapping,or shouldn't one mention a recent scene at the Lafayette(nous y sommes)when Gwiffin Bawwy stepped from Soil Erosion(with a drawingaccount)straight into Waterfowl Preservation(so the gunners can shoot them period)

& house moose wear yoor?

If a chap named David Diamond from Rochester New York who took the trouble to write a score(musical)for my ballet under that score(literal)by myself,with arrows pointing down from latter to former lest Choreographer Myaseen might take it into his Russian голова [head] to turn little Eva into topsy's granduncle—give him my best. Not that anything would seem less likely than that the original Tom should find itself produced in very teeth of Messrs Draper Kirstein Warburg and Draper's soviet epic,music by Nabokov,scheduled for appearance at ye Metropolitan Opera(& meanwhile Governor Landon was constantly being photographed surrounded with blossoming offshots. America,sir,is a fine environment)and don't let nobody kit use

eec

Coney Island's best to date:a "Loopoplane"

the "gondola",under the influence of a motor, swings back and forth &I then makes 3 compl● revolutions
          --after which it's stopped in position A for about ten seconds. I strongly recommend

Hiler: Hilaire Hiler (1898–1966), American painter and jazz pianist who was part of the circle of expatriates in Paris in the 1920s.

Antheil: George Antheil (1900–59), American composer and the subject of Pound's *Antheil and the Treatise on Harmony* (1924) (Gallup A25).

cigar: The dirigible *Hindenburg* made its first flight to the United States in 1936. It passed over New York City on 9 May.

bloody boat: The *Queen Mary*. Its maiden voyage took it to New York City on 1 June 1936.

Buchman: Frank Buchman (1878–1961) American spiritual leader and founder of the Moral Re-Armament movement.

Gwiffin Bawwy: Griffin Barry, American journalist active circa 1920–40.

Diamond: David Diamond (b. 1915), American composer.

Myaseen: Perhaps Léonide Massine (1896–1979), Russian-born choreographer.

Draper: Muriel Draper, the mother of the dancer Paul Draper Jr. A friend and former lover of Cummings. She ended their friendship when *Eimi* was published.

Kirstein: Lincoln Kirstein. "During the fall [of 1935], reports in the newspapers announced that Kirstein's American Ballet Company was going to present a ballet based on *Uncle Tom's Cabin* in the next season. Cummings thought that success had come at last and a composer was at work on the music, but when his publisher telephoned to find out the details, Kirstein told him that it was not Cummings' *Tom* but another version 'apparently by Kirstein, with music by [Nicholas] Nabokoff.' Rumors had it that Muriel Draper was involved in the production too, and Cummings let his imagination roam about the result: 'Kumrads Kirstein and Draper, Inc.' would end the ballet with a 'black and white chorus declaiming "Workers of the World Unite."' He was bitterly angry with Kirstein, and though the supposedly rival ballet never came into being, their friendship cooled to nonexistence" (Kennedy, 372). In a January 1936 letter to David Diamond, Cummings wrote, "thanks kindly for your music; and I'm glad Janet sent you a copy of 'Tom.' As for the question who is or isn't composing a score: Sessions was originally supposed to do it. Louis Siegel (whose music for Watson's extraordinary 'Lot' I liked) wanted to do it, and wrote me to that effect: I was obliged to write him that a composer had already been picked. Later, the American Ballet decided not to wait for Sessions, and tried to get Thomson; that fell through. Still later, Kirstein (who commissioned 'Tom') wrote me that the American Ballet couldn't put on my ballet. Then several New York etc. newspapers announced a production of 'Uncle Tom's Cabin' by the American Ballet; my publisher 'phoned Kirstein, who stated that the ballet was not my ballet but another ballet (apparently by Kirstein, with music by Nabokoff)."

Warburg: Edward M. M. Warburg (1908–92). From 1933 to 1936, Edward Warburg was a financial backer as well as the business manager of Lincoln Kirstein's American Ballet.

Nabokov: Nicolas Nabokov (1903–78), Russian-born American composer.

Landon: Alfred M. Landon (1887–1987), governor of Kansas and Republican nominee for president in 1936.

52. Pound to Cummings

TLS-2.

23 June 1936   Rapallo

> The Hiler howleth bitterly
> That the Kumrad unKumradly
>   Is and was ever and wont even answer a posCar.

Waaal: bo you have a gluttonness fer punishment/ alle sameee Wynd. Lewis in London. whaaar he STICK.

I dunno how you masochists do it.

Waaal, I am in'erested in Claudius Salmasius, and I wanna fine out a bit erbout the Monte dei Paschi. I mean more'n I know. And the Brit. Ital. Bulletin has printed a lot but. . . .

and nobody likes Mr Aberhart/ An let alone there not bein a Little Review

a Dial is not/

and wherewhenanHow do we eat?

Of course whether anyone has seen or read what I have said in the Bully Tin, I dunno.

But this IS the most civilized country/

You can go for several days without metting that baby stare wherewith the ang/ sax   greet ANY verbal manifestation of an idea.

I don't mean there aint any iggurunts. BUT . . .

the idea of mental movement is not absolutely unfamiliar to ALL the denizens.

Mebbe in time I will git roun to a canto. at present seems so much that ought to go INTO 'em.

needing historic digestion.

Know anyfink about the Alcestis press??

wot wants to print Cheever??

My relations with Faber are strained (20 pound strain . . plus the language).

Waaal, that AINT yr/ district.

e:e:c: and two pages monthly in Munson's . . .

other:alas manifestations unrecorded in transpitted scripts.

Not even a worried Quinn to say NO at the last moment.

Waal as the Boss said: "PerchE vuol' mettere i suoi idee in ordine?"

It may be an error. at any rate it MUST be inhuman.

An here's Mr Moron on front page Figaro/ and M.Jean touring in 80 days the world of J.Verne. Charlot and Miss Goddard.

benedictions. and to the lady

yrz EZ

Hiler: In a letter of 19 April 1936, Hiler wrote to Pound that "new york is a great place to see people, *I definitely don't think.* cummings has lived around the corner from me, not over two blocks away, for the last year and a half. he lives in a relatively tranquil little alley called 'patchin place' at number four (in case you don't know the address.) I wrote him two notes as he wisely has no phone. one when I was in my cups, the other in state of complete sobriety. assume that he received both of 'em as they never came back but I never saw him nor heard a word."

Salmasius: Latinized name of Claude Saumaise (1588–1653), French classical scholar. Pound refers to him and his *De Modo Usurarum* in *Carta da Visita* (Gallup A50a), "The Individual in his Milieu" (Gallup C1252), and Canto 87.

Monte dei Paschi: A bank in Siena founded in 1623. Pound discusses it in Cantos 42 and 43, where he celebrates it as a bank whose profits went back to the people of the community.

Bulletin: Gallup's *Ezra Pound: A Bibliography* notes that the "*British-Italian Bulletin* was issued as a supplement to *L'Italia Nostra,* a newspaper for Italian-speaking residents of Great Britain" (307). Pound contributed articles to the *Bulletin* during 1935 and 1936.

Aberhart: William Aberhart (1878–1943), Social Credit advocate who served as premier of Alberta, Canada, from 1935 to 1943.

Alcestis press: A small press founded in New York City by Columbia professor Ronald Lane Latimer. Latimer had published William Carlos Williams's *An Early Martyr and Other Poems* in September 1935. It was followed in September 1936 by *Adam and Eve and the City.*

Cheever: Probably Ralph Cheever Dunning (1878–1930), an American expatriate poet Pound had met in Paris in 1921. See Pound's "Mr. Dunning's Poetry," *Poetry,* vol. 26, no. 6 (September 1925), 339–45 (Gallup C681). Reprinted in *Paideuma,* vol. 10, no. 3 (winter 1981), 605–9 and in *EPPP.*

Munson's: Gorham Munson's Social Credit monthly, *New Democracy.*

Quinn: John Quinn (1870–1924), American lawyer and patron of the arts. His relationship with Pound is covered in Timothy Materer's *The Selected Letters of Ezra Pound to John Quinn* (Durham, N.C.: Duke University Press, 1991) and B. L. Reid's *The Man from New York: John Quinn and His Friends* (New York: Oxford University Press, 1968).

the Boss: Benito Mussolini. Pound was granted an interview with Mussolini on 30 January 1933. In *Guide to Kulchur,* Pound reports that at one point Mussolini asked him this question: "*Perche vuol mettere le sue idee in ordine?* (Why do you want to set your ideas in order?)" (182).

Mr Moron: Possibly Georges Duhamel (1884–1966), French poet, dramatist, and novelist. His article "Le Servitude politique" appeared on the front page of *Le Figaro* for 10 June 1936. In the article, Duhamel deplored an excessive interest in political questions on the part of savants. He concludes, "La France a longtemps lutté contre cette infection mortelle. Elle y succombe enfin. Les rares esprits indépendants qui ne désespèrent pas d'entretenir leurs contemporains, sinon des questions éternelles, du moins des grands problèmes de la science, de l'art, des lettres ou de la philosophie, ne tarderont pas à sentir que ces débats essentiels n'intéressent plus personne" [For a long time, France has fought against this fatal disease. She has finally succumbed. Those rare, independent souls who don't despair of maintaining (a dialogue with) their contemporaries—if not over eternal questions—at least about the great problems of science, art, literature or philosophy, will quickly sense that these essential debates don't interest anyone anymore].

M. Jean: Jean Cocteau. In *Le Figaro* for 9 June 1936 (p. 2) appeared a photograph of Cocteau with Japanese actors. The caption: "Le célèbre poète, qui accomplit actuellement un voyage autour du monde, s'est arrêté plusieurs jours à Tokio. On let voit ici, en compagnie du grand acteur japonais Kikugoro" [The celebrated poet, who is presently taking a trip around the world, stopped for several days in Tokyo. He is seen here in company with the great Japanese actor Kikugoro].

Charlot: Charlie Chaplin. Chaplin and Paulette Goddard were costars of *Modern Times,* then playing in Paris.

53. Cummings to Pound

TLS-2.

7th July [1936]   Silver Lake
                                                  (tel.:Madison)
                                                  NH

Dear EP—

seeing as how your latest Rapalloism suggests 6 lipdisked Ubangi stepping from the largest Egyptian pyramid in 1 Sears,Roebuck raincoat I submitted it to my learned colleague Professor Morehouse;who(with her not unusual virtuosity)translated same out of the original Pakrit into Choctaw:which being subjected to the radiance of the full moon for 2 hours 45 minutes 10 7/8 seconds and the merely a trifle arcane risiduum treated with saturated dolce-far-niente(patents pending)Hitler eventually appeared,speaking Hiler,and bowing from the ankles a la Joe Louis "do you" he guttered "know the very old one about the kike,with a soi-disant furcoat on one arm,pursuing a wouldnotbe customer of Nordic subtraction through the secondhandshop of the former;and the Nordic keeps backing up and the kike keeps bearing down until accidentally said furcoat comes in immediate contact with a functioning radiator:whereupon the Nordic(suddenly siezing his own nose)cries out "take it away! I tell you that coat's no good:smell it!" A nuance of horror traverses our wouldbe salesman's elastic physiognomy—and is immediately superceded by a kindly if not pitying smile. "That aint the coat" he objects,very gently "that's me. —Aint I the dirty sonofabitch!" Just at this moment,my friend the

Professor caught sight of a NY newspaper headline announcing that Dali appeared on a platform attired in a divingsuit and lectured the People of London on art through a loudspeaker which broke down. Tie that one,babe

now as for our earning one's living, it's simple;so simple it hurts(copyright):change your name to Shastakovich,you sadist,and S.Hurok(Inc.)will give you $5000 a week to tour the United Sates in an open bathtub complete with cellophane washcloths and rubberized soap not to mention hot water ad libido;you may or may not say anything you wish provided(of course)nobody misunderstands it,and I incidentally recommend among others the Minsky on Broadway circa 46th Street whose stripteasers part with sufficient urging with the eternal triangle with a smile without exaggeration withal. Bubs titties and nichons have the honour to call to your andsoforth the fact that andsoforth and sollicit your further patronage,expressing profound satisfaction andsoforth andsoforth and merely suggesting a plunge in Nipples

due [page 2]

Preferred(signed)Duggie

it seems to me that "Alcestis" had a mysterious editor,willfully anonymous & all that,probably a Princeton Man at worst? They do not specialize in misprints but will make a great effort to supply you within reason,especially the square kind with round earmuffs;presumably based on a misquoted text by Apuleius Assininus(5th century B.O.)relating to wedlock as practiced by certain less celebrated specimens of the immense lettuce family whose confusion with the conifers caused Darwin to explode Sir James Jean's ultrastellar cosmogonensis or tryptichery,sans so much as a prego svp etc and very distinctly to the deciduous detriment of bilingual both;burp

IF

If Franklin were what Landon seems
And not the Farley of our dreams
But only Kansas crap and piss
How quick we'd chuck him. But he iss

do you know a fellow named Roger Roughton? I met him in Santa Monica. He'd driven across the continent as they call it loosely in something closely ressembling a fourwheeled tricycle,& confided to us that once a shoe blewout so he took off the wheel and then threw it away. (Americans substitute a spare). A charming chap of portly Marxian leanings but we apparently agree on Fair Play:at least I do

—hoping you are the same
eec

#deuxieme catastrophe
    a man without Dreyfus(sp?)
    saw Blums in a tree
    he neither took Blooms nor left Blames
    now comment peut cela etre?

Pakrit: Prakrit is "a term applied to the older vernacular dialects of India, such as were derived from, or kindred to, Sanskrit" (Henry Yule and A. C. Burnell, *Hobson-Jobson: A Glossary of Colloquial Anglo-Indian Words and Phrases, and of Kindred Terms, Etymological, Historical, Geographical, and Discursive*, new ed., ed. William Crooke [London: John Murray, 1903], 730).

Joe Louis: (1914–81), heavyweight boxing champion of the world 1937–49.

Dali: Salvador Dali (1904–89), Spanish artist. Works by Dali were included in the first International Surrealist Exhibition in London, held from 11 June to 4 July 1936 at the New Burlington Galleries. Dali gave a lecture, "Some Authentic Paranoic Phantoms," dressed in a diving suit. His words were inaudible and he nearly suffocated. See Meryle Secrest, *Salvador Dali* (New York: E. P. Dutton, 1986), 163–64.

Shastakovitch: Dmitry Shostakovich (1906–75), Russian composer.

S.Hurok: Sol Hurok (1888–1974), Russian-born American impresario.

Landon: As in letter 41, Cummings again parodies Kipling's poem "The Return."

Farley: James A. Farley.

Roughton: (1917–41), British editor. In 1936 Roughton founded a little magazine in London, *Contemporary Poetry and Prose*. Cummings contributed poems to it and Pound published a brief note, "The Coward Surrealists" (Gallup C1375), in the issue for November 1936. In December 1936 Roughton published a selection of poems by Cummings, *One Over Twenty* (Firmage A16). *Contemporary Poetry and Prose* ceased publication with issue 10 (autumn 1937).

Dreyfus: Alfred Dreyfus (1859–1935), French military officer of Jewish descent. His conviction on charges of treason began the Dreyfus Affair, a controversy that shook France from 1894 to 1906.

Blums: Léon Blum (1872–1950), the first Jewish premier of France (1936–37). He became premier in June 1936 as the leader of the Popular Front coalition.

54. Pound to Cummings

TL-2. On verso of a card listing a program of music at Rapallo. Pound typed on the program: "this is a local effort Rapallo."

[Postmarked 13 November 1936]   Rapallo

    Dear Estlin and consort:
        Is anyone still cheered
by such simple outpourings of the

middle aged mind?
Item re/ Charlie J// appeared in our morining pypers
    12 Nov. if you want the date.
        O CALiForny
            yrz EZ

& they allus say I got no ear fer ther varnacular

AS REPORTED ; Nov. 1936

Charles Johnson wuz 90 years ov age
In Los Angeles Californy
He wuz her maaan an' a doin' her wrong.

Fucked an frittered his life away
In Los Angeles Californy
His wife wuz only 83
but disapproved of adultery
In Los Angeles in Californy

an Charley wuzza doin her wrooooong

One night when Charley went ter bed
she got his razor
                and he BLED
in Los Angeles Californy.

If ever your bitch is 83
and still disapproves of adultery
      You take this live wire tip from me
and dont go to Californy

          Charley wuz old and habitual
          but he wuzza doin her wrong
mebbe in fact and mebbe in fancy
but old girls out there is teasy and chancey.

so don't doin' em wrong
Unless you want yer gullit ~~spi p split~~ ⟨slit⟩
in Los Angeles Califrony
Where the male prong is so horny.
                ~~Ninety years old and a doing her~~
Ninety years old and doin her wrong.
Just to show he wuz still stong.

In Los Angeles Californy.
Where the men are ornry and horny
~~And the wimmen are resentful and~~

She said Charley wuzza doin her wrooooong.

"A chasin' wimmen" wuz the phrase
she used to excuse her fer endin' his days.

EZ

55. Pound to Cummings

TCS.

[26 December 1936]   Rapallo

If you can do anything for the Globe, St Louis, I shd/ be pleased. Dont know
what point if ANY is in yr/ mutual circumferences.
                    rushin fer train fer Roma/
                         yrz EZ
                       buone feste
              26 Dec.

Globe: This magazine began publication in March 1937. It styled itself as present-
ing "intimate journal, travel, romance, adventure, world interest." It ceased
publication in 1938. In the first several issues, Hilaire Hiler wrote columns on
international cuisine. See also Pound's contribution, "Abdication" (Gallup
C1394), in the first issue, and eight others.

56. Cummings to Pound

TLS-3.

[December 1936]   [4 Patchin Place]
                                             December the which

Dear Pound—

"my" dentist told me a joke. Shortly after Mrs Wallis Simson became Lady
Wallis Fitzdavid,a reporter asked what she thought of her boyfriend. He may be
Edward the 8th to all the world,she answered,but he's only Peter the 3rd to me.

"My" dentist was also somewhat agog over Willard,The Man Who Stretches. Here in the States(I must inform you)we have somebody named Ripley who runs a daily newsfeature,called Believe It Or Not,bringing the public's socalled attention to miracles. Well,one of Ripley's latest—it seems—is a chap who,since he can remember,has been able to make any part of himself grow and ungrow without any apparent effort. All sorts of eminent specialists have examined him,without result;so naturally they are sore as Hell. Of course he makes a tidy sum in vaudeville,etc. But the interesting thing is that "my" dentist was on a party with Willard—a highly respectable party,allow me to add. And Willarsaid(holding out his middle finger),Watch. And it grew 3 or 4 or maybe 6 inches. The girl nearest Willard almost fainted but not "my" dentist. He asked to feel Willard's finger. It felt solid. Then Willard's finger returned to normal. Then Willard made one of his legs grow for everybody,and then the other. Then Willard's neck grew—quite a lot—and retired. I asked "my" dentist about Willard's ears;and the reply was,We didn't get that far. Is he married?I asked,Has he children? I don't know,"my" dentist whispered,I was wondering too. The "hygienist" flushed slightly

now I'll show you a "handy"(a joke which you make with your fingers). Confronting a friend—be sure of this—you say and you do as follows(using only one hand)

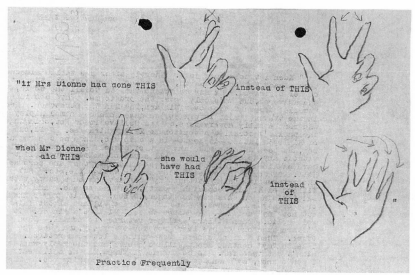

"if Mrs Dionne had done THIS   instead of THIS

when Mr Dionne did THIS   she would have had THIS   instead of THIS

Practice Frequently

VV your remarks in Roughton's mag! He should emit my slendrr volyoom pronto—& hope you'll enjoy;more especially since myself rudely insisted on being the selector

"Variety" reports that Shakespeare has no B.O. in flickers

Dolly goes WOW an present writing:you see,everybody can see it's queer
therefore Ort;and many people can even count the p-n-ses which are of course
really cucumbers or carrots or uno,so that's Oke&Jake—besides,Millit's Angle
Us has always been a Big Favorite with AngloSaxons of the nether variety.
There are at least 2 fairly good Picasso splurges current

Gielgud in Hamlet is like The Flying Cordonas;than which have no less
unspiral praise. Marion & I met him at a rout and were pleasantly amazed to
find he doesn't at all ressemble his reputation offstage either. But Leslie
Howard in the melancholy Dane . . . o my dear. Philadelphia(&Boston)"critics"
thought it 2 wonderful;naturally LH was upset when NY " [critics] panned him
into shit,so after each performance he makes a curtainspeech wistfully hinting
that certain gentlemen may be wrong;and the moviefans wilt with pleasure.
May I append the abovementioned Philly punks took a peep at G and
announced that he stunk by comparison? FLASH—lit—"Gone With The
Wind" sold its OneMillionth copy recently

I've telephoned Macy's to reserve 1 SantaClaussuit in case you're planning to
come down America's chimney this year;both are big enough for two

Marion sends love

                           —skol

                                          eec

Wallis Simson: Wallis Warfield Simpson, duchess of Windsor (1896–1986). She
    married the duke of Windsor in June 1937. He had been King Edward VIII of
    England from January to December 1936.
Willard: Clarence E. Willard (1882–1962). Willard's long and successful career in
    vaudeville depended on the abilities Cummings's dentist described. Robert
    LeRoy Ripley (1893–1949), American cartoonist, began his newspaper feature,
    "Believe It Or Not," in 1918. It featured unusual human and natural phe-
    nomena.
Mrs Dionne: Olivia Dionne, who gave birth to Yvonne, Annette, Cecile, Emilie,
    and Marie Dionne on 28 May 1934 in Ontario, Canada.
your remarks: Pound's brief article, "The Coward Surrealists," *Contemporary
    Poetry and Prose* (London), no. 7 (November 1936), 136 (Gallup C1375).
    Pound notes that the techniques of surrealism are to be found in earlier periods.
    "The XIIth century had surrealism in plenty." He goes on to condemn "mere
    flight and evasion of defined words and historic fact." Reprinted in *EPPP*.
volyoom: *1/20: Poems* (Firmage A16).
"Variety" reports: *Variety* (New York) is the weekly newspaper of the entertain-
    ment industry. "B.O." is its term for "box office." In the issue of *Variety* for 9
    December 1936 (p. 3) appeared an article under the headline, "The Bard A B.O.
    Washout." The article, by John C. Flinn, noted that "Hollywood had passed up

its option on William Shakespeare. . . . And whatever hesitancy there has been about looking the facts (which mean box office returns) squarely in the face after the public's reception of 'Midsummer Night's Dream' and 'Romeo and Juliet,' the lack of interest in 'As You Like it,' British-made and recently released in this country, has resulted in cancellation of any plans for future Shakespearean adaptation."

Dolly: Salvador Dali. Cummings may refer to an article ("The Angelus of Millet") by Dali in the magazine *New Hope* (New Hope, Penn.), vol. 2, no. 4 (August 1934). Dali finds in Millet's *Angelus* "the equivalent in painting of the well known and sublime 'chance encounter upon a dissecting table of a sewing-machine and an umbrella." Dali contends that "the tillable earth is the most advantageous of all known dissecting-tables, the umbrella and the sewing machine would be transposed in the *Angelus* under the form of a masculine and a feminine figure." Furthermore, "The umbrella . . . would be none other than the masculine figure [that] the picture seeks to dissimulate, merely rendering it more evident all the while, its state of erection through the shameful and compromising position of the hat."

Picasso splurges: Pablo Picasso (1881–1973), Spanish artist. Cummings's poem "Picasso," (*Complete Poems*, 95) celebrates his talent.

Gielgud: John Gielgud (b. 1904), British actor. He appeared in *Hamlet* in New York from October 1936 to January 1937.

Howard: Leslie Howard (1893–1943), British stage and film actor.

"Gone With The Wind": Margaret Mitchell's *Gone with the Wind* (New York: Macmillan, 1936), recorded its millionth sale in January 1937.

57. Cummings to Pound

TLS-1.

[1936]   4 Patchin Place NYCity

Dear Pound—

delighted to hear from you!

could you use anything obscene and antisocial?

I just bought a pair of shoes & a borsalino

Marion sends her best—

                                        eec

don't miss it an unattractive Jewish lad who failed to lay the boss's daughter despite a Christian nom de plume has written this epoch-making analysis of political and economic problems boldly throwing aside all such purely extrinsic factors as the psychological and fearlessly plunging the blunt rapier of his inferiority complex into world questions a poor little rich boy who died to become the only permanently paralyzed president of a merely temporarily terrorstricken republic solves every major issue confronting the civilized and uncivilized universe by rigid applications of the scientifically demonstrable assumption that strictly speaking human beings are neither more nor less than a function of their waterclosets many chapters of general interest to the confirmed crank and professional idealist including Fart And The World Farts With You and How Not To Stretch A Rubber Dollar Far Enough and Why We Should All Be Really Oneanother mutually antagonistic authorities like Benito Stalin and Vladimir Ilytch Mussolini have proclaimed this masterpiece by a sincerely secondrate opportunist the very phonograph record of the millenium remember mime is toney don't delay a single instant nobody can afford to be without

LAVABO AND OLD LICE
(by the author of
Jonah Exposed or,The Whale Had An Arsehole)

LAVABO: A play on the title of a novel by the American author Myrtle Reed (1874–1911), *Lavender and Old Lace* (1902).

58. Cummings to Pound

TLS-1. Enclosure.

28 January [1937]   [4 Patchin Place]

Dear Ezra—

some weeks ago,Marion & I were talking about you with Max Eastman & his(Russian)wife Eliena. Max asked if we thought you'd consent to come over here and lecture. We said,why not? Because if he would,said Max,I'm sure I could get him the money.

Today the enclosed arrived

whether or not you want to follow suit,why don't you drop M.E. a line of greeting? he's an old & dear friend of Marion's,a good & honest friend of mine—oddly enough—and admires you sincerely. Having just written a bestseller(The Enjoyment of Laughter)he's what's called In The Public Eye now;hence,if you did come,you'd probably do so on quote advantageous terms unquote. Madame is all wool & a yard wide:a swell gal, sans blague

—here's hoping

eec

PS)they're both confirmed Trotskyites

Enclosure: A letter from Eliena and Max Eastman, dated 26 January 1937, reporting that "(Colston) Leigh . . . said that he would guarantee Pound's expenses."
bestseller: *The Enjoyment of Laughter* (New York: Simon and Schuster, 1936).

59. Pound to Cummings

TCS.

9 Feb[ruary 1937]   Rapallo

ALL right, kumrad. Do I rate az a entertainment ? or only as a flat chested highbrow?
                                and will the above enquiry sent by this post to Leigh utterly blast and destroy my passage money OUT. ?

deevotedly   EZ

Leigh: W. Colston Leigh (1902–92), American lecturer's agent. Leigh, president of W. Colston Leigh, Inc., in New York, wanted Pound as a client and suggested that he sign with the agency for an American tour of ten or twelve weeks starting in October 1937. But Leigh and Pound were never able to agree about the date of the tour, the cities in which Pound would speak, or the financial arrangements.

60. Cummings to Pound

TLS-1.

3 avril [April 1937]   [4 Patchin Place]

Well

comrade,I understand(via hurried hello in the Grand Central Station from EK(alias Mme Max)that you're stalking amongst us the Spring after this . . . always putting the punishment off as long as inhumanly possible,like the sensitive soul you are! (Qui sait¿—maybe we'll get there first) regarding the question regarding your rostrum status,that all depends where you find yourself,isn't it? I guess a detatchable nez mightn't hurt during cities,but certainly wouldn't help elsewhere. Meanwhile Braddock doesn't seem to kind of want to sort of quote fight unquote Schmeling;so better tuck an Al Jolson in your trousseau for luck. And anyhow FELICITATIONS

I seem to have received on your authority a pleasant request to write something or other for some English magazine whose editor hints at reviewing Eimi! One person bought three watercolours & two individuals wish their portraits painted. If a punk named Seltzer can be kept on the alkaline side,Harcourt & Brace may still issue the threatened collected selection or is it selected collection In deep,things (with the sole exception of grippe)are apparently easing up around here:so the big bewailers waste other folks' socalled time letting their left do what their right knoweth & barking up the greebaytree copyright patent pending cave canem anonymous inc

Marion is that enthusiastic over your advent I fear I shall have to price me a couple of ceintures de chasteté over at Cluny soon

well,comrade,it's great to be in Madrid these days

eec

> (the only man woman or child who
> is just beginning to discover that
> Simple People Like Simple Things)

EK: Eliena Eastman.

Braddock: James Joseph Braddock (1905–74), American boxer and heavyweight champion of the world (1935–37).

Schmeling: Max Schmeling (b. 1905), German boxer and heavyweight champion of the world (1930–32).

Al Jolson: Born Asa Yoelson (1886–1950), Russian-born American singer and actor.

English magazine: Pound had written to Ronald Duncan on 10 March 1937, "In the case of cummings[,] I think you shd/ do article on EIMI, yourself[.] That someone shd/ notice Cumming's play "HIM" [and] Laughlin do the poems, esp. "No Thanks." Ronald Duncan was the editor of *Townsman*.

Seltzer: Thomas Seltzer (1875–1943), Russian-born American publisher. His firm, Thomas Seltzer, Inc., had published *Tulips and Chimneys* in 1923 (Firmage A3). Cummings was in the process of purchasing the copyright for *Tulips and Chimneys* from Seltzer.

Cluny: A town in France noted for its Benedictine abbey (founded in 910). The Benedictines at Cluny were noted for their strict observance of the Order's rules.

Madrid: From early November 1936 until the end of March 1937, the Republican forces in Madrid were under attack by the insurgents. The 15th International Brigade (which included the American volunteers of the Abraham Lincoln Brigade) participated in the fighting around Madrid, starting in February 1937.

61. Pound to Cummings

TLS-1.

15 Ap[ril] 1937   Rapallo

Revered Estlin
            DEElighted to see the LADY again, with or without ceintures
            BUT mme MAX seems to know what I don't. In the 1st. place it
wasn't ME that delayed. Whazzisname said AUTUMN 1938

I said why not in clean and decent weather. ⟨i.e. the fair and uffiz springe
tyme.⟩ His last letter appears not to want me at all, unless I do hick towns and
come in the dead of winter . . .
            whazza good of THAT?

Of course I like simple things bettern simple people, but what I don't like is
needless complications . . . and when it comes to blokes wot sez/
            "MOI, je suis l'ecrivain le plus COMPLEXE de mon siecle.."
            I paaasss. ⟨overheard in a (naturally) café⟩⟩

The pints I am raisin' or downing wiff Leigh ARE / a minimum fee per
squawk//
            a system that won't reduced my venerable hulk to complete
wreckage . . .

Wot Leigh seems to want is the maximum of sweated Leighbor/ along wiff li'l
boys like Spender and Auden . . . .

The term Al Jolson is a bit vague to me/ that shows how far out of touch I am
with my comPathriots. I reely dunno WOT iz a Al J.

            youah mean the fecetious touch/ the as it were un
Johnsonian (Saml) phrase now and again in the midst of seereeyus an
huplifting or puplifting discourse ??

I fergit who young Duncan says told him NOT to/ EIMI, I think it was Leavis
            so the yung Dunc/ nacherly is going to DO it. Bright lad.

I dont know what to dew erbaht Leigh . . . I though I might come over when the sun shone/ and preserve my respiration/ which just solidifies in icy=weather.

I love Marion dearly / but to die OF BRONCHITIS fer any damn wunnam in the 20 century !!
just AINT poetic . . .

                                                                        EZ

Whazzisname: W. Colston Leigh. In a letter to Pound dated 2 April 1937, Leigh indicated to Pound that "There is very little chance of using only the Spring for a lecture tour," that "a great many of the talks would be in small places," and that he was not in a position to guarantee Pound more than one hundred dollars per week.

Spender and Auden: Leigh sent Pound a brochure listing his agency's clients. Among them were Eleanor Roosevelt, W. H. Auden, Stephen Spender, John Spivak, Carl Sandburg, and Henry Seidel Canby.

Duncan: Ronald Duncan (1914–82), British poet and dramatist. Founder and editor of *Townsman* (Morwenstow, North Cornwall) from 1938 to 1945. In *All Men Are Islands: An Autobiography* (London: Rupert Hart-Davis, 1964), Duncan recalls his first meeting (1937) with Pound in Rapallo and notes that "Ezra taught me more in one day than I had learned in a year at Cambridge" (158).

Leavis: F. R. Leavis (1895–1978), British literary critic and editor of *Scrutiny* from 1932 to 1953.

62. Cummings to Pound

AL-1.

[April 1937]   [4 Patchin Place]

only come in Spring
        e.g. when you feel
i.e. don't auden your spender for any agent procurateur
item ⌠ "the more you shall ask, the more they will want" (Karl Pershing
idem ⌡   "stick to your guns, doughboys!" (General Marx)
re my error ("art is communication")

remember that all "political minded" people, including Eastmans

are simple people

"   "   "   simple people think

"   "   "   "   "   "   that they are

"   "   "   "   "   "   "   "   "   honest

which means nothing, which doesn't mean that they would trust you (or even me) with a red hot stove

{ When Count Keyserling toured America, a statement was forwarded to all
  concerned, telling exactly what & when he liked to eat drink & Leigh,
  advising of the minutest details—including laundry—& otherwise informing
  this country that somebody had arrived. That's how you should be handled
  kid & don't forget it

Marion is trying to get you better terms via some livelier publicity bureau. I'll write or wire if anything turns

Sois sage

(I'm tickled to hear about Duncan)

Al Jolson was the first kike to make a Big Racket out of singing mammy songs in blackface

Pershing: John J. Pershing (1860–1948) commanded the American Expeditionary Force in France during World War I.

Keyserling: Hermann Alexander, Graf von Keyserling (1880–1946), German social philosopher.

63. Pound to Cummings

TLS-1.

3 May 1937   Rapallo

Dear Estlin

Is there any use trying to "GET ANYWHERE" with Eastman by letter?

As preliminary ? any use trying to interest him in WHY his adored idiot Trotsk is in Mexico instead of MusQu??

Difference between me and Max is that I am interested in EFFECTIVE action and its causes.

Has he read ANY modern econ/ or only the gold rush 1848 etc.??

> miners' whiskers
> iz like Marx'x
>
> tickle nexes
> in all darkness

and SO forth

ever   EZ

Can any of the brethren git EATS out of GLOBE. Langston Hughes the star, with bro/ Fox doing noble on ROCKS
        (Frobenius' rox.

Hughes: Langston Hughes (1902–67), American poet. The second issue of *Globe* (May 1937) had for its lead article Hughes's essay "Just Traveling."

Fox: Douglas C. Fox's article, "Cultures in the Rock," appeared in the May 1937 *Globe* (pp. 11–16). Fox explained how Frobenius used rock paintings to study the indigenous peoples of Africa. He concludes, "In this short article I have tried to show that Leo Frobenius, almost alone among scientists (he was laughed at for years even in Germany) has looked and looks on these rock paintings as the only documents we have of ancient and extremely important cultures, enduring manifestations of traditions and customs, things that tell us far more of a people's way of life than can flint arrowheads and knives." Pound wrote Fox to look up Cummings when he and Frobenius were in New York. In a letter of 28 June 1937, Fox reported, "I met and liked Cumming [*sic*], saw quite a bit of Iris [Barry] and Dick who were very nice to the Boss and to me and sent the rest of the people you wrote me about invitations to the opening but heard nothing from them." On 1 May 1939, he wrote to Pound, "Lots of luck and my regards to Iris Barry and E. E. Cummings."

64. Cummings to Pound

TELEGRAM.

[5 July 1937]   Paris

SALUT 11 RUE DE LA BUCHERIE PARIS V EME ; COMMINGS MARION

65. Pound to Cummings

TCS.

5 Lug [July 1937]   12 via Marsala

Waaal, I spose thaar iz no
liklihood of purrsuadin you to
broaden yr/ minds by travel ?
    I shall be here till end
of this month/ Ef not settin
tight in Paris, whaar be you
thinkin' of ,?

                    yrz Ez

Bloke named Cory shd/ git to Paris some time
                    or other.

Cory: Daniel Cory, American philosopher and student of George Santayana. His
    "Ezra Pound, A Memoir," *Encounter* (May 1968), recalls his friendship with
    Pound from the mid-1930s to the time of his memoir.

66. Cummings to Pound

TLS-1.

[19 August 1937]   [Paris]

Cher Ezra—

well,there doesn't seem to be much to report;unless that we're leaving
tomorrow noon for Havre and the good ship Lafayette,due at New York
August 28

next time perhaps I'll have enough cash to budge from a street where
unbackboned drunks sink singingly into pissful oblivion almost underneath
Our Lady's rosewheel

expect you on other side soon

—luck always

C'gs

jeudi 19 août 1937

a street: The Rue de la Bucherie is on the Left Bank, close to the Seine and the Ile de la Cité. It opens on to the Pont au Double, a bridge whose other end connects with the square in front of the Cathedral of Notre Dame (hence Cummings's reference to "Our Lady's rosewheel").

67. Pound to Cummings

ACS.

[Postmarked 1 September 1937]   [Rapallo?]

Young Duncan seems to want to run a decent paper. have you a verse ⟨or PROSE⟩ or two??
R (not Raymond) Duncan at the moment
                Southole
                        Hartland
                                Devon
                Inghilterra

        yrz
        EZ
        to
        both

68. Cummings to Pound

TLS-1.

[30 September 1937]   [4 Patchin Place]
                                dayaftermichaelmas

Dear Ezra—

1,000,000,000 thanks for KUNG FU TSEU! in the immortal words of Marion "it reminds me of what I used to hear people say:Good things come in small packages" allow me,kind seer,to salute your celestial capacity for humbling without humiliating your fellowman,e.g. one who "goes beyond the mark" and speaking of learning;was it Ramakrishna who did not read and who did not write and who was not beclouded and who did discover that everyone may,via the very limits of his or her own religion,attain God?

New Hampshire is holier than I dreamed—you should meet Orion

yee newe granarye schoole stille keepse. Its principal, having slapped nein old men's collective puss with an(apparently)real mucker(1 Mongsewer Noir)has unlockinvared to Boise rhyming,my girlfriend tells me,with noisy. Round & round the infallible dais whereupon caper strictly synthetic yokels,weeping with unionized pleasure,kissing the rod and sparing the spoil and letting their ears tell them how unnecessarily soon everything will soon be unnecessary qed

I suppose you know the good old lowdown on Japan vs China? 1 Jap fired & killed 100 Chinese:1 Chinese fired & killed himself. 2 Japs fired & killed 1000 Chinese:2 Chinese fired & wounded each other severely. 3 Japs fired & killed 10,000 Chinese:3 Chinese fired & all escaped injury. 4 Japs fired & killed 100,000 Chinese:4 Chinese fired & almost hit 1 Jap. 5 Japs fired & killed 1,000,000 Chinese:5 Chinese fired & wounded 1 Jap very slightly. Half a dozen Japs fired & killed 10,000,000 Chinese:half a dozen Chinese fired & 1 unwounded Jap died of old age. Pretty soon the Chinese won the war;because there weren't any more Japs

have finished my "introduction" to "collected poems" & hope you'll like a couple of quirks. Should appear come January(out of Harcourt by Brace). Drop us a line when the mercies move use

—eec

KUNG FU TSEU: Pound's *Confucius: Digest of the Analects* (Milan: [Giovanni Scheiwiller], XV [1937]) (Gallup A44). "KUNG FU TSEU" was printed on the wrapper of this edition.

principal: Franklin Delano Roosevelt.

nein old men's: The justices of the U.S. Supreme Court, during the early years of the Roosevelt administration, handed down a series of rulings that declared unconstitutional various federal and state laws intended to expand governmental power for the public benefit. The term "nine old men" was coined by political columnist Drew Pearson.

Noir: Hugo Black (1886–1971), U.S. senator from Alabama 1927–37 and associate justice of the Supreme Court 1937–71. He was the first Supreme Court justice nominated by Roosevelt.

unlockinvared: Roosevelt left Hyde Park, New York, for the West Coast on 22 September 1937. He spoke at Boise, Idaho, on 27 September.

Japan vs China: Major fighting between the military forces of Japan and China began in July 1937.

"collected poems": E. E. Cummings, *Collected Poems* (New York: Harcourt, Brace and Company, 1938) (Firmage A17).

69. Pound to Cummings

TLS-1.

21 Oct. [1937]   Rapallo

Waaa l Brother

Az u kno; I am all fer axshun and orgumizashun.

I. Microfotos of inedited music ms/ as per various about to be printeds. But SLOW as hell gettin any replies out ov the U.S.

2. Doc F.Tweddell of Plandome. N.J. discovered a cure fer CONsumpshn, but instead of tryin to sell it at a dollar a bottle fer wots costs 1/2 ov one cent; he blurts out that six months cure wd. only cost two dollahs, so the curing industry has spent 20 years NOT consolidatin and tabulatin and making SCIentifik the doc's little deescovery

tho parts of it seem to have crept into use.

I dont spose you connect with Plandome/ but ef any friends have it like I beleev Crevel HAD, putt 'em onto the Doc. also he ought to git more publicity. ⟨To say nowt of Rockerfellr backing.⟩

3. Speakin of publicity I dont spose you care to announce ole Bull Wullmz's WHITE Mule to "Townsman" in a few trenchant.

The wooden Auden having declined to do likewise by EIMI I have told N.V. (ed. whats his name Grogson) to go to hell when he axd me fer MY opnyn of the said Awden.

Holy City 1937
O Paddy dear and dijuh hear
The very latest news
How British lads an sojers
Are dyin fer th jews
Out there in Palestine
By Jaffa and the like
Our valiant Thomas Atkins
Now displays hiz love ov kike.

> Oh its oil, oil; oil
> Oh its oil the oil day long
> Oh itz oil oil OIL
> Iz the burthen ov our song.

    yrz EZ.

And when Harcourt dont Brace/ try bro. Jas the Laughlin.
                                        Norfolk CoNN.
                                                    EZ

Microfotos: Perhaps a reference to the publication of a Vivaldi concerto. "Olga Rudge reproduced an entire Vivaldi concerto in the pages of *Broletto,* monthly magazine of the city of Como, and publicized the process herself in the *Townsman,* the *Delphian Quarterly,* and *Il Mare.*" Stephen J. Adams, "Pound, Olga Rudge, and the 'Risveglio Vivaldiano,'" *Paideuma,* vol. 4, no. 1 (spring 1975), 114.

Tweddell: Francis Twedell (1863–1939), Indian-born British doctor who lived in the United States from 1905 until his death. Tweddell's cure for tuberculosis involved breathing powdered gypsum. See Omar Pound, "Canto 113: Tweddell, Men against Death, and Paul De Kruif," *Paideuma,* vol. 22, nos. 1–2 (spring–fall 1993), 173–79.

Crevel: René Crevel.

WHITE Mule: William Carlos Williams, *White Mule* (Norfolk, Conn.: New Directions, 1937). Published June 1937.

N.V.: *New Verse* (1933–38), edited by Geoffrey Grigson.

Holy City 1937: Great Britain had been assigned the mandate for Palestine in 1920. The Peel Commission report of 8 July 1937 recommended that Palestine be divided in three: a Jewish state, an Arab state, and a British mandate territory. Arab displeasure with this recommendation led some Arabs to take up arms. "On the evening of 14th October a series of violent attacks were made on Jewish buses, trains, telephone lines, the IPC pipeline and military posts. These were mainly in the Jerusalem area." Yehoshua Porath, *The Palestinian Arab National Movement: From Riots to Rebellion* (London: Frank Cass and Company, 1977), 237.

70. Pound to Cummings

TLS-2.

18 Nov. [1937]   Rapallo

Dear e/e/

        England wrocked to its cradle/ AT last somfink has happened in the U.S. wich the BRITisch "mind" can grawsp //

Believing that I shd/ on ALL I MEAN ALL occasions be better informed than th wulgah

will you inform me WHAT kind of hair Max said Hem has on hiz buZZum??

/And seeing Eastman (if) will you find out whther the flop in Spain and the uncertainty (if that is what it is) in Russia has started cerebration??

ANYone know whether Stalin is in difFIculties because he is white hope of the London acceptance houses or because the banks suppose bolchevism to be anti=bank?

Trotsk capable of thought NOW?

observing the fact that he is NOT the ruler of Russia

is he just a kike blockhead and typical ass of the period,

or capable of examining the WHY of his exit not merely crabbing the "errors" of Uncle Joe??

Take a ten menute sere/ and try Max on these points onct again IF possible/ I mean if he can be tried in this way.

Money? WOT iz IT? will any Marxist try to answer?

and so forth.

I hear the yung are printin you in small doses.

on the other hand banging the star spanner as much as// I can but observe that yr/ more ample woikz IZ of other

and that them as do NOT Europe, dries, and HOW.

giv me luv to the laidy.

an say, we got fun, in the way of a levy on incorporated (not privik) capital.

wot does ole Trotsk say to THAT??

Also ole Wyndham way back in whenever '31 noted a few sparks in Adolf's manifesto . . .

on Loan capitaLLLLLLLL.

these here Marxbros/ is in backward an abySSSm.

yrs

EZ P

somfink: Perhaps a reference to the U.S. position during the Brussels Conference of 3–24 November 1937. Leading European powers and representatives of the United States met at the conference to discuss possible joint action against

Japan. Although Roosevelt in a speech on 5 October 1937 had spoken of a need to "quarantine" Japan, the position of the United States at the conference amounted to a policy of doing nothing.

Max said Hem: Max Eastman had reviewed Hemingway's *Death in the Afternoon* in the *New Republic* in 1933. Eastman commented that Hemingway seemed excessively determined to prove his masculinity: "But some circumstances seem to have laid upon Hemingway a continual sense of the obligation to put forth evidences of red-blooded masculinity. It must be made obvious not only in the swing of the big shoulders and the clothes he puts on, but in the stride of his prose style and the emotions he permits to come to the surface there. This trait of his character has been strong enough to form the nucleus of a new flavor in English literature, and it has moreover begotten a veritable school of fiction-writers—a literary style, you might say, of wearing false hair on the chest." "Bull in the Afternoon," *New Republic* 75, no. 966 (7 June 1933), 94–97. Hemingway felt that Eastman had called his masculinity into question. A few years later, on 11 August 1937, Hemingway and Eastman engaged in a brief fight in the office of Maxwell Perkins. This scuffle received considerable attention in the press.

flop in Spain: Pound may refer to recent victories by General Franco's armies over the Loyalist forces. In late October the government had been forced to move to Barcelona.

Stalin: Pound refers to the charges of treason and the show trials that were part of Stalin's purge of his former political colleagues, including Grigory Zinovyev, Lev Kamenev, and Nikolay Bukharin. The Great Purge (1935–38) also claimed thousands of other victims.

the yung: Ronald Duncan wrote to Pound on 30 October 1937 that Cummings had sent three poems for the first issue of *Townsman* (January 1938). These were: "The Mind's(," "american critic ad 1935," and "hanged" (Firmage B116).

a few sparks: See Wyndham Lewis, *Hitler* (London: Chatto and Windus, 1931). "And immediately this conducts us to the heart of the economic doctrine of the Nationalsocialist—namely, the absolute distinction between concrete and *productive* capital (great or small) upon the one hand, and Loan-capital (as the Hitlerists call it) upon the other. The arch-enemy is not *Das Kapital* pure and simple, as with Marx, but *Das Leihkapital,* or Loan-capital" (147–48).

71. Cummings to Pound

TLS-1.

[25 November 1937]   [4 Patchin Place]
                                        thanksgivingday '37

Cher cropper—

      as tu feel,suis all pour to relax et organically

1   there is an American(muckerjewrochester)composer,calling itself "David

Diamond";impoverished:86 Jane Street NYC. I should like to have published littlesnapshots of whose music e.g. for a somewhat apparently very untouchable ballet named Tom

2   thanks for data re New Jersey! It takes the Yankee to discover a cure for consumption socalled when a shallwesay world writheth with socalled production. (You'll see when you arrive babe). The prescence of 315 poems chez Quinn & Boden,printers giltedged to their imperial goys Harcourt Brace,tookme NJward a while ago:upshot—via -pertest of typographical "experts"—"owe boi yoo musda bin ona too wiks drung wida wumun wen yoo rode dad"

3   possibly(or vv)am will survive even English ignorings. I met the unfortunate wouldbe mrs Auden nay mann . . . William's pale ass needs doubtless no bush. Or at any rate your humble s vastly prefers steeplechase

4   speaking of kerosene,voici longagowords for erstwhile America's superhyperpopular worldwartune "Over There". Copyright in all seriousness including flotsam & jetsam

   stan-dard All-l-l
   stan-dard All-l-l
   stan-dard All stan-dard All stan-dard All-l-l
   don't let no-one Kid-you
   the in-di Vid-u
   al just-don't make-no-sense-at All-l-l
   stan-dard All-l-l
   stan-dard All-l-l
   stan-dard All stan-dard All stan-dard All-l-l
   but if you've pan-dard
   unto the Stan-dard
   why it's
      QUITE
     ALL
       RIGHT
        for
  it's All-for-standardoil

5   I hope the enclosed may amuse

       —sois sage

       C'gs

"David Diamond": Diamond had completed the music for the ballet of *Tom* in 1936.

315 poems: The poems of *Collected Poems,* published by Harcourt, Brace the following year.

mrs Auden: W. H. Auden married the daughter of Thomas Mann, Erika Mann (1905–69), in 1935 so that she could obtain a British passport.

pale ass: *White Mule.*

enclosed: Enclosure lacking.

72. Cummings to Pound

TL-1.

[20 December 1937]   [4 Patchin Place]

EP—

am enclosing 2 fullpage advertisements from a rather recent issue of "Town and Country",America's hyperfastidioos not to say sooperellygon or parexcellong della craim so to speak peeryoddycale. & if they don't tell you better about 127,000,000 than anybody you'll meet,Franklin Roosevelt not Shirley Temple is Whistler's Mother

e'er since(per Stalin's Peter Ingrateness)ye kumrads scismd into less Stalinists and lays Trotskyites,Mags(go East young)man has hibernated into an autobiography,courtesy of Schumann & Schyster:Macks is now in Elmira years&years&years ago,with generous true and fighting Christians;and naturally far nearer himself . . . the book sounds healthily guiltless. I humbly suggest that you Sebastian him directly with your monetary&otherwise arrowings?

a card for Joe Gould—by the way,he's supposed to inhabit Central Hotel 149 East 14th St—came here,and I joyfully read it and forwarded. Joe(who crashed both NY Tribune and New Yorker)wants to give me a souptonuts secondavenue orgy "for all of fifty cents"(for 2):am still in hiding. FLASH! the latter miscellany crowned your recently appearing Cantos with a kindofsortof shoottheworks boost via Miss Bogan,disappointed poetess of knowed. Bud dund resd,ywund slip ishe,em highr,lighk Vug,wudda muggasin

Abbie Anne it looks as if poor mister hear oh shit oh were trying to crawl into a full box of Swedish matches with one hand and play heilige nacht on eel dootchy's pas si sweet potato with the udder   kel errerr,as batpaXoi chorus

Be good!

Marion & I wish you BONNE ANNÉE

ps)she suggests you'll appreciate Armand;as for I,me no spiggada ink leash

20th of December '37

advertisements: Enclosures lacking.
Shirley Temple: Celebrated American child film star (b. 1928).
autobiography: *Heroes I Have Known: Twelve Who Lived Great Lives* (New York: Simon and Schuster, 1942). One of its chapters is titled, "Mark Twain's Elmira: The Influence of a Great Preacher and His Parish."
New Yorker: The *Fifth Decad of Cantos* (New York: Farrar and Rinehart, 1937) was published on 29 November 1937. Louise Bogan's review appeared in the *New Yorker*, vol. 13, no. 44 (18 December 1937), 94. "The wish 'to be free and general and not at all afraid—to feel, understand and express everything' fades out more and more from modern poetry. The crotchet and the creed will soon claim all. Ezra Pound has gone over to the Douglas Plan, for example. 'The Fifth Decad of Cantos' traces modern usury (familiarly known as money and banking) to its Renaissance beginnings. Pound transcribes real documents, and these, it must be said, are extremely tiresome. He finally rises into a hymn against moneylending which justifies all that has gone before. This hymn is later repeated in a related key; it sounds fine both times. Pound is also wonderful, as usual, with Italian and Chinese weather."
Miss Bogan: Louise Bogan (1897–1970), American poet and poetry editor of the *New Yorker*.
hear oh shit oh: Hirohito (1901–89), emperor of Japan 1926–89. Japanese expansionist policies in China led to open warfare in July 1937. Cummings's mention of Hirohito may have been prompted by the news of the attack on the U.S. warship *Panay* by Japanese naval airplanes on 11 December 1937.
chorus: The frog chorus in Aristophanes's *The Frogs*.
Armand: Enclosure lacking.

73. Pound to Cummings

TLS-1.

25 Jan[uary 1938]   Rapallo

Nart Amurkn Revoo
                    POETRY edtr/ Mr AUSSlander apologizes saying Funk
or Stunk or Skunk Wagonalls ENcyclopediah
sez I am ENGLISH
                    this after pantalettes Harvey stopped correcting errors
in N.A.R//

"Random House) dhirktet by Meestr CERF addresses me

"As one of Italian birth" you will doubteless be proud to possess a copy of this book (Eyetalians of N.Y. ù

//

wall estlin I am a MEMBER of what H.J. called a BODY. and on acceptin the elexshun I nominated mr E/E/ Cummings.

        com'n in IF the eel/ekt you. /it needs a little gun powder. And once in we can kick the so called Acad or a CAD (as long as Nic. But. is in it, ⟨demme!⟩ from near enough to make the boot felt.
        ol ov co 'se to M.D.G.

    yrz EZ

        an me luv to th lady

            EZ

AUSSlander: Joseph Auslander (1897–1965), American poet and poetry editor of the *North American Review*. Pound published "The Jefferson-Adams Correspondence" in the *North American Review,* vol. 244, no. 2 (winter 1937–38), 314–24 (Gallup C1422). In the "Contributors' Column" for that issue, Pound was identified as having been "born in the state of Idaho of English parents." Pound wrote to John Pell—the magazine's editor—on 24 December 1937, "My father is 79 and shd/ not be subjected to what he will consider gratuitous insult. He is NOT English, but American as was his father[,] father before him, and his grandfather and great grandfather etc/[.]" The managing editor replied on 12 January 1938, "We are sorry to have been so misinformed about your parentage and will of course correct the error in our Contributors' Column of the Spring issue. Funk and Wagnall's New Standard Encyclopedia, copyrighted in 1931, was the source of our misinformation."

Harvey: George Brinton McClellan Harvey, a former editor of the *North American Review.*

this book: Pound had received a form letter on Random House letterhead, signed by Bennet Cerf. "YOUR NAME [Ezra Pound, written in red ink] is in 'THE ITALIANS OF NEW YORK.' Under the auspices of the United States Government, the Federal Writer's Project has been engaged in compiling and writing a complete history of the Italians of New York, including an evaluation of the business, political and artistic achievements of those of Italian blood who live in or near New York City. By arrangement with the Government, we are publishing the result of this research under the title of 'THE ITALIANS OF NEW YORK.' As one of Italian birth, we believe you will take legitimate pride in owning a copy of this book. If so, please mail the enclosed postcard to us and we will immediately send you a copy." The volume refers to Pound once: "The expatriate, Ezra Pound, is one of the contemporary American poets who has virtually adopted for his own the culture of Italy, in which country he has lived for many years." *The Italians of New York* (New York: Random House, 1938), 166.

a BODY: On 4 January 1938, Henry Seidel Canby wrote to Pound informing him of his election to the National Institute of Arts and Letters. Among those elected along with Pound were James Boyd, Robert Hillyer, Henrik Van Loon, and Stark Young. In his reply, Pound nominated Cummings, T. S. Eliot, William Carlos Williams, George Santayana, Ernest Hemingway, Robert McAlmon, and Louis Zukofsky.

Nic. But.: Nicholas Murray Butler (1862–1947), American educator and president of Columbia University, 1901–45. He was also president of the Carnegie Endowment for Peace, 1925–45, and served as president of the American Academy of Arts and Letters, 1928–41. Pound regarded Butler as an obstructor of truth.

to M.D.G.: Pound uses the Jesuit motto, *Ad Majorem Dei Gloriam*. That is, to the greater glory of God.

74. Cummings to Pound

TLS-1.

February 26 '38   [4 Patchin Place]

Dear Ezra—

th lady,having translated your latest communique from rapalloese,submitteth to me that this "body" of which you're a "MEMBER" might even impossibly constitute reference to U of Columbia;something the party of the second part cannot but fail to succeed in believing,despite clue implied by disjunctive consyllable "Nic. But.". However(as one English Swede of Italian birth to another Hawaian Eskimo)the circular point isn't (a)that nothing ever joins me & v v (b)that samson is as samson does,plusorminus a navy of pillars or army of scissors;it's (c)that the hereinabove and thereafterthroughout undersigned,being 10/10 mistaken 9/16 souris 7/8 chauve or otherwise slightly as is,hopes to give ye proverbial jawbone a kick in ye sacrosanct ass until hell freezes over unquote. Placing which whole nutshell in a matter:please make twin improvements on bientôt due com(Harcourt comma Brace willing)plimentary copy of "collected Poems";viz.

> poem 26 "petticoat,drowsy in your" should be
>   *"*   *"*   is   *"*
> poem 309 "all the eyes of these   th listening" should be
>   *"*   *"*   *"*   *"*   *"*   with   *"*

here's trusting you'll like them a heavenofalot better than all my one hundred and twenty and seven and 000,000 compatriots never omitting there was an unfortunate deville who tried to shoot crap on the leville they returned from the ride with the eden inside and the face on the smile of the neville . . . come into the kindergarten,Mud

let me mention that Marion joins a great many bravos with a salut and enclosed to you your account;adding that our friend Gilbert Seldes,fired from NYJournal,became television. Since nothing can be done until next June anyway,if not at least two years,and meanwhile whensoever an automobile goes by the screen gets full of "snowflakes",but apparently nearly everyone receives fabulous salaries,her informant experienced some curiosity. Entering without trouble his confrère Cohen's(this is not a joke)palatial office,Gilbert asked "what do <u>you</u> do?" Mr Cohen woke and,opening a drawer,produced a bottle of asperin: "I take"(he answered simply)"these". It's almost as though we American seem to be pursued by asperin. In Tunis,Cummings & Morehouse met the asperine queen sic;her Roumanian husband(formerly a wouldbe poet)if that is the word drove us roaringly into the desert;there their German chauffeur halted,descended,broke out champagne and caviar,stood at superattention while his worsers were assuaged,&whereupon lordingly tossed the how emptiest bottle at 15 trillion quite unexcusably omnipresent a rabs. It's almost as if they still seem to be as it were fighting for it

—salut!

eec

PS what's Eeel Air Eel Air's current address? I mean,since he had those remarkable ears of his trimmed

"collected Poems": Cummings's *Collected Poems* (New York: Harcourt, Brace and Company), published 24 February 1938 (Firmage A17).
eden: Anthony Eden.
neville: Neville Chamberlain (1869–1940), British prime minister (1937–40).
kindergarden,Mud: Cummings parodies Tennyson's lyric, section 22 of *Maud*, beginning "Come into the garden, Maud."
Seldes: Gilbert Seldes had joined the Columbia Broadcasting System as "Director of Television Programs."
asperine queen: Cummings and Marion Morehouse visited Tunisia in September 1933. The "asperine queen" was probably Greta Knutson, Swedish-born wife of the Romanian-born Dadaist, Tristan Tzara (1896–1963). Knutson's pale skin prompted Louis Aragon to refer to her as "une femme d'un pay de neige venue."
Eel Air's: Hilaire Hiler.

75. Pound to Cummings

TLS-2.

21 March [1938]   Rapallo

My Dear(or h) Walt Whitman
                    The ripening Chas ALgernon Swnbn salutes
(in lack of patience to find a monumental) the (and to so many distressing)
free and unbottoned feeling
                    yes/ Harcut HAS sent it/ the vollum.
And ole Ez/ Algernon/ Chas/ iz a readin it/ and it WILL distress uncle Possum/
                    and, BOY, as a critic beleev ⟨you⟩ me you WUZ in to much
of a hurry to write some of 'em whereof the INSIDES is worth more care for
the outsides.
                    and some of IS bullseyes.
waal; HELL, so few have anything to git over/ and so few gits anything over/
that . . thanks.
                    and where do we go from here.⟨?⟩

as to yr/ earlier pisl/ the address of Hiler's ears (curled or uncurled) so far as I
know is co/ his paPAH as usual that is 200 W. 57th should reach him.
                    and Louis Rothschild has been pinched/ o WHOORAY a
tryin to skip wiff th swag/ has Mr Bronstein complained of this OUTRAGE to
the pee/or payrolitariat?

an bless yr lovin' bride.
the BoDDy is the Insteroot not CO/lumbia where there aint enough of 'em
⟨[illegible]⟩ to make a good Clam Chowder.

anyhow/ nothing EVER will join you save the fair and frail with an occasional
poigne de main from ole EZ.

who has (hath, why the HELL do you use these archaisms with no apparent
NEED) ~~corrected the~~ made the requested corrections of is and wi(th) 26/309
                    there once was a bank pimp named . . . .
                    who ought not to have been born but been p . . d on
well any how . . . thazzatt//
                              Hickery dickery dickery dock
                         let young men die for my bank stock.
opening lines being
        Pretty Tony the beauty's son
            Married a bank and up he run
                Hickery d etc.

Did I submit the paraphrase of Possum on the passing of More?
              anyhow I cant DAMN find it at the momeng. ⟨I think it was
when Elmer died Mr Eliot wiped his feet on the Criterion floor
He felt that there had been other Elmers before.⟩
              yrs deevotedly.

                              EZ

AND SAH/ it iz this// ef you hadda listened to papa you wd NOT have written
better poetry / BUT some of youh poetry would have been BETTER
WRITTEN.
       Youh HAAAvud boyes/ dat iz you an Doc Eliot youh jes' gits plain
lowdown SHIFFless' when you aint got me to sit on youh haids.

some is damn good/ OLAF is damn good/ but the answer is to hell with
Usuriocracy/
              where is Max/? them bolos/ won't attack capital/ they
foozles about wiff a red herring property/ they attack property and do NOT
attack capital.
Lenin quoting Hobson was ONTO international finance/ loans/etc but not
onto MONEY/ Marx sticks on a lable/ materialist and goes into a metaphysical
huddle on value.

Possum: T. S. Eliot.
Louis Rothschild: Baron Louis de Rothschild (1882–1955), Austrian financier. On
    11 March 1938, German troops occupied Austria. He was arrested on 13 March.
    In April 1939 he was released. See Pound's "Rothschild Arrested," *Action,* no.
    111 (2 April 1938), 13 (Gallup C1449). Pound remarks, "And here is the Baron
    Luigi, pinched like any other absconding cashier with his cash in a suitcase. Pray
    God this be the END of an era." Reprinted in *EPPP.*
Mr Bronstein: Leon Trotsky.
Pretty Tony: Anthony Eden resigned as foreign secretary on 20 February 1938.
More: Paul Elmer More (1864–1937), American man of letters. He died on 9
    March 1937. The second line of the distich echoes a line from Eliot's "Aunt
    Helen": "He was aware that this sort of thing had occurred before." In *After
    Strange Gods* (New York: Harcourt, Brace, 1934), Eliot refers to "My friend Dr.
    Paul Elmer More" (30). Eliot had corresponded with More, and they had met
    several times in the early and mid-1930s. Eliot eulogized More in "A Commen-
    tary," *Criterion,* vol. 16, no. 65 (July 1937), 666–89.
OLAF: Cummings's poem, "i sing of Olaf glad and big" (*Complete Poems,* 340).
Max: Max Eastman.
Lenin quoting Hobson: John Atkinson Hobson (1858–1940), British economist.
    His *Imperialism* (1902) is cited by Lenin in *Imperialism, the Highest Stage of
    Capitalism* (1917).

Marx: Pound probably refers to part 1, chapter 3 of *Capital*, where Marx discusses the nature of money. See *Capital*, trans. Eden and Cedar Paul (1930; New York: E. P. Dutton, 1974), 70–128.

76. Pound to Cummings

tcs.

23 marzo [March 1938]   Rapallo

waaal naow I have enjoyed 'em and OLAF an Marj so much I have even got roun to writin somefink abaht 'em / fer th only edtr likely to print it/ AND I have even Xotikly Q/ writ to a nelderly Brit/ crik to urge similar castigation of some of his pet aversions who WONT like 'em (not that I feel sure he will) I have also axiomed
     fer ALL poesy
When metric is bad/ langwidg is pore
When metric is good ENOUGH it will erhabt
drive out other defects of langwidg.

up an Yatt 'em   Didi Ax yuh: jever hear ov Bill Mahl?
                                          yrz EZ

enjoyed 'em: Cummings's *Collected Poems* (1938).
OLAF an Marj: See Cummings's poems, "i sing of Olaf glad and big," "between the breasts," and "Marj" (*Complete Poems*, 340, 85, and 226).
writin somefink: Gallup lists no writings by Pound on Cummings in 1938.
edtr: Probably Ronald Duncan, editor of *Townsman*.
Brit/ crik: Unidentified.
Bill Mahl: William Mahl, American author. Pound read his *Two Plays of the Social Comedy. The Age of Gold: An American Historical Play; The Great and the Small: A Comedy of Contemporary Confusion* (New York: n.p., 1935). The first play portrays the life of Jim Fisk from 1867 to his murder in 1872. Fisk's jovial rapacity finds expression in such passages as, "But you've got to keep your mind on businesss. There's only one rule for success in this country! Keep your eyes open, grab, and—hold tight!" and "It's rough and tumble and devil take the hindmost. You've got to play it hard or take a back seat" (51). Various other characters see value only in money. These include Jay Gould, Boss Tweed, and "Speyer, a German Jew" (12). The play's second act depicts Fisk's attempt to corner the gold market in 1869. The next play, *The Great and the Small,* is set in a grand hotel in central Europe. The characters, wealthy Americans and Europeans, discuss money and politics. A communist revolution occurs and the hotel is temporarily seized by the insurgents. After a day of economic debate

between the captured guests and their captors, counterrevolutionary troops put down the revolt. In a "Literary Note," *New English Weekly,* vol. 7, no. 19 (20 February 1936), 380 (Gallup C1299), Pound remarks that "The plays of William MAHL treat Jim Fisk and economic questions with a good deal of technique, but make no venture into the danger zone of what might displease the financiers." Reprinted in *EPPP.* In "An Introduction to the Economic Nature of the United States" (1944), Pound added, "Novelists and playwrights, once in a while, give one a clearer idea than professors. One can learn more from Ernest Poole's *THE HARBOUR* about fast clippers; and from William Mahl's TWO PLAYS OF THE SOCIAL COMEDY about the attempt of monopolising the gold in 1869, than he is likely to learn from historiographers." Reprinted in *Selected Prose.*

77. Pound to Cummings

TLS-1.

26 March [1938]   Rapallo

Waal me beamish and WAYward

                                    ewe arenot PRACTical/ thankgorrfer it but
yew air nawt prattikul/ and Duncan's printer simpley wdn't set up youKUNT
                    ell
The Brit. PRINTER is reesponsible to the law/ and it aint Duncc's fault/
            Nor of course can he tie up Miss Nippon's pudendum
                        with referendum

BUT he is a good lad/ fishin cadavers up on the Devon coast and SO forth/ with the burried man in his garden.

He fell down on JOE/ waaal I just give him some bits of JOE/ and didn't TELL him WHY/ and in any case it was Nude Erection's job

BUT fer cohesion/ YOU might write a nize lil peice say harft a page about Joe's ORAL hizzery
                    and mebbe that wd/ start somfink IF you make it clear and
EGGs plain WHY Joe izza hiz
                        torian ⟨after all Dunc is yung. if you dont
edderkate 'em oo will⟩

wot yew boyes LAKK is not cock but PURRsistance.

Anyhow it is somfink to print Hilaire and my Villon and the kid deserves well of the breverm/

his other wants are supplied, I think quite efficiently
at lease she look as if he wd/ stay home at night

It is something to have got his mag MOST disliked in Eng with so little
typographic display.
and there is a grrrreat deal he don't and WON'T print.

> recommendin me to yr/ mercy.
>
> I remain

> O ROLLE ye deep blue logg
> of ROLL .
>
> E

youKUNT: Ronald Duncan had written to Pound, probably in January 1938, "Oh
damn me, but can you or we or they do some monthly NEWS POEMS TO BE
PRINTED A WEEK AFTER THE WRITING OF?" Pound must have alerted
Cummings, because Duncan reported to Pound that he had received a "news
poem" from Cummings. Duncan, however, found it unprintable.

> little miss nippon
> O please get hot
> I'll give you a ribbon
> to tie up your twat

> little boy black and
> blue pull in your horns
> jill's gotta have jack and
> a shoe's on the corns

> (little red riding
> hood powder your nose
> the bedbugs are hiding
> chez lein & joes)

> little brown pedant
> go learn to paint
> asleep at the didn't
> with your was in the aint

> little miss muffet
> sat on a wall
> and all the other currencies
> didn't begin to fall

Duncan wrote to Cummings on 11 August 1938, "Couldn't print your last poem because of 'twot' in it, and the *twaddle* in the B. B. printers here."

fishin cadavers: In *All Men Are Islands: An Autobiography* (London: Rupert Hart-Davis, 1964), 189-93, Duncan recalls his delight in salvaging flotsam and jetsam from shipwrecks on the coast near his Devon home.

burried man: This and the previous reference seem to point to Eliot's *The Waste Land*. Duncan knew Eliot.

JOE: Joe Gould.

Nude Erection's: New Directions.

Hilaire: Hilaire Hiler.

Villon: "'Heaulmiere' from the Opera Villon by Ezra Pound," *Townsman*, vol. 1, no. 2 (April 1938) (Gallup C1448). Reprinted in *EPPP*.

she: Rose Marie Hansom. She and Duncan visited Pound in Rapallo in February 1938. They married in 1941.

O ROLLE: Pound parodies Canto IV, stanza 179, of Byron's *Childe Harold's Pilgrimage*.

78. Pound to Cummings

TL-1.

27 Marzo [March 1938]   Rapallo

Dear East Lynn
                        NOW/ vide enc/ we KNOW where the pissheaded cod fish
who WAS in the gnu yukk customs johouse has GOT to
He went to England and was made cure/eater of the Millbank Lavatory/
                        BUT the contents of my own greater intestine is⟨/are⟩ insufficient
to meet the case/
                                        can YOU start a little American
vituperation of Man/son
                                        what the female component that produced him
was I can not imagine/
                                        barbary ape hardly meets the case/ but
hybrid WHAT. . . . ⟨??⟩ you are nearer a zoo than I am/ chameau chamelle
buggared by an cocodril with bluebehinded mandril intervening/
                        I dont suppose you cd/ say it in PRINT
                        yrz
⟨oh to be in England now where buggars are in office⟩

enc/: Enclosure lacking.

Millbank Lavatory/: The Tate Gallery.

Man/son: James Bolivar Manson (1879–1945), director of the Tate Gallery (1930–38). It seems that Manson had prohibited a work or works by Brancusi from being exhibited at the Tate. Pound wrote to T. S. Eliot on 25 March 1938, "As an EDITOR and man of influence/ you might kill that LOUSE at the Tate lavatory who is keeping Branc OUT as not being ART/ after all you are a citizen of the damn country and paying takes to keep sh such SHIT in a government office. his name is MANson."

chameau: *Chameau* and *chamelle* are, respectively, French for male camel and female camel. *Chameau* is a term of insult in French.

79. Cummings to Pound

TLS-1.

[April 1938]   [4 Patchin Place]

Dear Ezra—

if I had an extra copy of εἰμι should send it to your Broletto with considerably less than unpleasure;if can dig a few surplus $(regular allowance,via mother,per month - 125;minus 70 for rent −55−1.83 1/3per day for two persons;but some months have thirtyone days)shall angle an Nth-hand sample. Pat Covici isn't my publisher,not to mention friend;nor,fortunately,my remainderer as of yore. Meanwhile here's to beholding e.g. the Vergil debate on measurable vs immeasurable,lightyears vs seraphim,in the solar lingo of my lord Dante

thanks much more than kindly for your letter and card re CPs! better can best best any time;man may eat bread,but bread eats love

as to the inevitable eengleesh cannoting to print miss nippon:why not set her up with "twot" spelled "tw-t" or,if that's this, just "*" and at the bottom of the page "*censored"? #

you ask me if I've seen "Mahl". I merely appear to remember being once in Madrid and buying a book once published in Germany;said book revealed a socalled translation of a socalled Frenchman's essay re(once)Picasso;said socalled essay contained a socalled translation of a socalled dictum by a fellow named Leonardo;and, since I spoke neither German nor Spanish,said socalled translation still says to itself der Mahler der sich nicht zweifelt macht nur geringe Fortschritte

delighted to learn of Great Britain's Tate Ah Tate with Lil Art. Your pal Brancoosh once crossed in the same paquebot with myself;we were far too near to meet:that happened in Paris,through E. Livre—a sonorous chap of whom you impossibly may have heard

& to whom Marion sends the top of the season's greetings

eec

il faut take a chance some fois,n'est-ce point?

Broletto: In November, 1938, it published Edmondo Dodsworth's short essay on
   Cummings's *Collected Poems*. See the appendix.
Covici: Pascal Covici.
Vergil debate: Cummings appears to refer to the Dantean vision of the heavens
   surrounded by circles of light that are angels (*Paradiso*, Canto XXVIII). This
   conception of the universe is incompatible with a materialistic conception. In
   Purgatorio, Canto IV, Virgil gives Dante an astronomy lesson in terms of the
   "measureable."
a book: Unidentified.
Brancoosh: Constantin Brancusi.
E.Livre: Ezra Pound.

80. David Diamond to Pound

April 3, 1938   86 Jane Street, New York City

Dear Ezra Pound,

Last night I spent talking with Cummings. He showed me a copy of The
Townsman, - and I was so impressed by your very intelligent and musical
article on those old, incredibly wonderful men who will always have birds in
their music. So I first want to say thanks for this, and at Cummings suggestion
ask if you would like to see some of my music that might interest you and
Townsman readers. Cummings says he has written you about me, - I did his
ballet, "TOM" and since 1935, several of your early poems. Am very proud of
my setting of "Four Ladies" and they may well fit into the Townsman, or short
little excerpts from "TOM", or I may write something especially if you like my
music. So please let me know if you wish me to send you some things to look
over, - I shall be happy to send you whatever you desire.
Want to know anything about me? I'm twenty-three, have written great
quantities of music in all forms, played a great deal in America. Am a
Guggenheim Fellow this year and shall go over to Paris for the winter, and this
will give me the itch to go on and see you in Rapallo if you say yes. Then I can
bring you the big orchestral score of my setting of your "Night Litany" for
Tenor Solo, Chorus, and Orchestra. I'd send it in advance, but I fear it is so
large, it may cost a fortune when I can bring it instead.

I hope you'll write soon and say you want to know my music.
>   With kindest regards and
>   sincerest admiration,
>   David Diamond

musical article: "'Heaulmiere' from the Opera Villon by Ezra Pound," and "Villon and Comment," *Townsman*, vol. 1, no. 2 (April 1938), 12–18 (Gallup C1448). Reprinted in *EPPP*.

"Four Ladies: Music for voice and piano. Pound's poem "Ladies" (from *Lustra*) is the text. Gallup E4q.

"Night Litany": First published in *A Quinzaine for This Yule* (Gallup A2), and included in *Personae*. Diamond has not published this score.

81. Pound to David Diamond

TL-1.

[April 1938]   Rapallo

Dear Mr Diamond
                    I doubt very much if any man who has been passed by
Erskine and the Guggenheim committee can do anything that wd/ interest me.
                    At any rate there are only about 200 dollars avialable
for work of men NOT subsidized by Moe and Aydelotte. And as these
scavangers have always opposed any efforts of mine and the work of any and
every good artist whom I have recommended to them BEFORE said artists
were very well and widely known
        I don't honestly think I can be botherd with any of their favorite
composers.

Put it this way: Until some, any, American institution spends a little money on
something I believe in I am god damned if I am going to meet any more
Americans.
                    yrs all too frankly

Erskine: John Erskine (1879–1951), American novelist and teacher. President of the Juilliard School of Music from 1927 to 1938.

Moe: Henry Allen Moe (1894–1975), secretary of the John Simon Guggenheim Memorial Foundation.

Aydelotte: Frank Aydelotte (1880–1956). Aydelotte helped formulate plans for the Guggenheim Foundation. He served on its advisory board from 1925 to 1948.

82. Cummings to Pound

TL-1.

May 10 1938   4 Patchin Place
                                                   New York City

Dear E—

a,b;c:d.

(a)David Diamond is a Jew of(he tells me)the lowest(according to Jews)breed,& born(moreover)on the wrong side of the tracks(as we say in democratic America)

(b)I happen to know that his wrestlings with the angel of poverty were immeasurably complicated by a steadfast refusal to kiss the reigning arse of(proJew)Roosevelt II

(c)if Marion hadn't found him 2 poorlittlerich goygirls who were willing to toss some crusts until our very young(22)friend "made good"(i.e.Gug)he probably wouldn't be almost alive but he certainly could be nearly dead

(d)I don't know what he wrote you,but he wrote you only at my suggestion & after expressing excitement not to say wonder re your music criticism in Townsman(we have no critics here);what hurt him most of your letter was the fact that you didn't write him,not the fact that you wrote somebody else(a racketeer,a punk,a coward,an A-for-american)
                              —a is for
                               Artist

                                        e

goygirls: Helen Stewart and Dorothy Case. "Later, in 1939, Helen and Casey provided money, through their fathers, for David Diamond (at Cummings' suggestion) at a time when he was in desperate financial need" (Kennedy, 375). Cummings's letter indicates help had been forthcoming before 1939.

83. Pound to Cummings

TLS-2.

Rapallo

20 May [1938]

All right my dear Estlin/

If Dave [Diamond] had writ BEFORE
those godallshitten Goog's were feeding him, I might have pity.

But what I cant seem to get EVEN into your head is that I get no goddamn
support from American endowments/ and that they nearly all IMPEDE every
intelligent action I undertake/

and the sense of organization is so lacking even in the five or six of you
who have some sense that NO effort is ever made (with the ONE move of you
and Eastman to get me into circulation) to put me in a position where I could
be effective.

Even the mangy Poetry in Chicago which I have done as much as
anyone to create does NOT uphold me for nuts.

What the hell is the good of all this flooding of the field with highschool
graduates IF all material careers are a dead end/

IF having picked the winner time and again NO attention is paid to one's
nominations.

These goddbuggared and allshitten endowments are of value ONLY in relation
to the intelligence of their selecting committees whereon I ⟨NEVER⟩ am.

I may be a fuckin saint/ but even my patience has an end/ and for
a goddam kike with 1500 dollars to come to me when NONE of my
⟨nominees⟩ ever get ANY of the bacon, is merely an irritation/

esp/ as his letter was NOT a composition to melt the heart.

It is IMPOSSIBLE evidently to get
anyone in america to understand baccillae/ and to be made to understand
WHEN a given biped, listed as human in the census records OUGHT to be
disinfected and burnt out.

hence all the key positions are in possession of bubonic plagues like the
hackneyed example of Nic Butler.

Bugger a kuntry that don't send me 500
bucks per annum/ what arsing encouragement, indeed what honesty is there in
hencouragin, the young to participate in the arts when they are unlikely to
have any livlihood save from interrupting any sort of sane activity and pleasing
the sheer poop which runs things. Let him (young Dave - see Serly, and find
out what Serly thinks of him.

devotedly but not suavely/ and love to Marion.

EP

Butler: Nicholas Murray Butler.
Serly: Tibor Serly.

84. Pound to Cummings

TCS.

[September 1938]   Rapallo

Renat Borgatti coming N.Y. this autumn/ meet her. ole pop aint yet told you
wrong.
                        EP

Borgatti: Renata Borgatti (1894–1964), Italian pianist. Pound gave her a favorable
  notice in "Stagione musicale del Tigullio: I concerti di Febbraio: Renata Borgatti
  pianista," *Il Mare*, 31, 1508 (8 January 1938) (Gallup C1437). A translation of
  the article appears in R. Murray Schafer's *Ezra Pound and Music* (New York:
  New Directions, 1977), 429–31.

85. Pound to Cummings

TCS.

[Postmarked 17 October 1938]   Rapallo

Mr DILLON, OF poetry/ CHIkago expresses due an proper sentimengs abaht
printin you's and me's woiks. I think this may be worth 100 bucks to you if
you have anything that can without shocking Cicero Ill. too greatly at least not
legally//

I know post mortemz has been pronounced but Johnnie writes me better than
what the young tell me abaht him/
why not us giv him a chant
I am ritin this coz it jus mightnt oKKur to yuh
⟨& regards to a lady⟩
                        EZ P

DILLON: George Dillon (1906–68), editor of *Poetry*. Pound had written to him
  on 17 September 1938, "Now to get down to brass tacks/ Do you agree with me
  that Poetry wd/ be in a more active sense the LEADING poetry magazine, and

that it wd/ continue the fight it was started for, I.E. the fight against the old crap and the mercantilists standards of Harpers, Century Scribner the thrice damned stuffiness of Ellery Stinkeivitz of the Aylan etc/ IF it contained every year a concrete indication of the state of activity of Eliot, Williams (Bill not Oskaaaar), Marianne, cummings and the undersigned." Dillon replied on 3 October 1938, "Thank you for your interesting letter. I look forward to going over it again when I have more leisure, and shall keep it at hand for the suggestions and advice it contains. For the present, let me say I agree heartily that POETRY should continue to feature new work by the poets you name. And let me say too that we are always glad to have your comments and criticism, even if we do not always have time to reply as we'd like." On 21 November 1938, Dillon wrote to Cummings, "Thank you for sending us the new poems, which I was very happy to find on my return from a trip. It will be a pleasure to print this fine and characteristic group. In fact there is no one whose work I would rather have for POETRY." Seven poems by Cummings appeared in the January 1939 issue of *Poetry* (Firmage B120). These poems were awarded *Poetry*'s Helen Haire Levinson Prize for 1939.

86. Cummings to Pound

TLS-1.

December 2 '38   [4 Patchin Place]

My arse true

—as they say it à la Salle Standardearl

"Poetry" is taking verse(january)
Laughlin wants me to unlock Catulle(subito)—

                                            thank!you!

                            C'gs

verse: "Seven Poems," *Poetry,* vol. 53, no. 4 (January 1939), 169–75. 1. "mortals)";
    2. :"these children singing in stone a"; 3. "nouns to nouns"; 4. ")when what
    hugs stopping earth than silent is"; 5. "up into the silence the green"; 6. " six"; 7.
    "love is more thicker than forget." Firmage B120.
Laughlin: In a letter of 24 November 1938, James Laughlin proposed that Cum-

mings translate Catullus. By February 1939, however, Cummings had decided to forgo the project.

87. Cummings to Pound

TELEGRAM.

[20 April 1939]   New York

To EZRA POUND REX
     WELCOME
     MARION & CUMMINGS

REX: The Italian ocean liner on which Pound sailed from Genoa to New York. It arrived in New York on 21 April 1939.

88. Pound to Cummings

ALS-1.

16 May [1939]   [Boston]

Dear Estlin et M.
when be you
goin to be
       whaar?
Called @ 4 Patchin
       but found
       only D.D.
              yrz
              EzP

Postal address
c/o
F.S Bacon
80 Maiden Lane
New York

D.D.: David Diamond.

89. Max Eastman

"MEMORANDUM ON DINING WITH EZRA POUND AND E. E. CUMMINGS"

24 May 1939

Cummings took us to dine with Ezra Pound—at Robert's on 55th St. "I prefer to eat good food and less of it," he [EP] said, and counseled us to order something "moderate." Then suddenly deciding that he liked us, he ordered the most expensive dish on the menu, and spent $32.50 on a dinner for six. A tribute to me [Eastman], Cummings said afterward, "and a nice one." At any rate a thick and sanguinary steak and exquisite red wine. He [EP] had a stupid man named "Hickock" with him, and is himself one-eighth as clever and all-sidedly alive as Cummings. He seems to subdue Cummings, though, being burly and assertive beside that slim ascetic saint of poetry. He [EP] is attractively curly-headed, almost rolly-polly, and with lots of laughter in the corners of his eyes—nervously restless, however, with the insatiable thirst of the self-infatuated "great man." He can listen, but he assumed I knew all about some recent contretemps. I found him sweet and likeable withal.

Eliena asked him if they hadn't stopped singing in Italy, and he was instantly and rather nervously on the defensive. Cummings, thinking Eliena had intuitively struck the tragic part about himself [EP] as well as Italy, kept murmuring, "plus tard, plus tard," but Eliena kept right on, and made being a fascist and a poet rather hard for him. As I consider him—intellectually—a mountebank, I watched him squirm under her questions with amusement.

"Don't you as an alien escape the regimentation wh. is the essence of it?" I asked. "I wouldn't say you would greatly enjoy being regimented yourself."

"Fascism only regiments those who can't do anything without it," he said. "If a man knows how to do anything it's the essence of fascism to leave him alone." Which is a sufficient measure of his intellectual acumen.

Cummings said afterward that he pitied him.

Speaking of the "boys"—Auden, Spender, MacNeice etc.—Pound said:

"For a man to pose successfully as a poet he's got to be at least one-eighth man or one-eighth poet!"

Hickock: Guy Hickock, formerly Paris correspondent of the *Brooklyn Daily Eagle.* Pound had published his work in the first number of the *Exile* in 1927.

90. Cummings to James Sibley Watson Jr.

AL-1.

decoration day [30 May 1939]
[extract]

you may be surpised to learn that the recently endowed beyond its fondest
hopes (& I don't mean peutêtre) Patchin Institute has been studying an Ezra.
We don't know if he's a spy or simply schizo, but we do feel he's incredibly
lonesome. Gargling antisemitism from morning till morning doesn't
(apparently) help a human throat to sing. He continually & really tackles
dummies, meanwhile uttering ferocious poopyawps & screechburps, as though
he suspected somevastinvisible footballgameaudience were surrounding bad-
guy titan-him. Etc if you don't know money you don't know nothing & if
you've studied economics in college of course you're ignorant etc and all of
which pleasureless unbecoming being made of the very impurest timidity. I
succeeded in asking if he'd like to see you & yes indeed he only wondered if
you'd like to see him he'd be at Hamilton College you could drive there but
whereupon his attention disappeared: which generally does. A youthhood pal
W Carlos W came to Ford Maddox Wiffer's for the express purpose of
reencountering Pound & I find poor Pound on his back on the
frontroomcouch looking like a derailed fast freight & gasping it was too hot to
telephone, but when I offered to invite Williams over here the patient weakly
said no. He's very fond of me, incidentally

91. Cummings to Pound

TLS-1.

[July 1939]   4 Patchin Place
                                                     Thursday

Dear Yank—

we returned last Sunday;since when(your warship being at sea)the enclosed
envelope has roosted on our door,waiting to crow. Much as I mostly loathe all
joiners gettogetherers civilizationsavers and friendsofwaterclosets,more am glad
that Ezra Pound has met the only living American young composer;and tickled
it is je suis that your incorruptible shallwesay unconscious led you straight to
the Jew whom Signorissimo Xly Patriate once refused to shake by hand because
the filthy Pagan was temporarily eating thanks to accursed Gug

we still wake up circa noon and still fall asleep toward dawn and still want to
hear about a certain district known but not loved as of Columbia so why not

'phone GR 7-3918 beginning Saturday if you're still possessed of the twentieth
part of a fin

Marion sends her best
-high
eec

envelope: Envelope lacking.
composer: David Diamond.

92. Pound to Cummings

TLS-2.

26 Oct[ober 1939]   Rapallo

dear Estlin
        As far az I can make out Germany is about 90% right in the
present show. Cuff=Pooper having done his damndest to start a war has now
escaped to the U.S. to "lecture" far from the blooding shells.
        I think you might in verse animadvert following yr. touching
tribute of Spaudin and Ender. ⟨to hell wif μετα τα φυϛικα⟩ ["After the
Physics," the title given to Aristotle's writings on metaphysical subjects.]

And with moderation I think one ⟨material⟩ egg (as minimum) might well be
heaved at EVERY lecturer, whether yittisch or brittisch or whoseeverbloody son
in law be he. with we hope the benefit of baseball training beeforheave
whenever such "lecturer" try to git the boys over to yourup to fight for the
interest on britisch loans, Das Leihkapital, Das WucherReich etc.
        In fact I think Cuff=Duper's moog will probably arise such
thoughts in several booZums once they see him. but you never can tell.
        At any rate Unc. Joe wdn't do their dhirty work for
them./
        and if the jews felt it wuz time to leave Mr Roosevelt / ETC.

Waaal, Meridiano, wot I senk you a kawpy OF, is takin on Broletto
communications çoivis; so IF any decent buks are pubd in AM. send 'em over
to EZ and they will reviewed be.

Any gnus of WHERE I can sell any printed matter wd. beeeee welKum.

but you neednt limit yr/ epistulary to prakkikal matters am allus glad to hear of the brig drifts in Amurikum sentimug

The venbl Possum is gittin my canters into page proof

but gornoze how much further. Apparently you mustn't say Rothschild in England; not even under yr breff. wich reflex on the freedumb of the Britisch press or do it not so?

waal giv me luvv to th Missus

yrz Ez P

and of course the effek of the gunus of the Hun/Russ pack on yr enTOUrage wd. be good subjekk matter

Cuff=Pooper: Alfred Duff Cooper (1890–1954), British statesman. Secretary of state for War, 1935–37; First Lord of the Admiralty, 1937–38; minister of information, 1940–41. Duff Cooper strongly urged an increase in naval construction during his tenure as First Lord of the Admiralty. He resigned his position after the Munich Agreement of September 1938. He lectured in the United States from October 1940 to March 1941.

touching tribute: Cummings's poem "flotsam and jestsam" first appeared with the title of "Dirge" in *Furioso,* vol. 1, no. 1 (summer 1939) (Firmage B121). In later printings, Cummings dropped the title.

Leihkapital: Loan capital.

WucherReich: A state based on usury and profiteering.

Unc. Joe: Joseph Stalin.

Meridiano: The periodical *Meridiano di Roma,* to which Pound began contributing in April 1938.

Broletto: A periodical published in Como, Italy, to which Pound contributed three articles in 1938.

my canters: *Cantos LII–LXXI* (London: Faber and Faber, 1940) (Gallup A47). Published 25 January 1940. References to the Rothschilds in Canto LII were replaced by thick black lines, because Faber and Faber feared suits for libel. At the time, Pound thought it his "best book" (Norman, 375).

Hun/Russ pack: The German and Soviet governments signed a nonaggression pact on 23 August 1939.

93. Cummings to Pound

TL-2.

[Late November 1939]   [4 Patchin Place]

                                                            Walden

Dear Ezra—

If anything ail a man,so that he does not perform his functions,if he have a
pain in his bowels even,—for that is the seat of sympathy,—he forthwith sets
about reforming—the world. Being a microcosm himself,he discovers,and it is
a true discovery,and he is the man to make it,—that the world has been eating
green apples;to his eyes,in fact,the globe itself is a great green apple,which there
is danger awful to think of that the children of men will nibble before it is
ripe;and straightway his drastic philanthropy seeks out the Esquimaux and the
Patagonian,and embraces the populous Indian and Chinese villages;and,thus,by
a few years of philanthropic activity,the powers in the meanwhile using him for
their own ends,no doubt,he cures himself of the dyspepsia,the globe acquires a
faint blush on one or both of its cheeks,as if it were beginning to be ripe,and
life loses its crudity and is once more sweet and wholesome to live. I never
dreamed of any enormity greater than I have committed. I never knew,and
shall never know,a worse man than myself

                                                —affectionately

                                                            Henry

                                                            New York

Signor Ezra Pound
Rapallo,Italy
My very dear sir—

in the Bell Telephone Laboratories in New York,in a "time vault" whose
temperature is maintained within 1/100 of a degree,at 41 centigrade,are the
most accurate clocks in the world—the four quartz crystal clocks. This
seemingly inanimate mineral is alive with the pulsations of time—vibrations so
precise that they can be harnessed to regulate and dictate time intervals to
other clocks. When properly cut and inserted in a suitable circuit,they will
control the rate of electric vibration to an accuracy of one part in a million.
Thus huge electric generators are paced to deliver exactly 60 cycles a second
and in turn hold your electric clock to accurate time.

Again,these remarkable crystals are the master controls which regulate the
frequencies of radio stations so that they will "stay put" and not stray away to
spoil your favorite program.

Independently operated and checking each other for more than 10 years,these clocks are further checked with the U.S. Naval Observatory at Arlington. That's why when you call MEridian 7-1212 for the correct time you get it every 15 seconds from the world's most accurate clocks

—respectfully

New York
Telephone
Company

[Note in Pound's hand: "recd from eec 5 Dec XVIII"]

Walden: The first part of Cummings's letter is a quotation from a passage near the end of the "Economy" chapter of Henry David Thoreau's *Walden*.

Bell Telephone: The second part of Cummings's letter is a quotation from a leaflet sent to its customers by the Bell Telephone Company. The same leaflet helped inspire Marianne Moore's poem, "Four Quartz Crystal Clocks."

94. Pound to Cummings

TLS-1.

17 Dec [1939]   Rapallo

Vurry interestin, my yung GOliath ⟨? goy-lieth⟩
    Dew yew figger Mr Thoreau wuz a onanist or an eunuch? or wot ministered to his pleasaures thaaaar in th' wildurness?
                footone / in 1902 anno dumuni, Mr Feignebaum was known to his fellow students at U.P. as FuK=a=tree

Waaal a mild kewreeosity as to th workins has ministered to the evolution of them remarkabl crystals. so sez we/ let's be curious and/or
        sez Mr whoosis M/C/ to Mr Whatzis M/C/ after the crime of '73
"Did yew know it wuz loaded? I didn't know it wuz loaded."
        i;e; the demonitization of silver. and so gozit. ⟨or don't set on the railway track so insouciant.⟩

I am for reasons not wholly clear to msf sending ⟨you i.e. to you gornoze why⟩ a 2d. pamphlet (pubd. last summer in my absinths and needing two corrections . . included in copy forthwith) and also requesting that one technical term be understood as it wd. be in context with other B.U. pamphlets. re/ articulation and responsibility.

and so forth, appy gnu year

an luv to the lady   EZ.

tell Max an attack on private ownership that leaves interest (% usury) free to corrode is NOT the answer.

⟨& even you are so old you once wrote a sonnet on Froissart (better than most)⟩

Feignebaum: He is mentioned in Canto 28.

crime of '73: An act that decreed silver dollars could no longer be produced by the director of the Mint. To the advocates of silver coinage it became known as the "crime of '73." Alexander Del Mar's *Barbara Villiers or, A History of Monetary Crimes* (1899) has a short chapter entitled, "The Crime of 1873."

2d. pamphlet: *What Is Money For* (London: Greater Britain Publications, 1939) (Gallup A46).

B.U. pamphlets: British Union of Fascists.

Max: Max Eastman.

sonnet on Froissart: Jean Froissart (1338–1410?), whose *Chronicles* are a history of his own time. Pound refers to the sonnet beginning, "Thou in whose sword-great story shine the deeds." It was first published in *Eight Harvard Poets* (1917) (Firmage A1), subsequently in *Tulips and Chimneys* (1923) (Firmage A3), and in later collections of Cummings's poems. *Collected Poems*, 139.

95. Cummings to Pound

TLS-1.

February 10,1940   4 Patchin Place

Cher cropper D. looks—

a wisdom wave(straight from the Orient girls!)exemplifies unerringly my 'tis of's latest slavver in a rage for permanents:1st we observe ye Saturday socalled Evening Post boosting ye Saturday Evening socalled Post per photo of o'erwrinklingly bemandarinhatted supergenial hyperaged headon celestial,spectacles retouchedout,whose subkindly grin translates a viceversa caption upwinging "Chinaman say" say being doubtless pigeon. Pretty quick Chinaman say appeared practically everywhere;what he "say" conveniently varying(with strictly scientific accuracy)according to product to be bloated. Yesterday—strolling the 14th vista—beheld lots of odd things and even including a downtown departmentstore not so unrecently purchased by choisis,oirish title and all:here came your correspondentifrice arsi to arsi with

quite the presumma cum laude or ultimum thulum of guaranteed 3fisted
absolute furbelow viz.

"CONFUCIUS SAY
wise man save his
appetite until Hearns open
<u>NEW SODA BAR</u>

Snacks,Salads,Sandwiches,Sodas
at Very Modest Prices!"

obscurely turning from pellucid offal—I quoted you the Thoreau,neither
because he did or didn't suck his own ignoble prick nor because nobleness
only is what this world's good for;I quoted that passage because it is noble to
feel:if you cannot feel,Chinaman say 2

your friend(psych-)Lewis and his wife are courteous i.e. extraordinary id est
gentle,folk. Merci. Also am only gradually recovering from an "Italian Letter"
of last Sunday's NYTimes(the sheet with the slogan All The News That's Fit To
Print)which told through a few paragraphs who a poet is,accidentally doing my
the deep honour to name self

Marion inserts hello

—roses &

eec

Lewis: Writing to Pound in April 1947, Lewis asked, "Have you been visited in
   your retreat by any literary lights? Cummings for instance? I saw him when I
   was in N.Y. But he was such a jumpy and peppery little creature it was impossi-
   ble to talk to him much. He has succeeded in writing some very excellent
   verses." *The Letters of Wyndham Lewis,* ed. W. K. Rose (Norfolk, Conn.: New
   Directions, 1963), 404. See also letter 160.
"Italian Letter": No such document exists in the microfilmed record of the *New
   York Times* for this date.

96. Pound to Cummings

TLS-1.

20 March [1940]   Rapallo

Honourd Estlin
               by dint of my characteristic unpleasantness / or at any rate
POST if not propter/ the t/reasurer of the Insteroot ⟨ov Awts n Lers⟩ has
printed a REEport/

they have MONEY/ not more thet $500 a year to any one purrsen.

If a polite member indicated Joe gould/ I spose Joe cd/ use it. whether it is
infra dig yr/ digs/ I leave to you.

My remarks on their not eeelectin' you a member (Arch sez he has nominated
yew regular ever since HIS eeelection five years before mine) etc/ etc/ may or
may not have lubricated.

at any rate why shd/ the ooof stay in the vaults of a rust
company// ⟨? question⟩

now abaht mr thoreau/ thazz O.K. for mr thoreau/ or Doc Williams. and I
dont deeny it/ sitting by ⟨the⟩ of wealth and talents/
etc/

Arch shd/ know the ropes/ I doubt if treasurer ever before issued a reap/ort. or
ab/ ⟨majuscule for that A⟩ ditto/ but still. it arruv this a/m/. ⟨I mean the
report.⟩
dont try to hand out the sandwich to ALL yr/ most undesirable acquaintances.

Oh yes, Disney was not elected in the <u>literary</u> section/ I admit I suggest the
plastic blokes ought to take him in THEIR compartment, and he dont need the
suuprt of Nic Butter or Dottery Tumpysun. I mean it will be all right with
Walt anyhow/ mebbe he withdrawd/ The quality of membshp aint rising. and I
spose now that dollar reaport is out there will be rush to the guichet.

do relieve yrself (and Joe) if or before you aint ⟨or⟩ are become too old to with
dignity.
                              ever happy to serve/ if that's what it might be/ or
at any rat meant well
                              EZ. P.

Insteroot address/ 633 W. 155 th St. sec/ H.Seidel Canby
they say he means well. he has only asked me to resign onct so far.
                              ⟨& luv to lady⟩

Arch: In a letter of 13 November 1939, Archibald MacLeish informed Pound that
    "I have sent your nomination of Cummings along to the Institute. I am afraid I
    am not a very good member of that august body but I have certainly been
    nominating E. E. Cummings every year since I can remember."
Disney: Walt Disney (1901–66), American film animator and movie producer.
Nic Butter: Nicholas Murray Butler.
Dottery Tumpysun: Dorothy Thompson (1893–1961), American journalist.

Canby: Henry Seidel Canby. Pound probably refers to a passage from a letter Canby wrote to him on 14 March 1938. "The Institute was glad to recognize your services to literature by an election to its membership, but if you do not like its scope and activities, as to which you do not seem to be very well informed, it is always possible for you to resign. In any case, I would suggest that scurrilous attacks upon its members and officers are not the best means of elevating American culture."

97. Pound to Cummings

TCS.

20 Ap[ril] 1940   Rapallo

Who"z this bloke BOAKE Carter?
seems hep.
                    yrz EZ

I got a line of hope fer the venerabl Eastman
if he will answer a question in exchange
                    EZ P

Carter: Boake Carter (1898–1944), British-born American journalist and radio commentator. Carter had a daily, fifteen-minute radio program that was broadcast nationally over the Columbia Broadcasting System. He also wrote a syndicated newspaper column, "But. . . ." In *Why Meddle in Europe* (New York: R. M. McBride, 1939), Carter observed that if war should break out in Europe, "There is nothing in the facts, or in sound logic flowing from them, which indicates any good reason why we should again repeat our colossal folly of 1917. We shall profit enormously by staying out. We shall lose enormously by going in" (205).

98. Pound to Cummings

TLS-1.

5 or 6 Maggio [May 1940]   Rapallo

Dear Estlin
                    Haow are the norweeguns feelink abaht the feller wot painted
your bog?

Nooz of the murkn liter⟨ar⟩chy front seems to bee the orange covered house of
Mr Hemnwy amid the banana trees "surrounded by a tropical ammosphere".
waaal
if you indite any more verses send 'em on/ i am more in favour ⟨wif⟩ editers in
the ole contynong in purrperschun as the s/o/b/ in Morgenthalia get more and
more lousy.

Pity my talentz is gittin so lorst to me native tongue
BUT still, I spose the furriners profit. Tho it will putt a strain on the
bilbuliographers/ the wot you call bib/ what the cheezus
              I dunno wot drives me to writin ⟨this letter⟩ except fatigue and of
course a thurst fer nooz of the further outposts

I don't spose young Jas/ can be accelerote, or that it wd/ do any savin
        wall love to the Queen of Patchinia,and do send on news of the local
cultures.
                          as ever Ez Po
I have told TWO, no, THREE blighters to review Eimi and yr/ poEms, but they
dont git on with it/ I spek EIMI is a fair buggar fer them as is not born to the
langqidg.

⟨Do take pore ole Bull Wms something sweet, or a nice soft steak fer his
dinner⟩

your bog: German military forces invaded Denmark and Norway on 9 April 1940.
  Although British ground forces were landed in Norway, they were evacuated on
  2 May.
      The reference to the "bog" is repeated in letters 119, 129, and 143, but I do
  not know what Pound means.
house of Mr Hemnwy: In the spring and summer of 1940, Hemingway was living
  at Finca Vigia (Lookout Farm), twelve miles outside of Havana, and finishing
  For Whom the Bell Tolls.
s/o/b/ in Morgenthalia: Henry Morgenthau Jr. In "The First Page: And a Mission
  for England," *Action,* no. 147 (10 December 1938), 8 (Gallup C1487), Pound
  urged his English readers, "Clean your own house. Ged rid of the gold-brokers
  who have formed the mind of Mr. Morgenthau, Junior." Reprinted in *EPPP.*
Jas/: James Laughlin.
Queen: Marion Morehouse Cummings.

99. Cummings to Pound

TLS-1.

treize mai [May 1940]   [4 Patchin Place]

Dear Ezra—

have done what less I could to more your most generosity around little joe. Eg
wrote Can(unquote)by;pas d'answer. Then a pleasant ba from Stephen Rose
Benet,at whom had officially been referred my naked suggestion,claiming
ignorance of & curiosity re j g :replied phenomenon vide CPs twosixtyone
must however be viewed to be perceived,gave its address. Coached Joe,which
expressed willingness sans astonishment con skepticism but(to undersigned's
delight)announced Steve was "up my alley" apparently via John Brown's body a
certainly bookofthemonthclub selection probably for years ago. Ye candidate
once depuis materialized;there'd come no word from fame

Marion and I've glimpsed intermittently that steady admirer of your warship
named Fox. A sort of tortoise,I like them. Full of kangaroo. Beaucoup frendlich

also rabbits. John Reed. Popped en route to Canada. You saved his mangled
life. You did a good job

high see can't casts no shadow itler & itler

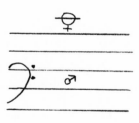

Estlin

[On the verso of the letter Marion Morehouse Cummings added the following
message.]

Boake Carter is a radio commentator, lecturer & columnist. He's an
Englishman, but has lately been made a citizen of the U.S.A. He's very anti-B.
now and is forever reminding the Americans that the English usually think of
us as LOUTS, SLOBS & BOOBS; its only when they need us that we are
permitted to join them in saving the world for something or other.

M.

Can: Henry Seidel Canby.

Benet: Cummings conflates the names of Stephen Vincent Benét (1898–1943), American poet and novelist, and William Rose Benét (1886–1950), American poet and critic.

CPs twosixtyone: Poem 261 of Cummings's *Collected Poems* (1938) is "little joe gould has lost his teeth and doesn't know where." *Complete Poems,* 410.

John Brown's body: Stephen Vincent Benét, *John Brown's Body* (Garden City, N.Y.: Doubleday, Doran, 1928). In 1928 and 1929 it sold 130,000 copies. It also earned Benét the Pulitzer Prize for poetry. Carl Brandt, of Brandt and Brandt (the same literary agency that represented Cummings), was Benét's literary agent. Benét was elected to the National Institute of Arts and Letters in 1929. In 1937 he became chairman of the nominating committee for the literature section. Benét's opposition to the policies of Nicholas Murray Butler is covered in Charles Fenton's *Stephen Vincent Benét: The Life and Times of an American Man of Letters* (New Haven: Yale University Press, 1958).

Fox: Douglas C. Fox.

John Reed: John Reid (1915–85), Canadian novelist. He lived in Rapallo, Italy, for nine months in 1938–39 in order to learn from Pound.

100. Pound to Cummings

TLS-1.

8 Giugn [June 1940]   Rapallo

Dear estlin AND M///
                         Waal as to ole Ez" hiz rightness. Do we perceive a
tenDENcy to perceive that the choice is between a republican (in the old sense)
             with strong executive form of govt. (at least as strong exec. as
Tommy Jeff//)
WITH an organic insides wherein every bloke is represented by a bloke of his
own trade or profession.

             AND on the other an bloody 'and a dictatorship by and for
usura, run by figureheads working for money lenders ?

Thank M/ fer Boake clippin' / I shd. like rather more ⟨clippinz⟩ when the
fambly finances run to spare pustal stampps.

Also a bit of classy curiosity re/ purChase of gold by the gummyment seems to
me timely. Whether I can kyristalize me thorts on that, who noze.

anny howe here'z fer a birght new world, with no Butlers ⟨nicking⟩. In fak I cd/
omit several bloated objects from the scene. Mr Eliot did not arrive here, after

having sent careful schedule ⟨of days where from genova to Palermo⟩

I hear they are to murder his cathedral, or may by now have done so in the teeyater of the uniwurstity of Roma.

yrz EZ

⟨& O how you like the choo choos & centeneral pustal stamps⟩

clippin:' Enclosure lacking.

Mr Eliot: On 9 May 1940, Eliot wrote to Pound that he hoped to stop overnight in Rapallo on 8–9 June 1940. In a letter of 20 May, Eliot informed Pound that his visit to Italy would not occur.

choo choos: Italian postage stamps—depicting locomotives—celebrating the centennial of the Italian railroad.

101. Cummings to Pound

TC.

[Postmarked 29 June 1940]   [Silver Lake, N.H.]

thank you most kindly for the choochoo-message of Good Cheer dont j'avais besoin(see obverse)Et Comment. M is sending you Life Time and Colliers but the greatest of these is

obverse: An illustration of a giant fish pursuing a man, with the caption "The fish keep you busy here."

102. Pound to Cummings

TL-1. Carbon.

19 Lugg XVIII [July 1940]   RAPALLO

Dear Estlin

DAMN nuissance having no mail or papers from U.S. Any gobt. not made of 99% snot wd/ have used bargaining power to maintal postal service. who pays for their stinking navy? Note fer poetic use/ TEN billion given gold sellers/ 4 billion velvet/ sheer steal / nacherly farmers is poor, and mortgaged.

as to eddikatin the boyes you mean are unrefined/ wot about Adolf's "Bauernfahig" ideas/ men on land who can WORK it/ not to be putt off it, leave it to son who can grow crops/ NOT split it up one kid bauer fambly stays bower/ others can go be whatever.

The SHIT of the brit/ mutts citing Jeff, and Lincoln, to get young Patchin etc/ to die fer Lazard's mortgages/ [H]ambro damn kike, wanting to putt his bumbailifs into Norway// nackerly pore brits: not very keen on fighting for sheeny (Rothschild) mortgages on England.

as fer U.S. being governed by foreign jew agents etc/ WHY? will they NEVER learn the country was sold up by Sherman and Ikleheime[r] in 1863?
                        Nuther point is yr/ getting ALL yr/ european news from news=sellers; and believing jew agencies, Reute[rs,] [H]avas, owned by Rothschild, Lazard etc . . . Ask the poor kike WHY he lets big kike produce pogroms. The big kike nearly always gets to Portugal with 14 automobiles. Wonder has Wheeler any monetary ideas/ If you send clippings, or get someone to send em to Kitasono he cd/ forward 'em to me. It takes time, but air mail is too eggspensive. What about this noo noozwyper P/M? and what is the N.Y. enquirer . . . If you are too weary to answer, pass on this note to Angold, or to young McPherson (D.McPherson? p:o:box 217 Philadelphia)/ mebbe you better pass it on anyhow/ and get one of them to answer. ANY publishing being done in U.S.?
Am I right that rip van Wendel has slept for 20? // Can you delouse Frankie? and have Farley and Garner really been scraped off; or is that all eyewash? The treasury is the WORST.

If you think CoopDuffer is democracy OR the red flag, why ??
good bilingual series started in Barcelona/ Poesia en la Mane/ only I dont see yr/ spanish translator yet. do you hear from Kit Kat (=ue). I had orter have got up stairs to see them pixchoors; but nevr wuz at 4.Patchin with necessary energy to git up stairs/ have noted lacuna since.
                        waaal, benedictions/ Have you met Johnnie Slocum/? agency Russel, Volkenning, 522 Fifth Ave. might be of use, to you or someone/ might also be of use to me IF you ever cd/ move 'em. I have sent 'em several ms/ purrzoombly NOT wot they want.

                    bless the lady   yrs

unrefined: A reference to Cummings's poem "the boys i mean are not refined" (*Complete Poems*, 427).

"Bauernfahig": [*bauernfahig*] "Fit for farmers." Perhaps a reference to Nazi plans to create new entailed farms owned by proprietors with the title *Bauer*. See David Schoenbaum, *Hitler's Social Revolution* (Garden City, N.Y.: Doubleday, 1966), 164–66.

young Patchin: Probably Kenneth Patchen (1911–72), American poet.

Lazard's: The international banking and investment house of Lazard Frères and Company.

Hambro: Sir Charles Hambro (1897–1963), British merchant banker. He established the Hambros Bank in 1921 and was elected a director of the Bank of England in 1928. When World War II began, he joined the Ministry of Economic Warfare.

Sherman and Ikleheime[r]: Probably a reference to the National Banking Act of 1863, which effectively eliminated state bank currencies in favor of the national currency. It also strengthened national banks and weakened state banks. John Sherman (1823–1900), United States senator from Ohio (1861–77 and 1881–97) and secretary of the Treasury (1877–81), strongly supported the National Banking Act. In "A Visting Card" and "Gold and Work," Pound cites "a letter of Rothschild Bros., quoting John Sherman, addressed to the firm of Ikleheimer, Morton and Van der Gould, dated 25 June 1863" (*Selected Prose*, 311 and 339).

Reute[rs,] [H]avas: News agencies. Reuters (founded 1851) based in London; Agence Havas (founded 1835) in France.

Wheeler: Burton K. Wheeler (1882–1975), United States senator from Montana (1923–47). He was a leading proponent of U.S. isolationism. Pound had met him in Washington, D.C., in 1939.

Kitasono: Katue Kitasono (1902–78), Japanese poet. His relations to Pound are covered in Sanehide Kodama's *Ezra Pound and Japan* (Redding Ridge, Conn.: Black Swan, 1987). On 22 August 1940, Kitasono wrote to Pound, "I am sending a copy of VOU each to Mr. Juan Ramon Masoliver and to Mr. E. E. Cummings. I have often tried to translate Cummings' poems, but never succeeded" (*Ezra Pound and Japan*, 92).

P/M: A new afternoon New York newspaper of left-wing sympathies.

N.Y. enquirer: A New York Sunday afternoon newspaper founded in 1936. Its founder, William Griffin, professed great admiration for the editorial policies of William Randolph Hearst. In a 1947 speech, Griffin claimed that "The Enquirer has championed strict adherence to the Constitution, as the indispensable guardian of our American rights, liberties and privileges." In the mid-1950s, the *New York Enquirer* became the *National Enquirer*. The files of the New York Public Libraries contain no issues of the *Enquirer* prior to 1949.

Angold: J. P. Angold (1909–43), British poet. He was a proponent of Social Credit and contributed to the *New English Weekly.* He also was associated with the magazine *Prosperity* (London), in which appeared Canto 45 ("With Usura") (Gallup C1293). Angold was killed in World War II.

McPherson: Douglas MacPherson, a young Philadelphian who had written to Pound in 1939 about a magazine that he proposed to start. On 25 February 1940, MacPherson wrote to Pound, "I am enclosing some documents. Two from PHILA. RECORD, owned by the jew Stern; RECORD is a Democrat (New Deal brand) paper. Other clipping from PHILA. INQUIRER (Republican), owned by the jew Annenberg (Moe). The latter paper's editorial reveals the anti-British sentiment that is rapidly developing in U.S."

rip van Wendel: Wendell Willkie (1882–1944), Republican nominee for president in 1940.

Farley: James A. Farley.

Garner: John Nance Garner (1868–1967), vice president of the United States (1933–41).

CoopDuffer: Alfred Duff Cooper. See letter 92.

them pixchoors: Paintings by Cummings.

Slocum: John J. Slocum (b. 1914), American scholar and diplomat. Slocum had known James Laughlin since they were at summer camp together. Slocum was also president of the Harvard *Advocate* in 1935. Pound stayed at Slocum's apartment on East Seventy-Fourth Street during part of his American visit. During 1940 and 1941, Slocum was listed as the "Secretary" in the literary agency of Russell and Volkening, Inc. "Russell" was Diarmuid Russell, son of the Irish poet, George Russell ("A.E.").

103. Pound to Cummings

TLS-1.

14 Nov. 1940   Rapallo

Dear Estlin; to wile away ye longe winterr nightes, knowe thenne that "Mr Canby thinks he ought to be IN" / thus from sekkerterry of the said Sidling Can/be but unlikely. in the words: "Unfortunately yr/ nomniation arrived too late (from ye perriles of ye sea etc.) to bee putt on this yeare's ballottt". However Mr Canby etc/ ut supra.   . . . and thatte yr/ nomination wille bee keppet for nexte yeare . . . .   let us praye. and considering that Arch Mc Loosh has (so he says) been nominatin yuh ever since he (the MacLoosh) got INNE. ;;; and so forth/ as to what Nic Whole Ass ⟨Merdy⟩ Butter thynkiet eye knowe notte. But I whope WHEN, you wont snot 'em. as Hen Adams; Hen. James, and Brooks Adams didde not snotte the said insterooshun, but even in theyre darke and dysmale pea/riod ye/ end of pea/tyme feel at least that amount of civic urage/ besides which there is some money, and Nic Whole ass is yes even now makiyng two backs/ or trying to rush it from controll of Damrosch/ etc. and there wille allus be some Joe Gould or whomever shd/ have it and won't get it unless a few, minimum etc of clean men get in, and poop the sons of hell.

Not alll the above shd/ be considered quote from Felicia Geffin (sec. to Cby/) What canyou saye of Leverett S. Lyon and V.Abramson ? whose worke is sent me by the heavy endowment/ ye/ Falk, vs/ ye Brookings vs/ ye socalled Acad of

Polecatical science ?? no connection of the Insteroot Can/bee. and will any send me news ⟨mews⟩ of the late eeeel/ections / and hath any news of the Eleatic Elyot or other survivors of the licheraty and/or versific epoch?

Love to the ladye / and I remain. yr EZ

that this is worth 20 cents; I doubt/ but you can reply by ornry post as Dillon's gazette/ Leverett Lyon/ the Annals of the Ac/ pol sci etc/ seems to arrive by plain post/ being I spose passed by the nonsener. and so to etc.

I thought the news from Geffin wd/ etc. brighten ye walles of Patchin. and of course relieve breathless anz/ierty. Yeezus my Jayzus. an anyhow you wuz allus a hellyun fer style. some jems whereof still drop from the onconschus crucible of etc.
⟨them as least [illegible]⟩

Ezra Pound

Damrosch: Walter Damrosch (1862–1950), German-born American conductor and composer. He was awarded the gold medal of the National Institute of Arts and Letters in 1938.

Lyon: Pound evidently had received the Brookings Institution publication *Government and Economic Life: Development and Current Issues of American Public Policy,* by Leverett S. Lyon, Myron W. Watkins, and Victor Abramson (Washington, D.C.: Brookings Institution, 1939–40). This was a two-volume, thirteen-hundred-page examination of U.S. government regulation of private enterprise. In vol. 1, p. vii, the authors noted that "The study upon which this report is based was made possible by the Maurice and Laura Falk Foundation of Pittsburgh." Maurice Falk (1866–1946), a Pittsburgh businessman, had established the Maurice and Laura Falk Foundation in 1929. It was capitalized at $10 million and the funds were to be expended within thirty-five years. The directors of the foundation funded many projects devoted to economic research.

Acad of Polecatical science: The Academy of Political Science, founded in Philadelphia in 1889, is an organization that, according to its own description, "promotes the cultivation of the political sciences and their application to the solution of social and political problems." In 1940 its headquarters were at Columbia University. Pound was a member.

eeeel/ections: The national, state, and local elections of 5 November 1940.

Elyot: T. S. Eliot.

Dillon's gazette: *Poetry* (Chicago).

Geffin: Felicia Geffin, secretary to Canby.

104. Cummings to Pound

ALS-1.

[December 1940]   4 Patchin Place

Dear Ezra—

your 14 Nov. (adorned with six Pegasus & 2 settingupexercise) greeting crashed
Patchin on Monday December nine. To Hell with subrosa & autrement
sororities or fraternities, very particularly the pythian orders of moose. When
callow thou hast attained my humble servant's exparience, all thesey thosey
gettogetherys merely mean goosing one's self into a plentifully [pugforested?]
brownpaperbag, the worser to swim winedark Hellesponts inc.

now something different's a fellow gets word to pay 250 $ or hear a jailsentence
or fulfill his jury-"duty" (which he's already succeeded in dodging once)—the
poor guy "serves". At least I did. And that's a distant mil from muttering
thankyouplease to the Kore Wheeler Markham chair of contaminated
desuetude in Archibald Benet's parlor de burys

swam at "Times Square" last "election eve" to watch me lose 15 berries re
W.W., having (also to please my family) once voted for the gent with artificial
teeth that fell asleep president & awaked Hughes. Mob = 42nd - 48th. 3 (three)
its looked as if they were trying not to be blown by horns: otherwise nothing
did everyone whatsoever at all.
Jim Angleton has been seemingly got hold of by an intelligent prof &
apparently begins to begin to realize that camp mil ser might give the former a
respite from poisonal responsibility . . . maybe he's developing? Per contra: last
summer Ted Spenser dropped up with two dubs, one the farflung Bessemer
gonzesse yclept Laughlin; which mistakenly afterward wrote addressing me as
"immortal and rustic bard"—Who promptly announced "What I need is a
thousand dollars and when I need it is now"; celui-la muy languidly replies
that so would everybody including him like a thousand dollars. Lighthouse
Robbie was correct
            The full is so world of a thingful of numbs,
            I all we should think be as finger as thumbs
Beside "Treasure Island" I put "Lorna Doone"

Spring is coming. Two penguins salute you from our mantlepiece. The lady
sends love and the elephant wishes bonne chance

                                                        —eec

PS and right soon

Pegasus . . . settingupexercise: Italian postage stamps.

W.W.: Wendell Willkie.

Hughes: Charles Evans Hughes (1862–1948), American statesman. Republican nominee for president in 1916, Hughes was narrowly defeated by Woodrow Wilson.

Angleton: James Angleton. See the Biographical Notes. Robin W. Winks's *Cloak and Gown: Scholars in the Secret War, 1939–1961* (New York: William Morrow, 1987), 336–37, lists several "intelligent profs" whom Angleton admired: Norman Holmes Pearson, Filmer S. C. Northrop, Arnold Wolfers, Angelo Lipari, Arthur Mizener, and Andrews Wanning.

Spenser: Theodore Spencer (1904–49), professor of English at Harvard University. Spencer was an admirer of both Cummings's and Pound's poetry.

gonzesse: French slang, meaning "girl," "bird," "chick." Cummings also uses the word in the last chapter of *The Enormous Room:* "Jean's letter to his *gonzesse* in Paris still safe in my little pocket under my belt."

Laughlin: James Laughlin. In a letter dated 2 July [no year], Laughlin wrote to Cummings, "Immortal & Rustic Bard: Being always too embarrassed to discuss business in public I didn't get around to finding out (while breaking your crockery) whether you have any astounding material with which to astound the small public that limps, halts and gropes to the lip of my diseased publication????? [Laughlin refers to *New Directions in Poetry and Prose.*] I don't particularly want (for this) poems, but something new, strange and wonderful, never before seen by eye of man, beast or eskimo in this world or the succeeding. At a later date, I would like to do a group of poems in our new pamphlet series, say in about a year or two. Wot's time? You have a swell place up there. With regards." In a letter most probably subsequent to this one, dated 21 August 1940, Laughlin said, "Dear Cummings— Respectfully speaking BUT you are so ambiguous. I ask you have you anything written for me to look at and you tell me you want 1000 bucks. I want 1000 bucks, too. I guess most people do. But to get back to fax - have you anything I would like? Ted Spencer speaks most highly of a poem, about your revered parent. Yours, J. Laughlin."

Lighthouse Robbie: Cummings parodies the first two lines of Robert Louis Stevenson's poem, "Happy Thought" (poem 24 of *A Child's Garden of Verses*): "The world is so full of a number of things, / I'm sure we should all be as happy as kings."

"Lorna Doone": *Lorna Doone: A Romance of Exmoor* (1869). A historical novel set in late seventeenth-century England, by Richard Doddridge Blackmore (1825–1900).

the elephant: A sculpture at the 4 Patchin Place apartment.

105. Pound to Cummings

TLS-1.

16 Sett [September 1941]   Rapallo

Dear Estlin/ I haint had no news/ not wot you wd call NEWS since Russia
started savin democracy, and Kit Kat per force stopped writin, or his stuff
comin' in. Last was a pretty ideogramic an' kana ⟨version⟩ of my cat mousin
quince blossoms (at least I spose the blighter translated it correctly, I aint had
the patience to verify.

Well now wot the hell do we think of it all/ If I aint a seein' it clear and whole,
and hole, I wanna be told and told. I can't git any american news worth a pea
hen/ And when I do see a american peper it is full of goof, and nothing about
the few raminin distinguished figgers on the american seen. I try to tickle up
ole Max now and then/ wot does HE think of the shindy/ in fact what do you
or does ANYone think of it?
        If NObody'z got 30 cents fer an air mail/ send on a response ordinary
with a pretty pixchoor on the stamp for philatelists.
                Gawd/ I been impelled to translate a novel (that is a prose
book, that wuz worth it, by Enrico Pea (not pronounced Peee) I spose it wd/
take a war to drive me to finding a PROSE book and an author/
                        specially as I had seen the bloke walkin
along the sea front ten years ago . . . No he aint exactly a neighbor; but I have
looked into his macubine eye since I traduced him. Any way to git the ms/ to
Amurika and into print?
        you might ask Slocum (fergit if you know Sloc?) J.J.Slocum co/ Russel
Volkenning/   , at any rate, I shd/ like to know if he got my henquiry about
Henry's ⟨P's⟩ volume. We are also gittin Tom Hardy traduced into the local
idiom   / wich may strike you as archaic. but still, it do pass the time
pleasantly.

waaal love to her highness: and so forth   yrz/ EZ
                                                az uzual
                                                Ezra Pound

⟨Haow are th breveren any how?⟩
I shd/ probably accept any advice thet you giv me. wich you certainly wont
UNLESS I keep on asking fer it wich I now do.

Russia: War between Germany and the Soviet Union had begun on 22 June 1941.
Kit Kat: Writing to Katue Kitasono of 25 March 1941, Pound had included a
    haiku, "Mediterranean March." The letter in which Kitasono sent his transla-

tion is dated 28 May 1941. In it Kitasono remarks, "I translated your Hokku 'Mediterranean March' and wrote it in my own poor hand." Both letters are printed in Sanehide Kodama's *Ezra Pound and Japan*.

Mediterranean March
Black cat on the quince branch
mousing blossoms

a novel: Enrico Pea (1881–1958), Italian novelist, was the author of *Il romanzo di Moscardino*, a tetralogy consisting of *Moscardino* (1922), *Il Volto Santo* (1924), *Il servitore del diavolo* (1931) and *Magoometto* (1942). Pound's translation of the first of these was published in *New Directions in Prose and Poetry 15* (1955) (Gallup C1742). It was reprinted separately the following year in Milan by Vanni Scheiwiller (Gallup A71). See Enrico Pea, "Thank You, Ezra Pound" (trans. David Anderson), *Paideuma*, vol. 8, no. 3 (winter 1979), 442–45.
Slocum: John J. Slocum.

106. Cummings to Pound

TLS-1.

October 8, 1941   [4 Patchin Place]

Dear Ezra—

whole,round,and heartiest greetings from the princess & me to our favorite Ikey-Kikey,Wandering Jew,Quo Vadis,Oppressed Minority of One,Misunderstood Master,Mister Lonelyheart,and Man Without a Country

re whose latest queeries
        East Maxman has gone off on a c-nd-m in a pamphlet arguing everybody should support Wussia,for the nonce. "Time"(a loose)mag says Don Josh Bathos of London England told P.E.N. innulluxuls that for the nonce writers shouldn't be writing. Each collective choisi(pastparticiple,you recall,of choisir)without exception and—may I add—very naturally desires for the nonce nothing but Adolph's Absolute Annihilation,Coûte Que Coûte(SIC). A man who once became worshipped of one thousand million pibbul by not falling into the ocean while simultaneously peeping through a periscope and sucking drugstore sandwiches is excoriated for,for the nonce,freedom of speech. Perfectly versus the macarchibald maclapdog macleash—one(1)poet,John Peale Bishop,holds a nonce of a USGov't job;vide ye newe Rockyfeller-sponsored ultrarumpus to boost SA infrarelations. Paragraph and your excoed Billy The Medico made a far from noncelike W.C. of himself(per a puddle of a periodical

called "Decision")relating how his poor pal E.P. - talented etc but ignorant ass
who etc can't play the etc piano etc . . . over which tour d'argent the wily
Scotch duckfuggur Peter Munro Jack 5 Charles Street NYCity waxed so wroth
he hurled at me into New Hampshire a nutn if not incandescing wire
beginning "stab a man in the back but do it three years too late":'twould hence
apper you've still some friends,uncle Ezra,whether vi piace or non

now to descend to the surface;or,concerning oldfashioned i:every whatsoever
bully(e.g. all honourless & lazy punks twerps thugs slobs politicos
parlourpimps murderers and other reformers)continues impressing me as a
trifle more isn't than least can less,and the later it's Itler the sooner hit's Ess.
Tune:The Gutters of Chicago

> ("make haste" spake the Lord of New Dealings
> "neutrality's hard on my feelings"
> —they returned from the bank
> with the furter in frank:
> & the walls;&the floors,&the ceilings)

.   As my father wrote me when I disgraced Orne—forsan et haec. And the
censor let those six words through

hardy is as hardy does

—salut!

eec

a **pamphlet:** Perhaps Max Eastman's *A Letter to Americans* (New York: Rand
School Press, 1941). Eastman argues that "if Hitler wins this war totalitarianism
will triumph over democracy throughout the world" (13). Therefore, he goes
on, "If we are ready to make an open gift of all help to England . . . we ought
also to be ready, in case of certain need, to fight by England's side" (14).
Nowhere in this essay does Eastman speak of supporting Russia. Cummings
therefore may have had an incorrect impression of *A Letter to Americans.* Or he
may be speaking of another, unrecorded publication by Eastman.

Bathos: John Dos Passos had attended a PEN conference in London. According to
Time, "U.S. delegate John Dos Passos (who arrived late with Thornton Wilder)
declared: 'Writers should not be writing at all now.'" *Time,* vol. 38, no. 13
(September 1941), 88.

A **man:** Charles A. Lindbergh (1902–74), whose solo flight across the Atlantic
Ocean in 1927 had made him an international hero. Lindbergh campaigned
actively to keep the United States out of World War II. In a speech at Des
Moines, Iowa, on 11 September 1941, Lindbergh listed three groups that were,
he said, pushing the U.S. toward war: the British, the Roosevelt administration,

and the Jews. "No speech by Charles Lindbergh or by any other noninterventionist speaker before Pearl Harbor provoked such widespread controversy and criticism." Wayne S. Cole, *Charles A. Lindbergh and the Battle against American Intervention in World War II* (New York: Harcourt, Brace, Jovanovich, 1974), 162.

macleash: Archibald MacLeish was a friend of Felix Frankfurter. He served as Librarian of Congress from 1939 to 1944. MacLeish advocated aid to Britain and the building up of U.S. armed forces. He was also one of President Roosevelt's speechwriters.

Bishop: During 1941 and 1942, Bishop lived in New York City and was employed as publications director for the Office of the Coordinator of Inter-American Affairs.

ultrarumpus: Nelson A. Rockefeller (1908–79) was appointed head of the federal government's Office of Inter-American Affairs in 1940. The OIAA strove to further Latin American economic development and to promote cultural exchange between the United States and Latin America.

Billy The Medico: William Carlos Williams. Cummings refers to "Ezra Pound: Lord Ga-Ga!" *Decision*, vol. 2, no. 3 (September 1941), 16-24. In this essay, Williams acknowledges that Pound is a "great poet." But he is also "a stupid ass," "a spoiled brat," and "tone deaf." Furthermore, "Pound has missed the major impact of his age, the social impetus which underlies every effort toward a rebirth, he has missed it largely through his blindness and intense egotism, a complete reactionary." Finally, "because Ezra is rooted in nothing more than the literary and ghostly past he has missed knowing anything of the living springs of today."

Peter Munro Jack: Peter Monro Jack (1896–1944), Scottish-born American literary critic. His literary reviews appeared in the *New York Times Book Review* and other leading journals and newspapers of the era. He reviewed Pound's *Guide to Kulchur* in the *New York Times* (26 February 1939, 14).

furter in frank: Felix Frankfurter (1882–1965), associate justice of the U.S. Supreme Court (1939–62).

when I disgraced: In *The Enormous Room* (1922), Cummings describes his stay (with Slater Brown) in the Depot de Triage, which was located in the village of La Ferté Macé, near the town of Bagnoles-de-l'Orne. Cummings's letters home from the detention center were headed, "La Ferté Macé, Orne." The Latin quotation he refers to is from Virgil's *Aeneid*, Book 1, line 203: "forsan et haec olim meminisse juvabit" [Perchance even this distress it will some day be a joy to recall].

107. Pound to Cummings

TLS-2.

Anno ~~XVIII~~ ⟨XX⟩; and a nother new Fascist year
Rapallo
                has been born.
                    6 Nov. [1941] or thaaar abouts

Revered Estlin/
                            And alas that nowt bores me like
changin typing ribbons.   /waal give me lovv to the Princess and as
fer Josh Bathos, I spect he has caught it from Hem, who has long thought that
writers shouldn't think/ Thinkers being prohibited toewrite ANYhow in all
angry=saxon cuntries.

/   waaal old Doc Willyam anonimo who don't "want his name mentioned"
wrote me he has done so, and had sent a note of mine to the redaction as
counterblast/ which nacherly they do not print/ at least not if I know 'em.
However, noble Jack, lets hope he allus has some.

Now it wd/ be Halifax to suggest that I onnerstn ALL of yr/ letter other than
that J.Pealed Bishop has a job/ for which let us be thankful.
                    I am translatin Confucius, really this time, having erred
in trustin a possibly scotch, but at any rate parson and frog savant/ and to keep
ones wits and peker up in the presence of a tiger does NOT mean
        deliberation whatever the earlier mistraducers of ideogram may have
said.

In fact in recrd time I propsed a nedition on a Monday, and got it approved on
A Tuesday, and had the first chapter of chink in the zincographers on
Wednesday; and is now in print: though the accompanying traduction contains
one bad error/ mine/ one oversight also mine/ and one gawdawful emendation
of me colleague. me unbeknownst
and dont say I have no country. Wot about Malta?

At any rate I haven't set up a provisional government of the U.S.A. and am not
calling myself the American people. Not YET. Tho I wish I cd/ get some
definite replies to what I SAY.

if anyone ever listens to it.
My old line that civilization orter to be kep UP, even if only six people have
any. Most of 'em being here or in the far orient.
Ole E.P. meaning En= rico Pea   seems to have some/ and to be a addition.
An then we gotter li'l kulchural revival in this Vivaldi industry.

Wots ole Fox up to? compleatly burried in a dead museum instead of living among the aborigines/ or is he morphologizing the primitive strata of Manhattan?

No I don't hold with Mr Thoreau, and I think Max will have a bit of a plug to chaw if he wants to support all the mujiks.

Why dont he stake out a little farm in the Ukraine if he likes farmin?

I allus thunk he didn't like WORK/ whether with plow or on technik of writin/ in fact now you come to think of it, they tukk the 'ammer and sickle: not the plow/ not the productive end of the bizniz; but the rake it in and knock/

I admit I have neglected some opportunities/ Mediterranean mackerel, and a fish called volpino, of the seatrout to shad variety / that I might have been eatin fer years, if I hadn't been so lazy about eatin small bones/ and the cookin improvin.

Now I have started on a bilingual Dai Gaku ⟨alias Ta Hio⟩ I shall go on to do Mencius if so be gawd spares me, etc. that will take about three years unles I bust meself sprintin/   I wonder has Hollis or McN Wilson or any of the men who EVER thought about anything uttered a pipsqueak for the past 2 years/ Ole Puddin Wells is fairly loony/ as allus.

You can see by the printed date on this paper, that me stationary aint used as fast as it onct wuz.

                         EZ
                         Ezra Pound

Willyam: William Carlos Williams.

parson: James Legge (1815–92), was born in Scotland and prepared for his missionary work in China at Highbury Theological College. Between 1840 and 1873 he lived in China. Pound used his multivolume translation *The Chinese Classics* (1861–93).

savant/: Jean Pierre Guillaume Pauthier (1801–73), translator of Confucius: *Doctrine de Confucius; ou Les Quatre Livres de Philosophie Morale et Politique de la Chine* (Paris, Libraire Garnier Frères, [1852?]). Pound mentions him as a translator of Confucius in *Guide to Kulchur*. Pound also refers to him in the prefatory note to his translation, *The Confucian Analects* (1951).

deliberation: Legge's translation of section 2 of *The Great Learning* (which Pound calls *The Great Digest*): "The point where to rest being known, the object of pursuit is then determined; and that being determined, a calm unperturbedness may be attained to. To that calmness there will succeed a tranquil repose. In that repose there may be careful deliberation, and that deliberation will be followed by the attainment *of the desired end.*" *The Chinese Classics* (Hong Kong: University of Hong Kong, [1960]), 1:356–57. Pound's version of the same passage:

"Know the point of rest and then have an orderly mode of procedure; having this orderly procedure one can 'grasp the azure,' that is, take hold of a clear concept; holding a clear concept one can be at peace [internally], being thus calm one can keep one's head in moments of danger; he who can keep his head in the presence of a tiger is qualified to come to his deed in due hour." *Confucius: The Great Digest, The Unwobbling Pivot, The Analects* (New York: New Directions, 1969), 29. The character that Legge translates as "deliberation" could also be translated as "deep thinking" or "consideration." Pound added the comment about the tiger because this character is closely related to the character for tiger. The difference is that the radical meaning "heart" that is at the bottom of the "deliberation" character is not present in the "tiger" character; a different radical is present at the bottom of the tiger character. (The ancient Chinese considered the heart to be the location of mental operation, hence the presence of the "heart" radical in the character meaning "deliberation.")

Vivaldi industry: Antonio Vivaldi (born ca. 1675–78, died 1741). Besides arranging the performance of works by Vivaldi at the Rapallo musical concerts, Pound had encouraged Olga Rudge to research and write about the composer.

Fox: Douglas C. Fox.

bilingual: Pound's *Confucio: Ta S'eu, Dai Gaku, Studio Integrale* (Rapallo: Alberto Luchini, 1942) (Gallup B46).

Hollis: Chrisopher Hollis.

Wilson: McNair Wilson.

Wells: H. G. Wells. In a letter to Wells dated 31 January 1940, Pound had charged, "So far as I know you have lived in a sausage tower, oblivious of 20 years thought. AND stayed stuck with the ass Kiplings concept of world govt. I doubt if you can give, even now, a valid definition of money."

108. Cummings to Pound

SOURCE: Dupee and Stade, *Selected Letters of E. E. Cummings.*

March 21 [1942]   [4 Patchin Place]

Dear Ezra—

today is March 21,the First Day Of Spring;we honour you and it,as(of November 6)you honour it and us. Beauty also sends love

I have no and never had any and never shall have until having's obligatory(which God forbid!)radio. This is not out of disrepect for you;it's into respect for me. So happens the latter individual doesn't begin if abovementioned endlessness occurs. Maybe he's odd. Or maybe to corrupt—

i.e. spiritually betray—more people most quick equals the instrument of delusion beforementioned. As for de gustibus,all you young sprigs are plumb unlucky:I,per contra,had as a kid a real musicbox

oldage entails,of course,socalled disadvantages. E.g. have spent some months wrestling with(1)a game leg—"sciatica"(2)a bum back—"sacro-iliac";both were eventually diagnosed(via Xrays)as "arthritis". Am now up,& somewhat about,in a most imposing corset;which I hope to be rid of before the time when birds migrate. Maybe all said nonsense might be blamed on the war? Anyhow,something's taught me what I never suspected:that health is a thing of wonder;yes,all healthy people are per se and incontrovertibly miraculous

"health and a senseofhumor"—that's my 82year mother's favorite slogan. And speaking of humor,Fox wrote me a high letter;his first museum job's(guess)arranging a May Day ikon show;Litvinov will appear in person. Why not? According to "Time" mag,that very museum is very very advanced:every gallery being wired for sound,pictures are interpreted while you gaze at them;I gather nobody so much as drops a nickel in a slot,the wisdom just gushes . . . and harken—by way of hoisting the maninthestret out of lamentable ignorance & through Art's Portals, what do you suppose? Perfumes. Yes,the public's nostrils are approached:did I say approached?tittilated. Now match that,Mencius Praecox

shall presently hazard a prepliocene quatrain;mightily begging you to vastly believe(a)that all characters and incidents thereof,being purely fictitious,are not intended to refer to,and do not refer to,any existing or extant person or persons(b)for the simple reason or effective cause that—as thou likely wottest not—such unfolks never were ever alive at all at all. I've translated out of the original pakrit,running asterisks wherever plausible

> life might be worse
> no mouth can cr*p
> but somebody's ears
> are licking it up

which happily is seldom

Litvinov: Maksim Litvinov (1876–1951), Russian revolutionary and Soviet diplomat. Soviet ambassador to the United States, 1941–43.
pakrit: See the note to letter 53.

109. Cummings to Pound

TLS-1.

September 10 1945   Silver Lake,New Hampshire

Dear Ezra—

wal(as you would say)having sought with signal nonsuccess the slightest clue to your now both distinguished and notorious whereabouts,have wrongly or rightly decided to address the maestro in his unnative Rapallo:hoping that,if you've moved,the censor will humanly forward this my innocent greeting;while rather more than suspecting that a lot of people who aren't you have done considerable moving. Anyhow:hearty salutations from Marion and me,& here's hoping you've enjoyed your Enormous Room as much as the undersigned did his

during our second late unpleasantness,it has been my inestimable priviledge to occasionally go on record as maintaining that friendship is thicker than blood,creed,or color;& please believe that I say this less proudly than humbly. For the rest,lays intellectualissimi(& -mae)have been keeping the yammer&trickle awaving(& hewing to the chips let the line fall where it may)with a by naif myself quite unimagined fidelity. Of course not everyone is born a contortionist,so here & there you meet some dazed bloke who harbors something remotely ressembling a demidoubt as to whether Kumrad Stalin is really & truly "just a sweet old gentleman". But why worry? As Kenneth Patchen observes "every doggerel will have its day"

I profoundly hope that when we meet again(which I hope profoundly will be my unnative Paris)you'll appear not quite as conscientiously as possible concerned with the shallwesay wellfare of quote mankind unquote. The younger our nonhero grows,the duller all sciences,including atomic sociology & economic bombery,become. At ye present instant wouldn't give you a ton of Chinese paperdollars for government of by & for the feeble. Your good friend Kung(by the Tao)has on the other hand cheered me mightily during my quite unpremeditated isolation;to Lao & to him,deep bows

                    —vive l'âme
                         Estlin

Kung: Confucius, Chinese philosopher of the sixth century B.C.
Lao: Lao-Tzu, Chinese philosopher, a contemporary of Confucius and founder of
    Taoism.

110. Cummings to Pound

TLS-1.

December 6 1945   4 Patchin Place
                                         New York City

Dear Ezra—

welcome home!

I wrote you at the old Rapallo address last August or September;my letter was
not returned:probably,however,you didn't receive it. The book which Mr
Cornell is kindly bringing you comes from Charles Norman,the man who did
you proud in "PM". Why not drop him* a line?

Marion's been in the hospital a year with one kind of arthritis;I;ve
entertained(off & on)another kind,chez moi,for 4 years. Now we're both of us
much better,and shall leave for Arizona—c/o Mrs Hubert D'Autremont,South
Arizona Bank,Tucson—whenever a train will take us. If,in the meantime,our
mutual state of health permits,we'll naturally stagger down to Washington &
say hello to you & stagger back again. But if not,here's our love

vive la vie!
                        —Estlin

*66 Bedford Street
NYCity

Cornell: Julien Cornell (1910–95), a New York lawyer who was representing
    Pound. See his *The Trial of Ezra Pound* (New York: John Day, 1966; Faber,
    1967).
Norman: Charles Norman (b. 1904), American poet, literary critic, biographer
    and journalist. His article, "The Case for and against Ezra Pound," in *PM*
    appeared on 25 November 1945. It is reprinted in *EPPP*, 8:255–65. See the
    Biographical Notes.
D'Autremont: Hubert and Helen d'Autremont were the parents of James An-
    gleton's wife. Estlin and Marion's winter stay at their home is covered in Ken-
    nedy, 396–98.

111. Pound to Cummings

ALS-1.

17 Dec. [1945]   gallinger Hospital, Wash. D.C.

Dear E & M
        Thanks for flowers & all - no substitute for Marion's presence. =
Got your other letter in D.T.C. = near Pisa I most certainly never "adhered to
the Kingdom of Italy against the U.S." - but how the hell to make anyone
understand ANYthing - without educating 'em from age of 6 to 60 - beats me.
20 years work to prevent the damn war starting - etc. god bless the survivors.
                Yours
                  E

Ezra Pound.

to Mr & Mrs E.E. Cummings
        co. Mrs N. D'Autremont
        S. Ariz. Bank
            Tucson.

"**adhered to . . . the U.S.:** Pound paraphrases the District of Columbia Grand
Jury's indictment, which says in part that he, "a person owing allegiance to the
United States, in violation of said duty of allegiance, knowingly, intentionally,
wilfully, unlawfully, feloniously, traitorously and treasonably did adhere to the
enemies of the United States, to-wit; the Kingdom of Italy and the military allies
of the said Kingdom of Italy."

112. Pound to Cummings

ACS.

[Postmarked 25 January 1946]   [Saint Elizabeths]

I like getting
        letters

                E.P.

S. Liz

113. Pound to Cummings

AL-2.

[18 February 1946]   St Elizabeths Hosp. D.C.

Dear Estlin

I cdnt write to Norman (or rather started & got muddled.) & now have no
addresses or any letters antedating this abode =
                    was he Engl or Am.—

re the Cerf. Cerval or wood-puisie -
after 1918 Three Mts. & other presses broke the monopoly & suppression
printing <u>luxe</u> what the Shit & usury poopers wd/ not print

Then the Shit the blonde fahrt made a de luxe Trust & stopped ⟨the⟩ print of
real stuff in the U.S. - in de luxe
= Hence his present <u>fahrts</u>.

<u>p. 2</u>

venom & general <u>pustulence</u>
but it aint fer me to <u>say</u> so.
non dimeno. it cd. <u>be known</u>
                    <u>quietly</u>

of course NO one ever NOTICES anything -
life in trailors -
            rootless -   18 <u>Feb</u>
or burocrag. piznfish
            Love to M.

Cerf: Bennett Cerf (1898–1971), American publisher. Shortly after becoming an
  independent publisher, Cerf went to England in 1926 and arranged with Francis
  Meynell to become the American distributor of Meynell's Nonesuch Press. Over
  the next few years, Random House "became the leading distributor of press
  books in the United States. We had the Golden Cockerel Press, the Spiral Press,
  the Fountain Press, the Shakespeare Head Press and many others. All of these
  private presses came begging us to take them on, since they would then be
  basking in the reflected glory of the Nonesuch Press, which was the established
  name in limited editions. By 1929 we had a catalogue of about thirty limited-
  edition books each season." Bennett Cerf, *At Random: The Reminiscences of
  Bennett Cerf* (New York: Random House, 1977), 77.
Three Mts.: The Three Mountains Press (1923–26), owned and operated by
  William Bird. Its first publication was Pound's *Indiscretions or Une revue de deux*

mondes. Subsequent Pound titles Bird published were *Antheil and the Treatise on Harmony* and *A Draft of XVI Cantos*. Bird also published works by Ford Madox Ford, William Carlos Williams, and Ernest Hemingway. See Hugh Ford, *Published in Paris: American and British Writers, Printers, and Publishers in Paris, 1920–1939* (Yonkers, N.Y.: Pushcart Press, 1980), 95–116.

114. Pound to Cummings

AL-1.

4 March [1946]   St Elizabeths Hosp.
                                                             Wash DC

Dear EEC

Who the hell lives in this hemisphere? Joe Gould. Sadakichi Hartman (? alive or defunct)
people give me high brow toil by ~~whom dont know~~ who try tell what they dont know. & crit what they have not read/ -
old Fordie saw more than we gave him credit for. also must have
inseminated—& so on
forget what else, but do write.
Also certn program vs Time bloody
                              LAG
love to Marion

Hartman: [Carl] Sadakichi Hartmann (1869?–1944), poet and critic. Born in Japan of a German father and Japanese mother, who sent him to the United States in 1882, where he became a naturalized citizen (1894). He became acquainted with Whitman and published a book about him, *Conversations with Walt Whitman* (1895). Pound and Hartmann corresponded during the 1930s. In one of Pound's last letters to Hartmann, he urged him to apply for funds from the American Institute of Arts and Letters (Paige, 341).

115. Pound to Cummings

ALS-1.

6 March [1946]   St. Elizabeths

eec. HELL. There is or was civilization or @ least coordination - and 25 to 150 years Time lag. as per all U.S. highbrow pubctns. save a few lines by e.e.c. (& ? x - y - (improbably Z). dont Fox or anyone ever do anything.

& in any case why not

yrs
EP

4 or 5 definite jobs
Frobenius.
Gesell. B.Adms.
V Buren

Frobenius: Leo Frobenius.

Gesell: Silvio Gesell.

B.Adms: Brooks Adams (1848–1927), American historian and younger brother of Henry Adams. Pound thought Brooks's contributions to civilization exceeded those of his more famous brother. "Henry Adams warned his brother Brooks Adams that he might be martyred. Brooks didn't much care, and he died at a ripe old age, but the public is still nearly unaware of his books, in especial of 'The Law of Civilization and Decay,' and 'The New Empire.'" "Letter from Rapallo," *Japan Times and Mail* (Tokyo), 12 August 1940, 8 (Gallup C1568a). Reprinted in *EPPP.*

V Buren: Martin Van Buren (1782–1862), eighth president of the United States. Pound considered him to be one of the key defenders of economic liberty in America during the first half of the nineteenth century. "Van Buren had the transitory honour of being called THE LIBERATOR OF THE TREASURY. But his decade has disappeared from American history." "An Introduction to the Economic Nature of the United States," *Selected Prose,* 179.

116. Cummings to Pound

TLS-1.

March 10 1946

4 Patchin Place
New York City

Dear Ezra—

thanks for the blast. "It" must be lousy. But even the undersigned can imagine far worse;farfar en effect

Charles Norman(about whom you inquire)was the fellow who staged a "symposium" re yourself in a(usually kumrady)NY paper called P.M.. His address is 66 Bedford Street,New York City

I now suggest that you send Ted(Professor Theodore)Spencer—3 Warren House,Harvard University,Cambridge,Massachusetts—a word;some,any:or even

a groan or three. He recently wrote me that he'd erstwhile dropped you a line
sans result. Ted's a pal-&-admirer of Tears Eliot,from whom I got(while at
Arizona)a much-concerned-concerning you epistle;which was duly answered to
the shall we say best of my unability times Marion's skill

M & I still find "arthritis" an fing nuisance. But NY's variegated violence seems
mighty sweet after Tucson's monotonous mediocrity! The lady sends you her
best

—sois sain

eec

"symposium": See the note to letter 110.

Eliot: Eliot's letter (10 December 1945) is the only letter from Eliot to Cummings
in the Cummings papers at the Houghton Library. Eliot asked two favors of
Cummings: first, that he go to St. Elizabeths and report on Pound's mental
state; second, that Cummings immediately notify Eliot if and when Pound was
sentenced (so that Eliot could coordinate support by certain eminent English
writers for an appeal for clemency).

117. Pound to Cummings

ALS-1.

[March? 1946]   St Elizabeth Hospital
                                       Wash DC
                                       M

Then there is the case of Eastman Mx Digested by Literary's Bainbridg'd
Wallace.
also old song Dye Ken J. Peel.
answer in affirmative. & love to the lady if still the same. wd. he appreciate
answer?

=

Then of course
o hell!! but dont anyone ever mention a BOOK in these FKn. weaklies &
literaries??
if the buggars wd once read a Book instead of advertised sawdust
etc.
love to Marion
& to
E.P.

Eastman: Max Eastman.

Wallace: The *Reader's Digest* had been founded in 1922 by DeWitt Wallace (1889–
1981). He hired Max Eastman as one of the magazine's "roving editors" in 1941.
J. Peel: Pound refers to the song "John Peel," by John W. Graves (1795–1886). Its
first line: "D'ye ken John Peel with his coat so gay."

118. Pound to Cummings

ALS-1.

12 M[arch 1946]   S. Liz.

Told ⟨wrote⟩ Ted S hadn't recd. but mebbe he meant LONG AGO.
                         C A T
"a domestic animal" sez
                    S Johnson -
definition inadequate.
& thats what YOO do.
          =
I dont need cameos. but want to know who has survived.
wot 'bout the Wyndham fer zample
& Marianne & other inhabitants
no one ever meets Anyone else   yrs
                                                 EP

Ted S: Theodore Spencer.

119. Pound to Cummings

ALS-1.

15 M[arch 1946]   St Elizabeths

Dear estlin
                    Thanks for 'Wake'. So hard to people a world after diluvium.
Wot fer zmpl become of the bozo who painted the bog-seat red?
       -
& an IDIOM whence? in an Archikulchur based so Xclusivly on Ecuador &
Croatia.
                         -
Do you know a bloke named Ch. Olson who is or wuz? @ <u>Commodore?</u> Hotel.
if not why not ⟨phone⟩ & invite him to tea?
          love to Marion
                    EZ

'Wake': The *Harvard Wake*, no. 5 (spring 1946), was devoted to work by and about Cummings.

bozo: See the note to letter 98.

Olson: Charles Olson (1910–70), American poet. He first visited Pound at Saint Elizabeths on 5 January 1946. The relationship between Pound and Olson is covered in *Charles Olson and Ezra Pound: An Encounter at St. Elizabeths*, ed. Catherine Seelye (New York: Grossman, 1975).

120. Pound to Cummings

ALS-2.

18 M[arch 1946]   S. Elizabeths

Dear e:

        There are several persons whom I cd hear OF.

H. Gregory. whom I hadn't time or nrg to see in '39

& H. Loeb, who did the <u>chart of plenty</u>

The original trouble with that pile of cow shit Cerf can not be set down to anti- sem. as there were three jews on my side of the fight from 1924-'27 & since

        Of course none of 'em large advertisers @ present moment in current magazines

Sorry you're arthritic - if it paralyzes the hand get M. Barnard ⟨or some manuens.⟩ to send on information re/ monde (or im—) licheraire.

& remember I have NO address book. & no addresses of anyone—save on letters recd since I came to present moated grange.

        =

        Forget whoever else ever wrote (as distinct from canning) save names already sent you.

believe I asked after the unique & only Marianne?

                  yrs

                  E. P.

Hem's superior beaver seems to be the only lit. item tolerated in the canned weaklies.

making penitence to the novelists d'antan -

by way. know anything current

Ayn Rand "Fountain something" = re/ press

        &

I.M. Morris "Liberty St."

      ?

he has heard of passports not 25 year time lag

And they took Freud instead of Frobenius#
  #now being Amy Low'd in Sunday Splmts

Gregory: Horace Gregory (1898–1982), American poet.

Loeb: Harold Loeb (1891–1974), American author and editor. Founder and editor of *Broom*. Pound refers to Loeb's *The Chart of Plenty: A Study of America's Productive Capacity Based on the Findings of the National Survey of Potential Product Capacity* (New York: Viking, 1935). In "Loeb Report (A Refresher)," *New English Weekly*, vol. 8, no. 17 (6 February 1936), 326–27 (Gallup C1295), Pound asserted that "No one of enough intelligence to keep out of a straight jacket can read this report and still believe in MATERIAL SCARCITY." Pound also recalled that "He [Loeb] asked me to baptize him with fire, and with fire I baptized him in the Cafe Voltaire, with the fire (liquid) off an *omelette au rhum* [in 1923]." Nevertheless, Loeb's report "is a masterpiece. It condemns the present system as an outrage, and any man who supports the system, the Bank of England, the Bank of France, Wall Street, or any aider and abetter of their infamies, as something duller than an ox has ever yet been considered."

three jews: There are a number of individuals Pound might have had in mind: Harold Loeb (see the previous note); Guido Jung, minister of finance in Italy 1932–35; Mordecai Ezekiel, whom Pound refers to as "the Jew . . . who has toddled first toward the economy of ABUNDANCE in his *2,500 Dollars a Year*," (in "The Revolution Betrayed," *British Union Quarterly*, vol. 2, no. 1 [January–March 1938], 36-48, reprinted in *EPPP*). Also, on 2 December 1938, Pound wrote to Louis Zukofsky, "so far as known, only ONE jew, Ernst Loeb is working for monetary decency. He is in Holland and I suppose will get about as much 'hand' from the local sanhedrin as Spinoza had./ E.L. is suggesting to his fellow Hollander jews and jew dutch that they stop diggin their own graves." I have been unable, however, to locate publications by Ernst Loeb.

Barnard: Mary Barnard (b. 1909), American poet. Her career and her meetings with Pound and Cummings are recorded in her book, *Assault on Mount Helicon: A Literary Memoir* (Berkeley and Los Angeles: University of California Press, 1984). See also the Barnard issue of *Paideuma*, vol. 23, no 1 (spring 1994).

Rand: Ayn Rand (1905–82), Russian-born American philosopher and novelist. Pound refers to her novel *The Fountainhead* (New York: Bobbs-Merrill, 1943).

Morris: Ira Victor Morris, author of *Liberty Street* (New York: Harper and Brothers, 1944). His novel, set in an unnamed Central American country in 1943, sympathetically portrays the plight of European refugees waiting for visas to enter the United States. The villain of the piece is a U.S. government bureaucrat.

Freud . . . Frobenius: Charles Olson reported that Pound remarked on 19 March 1946, "I just thought of a phrase: America, where people listen to Freud and not to Frobenius." See *Charles Olson and Ezra Pound: An Encounter at St. Elizabeths*, 82.

121. Pound to Cummings

AL-2.

29 March [1946]   St. Elizabeths

Dear Estlin
            Very encouragin that exists a Wake to print a serious ~~essay~~
piece of work like Rosenfeld's
            give him my congs.

Vague memory mix'd with B. Hecht but think R. was in Paris absorbin &
advertisin the almost as soft S Anderson in 192X?
say '22

Whom is he quotin on p. 34 bottom ??

---

incidentally I think Possum ⟨T.S.E.⟩ is ⟨elsewhere⟩ in error when he nearly
states all my ideas are cliches -- but - - - -
==   thazzanaside
as to Eimi - I think I sd/ so 20 or 19 years ago. i.e.
- what the laudatory are @ in Wake.
but NO perception of need of more than a 1 man job—
Vast prejudice in minor contributors == sorry if egregious Edmondo
Dodsworth's study not there - he bein wop of course it wd/ have been regarded
as damnd by most of the Those present -
      I must also have sd/ somewhat in 'Carta da Visita" ==
      I spose the 3rd of the 3 large vols - Ulysses; Eimi; & whats its name by
W.L. will be cited in another 15 or 20 years. ----
      & so on -
                  one dollar

Love to M.
            the initial matador a bit severe on W.C.W. but the deceased by
from bike or kike fallen Dodsworth gd/son of returning from India Briton
⟨with sense enough to not completely to Eng. return⟩ sd/ about the same.

piece of work: Paul Rosenfeld (1890–1946), American musical and literary critic.
    His "The Voyages," *Harvard Wake*, no. 5, pp. 31–44, is an essay on *Eimi*.
B. Hecht: Ben Hecht (1893–1964), American playwright and screenwriter.
S Anderson: Sherwood Anderson (1876–1941), American novelist and short-
    story writer. He and Paul Rosenfeld (a friend for twenty-five years) were to-
    gether in Paris in 1921.
p. 34: Pound refers to the quotation in this passage from Rosenfeld's essay: "For
    the idealist, the Divinity made the world to be outside Divinity; and the activity

in it is not completely God's. Complete determinism, predestination are absent from the world; Law by no means thoroughly rules it. It is impelled from within by the Ideas, its spiritual content, the provisions of this benevolent God; floats of its own force almost like an architecture in space; and Man is able to interfere with its energies. Curiously enough, this ability of his flows from the very fact that to a pronounced degree Man shares in the nature of God. Man's life extends to the beginning of creation; and 'within him is the soul of the whole, the wise silence, the universal beauty, to which every part and particle is equally related, the eternal One'; and the individual soul mingles with the universal soul, whose beatitude is accessible to us."

⟨elsewhere⟩: Pound probably refers to Eliot's essay on *Personae: The Collected Poems of Ezra Pound* (1926), "Isolated Superiority," *Dial*, vol. 84, no. 1 (January 1928), 4–7. Eliot praises Pound's formal mastery, but questions the content of the poems. "But of Pound I believe that in form he foreran, excelled, and is still in advance of our own generation and even the literary generation after us; whereas his ideas are often those of the generation which preceded him." Eliot adds, "But Pound's philosophy, I suspect, is just a little antiquated."

Eimi: Pound probably refers to his comments on *Eimi* in "E. E. Cummings Alive," *New English Weekly*, vol. 6, no. 10 (20 December 1934), 210–11 (Gallup C1128). Reprinted in *EPPP*.

Dodsworth's study: Edmondo Dodsworth's "E. E. Cummings," *Broletto*, vol. 3 (November 1938), 19–21. See appendix.

'Carta da Visita': *Carta da visita* (Rome: Edizioni di Lettere d'Oggi, 1942) (Gallup A50). Pound reprints Cummings's poem "Dirge" ("flotsam and jetsam") in *Carta da visita*.

whats its name: *The Apes of God* (1930) by Wyndham Lewis.

matador: None of the contributors to the *Harvard Wake* issue devoted to Cummings denigrated Williams. Perhaps Pound meant to write "E. E. C."

122. Cummings to Pound

TCS.

[Postmarked 4 April 1946]   4 Patchin Place
                                             NYCity

glad you enjoyed "Wake"—for which a Philippine-American poet named José Garcia Villa was entirely responsible:he announced(one afternoon)that I should & would be "honoured";& all protests proved unavailing. Am myself still dazed by the generosity of nearly everyone concerned—should hate to be called on for an equivalent job

Marion sent you a copy of "The Sewanee Review"—hope you received it. That number's the last edited by Allen Tate,who's now in NY acting as poetry-editor

for Henry Holt. Quel metier! But I understand the "SR" backers were mighty
pernickety . . . & de gustibus non

eec

Villa: José Garcia Villa (b. 1914), born in Manila, has spent most of his adult life in
New York City.
"The Sewanee Review": The *Sewanee Review,* vol. 54, no. 2 (April–June 1946),
216–21, contained Cummings's essay, "A Foreword to Krazy." Tate edited the
Review from the summer of 1944 to the fall of 1945.
Holt: The New York publishing house.

123. Pound to Cummings

ALS-1. Enclosure.

4 Ap[ril 1946]   S. Eliz

Dear Estlin

ever since you sent me the "Church Seat" & other expressions of the "spirit" I
have wanted to do something in return -
    Perhaps the "enc" is the long hoped opportunity

yrs Ez

& lov to Marion

"Church Seat": Unidentified.
"enc": A clipping headed "Clarence Day 1874–1935." "The death of Clarence Day
on December 28, 1935, was not only a loss to American literature; he was an
example of courage and integrity such as we can ill afford to spare. For more
than thirty-five years Mr. Day was an invalid suffering from arthritis. Yet during
all those years he not only enjoyed a rich creative life, but maintained a wide
circle of distinguished friends with whom he carried on lengthy conversations
and correspondence, with never a hint of his suffering. He did, in a sense,
conquer his disabilities, for he made them a minor aspect of his life, and he
made his humor, his grace, his charm and his wisdom manifest in the writing
that was the major aspect of life to him.
    Born on November 18, 1874, the son of Clarence S. Day, of the New York
Stock Exchange, and grandson of Benjamin Henry Day, founder of the New
York Sun, he grew up in the city of his birth, was educated at St. Paul's School
and Yale. He entered the brokerage business, disliked it, resigned and enlisted in

the United States Navy. It was there that he became ill and was forced to retire to a physically inactive but intellectually energetic existence. When he died he was at the very height of his power and his success."

124. Pound to Cummings

ALS-1.

27 June [1946]   St Elizabeths

Dear eec

Wd like <u>yr. version of pow-wow</u> -
Lost @ least 8 years—(or 40.)
damn fools (re Frobenius, & insu-bloody-larity) don't realize that man who translated 'Lute of Gassir" was, among other things, a gt. poet.
                    Where the fahrt'nhell is Fox.

                              Ez

love to Marion

pow-wow: James Laughlin wrote to Cummings on 7 June 1946, "TS Eliot is here and he is very anxious to hold a council of strategy of those who are wanting to help Ez. P. He asked especially about you. Could you and Mrs Cummings join us for dinner the night of June 20th - Thursday? I'll let you know later where it will be. Does the Lafayette have any small private dining rooms? There will be just six or seven people." Cummings and his wife were at Joy Farm in June and so could not attend the meeting. Laughlin wrote later, in an undated letter, "What we concluded at the council—where you were greatly missed and highly spoken of—was that things must be done quietly. An attempt first to get him moved to better quarters in the hospital, then later his release, since he is incurable but harmless." Although Laughlin does not recall precisely who attended the meeting, he thinks it probably included Marianne Moore and Julien Cornell (in addition to Eliot).
'Lute of Gassir": See Leo Frobenius and Douglas C. Fox, *African Genesis* (New York: Stackpole Sons, 1937). This selection of African folktales includes "Gassire's Lute." According to Fox, it is the "best part" of an ancient North African epic of which only fragments remain. The most recent edition of *African Genesis* was published by the Turtle Island Foundation (Berkeley, California) in 1983.

125. Cummings to Pound

ACS.

[8 July 1946]   Silver Lake, New Hampshire

I like your motto!
we couldn't attend the conference, being elsewhere (here). But I gather that
'twas a success

according to my friend Allen Tate, your friend "Possum"'s around. Hast seen
such an animal?
                                Sois Sage
                                Estlin

motto: Pound's letter of 27 July 1946 was written on new stationery headed with
    Pound's name and the motto, "J'ayme Donc Je Suis."
conference: See the note to the previous letter.

126. Pound to Cummings

ALS-2.

10 July [1946]   St. Elizabeths
                                                  10 or what
                                                  Juglio
                                                  S. Liz.

Yaaas
        Possum seen on these premises. much more alive than in sad comic strip,
in the weaklies photod
_____

Sez wants meet You - incredible, but apparently had never - unless very
incomprendin - but am incredulo
_____

Of course the things others don't think of DOING beats me. & tend to drag
me into agreement with them wot 'as bugd me.
        I dont onnerstan. ⟨yrs is⟩ second note today tellin me to "sois sage" =
like they sez to the turkey stuffin

Can Allen sufficiently Dic- To git the possum to mobilize les douze = whoever
gets TO N.Y. & conjunk. please keep the Possum from eatin his Tail &
sleepin =

Poisonly think you cd/ custodiate me as well as the locale = any godddam coral stockaid with porus circumallation wd/ relieve --
      also any means yr. staff can take to git my MIND out of here, even if carcass remains vinculated.
                    Love to Marion

                    EZ

Is Lorca any good? I mean have you any of him. prefb. in orig?

Possum: T. S. Eliot.
Allen: Allen Tate.
les douze: Before his voyage to New York, Eliot had written to "twelve or fifteen poets, requesting their public support for Pound and asking them to provide private testimonials in the event that he should be tried and sentenced for his crime" (Peter Ackroyd, *T. S. Eliot: A Life* [New York, Simon and Schuster, 1984], 281). Pound may be referring to this group of poets.
Lorca: Federico Garcia Lorca (1898–1936), Spanish poet and playwright.

127. Cummings to Pound

TLS-1.

July 23 1946   Silver Lake
                                     New Hampshire

Dear Ezra—

thou little knowest our unhero's taste in wine("which never" as Ralph Waldo naughtily observes "grew In the belly of the grape,")if you think I'd waste God's time(or even A.Stone's timespace)treading a tome by Bull Billit. Not that Bull isn't a charming chap:I remember meeting this Mycenas at 4 Patchin(on whose rez-de-chaussée he'd personally erected a WC;still functioning,for which am grateful during the winter months)& him offering to receive all pictures painted by my,in exchange for a yearly payment to self—all this il-y a une fois("And besides" as Kit Possom wisecracked "the wench is dead").
However,'tis one grimly perhaps droll subject for meditation—the fact that "The Reader's Digest"(a title more than suggesting O.Spengler's natty notion that as a culture ends,i.e. a civilization begins,the unfortunate polloi become omnivorously overconscious of their nether organs)hath "condensed"(sic)Bull's latest lapsang in current "issue";meaning that 12(?have no head,as we say,for figures)million SuperMorons will learn to their horror that . . . my 4th in this

sentence . . . kumrad Steel 's no "nice old gentleman";or do we go too far? But guardez la chemise:doubtless the pronto following numéro will cancel all That by some seersucking sobbery conclusively proving The Great Man's invincible universality. And why is "America" sold on "Russia"? Well,if thous askest me:R represents everything A really is-without-daring-to-be. Such as? "Fascist"

now regarding TSMarlowe—we've(in thine ear;subsub rosa)met. But I never knew it until,one day,Marion discovered a "Cambridge Dramatic Club" playbill headed "Fanny,or The Servant Problem". "Do you remember" she asked me carelessly "playing the part of 'Ernest,the Second Footman' in 1913 before an audience of your peers?" "O yes!" I immediately cried "and Amy de Gozzaldi kissed me;and her mouth came off on my mouth,and billions cheered:I shall never forget." "What about 'Lord Bantock'?" suggested Marion. "never heard of him". "The hero." "O—hero;yes . . . why,let's see:a snob,cold,older than me,aloof,never sat with the rest of the cast at rehearsals,immaculately dressed;you know,a type"the frozen jeunesse dorée". "Then you Have met TSEliot" she remarked mildly "and you said you Never had"

finally,re Lorca:not having ever more than glimpsed him,in "translation"(sans effect)inquired of M "is Lorca good?" and she answered "good kumrad" & there the matter ends,for me who am(I trust)taking no plugged nickel with heads-snob slob-tails

all right;if you can't be sage,be careful(proverb)

                                                                —salut!

                                                                eec

Waldo: Cummings recalls the first lines of Ralph Waldo Emerson's poem "Bacchus": "Bring me wine, but wine which never grew / In the belly of the grape."

a tome: Here and below (in the reference to "Bull's latest"), Cummings means William C. Bullitt's *The Great Globe Itself: A Preface to World Affairs* (New York: Charles Scribner's Sons, 1946). Chapter 2 was condensed in *Reader's Digest* (July 1946), 145–76. See the note to letter 134.

Possom wisecracked: Cummings refers to the epigraph to Eliot's poem, "Portrait of a Lady." The epigraph is from Christopher Marlowe's play, *The Jew of Malta*.

natty notion: Oswald Spengler (1880–1936), German philosopher. In *Der Untergang des Abendlandes* (1918) Spengler discusses the inevitable change from a culture to a civilization. The "notion" to which Cummings refers seems to be Cummings's inference based on several comments by Spengler. "Culture and civilization—the living body of a soul and the mummy of it. For Western experience the distinction lies at about the year 1800—on the one side of that frontier life in fullness and sureness of itself, formed by growth from within, in one great uninterrupted evolution from Gothic childhood to Goethe and Napoleon, and on the other the autumnal, artificial, rootless life of our great cities, under forms fashioned by the intellect. Culture and Civilization—the organism born of Mother Earth and the mechanism proceeding from hardened fabric. Culture-man lives inwards, Civilization-man lives outwards in space and amongst bodies and 'facts'" (*The Decline of the West: Form and Actuality* [New York: Alfred A. Knopf, 1926], 353. "Hunger and Love thus become mechanical causes of mechanical processes in the 'life of peoples.' Social problems and sexual problems (both belonging to a 'physics' or 'chemistry' of public—all-too-public existence) become the obvious themes of utilitarian history and therefore of *the corresponding tragedy.* For the social drama necessarily accompanies the materialist treatment of history, and that which in Goethe's 'Wahlverwandtschaften' was destiny in the highest sense has become in Ibsen's 'Lady of the Sea' nothing but a sexual problem" (155–56).

TSMarlowe: T. S. Eliot. In the 1912–13 season, the Cambridge Social Dramatic Club produced Jerome K. Jerome's 1908 play, *Fanny and the Servant Problem* (the play was titled *Lady Bantock* in its American productions). Eliot played the role of Lord Bantock; Amy de Gozzaldi (1892–1981) played his wife, Fanny. "One of Estlin's first loves was Amy de Gozzaldi . . . . Cummings met her in . . . May 1910, and came to know her better when he played Ernest Bennet (the second footman) in Jerome K. Jerome's *The New Lady Bantock* in May 1913. One part of the action called for Cummings to kiss Amy . . . but she intimidated him by her sophistication. At rehearsals the director continually encouraged him to be more bold. At length, on the night of the performance he outdid himself in a kiss that he remembered for months. Cummings felt somewhat outpaced for Amy's regard by the elegant young man who played Lord Bantock, T. S. Eliot" (Kennedy, 86).

128. Pound to Cummings

AL-1.

25 Lug [July 1946]   S. Liz

Kontinuin
    BEEsides
think of the advantages he (Possum) has hed since (1915-20 in the gt city of
L-n-n
& heterodite.
                  I admit there wuz time when anyfink connected with T.T. &
Dial got under his skin - wot wiff you bein the whiteheaded & a Haaaavud
man n a umourist—buttttt he has got over that =

as to yr A. 'n' R. A haz got wot Johnnie Admz writ into Mass. const. namely
videlicet that tendenz to turn everything into a strawberry festival. wich the
Balkans cum messopotamia aint #

(incidentally Nancy thinks I ought to be short for not liberatin Spain &
hangin' priests in their own budelle.)
if you say look at ole Hi Rronk Wms of Rutherford ⟨he aint got this. the
answer iz vide verso⟩ OV[er]

[On verso]
He izza damn dago born on Ellis Island & costiv since wuz a cheeild.

T.T.: Pound probably meant to write "S.T." (Scofield Thayer).
Dial: The *Dial* (New York).
A. 'n' R.: America and Russia.
Mass. const.: John Adams's draft version of a new constitution for the common-
    wealth of Massachusetts was adopted, in large part, as the Massachusetts Con-
    stitution of 1780. Adams's draft called for a governor, a lieutenant-governor, a
    senate, a house of representatives and a governor's council. The draft also
    contains detailed instructions regarding election procedures, but it says little
    about the framing or execution of laws. Adams's draft can be found in volume 4
    of *The Works of John Adams,* ed. Charles Francis Adams (Boston: Little and
    Brown: 1850–56), 219–67.
Nancy: Nancy Cunard (1896–1965), British poet and publisher. Cunard had
    written to Pound, remarking that "Williams has called you misguided. I do not
    agree. The correct word for a Fascist is 'scoundrel.'" Anne Chisholm, *Nancy
    Cunard* (New York: Penguin, 1981), 366.
budelle: Italian for "guts, intestines."
Hi Rronk Wms: William Carlos Williams.

129. Pound to Cummings

ALS-1.

27 Lug [July 1946]   S. Eliz.

HELL
        I didn't expect you TO READ the Bastid ⟨even digested or excreted in the
Bitcherary BOWEL⟩
but as he is still fkn XT almighty IF you still speak to the super (sez you
charmin') plumber of blood red bog.
        Tell him to get me fkn out of here. I mean B.B.
                                        yrs
                                        EZ

                i.e.
before he makes

newer
morer
    maurer
error

Bastid: William Bullitt.
Bitcherary: *Reader's Digest.*
plumber: Max Eastman?
red bog: The Soviet Union? See the note to letter 98.
B.B.: Bill Bullitt.

130. Cummings to Pound

TCS.

[Postmarked 12 August 1946]   Silver Lake
                                               New Hampshire

"strawberry festival" is right! And the oddest
part of a sf(or so it seems to me)is,that each
participant KNOWS himheritself to be performing
(singleminded)a drama of such hyperultimate
superimport as makes Antony & Cleopatra(by one
William Shakespeare)seem pathetically not to say
innocuously <u>dull</u>

                              C'gs

131. Pound to Cummings

ALS-1.

[1946?]   S. Eliz

Dear e e c.
    Waal I never heard Chandler do anything except "Revere P." Whoopin it
up fer the consterooshun. a doggymint no one else appears to have heard of
except Charlie Giliberti the shover
                        to Mr Davies

                    Ez P

Chandler: Douglas Chandler (b. 1889), American journalist who broadcast prop-
    aganda from Germany during World War II. His programs began with

Chandler saying, "Hello, from the heart of Hitler Germany. Your messenger Paul Revere calls to you, my fellow countrymen and foes." After the war he was convicted of treason.

Giliberti: Pound read this passage in Joseph E. Davies's *Mission to Moscow* (New York: Simon and Schuster, 1941): "There is scarcely a day but what our American chauffeur 'Charlie' Giliberti is approached on the streets by some American who has taken out Soviet citizenship and who pleads that he intercede with the American authorities to help him to get back home" (111). *Mission to Moscow* was one of the books available to Pound at the Disciplinary Training Center in Pisa.

Davies: Joseph Edward Davies (1876–1958), American diplomat. U.S. ambassador to the Soviet Union from 1936 to 1938. Charles E. Bohlen, in his *Witness to History: 1929–1969* (New York: W. W. Norton, 1973), remarks that Davies "took the Soviet line on everything except issues between the two governments. He never even faintly understood the purges, going far toward accepting the official Soviet version of the existence of a conspiracy against the state" (44–45).

132. Cummings to Pound

TLS-1.

September 30 1946   4 Patchin Place
                                                        New York City

Dear Ezra—

only daybeforeyesterday we were honoured by the visitation of a brave & gay & loyal ἄγγελος [messenger];to wit,your charming son:congratulations!

& how dost thou like the possum's tribute via current issue of "Poetry"? Must confess I was amazed to find me in a canto

Marion sends her best!

—salut

Estlin

son: Omar Shakespear Pound (b. 1926).
tribute: T. S. Eliot, "Ezra Pound," *Poetry,* vol. 68, no. 6 (September 1946), 326–38. Reprinted in *Ezra Pound,* ed. Peter Russell (London: Peter Nevill, 1950).
a canto: Canto 80. A selection from Canto 80 was published in the September 1946 issue of *Poetry* (Gallup C1707). Cummings is quoted in the canto: "'a

friend,' sd/ mr cummings, 'I knew it 'cause he / never tried to sell *me* any insurance.'"

133. Pound to Cummings

AL-1.

1 Oct[ober 1946]   [Saint Elizabeths]

How the hell can I tell wot I think of wot the Psm's etc. if the Zabl or the who t ell runs it aint the decency to send me the

—   —   —   —

_____

mugs gazoon?

_____

as fer yr. amaze, wot else can I do fer the elite (pronounced e-light) in Posm's natal
                    Love to M.
By the way ole G.S. "Midl Span" has some 10 strikes

Zabl: Morton D. Zabel, former editor of *Poetry.*
"Midl Span": George Santayana, *The Middle Span* (New York: Charles Scribner's Sons, 1945). This memoir covers Santayana's life from the beginning of his postgraduate days to the end of his career as a professor at Harvard. Santayana mixes penetrating glimpses of people and places he has known with wide-ranging judgments. "The Greeks knew what it was to have a country, a native religion, a beautiful noble way of living, to be defended to the death" (6). "A string of excited, fugitive, miscellaneous pleasures is not happiness; happiness resides in imaginative reflection and judgment, when the *picture* of one's life, or of human life, as it truly has been or is, satisfies the will, and is gladly accepted" (8). "The ethos of an aristocratic society, I perceived, is of a very high order. It involves imaginative sympathy with those who are not like oneself, loyalty, charity and self-knowledge" (32). "[R]ebellion against convention has the advantage of springing afresh from the heart, the ultimate judge of everything worth having or doing" (75). "Courage and distinction will save a man in almost any predicament" (119–20). "[A] *deracine,* a man who has been torn up by the roots, cannot be replanted, and should never propagate his kind" (122). "It is, or it was usual, especially in America, to regard the polity of which you happen to approve as sure to be presently established everywhere and to prevail forever after" (129). "To be good morally you must first be distinct physically: you must not be an anonymous *it*" (177).

134. Pound to Cummings

ALS-1.

8 Ott [October 1946]   S. Elizabeths Hospital
                                        Wash. D.C.

Dr Estlin

I <u>think</u> you better dip into Mons. BULLITT'S big bk after all
                                        Ez
love to the lady

"Mr B. iz in hospital" (too)
"& not expected out for some time"
_____
nondimeno you might someday want to know why
                        several   v. verso

If I can read it you can
_____
there Z a reezun

hospital: Bullitt underwent surgery on his spine in September 1946.
big bk: William Christian Bullitt, *The Great Globe Itself: A Preface to World Affairs*
(New York: Charles Scribner's Sons, 1946). Bullitt argues that during World
War II Franklin D. Roosevelt "chose to gamble on his ability to convert Stalin
from Soviet imperialism to democratic collaboration" (20), with the result that
a powerful and aggressive Soviet Union was now bent on spreading Communist
dictatorship to the rest of the world: "The aim of Soviet foreign policy is
constant: to establish Communist dictatorship throughout the earth" (107).
Bullitt rejects, however, the proposal that the United States should destroy the
Soviet Union with atomic bombs. Rather, it is in the American interest "to use
our own economic, political and diplomatic power to help the democratic non-
Communist governments of Europe to preserve the independence of their
states" (178). Bullitt urges the creation of a "Defense League of Democratic
States" (204) to prevent further Soviet expansion. In his conclusion, Bullitt
foresees a day when "the people of the Soviet Union control their own govern-
ment and live like ourselves in freedom and democracy" (216).

135. Cummings to Pound

TLS-1. Enclosure.

October 13 1946
4 Patchin Place
New York City

Ezra—

all right,I'll get the lady to plumb
shallows of lendinglibraries for Bull
B's Roosky Revelations;& even toss an infra-
glance thereanent,weather permitting

we're still trying to find a copy of
that "Poetry" number which does you
honour:apparently the combination of EP &
the arboreal marsupial was too
much for even ye common man,who bought
like(as he'd say)crazy

did you know the EP issue of "PM"
sold out completely;which never happened
before?

—Marion sends love

eec

Enclosure: A newspaper clipping headed, "French Lament End of Famed Brothel in Paris." The clipping's first two paragraphs: "All day today a group of some-what seedy men carried furniture out of a tall building in Montparnasse. The furniture, which had just been sold at auction, consisted mostly of beds—handsome, deep-cushioned double divans. And the men who carried this furni-ture were assisting not only at an auction sale but also at the obsequies of a French tradition.

For the building that was being sold was none other than the famous Sphinx, most renowned bordello in Paris closed by reason of the new French law forbidding prostitution." The Sphinx had been in business since 1930.
arboreal marsupial: T. S. Eliot.
EP issue: The issue of *PM* for 25 November 1945, which contained Charles Norman's article on Pound.

136. Pound to Cummings

ALS-2.

15 Ott. [October 1946]   [Saint Elizabeths]

Red Sx 3
Cardinals 4
Dear Kumrad -

Yes. if you can't buy it. @ least know by theez preentz that Dillon valubly
testifys I did ⟨not⟩ corrupt his morale.

I spoze with 25 year time lag it will — or rather someone by then will tell the
———— that I was not @ any time sending axis puppergander — ⟨but my own⟩
of course the idea that a latin (i.e. civil) country wd/ permit author of
distinction to free speak on Cavourian or Mazzinian 'mike" as has in fact, & in
P.M., been stated wd. too gtly shock inferiorty cx of inferior potes

They jess cant believe it or onnerstan the printed statement.

you ought to collect on the P.M. sell-out. as were the one bright starr.

but never ascertaind if it was the London or ⟨some⟩ N.Y. Norman
=

my copy went into storage with papers I had @ gallinger—& never here.
        & so wan.
        lov to the lady
                EP

Red Sx: On 15 October 1946, the St. Louis Cardinals defeated the Boston Red Sox
  in the seventh and deciding game of the World Series.
Dillon: George H. Dillon, one of the editors of *Poetry*. See his "A Note on the
  Obvious," *Poetry,* vol. 68, no. 6 (September 1946), 322–25. Dillon takes up the
  issue of whether Pound should be published, in view of his wartime radio
  broadcasts and political beliefs. "This leads," Dillon writes, "to one of those
  'fundamental' questions: Can you reasonably refuse to publish a poem because
  of what you believe to be the pernicious effect of its ideas? The answer is that
  that is the wrong approach to the problem. The problem does exist: even a
  literary magazine must occasionally deal with it. But it can be said that ideas,
  however absurd, do not become pernicious in written form except through the
  medium of dishonest, and therefore bad, writing." Dillon also noted that
  Pound's broadcasts were, for him, matter for "amusement." "Pound, whenever
  we caught his performance, went on and on. But it was impossible to have any
  serious reaction."

Cavourian: Count Camillo Benso Cavour (1810–61), Italian statesman and the leading figure of the *Risorgimento.* He devoted himself to creating a united, independent Italy under the government of a constitutional monarchy. He was a moderate liberal.

Mazzinian: Giuseppe Mazzini (1805–72), Italian patriot. From his young manhood on, Mazinni worked for a free Italy with a government established on democratic principles.

137. Pound to Cummings

ALS-1.

16 r ? Ott. [October 1946]   S. Liz

eec

Consarnin' collaboratn & intrcommunicatn among the intellergezia. U.S.A
1946

each in his corner
facin' his individual wall
where cummings speaks only to Estlin
& Estlin not @ all

                       =

alias
who
kno
zoo   & iz
              Joe Brittan's still open
              roun deh cornah ?
              rekon Joe died befr you arruv

Brittan's: See the note to letter 47.

138. Cummings to Pound

TLS-1.

                                        [4 Patchin Place]
[Pound wrote at the top of this letter, "23 Oct '46]

Dear Ezra—
more than glad to be accused of noncommunication with any unworld's
omnivorously inexisting intelligentia unquote. M Voltaire said it in 3 words:of

all the cowardly fanatical demiarsed amourpropreridden nonproud unhumble superegocentric hyperpseudos embraced by that axetogrinding extraimpotence illimitably misentitled culture comma La Canaille Ecrivante smell least healthy taste most sickly feel look & sound by lightyears the feeblest

l'autre dull day I looked-up one MRWerner,erstwhile wellknown biographer("Barnum" "Brigham Young" "Tammany" "Bryan" etc)who during our twentyodd years of off&on friendship has to my knowledge never miscued concerning matters Americanly political;while during a similar period have never guessed right. "This is your year" he(a choisi by involition & a nude eeler per hypnosis)cried:thereupon plunging into the following direforhim prophecy—G.O.P. will win the forthcoming voteries by a majority as great as unless greater than any of USA history;will control "the house" & perhaps "the senate";& will make whoever-they-like "president" next time. "Don't" Morrie pleadingly threatened "vote for anyone but a Republican!" & I, as a noir-r,promised that wouldn't.

we've been enjoying tepid weather in the city of Mark Antonio;& rumor contends that Caesar's demise changed the gulfstream:but as a matter of fact I can scarcely recall a thunderinggood winter,so maybe ye hammer mit sickle's to blame. How did you like those goats surviving unclesam's latest Noble Experiment?

                              —sois careful
                                   EEC

mercredi

3 **words:** They appear near the beginning of chapter 21 of *Candide.*
MRWerner: Morris Robert Werner (b. 1897), author of *Barnum* (Garden City, N.Y.: Garden City Publishing Company, 1923); *Brigham Young* (New York: Harcourt, Brace, 1925); *Bryan* (New York: Harcourt, Brace, 1929); *Tammany Hall* (Garden City, N.Y.: Doubleday, Doran, 1928) and other biographies and historical studies. Cummings's portrait of Werner appears in Kennedy, following page 270.
noir-r: A "black" Republican is one who invariably votes for the party's nominees.
Noble Experiment: The *New York Times* (24 September 1946, 24) reported that "almost 2,500 travel-weary goats, pigs and rats completed a 13,000 mile round-trip cruise to and from the Bikini atomic bomb tests today. . . . About 4,900 animals were aboard the target ship in the Bikini Lagoon."

139. Pound to Cummings

ALS-1.

23, or 4 Ott [October 1946]   S. Liz

P.S.
you'll nver cure yr f/n arthritis Till you find 3 peepl fit to spik to.
       & don't tell gran'paw
thet in 140 millyum
                there
                    aint

Lov to a lady
       Ez P

mebbe the nation has polio? 2nd phase pollyana
I heard that Joe Gld hez still a cig. holder

pollyana: See letter 21, where Cummings's mention of "Pollyanna the Glad"
    clearly refers to Franklin Delano Roosevelt. Pound believed FDR's outlook had
    deeply influenced the nation.

140. Pound to Cummings

ALS-2.

24 Ott [October 1946]   S. Liz.

yes an Natalie sez fem. of ecrivain : ecrivisse

Who th ___ l said you shd. communic with canaille:
    ⎧ain
ec ⎨or
    ⎩isse

don't tell me there are no intelligent men who DONT (i.e. write.)

I never suggested you shd. con/sort /or /sert with 1/2 a/d writers.
-- git my meanin

    ―――

find Thee who etc. etc. some life in the <u>cian' dei co'umbi'</u>
    when did I imply you shd with etc

Can. Ecriv. !

       !!

no -- no --

I am not clear.

the precious grains of

    NOUS

also responsible -- if they

don't, you see (or shd. hv. saw) wot

has 'apnd

          Ez   Luv to the lady

request — :

    diagnosis

of J. Dos P___os.

I mean fer me privik

not interested in destruction — even of goats —

anybody can destroy

Natalie: Natalie Barney (1876–1972), American expatriate who lived in Paris and
had a famous salon there. She and Pound first met in 1913 and became lifelong
friends. See Ezra Pound, "Letters to Natalie Barney, Edited with Commentary
by Richard Sieburth," *Paideuma,* vol. 5, no. 2 (fall 1976), 279–95.

NOUS: Anaxagoras, a Greek philosopher of the fifth century B.C., held that all
things were governed by nous (mind), and that it was corporeal—although the
least substantial of all things.

Dos: John Dos Passos.

141. Cummings to Pound

TLS-1.

October 29 1949 [1946]   [Patchin Place]

Dear Ezra—

"anybody can destroy"—right. & bravo!

observation re national polio-polyanna:pertinent putting it mildly

diagnosis of undersigned's personal freezeup . . . masterly. Or,as I'd say:the last
guerre is to this as "La Ferte Macé" is to "arthritis"

all diseases are imaginary. An old man told me that he saw the Good people tearing a peasant's thatched roof apart(writes WBY;thereupon barkleying)another man would have seen a high wind. Now tell me frankly:how do you stand(or float)on(in)e.g. "A Vision"?

understatement:not all imaginings are diseased

if you suppose that I am not(haven't been,shan't be)looking for "3 people fit to spik to",you're—in proud and humble I's opinion—wrong. My(no doubt Ighly Coloured)notion of me equals a naturally both-solitary-and-social,i.e. healthy,individual;who's doing his unlevel best to celebrate To Kalon Kai Agathon beneath the cui lumen ademptum of a monstr' horrend' inform'ingens. Of course,the smart thing 's to disguise oneself as a hesheep & get counted out of ye cave:leaving cyclops to roar & heave(missingly)rocks. Well,maybe am not smart;or,again,perhaps even Vergil was born in a living— unkilled by radio—world

anyhow:late or soon,we get what we're looking for;so,deeply hope I am looking for Love

sub rosa,re Dos (1)he's a sweet(good,generous,healing—vs sour;evil,selfish,hurting)person (2)who's not unrecently turned a sombresaut gauche-to-droit (3)& whose books have I never read(nor could). He had a grandfather who was a Portugese shoemaker(in Madeira,whither Dos once conducted myself;& what a funicular:et les anglais!)—&,speaking of unworlds,"he made a pair of shoes" said D "whole shoes;for somebody . . . but now,everybody's just making parts of something:for anybody. That's the trouble everywhere!" My friend speaks many languages perfectly & reads Latin(also probably Greek)at sight—suffered all his life with "arthritis" until a couple of years ago(the right swing?)& partially-cured himself of nearblindness via Dr Bates(takeoffyourglasses)exercises;have seen him walk across 5th Avenue while brakes screamed,cheerfully oblivious

I still think "the nicest things happen by themselves"(Him) any further advice respectfully received. Marion sends her best

    —Vive La Vie!

       EEC

"La Ferte Macé": The French town in which Cummings was imprisoned from September to December 1917. His experiences there became the basis for *The Enormous Room*.

writes WBY: The passage is from Yeats's *Fairy and Folk Tales of the Irish Peasantry* (1888). "An old man told me he saw them fight once; they tore the thatch off a house in the midst of it all. Had anyone else been near they would merely have seen a great wind whirling everything into the air as it passed." *W. B. Yeats: Prefaces and Introductions,* ed. William H. O'Donnell (New York: Macmillan, 1989), 11.

To Kalon . . . : "The Good and the Beautiful."

cui lumen . . . : "Vix ea fatus erat, summo cum monte videmus / ipsum inter percudes vasta se mole moventem / pastorem Polyphemum et litora nota petentem, / monstrum horrendum, informe, ingens, cui lumen ademptum" [Scarce had he spoken when on the mountaintop we saw the giant himself, the shepherd Polyphemus, moving his mighty bulk among his flocks and seeking the well-known shore—a monster awful, shapeless, huge, bereft of light.] *Aeneid,* book 3, ll. 655–58. *Virgil,* vol. 1, trans. H. Rushton Fairclough (Cambridge, Mass., and London: Harvard University Press and William Heinemann, 1974).

re Dos: John Dos Passos.

Dr Bates: William Horatio Bates (1860–1931), American physician. Author of *The Cure of Defective Eyesight without Glasses* (New York: A. R. Elliot Pub. Co., 1915).

(Him): In *Him* (act III, scene i), Me says, "Now you are trying to feel things; but that doesn't work, because the nicest things happen by themselves." *Him* (New York, Liveright, 1970), 87.

142. Pound to Cummings

ALS-1.

30 Ott [October 1946]   [Saint Elizabeths]

Dear Estlin

No recollection what WBY put in that vol. = very little of anything he said ⟨in print⟩ after 1908 = But interested recent rev. of letters _to_ F. Farr _from_ him & G.B.S.

reviewer noting that Y. wuz the more serious character. = wich wuz tru.

      rest of yrs.   seen, vizd, approved

—————————————————

did I ask _how_ near youd got to finding 3 or list of 3 nearest approxs ? ?

—————————————————

   =

my bee in bt. - bein' plantin' the damn bois fer the blinkin rossignols.

   =

re Dos (yes, I kno) buttt friend wantin to kno if Dos wuz fit <u>reader</u> fer inedits
= of course if his gdpa wuz totalitarian <u>shoer</u> - there's a <u>basis</u>.
      & bless the lady

yrz
EZ

I aint vurry entertainin'

WBY: William Butler Yeats.

review: A review of Clifford Bax, ed., *Florence Farr, Bernard Shaw, W. B. Yeats: Letters* (New York: Dodd, Mead, 1942). Pound refers to the British actress Florence Farr (1860–1917) in Canto 28 as "Loica." Farr played the role of "Louka" in the first production of Shaw's *Arms and the Man* in 1894.

rossignols: That is, Pound wishes to create favorable circumstances so that poets may flourish.

friend: Unidentified.

143. Pound to Cummings

ALS-1.

4 Nov. [1946]
                                         S. Elizabeths Horsptl
                                         Wash D.C.

dear eec
      Furthrr
reflexn or queery
arthritis because
Bill B painted the
bogseat red instead of fixn
the drains?
      Hence my interest in Gesell

Wot 'bout this guy K. Patchin.
whose vury nyme seems to
alarm some.
        Luv to a lydy
EP

Gesell: Silvio Gesell (1862–1930), German economist.

Patchin: Kenneth Patchen (1911–72), American poet. On 4 November 1946,

Patchen wrote Pound briefly to say he was confined to his bed with severe back problems.

144. Cummings to Pound

TLS-1.

[10 November 1946]   [4 Patchin Place]

Dear Ezra—

sans doute 4 PP could be physiologically improved:aesthetically,no. And man lives(as little you-i distinctly perceived through a 3000mile only last winter trip to that superadvertized Lourdes of American "science" called Tucson Ariz)not otherwise than by aesthetics. By bread(etc)alone man merely undies. But feel sure you'll agree that an individual's natural interest isn't—unlike any unnatural soidisant "world"—in undying. Truth is a 3. 2dimensional(dying-undying e.g.)ideés fixes do belong to ye realm of the movies

rather shortly before the late pleasantness alias mandate,Marion entered a large local bookshop & asked for BB's opus. Horror! We don't have it! "Will you order it,then?" she asked. Doubts&frowning. "You see" her cool voice very clearly explained "I'm one hundred percent against Russia." Consternation!(sic) . . . Then a young pretty girl who assists the humanitarian nonfemale(not male)owners appeared;"yes" she said smiling at Marion,"I'll get it for you." & enfin 'tis here. So now shall peruse

far from needless to add:a "swing to the right"'s an unswing to the left(ye olde 2);what I hope may emerge is,a flight—out of flatness

—and love from the lady

Estlin

dimanche

mandate: In the congressional elections of 1946, the Republican Party gained control of the House of Representatives and the Senate.
BB's opus: Bullitt's *The Great Globe Itself.*

145. Cummings to Pound

TLS-1.

[12 November 1946]   [4 Patchin Place]

to E.P.

Memo(entre nous)

KP is an ample soft larval-looking fellow,sans intellect,goodhearted,a complete
pacifist(when the USGovernment told him to report to his draftboard
he,having gone to bed with an arthritic back,replied "come and get me"—&
nobody appeared)whose father was a coalminer. K,according to his wife(in any
other epoch,a big square servantgirl;who fanatically boosts her husband's
genius on all occassions(which is dull)but adores Marion,which is
touching)just-writes as "it" comes to him,without ever making any corrections.
This I believe;also that he superintends the printing of his books—which are
full of calligrammatic word- & type-arrangements—down to the most
microscopic detail. He told me once,casually,that he'd looked over the
verseforms used by ⟨other⟩ poets & decided there ⟨was⟩ "nothing in them for
me". So far as I can guess(since I faithfully subscribe to each new book but
cannot read it)his ebullitions are without any conscious structure. Perhaps for
this reason—assuming,as why not,an Epoch of Ultimate Confusion—they've
been compared by a throng of disciples to every great literary creation of past
epochs,or almost every anyhow. I like K(& don't the disciples);perhaps for no
reason,perhaps because he likes & respects me & my(such as it is)stance. If you
want to read his latest opus,say the word & shall send it along—otherwise not.
Let me finally add that K paints;as he writes.

("love" is his favorite word)

EEC

KP: Kenneth Patchen.

146. Pound to Cummings

ALS-2.

13 Nov[ember 1946]   [Saint Elizabeths]

Thanks re K. P. memo
who <u>inhabits</u> the country Anyhow?

No. I dont want any more books. exemplaires or other --
save yourn if any new

---

still regret fatigue that prevented my gittin' to top floor in '39.

---

but used the small portrait on mantle. -- doubt if you will be able ⟨ultimately⟩
to trace -- but acknowledge (herewith & by) the debt -

---

was day was unable to git round to pore Fordie's fer reuniun of Doc. Wms
satelites
                         etc.
               & ceterar

---

ever hear of a bloke Z. D. Sung - alive in 1935?
hope he still is.
               lov to th lady
                    Ez P

I dunno what Bunting you could get save what's in Active Anthology??

top floor: The top floor of Cummings's residence at 4 Patchin Place.

small portrait: Either a portrait of Loren MacIver (a friend of the Cummingses) or of an elephant.

Fordie's: Ford Madox Ford founded in early 1939 a literary club called Les Amis de William Carlos Williams. The group held only five meetings.

Sung: Author of *The Symbols of Yi King; or, The Symbols of the Chinese Logic of Changes* (Shanghai: China Modern Education Co., 1934). Sung contends that the symbols in the Book of Changes are in "perfect agreement" with "those of the algebric terms of the expanded expression of a binomial sixth power, and the concord in the numerical value of the two technical terms, assigned in their elementary forms, to the length of day and night of the two solstices in China" (i).

Bunting: Basil Bunting (1900–85), British poet. The poems by him in *Active Anthology* were "Villon," "Attis: Or, Something Missing," "How Duke Valentine Contrived," "They Say Etna," "[Yes, it's slow, docked of amours]," "[Weeping oaks grieve, chestnuts raise]," "[Molten pool, incandescent spilth of]," "The Passport Officer," "[Fruits breaking the branches]," "Chomei at Toyama," "The Complaint of the Morpethshire Farmer," and "Gin the Goodwife Stint."

147. Pound to Cummings

ALS-2.

26 N[ovember 1946]   S. Eliz DC

Sorry to be so d—n dull & purrsistent BUTT.

=

D'courre you got paint as alibi - so haz Wyndham - temperd ⟨in his case⟩ by
inf. cx. at bein' only non-univ among 3 flat chested (J.J., Possum, &
sottosciutto) - hence mass of undigested (as baboo) in insides WHEREAS you
wuz sterilized @ Hawud - nevertheless a page - now-n- then ?? whose - ??
in all these years <u>one</u> quote, one author unius Thoreau.

---

now do you ever read?
nifso, wot?
            Joe. G. still alive - have we between us force to git him printed, or
has he withdrawn thru hiz cig-holder into super-Estlinear silence?

---

of course I cant think of anyone in N.Y. whom you cd/ posbly read for
pleasure or even find legible ⟨chapter in Fordie's 'Last Post' is worth it⟩

                                    BUTT
not bein a pynter meself, I do occasionally & if a page lives in you semi-sub-
conscience do name it.
        lov to th lady
                    yrs Ez P

J.J.: James Joyce.
Possum: T. S. Eliot.
Joe.G.: Joe Gould.
'Last Post': The last volume (published 1928) in Ford Madox Ford's *Parade's End*
    tetralogy.

148. Cummings to Pound

TLS-1.

November 28 1946   [4 Patchin Place]

Dear Ezra—
sorry to be taciturn

Marion,who is my reader,suggests immediately

Firebrand(The Life of Dostoevsky)—by Henry Troyat(Roy
                              Publishers)
William Blake—by Mark Schorer(Henry Holt)
Concord And Liberty—by José Ortega Y Gasset(W W Norton &
                              Co)
                        especially
have also enjoyed the first volume of
      The Travel Diary of a Philosopher—by Count Hermann
                        Keyserling
                              (Harcourt Brace)
as usual,especially his Indian chapters;&have almost accomplished
Thomas Mann's Joseph ⟨regard the <u>Prelude</u> to Joseph And His Brothers⟩
cycle(Knopf),an extraordinary tour de sagesse of OldTestament
reinterpretation. Do you know
      The Livery of Eve—by F W Bain(G P Putnam's Sons)
?   Did anyone ever finish Oswald Spengler's Decline of the West (1
volume:Knopf)? You might try
      The Condemned Playground—by Cyril Connolly(Macmillan) he being
my English publisher(bringing out "1 × 1")& editor of the only lively extant
magazine(Horizon)- arriving today in NY unless I'm mistaken;or,on the other
hand,
      Curious Relations—by William D'Arfey(Jonathan Cape)probably 'twere a
social error to add
      The Wisdom of China & India—by Lin Yutang(Random House)but how
about Chuangtse?(p 625)

however,Shakespeare's still my favorite poet

                                          —vive la vie

                                          EEC
PS a ⟨learned⟩ friend of mine extolls The Aim of Education—by A N
Whitehead(Macmillan)

my "Santa Claus" has just appeared in book form;if you'd care for a copy,just
say so:no obligation
bien entendu

how did Polite Essays—by Ezra Pound(New Directions)strike your-honour?

<u>Caesar</u> Welcome to Rome.
<u>Antony</u>   Thank you.
<u>Caesar</u>   Sit.
<u>Antony</u>   Sit,sir.
<u>Caesar</u>   Nay then.

Firebrand: Henri Troyat, *Firebrand: The Life of Dostoevsky* (New York: Roy Publishers, 1946).

Blake: Mark Schorer, *William Blake: The Politics of Vision* (New York: Henry Holt, 1946).

Concord: José Ortega y Gasset, *Concord and Liberty,* trans. Helene Weyl (New York: W. W. Norton, 1946).

Travel Diary: Count Hermann Keyserling, *The Travel Diary of a Philosopher,* trans. J. Holroyd Reece, 2 vols. (New York: Harcourt, Brace, 1925).

Joseph: Thomas Mann, *Joseph and His Brothers,* trans. H. T. Lowe-Porter (New York: Alfred A. Knopf, 1934).

Livery: Francis William Bain, *The Livery of Eve* (New York and London: G. P. Putnam's Sons, 1917).

Decline: Oswald Spengler, *The Decline of the West,* trans. Charles Francis Atkinson (New York: Alfred A. Knopf, 1932).

Condemned: Cyril Connolly, *The Condemned Playground, Essays: 1927–1944* (New York: Macmillan, 1946).

Connolly: Cyril Connolly (1903–74), British editor and essayist. He had recently written, "Well, there are three writers whom I envy America: Hemingway as a novelist, Edmund Wilson as a critic, and E. E. Cummings as a poet." "Comment," *Horizon,* vol. 64, no. 80 (August 1946), 70–71.

"1 × 1": E. E. Cummings, *1 × 1* (London: Horizon, 1947).

Horizon: A monthly "Review of Literature and Art" edited by Cyril Connolly from its inception in January 1940 to its final issue (December 1949–January 1950). *Horizon* published poems by Cummings in February 1944 ("[what if a much of a which of a wind]"), October 1947 ("[to start, to hesitate; to stop]" [Firmage B150] and January 1948 ("[this(let's remember)day died again]," "[neither awake]," "[infinite jukethrob smoke & swallow to dis]," "[jake hates]," "[whose are these(wraith a clinging with a wraith)]," "[this is a rubbish of human rind]," and "[if(touched by love's own secret)we,like homing]").

Curious: William D'Arfey, *Curious Relations,* ed. William Plomer (London: Jonathan Cape, 1945 and New York: William Sloane Associates, 1947).

Wisdom: Lin Yutang, ed., *The Wisdom of China and India* (New York: Random House, 1942).

Chuangtse: Pages 625–28 are a brief introduction to the thought of Chuangtse, a philosopher of the third century b.c. A Taoist, he "was probably the greatest slanderer of Confucius" (625).

Aim of Education: Alfred North Whitehead, *The Aims of Education and Other Essays* (New York: Macmillan, 1929).

"Santa Claus": E. E. Cummings, *Santa Claus* (New York: Henry Holt, 1946) (Firmage A21).

Polite Essays: Ezra Pound, *Polite Essays* (London: Faber and Faber, 1937). Issued by New Directions in New York in 1940. Gallup A42a and A42b.

Caesar: From Shakespeare's *Antony and Cleopatra,* act II, scene ii.

149. Pound to Cummings

ALS-2.

29 Nov[ember 1946]   [Saint Elizabeths]

MYgorrrrd
     As to Spengl
all I know iz: I didn't. I saw a Eng. trans (was it by Cedar & Cedarine?) in wich
AKT was translated as "act".
     It is my impression that Whitehead ALONE of yr. list is free of a faint
stale aroma. = Conolly's mag. Saville Row. = saw peculiarly stale lavender tie. &
the supercilious sneeze of what the '90 are ascended to in 1946-- NO - mon
cher
it needs Ventilation =
     It was time fer communications to open wiff the outer air
     =
          take me back to 3 or 4 of Remy's more lucid remarks— thet hev
got lorst in the hinterim
          =
Cutting off Eng. from continong during Napoleonic-- p-----d
the island. & it has happened again.
          =
"neck & sa nektie."
Did you ever get copy of
Dod's wopsay on e.e.c?
                                   yrs
                                        Ez

Thank M. fer the
sad advices   OVER
P.S.
dam it all
it's revealing
Anyhow

Eng. trans: All English translations of *The Decline of the West* listed in the *National
     Union Catalog* are by Charles Francis Atkinson.
Cedar & Cedarine: Eden and Cedar Paul, British translators.
Saville Row: Savile Row in London contains the most fashionable men's tailors.
Remy's: Remy de Gourmont.
wopsay: Edmondo Dodsworth's essay on Cummings. See the note to letter 121.

150. Pound to Cummings

ALS-1.

30 Nov[ember 1946]   [Saint Elizabeths]

Dear eec
                    Meaning ÷ a list of
superior fads - whose
racket consists in avoiding
dangerous subjects =
                    Remy was not such -
That is the point which
the Rev. Possum misses.

                                        Ez P

Remy: Remy de Gourmont.
Possum: T. S. Eliot.

151. Pound to Cummings

ALS-1.

3 Dec[ember 1946]   S. Liz

Sorry to Purr sist
        or Per scratch.
But I want hellup in fog. Do yew mean that you two exist in abs/ vacuo (or
torcelliano) = no one whose mind of least interest.
One year in pays, no one admits havin a (mental) friend with whom ANY
point in Xporin any idear wotsodamnever.

H.J 40 years late with preface by Auden.

---

nothing thought untill 40 yr. t.lag.
                    ? ? ?
Pt. max vitality J. Adams-Jeff letters not since @ voltage

Two decencies in West's (x. Rocky) now Western
were   ⌐Autrs '46⌐
Jxn Maclow
        &
Stallman

wot bout
    Jxn?

Open writers
1. Remy
2. Frobenius
    der Geheimrat

    yz
    EZ. P

⟨even⟩ the young Omar
depressd by his list

───────

as was exacted by
earlier re/Canaille LIT

H.J: *The American Scene, together with Three Essays from "Portraits of Places,"* edited with an introduction by W. H. Auden (New York: Scribner's, 1946).

J. Adams-Jeff: Pound had noted the importance of the correspondence in "The Jefferson-Adams Letters as a Shrine and a Monument" (reprinted in *Selected Prose*).

West's: Ray B. West Jr. was the editor of *The Western Review* (formerly *Rocky Mountain Review*), published in Lawrence, Kansas, by the University of Kansas Press.

Maclow: Jackson Mac Low (b. 1922), American poet, composer, and musician. Pound evidently saw his poem, "The Lion House: Christmas," *Western Review*, vol. 11, no. 1 (autumn 1946), 44. Pound and Mac Low began corresponding in 1946.

Stallman: Robert Wooster Stallman, American literary scholar. Pound evidently saw his poem "Ghost Bow," *Western Review*, vol. 11, no. 1 (autumn 1946), 4. Stallman also contributed an essay on John Peale Bishop to the same issue.

der Geheimrat: German for "privy councillor." Pound appends this title to Frobenius in *Guide to Kulchur:* "I said to Frobenius: 'I shd. like you to drift round to an opera by my compatriot A.' 'Ah!' said the Geheimrat, 'that will interest my wife" (217).

152. Pound to Cummings

ALS-1.

19 Dec[ember 1946]   S. Liz DC

dear e.e.

1. But whether any relique is interested in Bill of Rights. i.e. any form of protecting the individual ??

───────────────────────

re Santayana on coral insects.

2. distinction betrween live thought & DEAD thought
& in yr Thoreavian pantosocracy can live thought be maintain'd solely by
telepathy without verbal communication?

Putt these in lady's Xmas nilon

yr Ez P

insects: George Santayana, *The Middle Span* (New York: Charles Scribner's Sons,
1945), 162. "Did the members of the Harvard Faculty form an intellectual
society? Had they any common character or influence? I think not. In the first
place they were too much overworked, too poor, too much tied up in their
modest homes. Nor had they had, like old-fashioned English dons, a common
education, and written Latin hexameters and pentameters. I believe there were
some dinner clubs or supper clubs among the elder professors; but I never heard
of any idea or movement springing up among them, or any literary fashion. It
was an anonymous concourse of coral insects, each secreting one cell, and
leaving that fossil legacy to enlarge the earth."

153. Pound to Cummings

ALS-1.

19 Dec[ember 1946]   [Saint Elizabeths]

To make up for recent perturbations of yr calm.
Try F T Cheng "china moulded by Confucius" re chinese painter.
        p. 256
                "He is never fashionable."
        yrs fr Xmas calm.
                Unc. Ez

F T Cheng: Cheng Tien-Hsi, *China Moulded by Confucius: The Chinese Way in
Western Light* (London: Stevens and Sons, 1946). Cheng attempts to describe
"the whole Chinese social system, or rather what may be called Chinese civiliza-
tion and culture," which, he adds, "is saturated with the teachings of Confucius
and those of Mencius, the sage next to him and the most brilliant exponent of
his doctrines" (23). The passage Pound refers to is from this paragraph: "The
Chinese artist, as I have said in connection with painting, always tries to inter-
pret nature rather than imitate it, and hopes to rise above it. He may be grand in
his conception and is yet patient in his execution. Nothing is too great or too
small for him: he may paint a river of myriad miles and yet will try to be faithful
even to a blade of grass that grows out of his brush. He aims at perfection and is

yet conscious that he may fall short of his aims; therefore he succeeds. He may be confident in himself and yet feels that there must be others who can do better than he himself; therefore he triumphs. He may be bold in his design, and yet will not go to the extreme; therefore his creation is in harmony with life and the universe. He is never fashionable and is indifferent to popularity: therefore he becomes a great master. His mind is at peace with the whole world; therefore what he produces is the embodiment of harmony and affection" (256).

154. Cummings to Pound

TCS.

December 21 '46   4Patchin Place NYC

well,I suppose there are two(roughestly
speaking)sorts of people:those who're
convinced that what's sauce for the goose
is sauce for the gander and those who're
aware that one man's meat is another man's
poison—the former frequently strike me
as fanatics;the latter invariably delight
me as humanbeings

                         eec

155. Cummings to Pound

CHRISTMAS CARD.

[December 1946]   [4 Patchin Place]

[Drawing of Patchin Place and printed greeting: "Merry Christmas And Happy New Year"]

                    &
                good luck
            Estlin & Marion
               Cummings

156. Pound to Cummings

ALS-1.

24 [December 1946]   S. Liz

Merry Xmas.
Remaining still one margin, or continong, of INcomprehension

---

never tried to pizon any man's gander = problem of communication - dislike
of seein poor geese pizon'd under impression that arsenic is cranberry sauce -
mi spiego?   [Chinese char]
praps knot = metaph - seems a bit feather'd not   [Chinese char]

[Chinese: "feather"]

W. E. Woodward (par ezpl) aint canaille licheraire =
4 bright young califs. arise etc.

<u>Hell</u>
communications aint
synonym for civic reform

Being about to destroy useless verso [the above] - when arrove the Patchin -

---

images gt. comfort in circs. = of course Patchin is less that colour than !!!
wottt'ell

---

various p.c. of Venice this day. every stone whereof - sings even in photo. to
the last damn gondolerpole =
egg strordinary impact of image on protoplasmic
waste of abs/ unorganized gelatine.

---

as to abandond argyment (verso), I never axd other to use my meat in pref. to
his own pizon or wotever -- or to try my so objected-to subject matter. (the
jeune califs. also object - (politely))
Love to Marion
ever Ez

Woodward: William E. Woodward (1874–1950), American historian. See the
note to letter 14.
young califs.: Possibly Robin Blaser (b. 1925), American poet; Robert Duncan
(1919–88), American poet; George Leite, editor of *Circle* (1944–1948); Jack
Spicer, (1925–65), American poet.
the Patchin: The Christmas card from the Cummingses with the drawing of
Patchin Place.

157. Marion Morehouse Cummings to Pound

ALS-1.

Jan[uary] 28 -47   4 Patchin Place
                                                           New York, 11

Dear Ezra—
                Glad you liked the Gogarty piece. And what did you think of
the Briarcliff mag. tribute to Bill W?
        Estlin has been ill with flu which is why you haven't heard from him.
And his mother died about 10 days ago just as he was beginning to feel better.
She was very old but we both loved her & miss her & that has depressed him
& me. Sewanee Review has all that I know of John Berryman but I shall ask
some questions & if I find anything will let you know.
                                        Affectionately
                                        Marion.
Himself sends greetings.

Gogarty piece: Oliver St. John Gogarty (1878–1957), Irish author. The "piece" is
    probably his memoir, "James Joyce: A Portrait of the Artist," which first ap-
    peared in *Tomorrow* magazine in January 1947. It is reprinted in Gogarty's
    Mourning Became Mrs. Spendlove (New York: Creative Age Press, 1948).
tribute: *Briarcliff Quarterly,* vol. 3, no. 2 (October 1946). This issue contained
    poems and prose by Williams, as well as photographs of himself and his family.
    It also contained Williams's "Letter to an Australian Editor," in which he
    discusses Pound.
Berryman: John Berryman (1914–72), American poet. The *Sewanee Review,* vol.
    55, no. 1 (January–March 1947), contained "Canto LXVI, a Poem," by Pound
    (56–67) and "Canto Amor, a Poem," by Berryman (68–70).

158. Cummings to Dorothy Pound

TLS-1.

April 14 1947   4 Patchin Place

Dear Mrs Pound—

thanks for your good letter!

please tell Ezra that I deeply appreciate his kindly thought of "adult" me in
connection with Rome's American(or America's Roman)Academy. Only last

night,I asked Ted Spencer about said edifice;he assured the undersigned that it concerns "archeologists,not creative writers"

if Arioste L should perchance be a finely blond youth sporting a vividly red chemise,he pleasantly materialized much too late one afternoon & promised to reappear;Olson hasn't appeared. But both Marion,who sends greetings,and myself are perfectly free to assert that Omar is our delight

the best of luck!

—sincerely

C'gs

Academy: The American Academy in Rome was founded in 1894 as the American School of Architecture in Rome. It soon expanded its scope to include a school of classical studies and to offer fellowships for sculptors and painters. See Lucia Valentine and Alan Valentine, *The American Academy in Rome, 1894–1969* (Charlottesville: University Press of Virginia, 1973).

Arioste L: Arioste Londechard, a pseudonym adopted by James Finley, a young New Yorker who corresponded with Pound and visited Cummings several times.

Olson: Charles Olson.

Omar: Omar Pound.

159. Pound to Cummings

ALS-2.

17 Ap[ril 1947]   [Saint Elizabeths]

Dear E.

Don' be a naz.

Ted is misinformed - it is fer painters. as well as excavators. & it dont matter what azzs think a thing is For. itz wot the blightrs can be led to. I didn't ax fer theory. I sez. Who iz runnin' the show. the babes on the spot don't know - = git sous inside. who controls the endow vast MT villa & studios - place dead on feet pleased when olga play'd fiddle fer 'em (that director now dead.)

&

dyin' fer live = it is fer architects - profs primarily - but ole aldrich cert/ thought it was fer painters -

only as nobody has thought of goin to Roma to study or practic awt ⟨pintin⟩ since Nat wrote the Mobile Fawn - there iz deseutude - Mr Behrenson (B) is sd/ the present directing menage is babes in wood.

I didn't do it. I aint met 'em cause where am I & where is B.B. -
So dont quote me as tube of qt.
                    love to Marion
                                                            EP
= family nooz. oh. yus, young Walter is born.
& my name is g-pop.
I spose the jeune Arioste was wearin the same shirt
I like colour m'self.

Ted: Theodore Spencer.
olga: Olga Rudge.
aldrich: Chester Holmes Aldrich (1871–1940), American architect. Director
    (1935–40) of the American Academy in Rome.
Nat: Nathaniel Hawthorne.
Behrenson: Bernard Berenson (1865–1959), Lithuanian-born American art his-
    torian. He and Pound met in Paris in the early 1920s and corresponded briefly
    thereafter.
Walter: Sigifredo Walter Igor Raimondo de Rachewiltz was born on Easter Mon-
    day (7 April) 1947.
Arioste: See the note to the previous letter.

160. Pound to Cummings

ALS-1.

22 Ap[ril 1947]   [Saint Elizabeths]

Flowers fer the K'rdz Table
"But he was such a jumpy and peppery creature it was impossible to talk to
him much. He has succeded in writing some v. excellent verse"

_____

      This in letter ⟨recd.⟩ ogg. from on the whole the most cerebrally active of
yr. elders.

@ any rate a few words must hv. bn exc'd.

I notice you scorrrun mere section numerals.
I spose it dont matter.
N.Y. 12
        14
or
?

Flowers: The quotation is in a letter to Pound from Wyndham Lewis. See Materer, 234. See also letter 95.

numerals: Postal codes for Manhattan.

161. Cummings to Pound

TLS-1.

April 25 1947   4 Patchin Place

Dear Ezra—

Hearty <u>congratulations</u> from Marion&myself on your <u>grand</u>fatherhood!!

As for Uncle S's Archeological Academia:I cheerfully grant that conceivably same might be rendered at any rate infracontemporaneous via perfervid activities of some 6fisted Sir Galahad(Launcelot,si tu veux)more than hypothetically ensconced,against sure suffocation,by—kindly allow me to mildly suggest—a seamless suit of stainless steel superarmor which(encore conceivably)12 "good" nonmen and women,all machine picked diplomatists of The New School For Soft Knocks,might semi-successfully(later)subtract with cautiously&how-orchestrated caressings of(putting it softly)an hyperblowtorch. Soit. Mais moi(esperons)je me suis pas—&,God willing,shan't be—so humanitarianistically de- or im-personalized as to glimpse in any search(even the abovementioned)irrevocable triumph of m over m as something remotely approaching major significance. Not that 'tisnt quite pleasant to know whence one's apres-demain(or demain,let us modestly say)meal arriveth. But more & more,as I grow,is the antedivulian undersigned delighted by Doctor Jung's terrafirma riposte when a desperate wouldbe dogooder demanded what can be done to make better the world?quote Jung,make thyself better. Truly a Greek might have said this(and did)yet imagine a Swiss! We're,Madame GStein announced just before her departure,in for a strange epoch—well,only a few days ago(when our nonunhero was worth 25bux)the very most vulgarest mag in even America offered him 500 for "right" to reprint,come next Xmas,a little moralityplay called Santa Claus—naturally I couldn't accept the(if such it were)compliment but that's neither ici nor la

                                                    eec

Academia: The American Academy in Rome.
New School: The New School for Social Research.

Doctor Jung's: Carl Gustav Jung (1875–1961), Swiss psychiatrist and author.

a Greek: Plato, *Protagorias,* 343b.

Gstein: Cummings may be recalling comments made by Gertrude Stein in "The New Hope in Our 'Sad Young Men'" (first published in the *New York Times Magazine* on 3 June 1945). Stein notes that the Great Depression and World War II have made Americans "a sad people," as were their ancestors before the Civil War. "I am completely and entirely certain," she writes, "that we are going to be more interesting again, be a sad and quiet people who can listen and who can promise and who can perform" (*How Writing Is Written: Volume II of the Previously Uncollected Writings of Gertrude Stein,* ed. Robert Bartlett Haas [Los Angeles: Black Sparrow Press, 1974], 143).

vulgarest mag: *Esquire.*

Santa Claus: E. E. Cummings, *Santa Claus* (New York: Henry Holt, 1946) (Firmage A21).

162. Pound to Cummings

ALS-1.

2 Magg. [May 1947]   [Saint Elizabeths]

DeaR K z

O.K. "Suiss" ef he wuz. Do you cert? in any c. 2500 years late.

"franchement ecrive ce qu'on pense' but fer over 20 yr. noWHERE that 4 did or cd/ -   n.

pro (or de)-motin' you to vacancy long unfill'd by late Jz is not. =

In fak only the uncorrupted (?) embalmers & the caterers union fillin the eggspanzz

Love to Marion

EP

re the villat on 7th or 17th hill. I think you καθ' without ἕκαστα (if thatz th spellin)

franchement . . .: See the note to letter 317.

late Jz: Probably Henry James, author of *The American Scene.*

villat: The American Academy in Rome.

καθ' without . . .: Pound plays on the phrase καθ' ἕκαστον ("singly, by itself").

163. Pound to Cummings

ACS.

22 May [1947]   S. Liz

Trust haaavud reunion passd happily on <u>Both</u> sides
                                                     yr Ez

reunion: A meeting between Cummings and T. S. Eliot in New York.

164. Cummings to Pound

TLS-1. Enclosures.

May 27 1947   4 Patchin Place

Dear Ezra—

re latest letter:having microtelescopically explored the hypereinsuperstein
expanding-&or-contracting universe of finitebutunbounded chinoiserie which
only our illimitable contempt for soi-disant fact impells us playfully to
misnicname your handwriting,Marion & I must conclude(not before frequently
crashing through the skylight of script & discovering each other in the cellar of
ignorance)that you pay me a multidimensional compliment. Bien merci

concerning subsequent postcard:its absolutely decipherable queery regarding
the recent juxtaposition of 2 Harvard graduates somehow suggests (z)a
pronumicamento of JFGould viz "the only reason a woman should go to
college is so she can never say O if I'd only gone to college" & (a)DHThoreau's
description of the shantih Irishman. I found your friend wearied(as was
natural)& kindly(as is surprising)

you might be enlightened to learn that the other day,at what amounts to a
bookseller's banquet-to-publishers somewhere uptown,Mrs WWilkie & Mr
CCanfield & similar ultraintellectuals exhorted fortissimo any & all caxtonians
present to (1)delete "intolerance" from,& (2)insert "tolerance" in,all & any
manuscripts submittedby aspiring & other authors. The ample audience(quoth
my trusty informant)swallowed its lambchops sans blush

& how did you like Mr Watts'elucidation of your current idiom in the Yale
Poetry Review?

                                        —love from The Lady
                                               eec

Enclosures: (1) A clipping of the column "Powerhouse," by Jimmy Powers, from the *Daily News* for 26 May 1947. Powers discusses cheating in sports and concludes, "There used to be a celebrated verse hung in most athletic club-rooms, which said, in effect, 'It matters not whether you won or lost—but how you played the game.' That has disappeared in the raucous laughter of some of our high pressure managers, coaches and leaders of impressionable youth. Come to think of it, the Commies are 'tricky' and the Japs were 'wily,' but the books show that few foul fighters ever got on top. They say our society is sick, our social order is collapsing, our morals are degenerating. And there are statistics to prove it. If this is so, is this the time to encourage youngsters to 'get in there and win—only the nice guys are in last place'?"

(2) A clipping from the *New York Herald Tribune* for 26 May 1947, headed "Japanese Storytellers to 'Bury' 20 Old Tales." The text of the article: "Tokyo, May 25 (AP).—Japan's professional story-tellers, who have a wide popular following, plan to hold 'burial services' this week for twenty old stories which their screening committee has purged from their repertories as undemocratic. The services are to take place at the so-called 'Story Mound' in the Honpo Temple at Tokyo. The banned tales deal with warfare and feuds. At the same spot last fall the story-tellers cermoniously resurrected fifty-three stories which Japan's war-time leaders had forbidden as too frivolous or risque. These fifty-three are regaling large and appreciative audiences."

Harvard graduates: T. S. Eliot and Cummings.

Irishman: In the "Baker Farm" chapter of *Walden,* Thoreau gives an account of an Irish immigrant, John Field, and his family.

Mrs WWilkie: Edith Wilk Willkie (d. 1978), wife of Wendell Wilkie from 1918 until his death in 1944.

Mr CCanfield: Cass Canfield (1897–1986), American publisher. At this time he was chairman of the board of Harper and Row.

Watts'elucidation: Harold H. Watts, "Pound's Cantos: Means to an End," *Yale Poetry Review,* no. 6 (1947), 9–20.

165. Pound to Cummings

ALS-1.

29 M[ay 1947]   [Saint Elizabeths]

Dear eec

The intention wuz in both (avoiding if poss- the fulsome) to convey
A. recognition by one of few surviving active (ie. W.L.) of activity in poss. frère but cert. *not* semblable.

B. (postcard) ⟨to report⟩ conviction of integrity of Kumrad by ⟨i.e. on part of⟩ the cadaverous Possum.

=

in fact the ever so slightly (as now seen) but, once the more so, junior. by 3 items of once quadrumvirate (of antipodes i.e. each of tother) the oirish item having pass'd on.

Love to the lady
EP

#vide infra verso

re yr. final- it was time somebody took part of the carp out of the carpet & started looking for pattern. (? one T or two. I dare say its two).
P.S. you are about the age of J. Adams when Bastun was objecting to his anon. writing , a "of this young" man

W.L.: Wyndham Lewis.
Possum: T. S. Eliot.
quadrumvirate: T. S. Eliot, James Joyce, Wyndham Lewis, and Ezra Pound.
oirish item: James Joyce.
J. Adams: John Adams. Pound most likely refers to his *Discourses on Davila, a Series of Papers on Political History,* published anonymously—though their authorship soon became known—between April 1790 and April 1791 in the *Gazette of the United States* (Philadelphia). Adams was fifty-five in 1790, Cummings turned fifty-three in 1947. The slight difference in age seems compatible with Pound's remark that "you are about the age of J. Adams when" *Discourses* was published. Pound's further comment, that "Bastun was objecting," reflects the widespread dissatisfaction with the *Discourses.* They were taken as expressing views inconsistent with republican government. As Adams himself noted in a marginal annotation to the *Discourses* in 1812, "This dull, heavy volume, still excites the wonder of its author,—first, that he could find, amidst the constant scenes of business and dissipation in which he was enveloped, time to write it; secondly, that he had the courage to oppose and publish his own opinions to the universal opinion of America, and, indeed, of all mankind. Not one man in America then believed him. He knew not one and has not heard of one since who then believed him. The work, however, powerfully operated to destroy his popularity. It was urged as full proof, that he was an advocate for monarchy, and laboring to introduce a hereditary president in America" (Charles Francis Adams, ed., *The Works of John Adams* [Boston: Little and Brown, 1851], 6:227). The reference to "this young man" seems to be drawn from another note to the *Discourses* by Adams: "See the review of this work in the *Anthology.* The writer was 'a young man; a forward young man'" (*Works,* 6:229).

166. Cummings to Pound

ALS-1.

June 13 1947   Silver Lake
                                               New Hampshire

Dear Ezra—

(1) What do your caps mean in "recognition by one of few surviving active. (ie W.L.)"?
(2) is Yeats "the oirish item" now "pass'd on" of "once quadrumvirate"?

here's hopin the (recently doctored) melancholy marsupial ignores fact that Harvard (& the selfsame year Yale) conferred an "honorary" degree on Walt Disney, "creator" of Mickey Mouse

"the trouble with Joyce" remarked Marion last night (when I objected there's a muchtoomuchness of Mr Bloom's unc throughout nighttown episode) "was that he didn't have Ezra to cut him in two"

                    —good luck

                              eec

doctored: Harvard University conferred an honorary degree on T. S. Eliot in June 1947.
nighttown episode: The "Circe" chapter of *Ulysses.*

167. Pound to Cummings

ALS-1.

[15–17? June 1947]   [Saint Elizabeths]

Pollical cats chasing Mickey.
        MOST Havpropriate.
                 _____

        item celtic.
the 4th was J.J.
Unc. Wm. was ov earlier bilin. not of the "quad"
                 _____

why shd I have trimmed a back-looker.

the <u>end</u> of a era.
but 1st of Trilogy

EIMI

Apes of G.

yr EZ.

"hope the note on "Subservience" sting you.
P.S. write often.

Pollical cats: T. S. Eliot's *Old Possum's Book of Practical Cats* (London: Faber and
   Faber, 1939), contains a poem about a battle between two breeds of dogs, the
   Pekes and the Pollicles.
Unc. Wm: William Butler Yeats.
Apes of G.: Wyndham Lewis's novel, *The Apes of God* (London: The Arthur Press,
   1930). The first book in the "trilogy" is *Ulysses.*
"Subservience": Probably an item in an enclosure now lacking.

168. Cummings to Pound

ACS.

[Postmarked 21 June 1947]   Silver Lake N H

thanks for the "<u>subservience</u>" datum!
glad to get your 4th item straight
shall try WL's Apes
weather ashey here; some blame a.b.
Marion sends love

                        eec

P.S. did you authorize one D.D. Paige to edit your correspondence for
publication? He says so

a.b.: Atomic bomb.
Paige: Douglas Duncan Paige. His edition of Pound's letters appeared as *The
   Letters of Ezra Pound, 1907–1941* (New York: Harcourt, Brace, 1950). For an
   account of Paige's editorial efforts, see Norman, 433–35.

169. Cummings to Pound

ACS.

July 10 1947   [Silver Lake, N. H.]

"Confucio Studio Integrale", "Carta da Visita", & "Lettere d'Oggi" (numero 6–7, Marzo–April) here came; & am exercising my feeble Italian with, let's hope, profit. How's Omar enjoying Hamilton? He wrote us a nice letter, regretting his inability to drop up before scholastics. And what do you think of the "flying disks" seen—& strenuously denied per Science—by groups & individuals (including experienced air-pilots) all over USA? Marion sends love

—eec

Confucio Studio Integrale: Ezra Pound, *Confucio: Ta S'en Dai Gaku Studio Integrale* (Rapallo, 1942) (Gallup B46).

Carta da Visita: Ezra Pound, *Carta da visita di Ezra Pound* (Rome, 1942) (Gallup A50).

Lettere d'Oggi: Gallup lists no contributions by Pound to this issue of *Lettere d'Oggi* (Rome). This literary periodical was founded in 1940 by Giambattista Vicari (1909–78).

Omar: Omar Pound was an undergraduate at Hamilton College, from which his father had graduated in 1905. Hamilton also awarded Pound an honorary degree in 1969.

flying disks: On 24 June 1947, Kenneth Arnold, piloting a private plane in the state of Washington, said he saw a number of "saucer-like" flying objects moving at high speed through the air. This report was followed by a rash of similar accounts of observations of unidentified flying objects in the skies over the United States. Charles Norman recalls a visit to Joy Farm during which, in the middle of the night, he was awakened by Cummings, who then said: "Would you like to see a flying saucer?" Norman believed the object they viewed that night was a meteorological balloon, but the Cummingses insisted that they had witnessed a visit by extraterrestrial beings: "Little men from another planet." See Norman's *Poets and People* (Indianapolis: Bobbs-Merrill, 1972), 275–77.

170. Pound to Cummings

ACS.

12 Lug [July 1947]   [Saint Elizabeths]

'dying flisks!' la jante!! merely another device to keep peeple from reading Sophokles or anything decent.

yr Ez

Luv to M

I spose you'll onnerstan part of p. 35/6 Carta d.v?

Yes! D.D.P. dee cidedly iz & not a Ph. =
D.D. =
Doubly Deserving.

I say that.

p. 35/6: Pound comments on and prints Cummings's poem, "flotsam and jetsam."
   Carta da visita was translated and published as "A Visiting Card" in 1952
   (Gallup A50b). "A Visiting Card" was reprinted in *Selected Prose.*

171. Cummings to Pound

TLS-1.

October 11 '47   4 Patchin Place

Dear Ezra—

below,you'll find some information about the socalled world. When you read
these harmless sentences perhaps you'll remember that Mr A said to me in NH
"nobody can possibly imagine a world as crazy as the world which the new
physics compels us to assume". The Russians are supposed to have one
superscientist in A's "field"; otherwise he's supreme therein

as for young Mr Lowell:he dropped over to the Marsupial's table when my
friend Allen Tate was dining his idol&(at Tate's urgent request)me,a l'hotel
Lafayette;the y Mr L seemed like a pleasant chap,in fact quite human

Ted Spencer spoke of seeing you not unrecently. Marion sends love. Sois sage

                        —et bonne chance!

                                        eec

"We are going ahead with our experiments with absolute zero. My latest plan is
to make a phonograph record of the chatter which the atoms talk when they
get down there,and if it works I'll send you one. Of course we still don't know
what absolute zero is and whether even any of the atoms are really there. What
we hear is the noise some of the atoms make(in protest maybe)when some of
their neighbors temporarily drop out of contact with the world due to the
excessive cold to which we have subjected them. They suddenly are
inaccessible,not touched or touching their fellows,really just as if they had

passed into another world or dimension,but they come back when the whole metal is warmed up again.

"It's when the atoms or electrons are bridging two worlds that radio waves are picked up and come out of the speaker unexpectedly. So I'm trying to persuade the atoms to tell me where they go or where they have been. But all this chattering is a language which nobody yet is able to understand."

> (latest letter from the man I call "the
> master of absolute zero"—whose real name is
> Donald Hatch Andrews)

Mr A: Donald Hatch Andrews (b. 1898), professor of chemistry at the Johns Hopkins University.
Lowell: Robert Lowell.
Marsupial's: T. S. Eliot.
Spencer: Theodore Spencer.

172. Pound to Cummings

ALS-1.

Nov[ember] 16 [1947]   S. Liz.

Appy birf day.
if a bit late

---

as to yr. friend I dunno if <u>he</u> is doin it fer bon motif

----

hibernating of course. thazz wot they're doin. ⟨them atoms⟩

#send him this letter head

                                                Ez

= all very there since -
per plura diafana
lux enim   Theology

friend: Donald Hatch Andrews.
letter head: Pound's letterhead: "J'ayme Donc Je Suis."
per plura . . .: "Through more things diaphonous . . . light shines." See the notes to letter 174.

173. Cummings to Pound

TLS-1.

[18?] November 1947   4 Patchin Place
                                                       New York City

Dear Ezra—

thanks for your birthday greeting!
When were you last born? Anthologies
merely give years

it's months since our zeroid friend was
last seen:hope he's not flat on his
back. Your letterhead might help;but
(as am one of the more vastly ignorant
of small humanbeings)please theologically
elucidate "per plura diafana lux enim"

Marion & I hope to share our Thanksgiving
dinner(which NewEnglanders call supper)
with your friend Omar

                              —skol!

nice chap,your letter-gatherer

friend: Donald Hatch Andrews.
Omar: Omar Pound.
letter-gatherer: D. D. Paige.

174. Pound to Cummings

ALS-1.

20 No[vember 1947]   S. Liz

az purr
            ⎧ S. Erigena
            ⎨ Grosseteste
            ⎩ G. Cavalcante (Ez notes on)
              Ez. Canto the whichever

yr. Zerite aint got nowt new in mind
however laboratoriously novel in the beanery =

yess DDP a good guy - glad you like.
    R.L. mellowin?
Thanks giv. & lov. to M.
                yrz EZ

Erigena: Johannes Scotus Erigena (ca. 800–ca. 877), medieval philosopher and
    theologian.
Grossteste: Robert Grosseteste (ca. 1175–1253), British bishop and theologian.
    The Latin phrases in Pound's letter of 10 November 1947 are from Grosseteste's
    short treatise *De luce.* For Pound's use of Grosseteste in his essays and in the
    Cantos, see Carroll F. Terrell, "A Commentary on Grosseteste with an English
    Version of *De luce,*" *Paideuma,* vol. 2, no. 3 (winter 1973), 449–70.
Cavalcanti: Guido Cavalcanti (ca. 1250–1300), Italian poet. Pound's "notes on"
    him are in the essay "Cavalcanti" (reprinted in *Make It New* [1934] and in
    Literary Essays of Ezra Pound [1954]). There Pound suggests a tradition of which
    Cavalcanti's "Donna mi prega" is a part. "From this poem and from passages
    elsewhere it would seem that Guido had derived certain notions from the
    Aristotelian commentators, the '*filosofica famiglia,*' Ibn Sina, for the *spiriti,*
    spiriti of the eyes, of the senses; Ibn Rachd, *che il gran comento feo,* for the
    demand for intelligence on the part of the recipient; Albertus Magnus, for the
    proof by experience; and possibly Grosseteste, *De Luce et de Incohatione For-*
    marum, although this will need proving" (*Literary Essays,* 158).
Canto: Canto 83, which links Erigena and Grosseteste:

        "lux enim
                ignis est accidens   and,
        wrote the prete in his edition of Scotus
        Hilaritas   the virtue *hilaritas*"

Zerite: Donald Hatch Andrews.
DDP: D. D. Paige.
R.L.: Robert Lowell.

175. Cummings to Pound

TLS-1.

vendredi [28? November 1947]   4 Patchin Place

Dear Ezra—

your classical enlightenment's welcome. I agree re scientia Et Comment when last beheld,our absolute zero friend seemed more hunted than ever:talked about Clerk Maxwell's(imaginary)demon who reaches into matter & redistributes the atoms—result,time flows backward—& promised he(our friend)would send me a phonographrecord of his own "chattering" atoms,while politely explaining he had no idea what would happen to someone who dared play it

yesterday Omar arrived,bearing a whole treasury of gifts:they're delicious;he's delightful. Please allow my & me to thank you & yours far more than kindly for him & for them

      —bonne chance!

                eec

PS my laundryman's sure that as long as people enjoy "slinjing" mud at each other "you and I will suffer,Mister Cummings"

friend: Donald Hatch Andrews.
Maxwell's . . . demon: James Clerk Maxwell (1831–79), British scientist, hypothecated an intelligence capable of detecting and reacting to the motions of individual molecules. The second law of thermodynamics states that heat does not naturally flow from a cool body to a warmer; work must be expended to make it do so. Maxwell conceived of the "demon" as a necessary principle of selection that would allow *(a)* the transfer of fast-moving molecules from a warmer body to a cooler, and *(b)* the transfer of slow-moving molecules from the cooler body to the warmer.
Omar: Omar Pound.

176. Pound to Cummings

AL-1.

8 Dec[ember 1947]   S Liz

O.P. sez Jo iz nut. wot erbout this? strikes me as most unlikely -- But yet again
- - -
love to Marion.
O. sez she cooks.

O.P.: Omar Pound.
Jo: Joe Gould.

177. Cummings to Pound

TLS-1.

samedi [December 1947]   4 Patchin Place

Dear Ezra—

the question Is Joe Gould Crazy strikes
me as,putting it very mildly,irrelevant.
For "crazy" implies either(crazy)or(not).
And badold goodyoung either—or is okay for
movie—i.e. 2dimensional—"minded" mobsters;
be they "intellectuals" or be they "proletarians"
or be they neither or be they both or etc.
But Joe happens to be 3dimensional:i.e. human

                                        —Marion
                                          sends her
                                          best

                                                    eec

178. Pound to Cummings

ALS-1.

[December 1947]   [Saint Elizabeths]

Sech indeed I had sposed the case
        1. YET considering the young az oracles.
        2. having no data other than ms/ of early J.G. vintage
                                        pre-bellic
        3. & also desiring orientation fr. oracles.

how come bulls? nostalgia of antique? or wottell. Left-hand Wagon-wheel Bull
collegue in jug - has no Xplain.
N.B. or (foot)
L H W-W B
gd. s. of sittin'
                yrs Ez

bulls: Pound had affixed a 1947 Christmas Seal stamp to his letter. The stamp depicts bulls hauling a load of Christmas trees through a snowy landscape. **L H W-W B:** Left hand wagon-wheel bull.

179. Cummings to Pound

ACS.

[Postmarked 25 December 1947]   4 Patchin Place
                                                               New York City

More than likely these "bulls"
are meant for oxen. Don't
forget this is The Age of Confusion

                    —Merry Christmas!
                           E

180. Cummings to Pound

TLS-1.

February 28 1948   4 Patchin Place
Ezra—

thanks for the timesly proof of Great B's nonexistence

master eXei; from Texas writes that you don't believe several persons(e.g. I)'ve
ever essayed Milton's Aereo. Correct. But,only last year,Marion & the
undersigned were 2 of a-select-many literally locked—by uniformed
gun(sic)men—into Frick's 5th Avenue museum while Dr Thos Stearns
congratulated himself on finding paradise lost

note that Rudyard's ours-qui is out walking again

                                      —sois
                                       très
                                       sage
                                             E

Great B's: Probably a clipping from the *London Times,* if "Great B" means "Great Britain."
master eXei: Dallam Simpson (also known as Dallam Flynn), American poet and publisher. Pound used Simpson's periodical, *Four Pages,* as an outlet for his

views. The stationery on which Simpson's letter was written was headed with a quotation in Greek: Οὐ ταῦτα πρὸς κακοῖσι δειλίαν ἔχει. The quotation is from Sophocles' *Electra*. Mary de Rachewiltz recalls her father speaking this line, and she translates it: "Shall we to all our ills add cowardice?" *Discretions* (Boston: Little, Brown, 1971), 306. The letter from Flynn is as follows.

"Dear Mr. cummings: As I wrote you, one of the aims of the leaflets is to lighten old Ez'z hours in the Hoosegow. Dr. Williams' essay seems to have been eminently sucessful ('Obligato on the roasting of the Possum, now spelled pos O.M.).

It is believed that your version of 'Milton, thou shdst be living (?) at this hour,' would get Ez through another ash wednesday, or failing that, the translation of a few lines of the Areo-plug-jet-ica* into either the english or american language would help.

Deferentially yours,

Dallam Simpson

*Ez don't believe Bill Williams or Mr. Eliot (Dec 7) or e.e.c. have ever read a page of it."

Issue number 2 of *Four Pages* (February 1948) contained William Carlos Williams's essay on T. S. Eliot, "With Forced Fingers Rude."

Milton's Aereo: John Milton, *Areopagitica; A Speech of Mr. John Milton for the Liberty of Unlicenc'd Printing, to the Parlament of England* (1644).

Frick's: Henry Clay Frick (1849–1919), American industrialist, art collector, and philanthropist. At his death his mansion in New York City became a museum housing the Frick Collection—artworks he had accumulated in his lifetime.

Dr Thos Stearns: T. S. Eliot lectured on Milton at the Frick on 3 May 1947.

Rudyard's ours-qui: In Kipling's poem "The Truce of the Bear," a blind beggar warns hunters about "The Bear that walks like a man." *Ours* is French for "bear." Cummings may also be punning on "Russkie." Just days before the date of this letter, the Czech Communist Party had taken control of the government.

181. Cummings to Pound

TLS-1.

March 29 1948   4 Patchin Place

Dear Ezra—

thanks for a very fine gift;conveyed by a most refreshingly cheerful young man named Fjelde

although can't judge Ted's opus,can(entre nous)whisper it's excellent sailing till scholarship docks,in latter few pages. His devout world-state-individual trinitarianism must more than delight your current Confucianist demon

news(?)-that,having sold usa Hoi a hyperriproaring trip on the Soviet
superhearse,sellers are trying to get into reverse without stripping gears. Joseph
Ferdinand says "a war with Russia would mean a civil war in every country
that fought her". And "why not in Russia?" asks Marion

one hears Italia's hostels are 2/3 unreserved;grace à tourismo's misdoubts re
forthcoming plebescite. Imagine having the chance to see that show & staying
hereabouts! But one mustn't forget that by going abroad one would meet
everyone one most wished one had never beheld

—vive le
printemps
!

C

Fjelde: Rolf Fjelde, one of the four cofounders (in 1945) of the *Yale Poetry Review*.
The sixth number of the *Review* (1947) was an "Ezra Pound Issue" in which
Canto 83 was published (Gallup C1709). Fjelde visited Pound in late January
1948. The "fine gift" carried from Pound to Cummings was probably Theodore
Spencer's book. Fjelde wrote to Pound on 4 April 1948 that he had visited
Cummings the previous week and left a "copy of Spencer's book." Cummings,
wrote Fjelde, "was most pleased with it."

Ted's opus: Theodore Spencer, *Shakespeare and the Nature of Man: Lowell Lectures,
1942* (New York: Macmillan, 1942). Spencer examines Shakespeare's plays in
terms of "the proper balance between the individual, the state and the forces
behind Nature" (213).

Joseph Ferdinand: Joseph Ferdinand Gould.

plebiscite: Cummings probably refers to the national Italian election of 18 April
1948. The Christian Democrat Party received over twelve million votes, while
the People's Democratic Front (a coalition of the Communist and other leftist
parties) received over eight million votes.

182. Pound to Cummings

ACS.

[1 April 1948]   [Saint Elizabeths]

blessed be she amung wimmin
yaas.

Thazz the white hope

Ez

1 Ap.   unintention

she: Marion Morehouse Cummings.

183. Pound to Cummings

ALS-1.

25 Ap[ril 1948]   S. Liz

Cheeus
Visitin howyers fr. 1-4 P. Hem.
you gotter write fer permishn to Superintendent.

_____

nobody else come in on Mondays. Thurs. Fri.

_____

But youze is welcome any time
nowt to conceal =
                        yrs Ez

                    P.S
wot do you know about a loopy loose head named D. Macdonald.
brief vignette wd/ be welcome:
Lov. to th lady
                        EZ

Superintendent: Dr. Winfred Overholser.
D. Macdonald: Dwight Macdonald (1906–82), American literary and cultural
   critic. Macdonald was on the staff of Henry Luce's magazine *Fortune* from 1929
   to 1936. In 1948, however, Macdonald was editor of *Politics,* a periodical he
   founded in 1944 and which ceased publication in 1949. The spring 1948 issue of
   Politics was devoted to essays about the Soviet Union. Macdonald noted in his
   introduction to the issue that "Most of this issue deals unfavorably with the
   Soviet Union. . . . In general, it may be said that, in the judgment of the editor,
   and of some contributors, USSR today is in the same position as Nazi Germany
   was a decade ago: i.e., it represents the main threat to socialist and liberal
   values" (75).

184. Cummings to Pound

TLS-1.

May 22 1948   4 Patchin Place
                                                   New York City

Dear Ezra—

yesteday,Marion made an uptown pilgrimage,returning with handsome
gifts:The Pisan & your other Cantos. JJL's subordinates explained that the boss
wants both books to appear simultaneously,& embellished by jacketblurbs
recommending same highly;hence(as nearly as my lady could determine)the
delay in publication. A chap named Bowra or Bower told her he was present
when "review copies" of 1 × 1 came back to the publisher(Cyril Connolly),for
it seems the recipients—O merrie Englande—didn't believe my humble
attempt was reviewable

have taken the excessive liberty of sending yourself a copy of a cheap little
poetry anthology(edited by master Selden Rodman)solely because you're fairly
represented. I've been seeing a lot of Joe G lately & wondered why;paraît que
his erstwhile refugee-backess decided she'd put her dollars on the foreign
poor,pour changer perhaps:or maybe Gould got fresh?

the temps hereabouts leaves proverbial quelque chose to be desired. I hope my
iceman(nay Dominic)'s right,he says "Yoo no-wheye?kawz soe-mennie Bad
peepl"

                                                   —be good!

                                                   eec

love from m

The Pisan & your other Cantos: *The Pisan Cantos* (New York: New Directions,
    1948), Gallup A60, and *The Cantos* (New York: New Directions, 1948), Gallup
    A61.
JJL's: James Laughlin.
Bowra or Bower: Anthony Bower, a subeditor at New Directions.
1 × 1: E. E. Cummings, *1 × 1* (London: Horizon, 1947) (Firmage A19b).
Connolly: Cyril Connolly. Cummings wrote to his mother on 5 January 1947 that
    "Cyril Connolly,the editor of "Horizon" magazine(much the best periodical
    concerning socalled literature;&published in London)has been wining-and-

dining Marion and me in celebration of a(let's trust)soon-forthcoming English
edition of 1 × 1" (*Selected Letters,* 171–72).

anthology: Probably *100 American Poems: Masterpieces of Lyric, Epic, and Ballad,
from Colonial Times to the Present* (New York: New American Library, 1948).

Rodman: American poet (b. 1909).

refugee-backess: According to Joseph Mitchell, Gould received sixty dollars a
month from the spring of 1944 until December 1947. His benefactor remained
unknown to Gould, since she transmitted the money through a third party. See
Joe Gould's Secret (New York: Viking, 1965), 151–68.

185. Pound to Cummings

ALS-1.

[Postmarked 28 May 1948]   [Saint Elizabeths]

Thanks. Mr. S. R is
merely another liar -
who lies is hog
ignorance. having
derived his intellectual
chicko from
Winchell & co.
         benedictions-

               EzP

begin his (R's)
education, when /&/or if
you think
possible

Mr. S. R: Selden Rodman. See *War and the Poet: An Anthology of Poetry Expressing
Man's Attitudes to War from Ancient Times to the Present,* ed. Richard Eberhart
and Selden Rodman (New York: Deven-Adair, 1945). Eberhart and Rodman
used sections 4 and 5 of *Hugh Selwyn Mauberley,* although this extract was
identified only as being "from Ode Pour L'Election De Son Sepulchre." In his
note to the poem, Rodman commented, "His [Pound's] reaction to World War
I was passive and literary; he was living in England 1917–19, serving as London
Editor of the *Little Review* (Chicago). His reaction to World War II was non-
literary but active; in 1941 he began those Fascist propaganda broadcasts by
short-wave from Rome for which he was subsequently indicted for treason.
'There died . . . ,' written at the peak of his powers in the 20's, perfectly
expressed the disillusionment with the first war and its peace then widely felt"
(224).

Winchell: Walter Winchell (1897–1972), American newspaper columnist and radio commentator.

186. Pound to Cummings

ALS-1.

30 <u>May</u> [1948]   S. Liz

<u>later</u>

Dear Estlin———

Hope I didn' keep you settin bolt up fer too long
- one never does think of wot may be to other.

___

omission (a) fr/ narrative
=
Jap cultural attache when I was tryin sell him Kit-Kat# & co.
"B--u--t, to tellyouthe Truth- we can't unnerstan' a singl' word these young
men write." (end qt)

___

#Kitasono of Vou club

___

best beloveds to M.
yrs Ez

Kit-Kat: Katue Kitasono.

187. Cummings to Pound

TLS-1.

July 15 '48   [Silver Lake, N.H.]

Dear Ezra—

the back cover of "Spring and Summer" "Sears,Roebuck And Co." catalogue
bears one big ad;headed "GOOD,CLEAN,WHOLESOME READING FOR
SALE",& telling all about "The People's Book Club,which is Sears-owned and
Sears-operated." It seems that "We believed there was a place for a club that
could supply decent reading material at a fair price" & the "Club"'s the
result—"with hundreds of thousands of members."

"Providing 'best sellers' at less than normal prices is one of the benefits of
membership" but "is far from the sole advantage." "The standards by which

our editors and critics judge literature contain this one very vital <u>must</u>. The books must be readable by every member of the family."

"We will always believe that good,clean,wholesome reading serves to strengthen family ties;that books read together,discussed together, enjoyed together bring the family closer together in a common interest. It was because of this belief that we brought such outstanding books as "The Robe" and "Green Grass of Wyoming" to our book club members."

& now please note the following sentences.

"We cannot control what authors write,but we can and do control what books we offer." Paragraph. "So if you would like to read without blushing,without tearing pages out before passing the book on to the younger members of your household,we invite you to turn to page 620" etc. "We think you'll be particularly interested"(the next paragraph begins)"in the bonus book supplied new members this season. It is the inspirational novel'Miracle of the Bells,'destined,we believe,to live with the famous books of history. The enrollment book,'Hope of Earth,'is in the same key and promises to be one of the best of the 1948 novels. The Peoples Book Club price for both to new members is only $1.66."

& now comes windup.

"For the best value in the best reading we again urge you to turn now,this very moment,to page 620. You'll be glad you did."

many paragraphs. Marion & I hope the heat's not too horrifying where you're;& that your work goes well

—Xaîpe

Estlin

188. Pound to Cummings

ACS.

19 Oc[tober 1948?]   [Saint Elizabeths]

Hyper WHAT?
why don't you larn

PRINTIN'?
luv to deh loidy

                    EZ

189. Cummings to Pound

TELEGRAM.

25 December 1948   New York

LOVE AND A MERRY CHRISTMAS TO YOU ALL
            MARION AND ESTLIN

190. Pound to Cummings

ALS-1.

27 Jan[uary 1949]   [Saint Elizabeths]

An nex time I spose they'll fer clarity spell it Ay MEE.
                         or ai - or whatever
with thanks to the complimenting author.
               & enclosed the coincident stuffing of case (no kid'n). it wuz
Ed.

_____

&, ever annoying, do you think W. Sloane capable of <u>further</u> utility in
pub/g other in BASIC (eng. or wotever. fer zampl the‾‾‾
late Leo's Continents Livg.
            love to Marion
                         ever Ez

nothr much kneeded reprint is Ah Chin Le. or the Civilization of the Western
Barbarians particularly of the English
Lee Shepard (Bostun) 1876.

Ay MEE: Pound had evidently received from Cummings's publisher the second
    edition of *Eimi* (New York: William Sloane Associates, 1949) (Firmage A13b).
stuffing: Enclosure lacking.
Sloane: William Sloane, American editor and publisher. He had been an editor at
    Henry Holt when that firm was publishing works by Cummings. He started his
    own company, William Sloane Associates, in 1946. It went out of business in
    1952.

late Leo's: Leo Frobenius's seven-volume *Erlebte Erdteil:* (1) *Ausfahrt: Von der Völkerkunde zum Kulturproblem* (1925); (2) *Erschlossene Räume: Das Problem Ozeanien* (1925); (3) *Vom Schreibtisch zum Äquator* (1925); (4) *Paideuma* (1928); (5) *Das Sterbende Afrika* (1928); (6) *Monumenta Africana* (1929); (7) *Monumenta Terrarum* (1929).

Ah Chin Le: *Some Observations upon the Civilization of the Western Barbarians, Particularly of the English; Made during a Residence of Some Years in Those Parts, by AH-CHIN-LE, Mandarin of the First Class, Member of the Enlightened and Exalted Calao,* translated from the Chinese into English, by John Yester Smythe, Esq., of Shanghai, and Now First Published out of China and in Other Than Chinese (Boston: Lee and Shepard, 1876). Both Ah-Chin-Le and John Yester Smythe were pseudonyms for J. B. Swasey, British author. Swasey uses the figure of Ah-Chin-Le to condemn many aspects of Western civilization. The flavor of his commentary is suggested by the following quotations: "The most monstrous thing which the diseased human imagination ever created—the Jew-Jah theology and worship!" (122); "It [London] is gloomy, morose, huckstering, repulsive. Huge it is, like the English barbaric power; but incoherent, uninformed, unloved, without the beauty of refinement" (265).

191. Cummings to Pound

TLS-1.

dimanche [February 1949]   4 Patchin Place
                                                           New York City
                                                                11

Dear Ezra—

glad my book arrived all right.
Thanks for the stuffing!

I have small confidence in any
publisher's even intelligence
(taste being out of the question)
but will pass your suggestion
along

Marion sends love!

                        —sois sage

                eec

192. Cummings to Pound

TELEGRAM.

20 February 1949   New York

HEARTY CONGRATULATIONS TO CAPITALIST SYSTEM IN PARTICULAR
AND ANDREW MELLON IN GENERAL
                    MARION AND ESTLIN

CONGRATULATIONS: The award to Pound of the Bollingen Prize for Poetry was
   announced in the nation's newspapers on 20 February 1949.
MELLON: The Bollingen Foundation was funded by the Mellon family.

193. Pound to Cummings

ALS-1.

21 Feb[ruary 1949]   [Saint Elizabeths]

itz th last step that counts.
_____

        and now
ef I cd/ in'erest the
        lady an' gent
             in
             the
Constitution -- --

of course e.e.c's was bettern their'n more'n 3 yrs ago

                         yrz
                            Ez

e.e.c's: Perhaps the award Cummings won in 1944, the Shelley Memorial Award of
   the Poetry Society of America (Kennedy, 405).

194. Cummings to Pound

TLS-1.

mercredi [February 1949]   4 Patchin Place

Dear Ezra—

if I don't misunderstand your epistle to one a merry canny, it harbours a great compliment for myself. Thank you!

& what about "the" constitution?

Marion has often urged your h s to take a peep at G's c,& I've only 2 objections. Alpha's that you have to be pretty rich to escape radio—which does me in 3times quicker than everythingelse. Omega's that with a bumback you need good beds(not hard,not soft)& good means soft(as hard means bad)in ye shallwesay δημοκρατία [democracy]

let's not

—salut!

eec

G's c: God's country.

195. Pound to Cummings

TL-2. Enclosure.

[Postmarked 6 March 1949]   [Saint Elizabeths]

e/e/c

communique strictly ANONymous

FURthest from the utmost reach and bound of imaginable thought that the Kumrad shd/ suppose that io credesse that ANY physical displacement whatsodAM Wd/ be required

nay but rawther that the MIND leaping up and back thru the horrors already experienced, the waves underwhich already inundated the frail barque had wallowed

a companion wollum

1 (no "Blimey th' Limey," or other subject requiring exploration of the yet unsuffered and unpercolated)

BUT the native, the indiginous

(or howso yew spellit)

the since nativity circumvolent

etc/

shd/ purrived theme and HOW and detail and howtell

(documentation ?? waaal vid/ enc/ wich in so far as it concerns a pair of anarchists, may etc/ yr/ experience of the doctrinaire /

2

//

Now as to the BASIC issue/ wich bein' the ONLY barrier left between man and servitude/

THAT is (or wuz) procurable, ef I reemembur fer 10 cents, in a brochure adorend with Unc. S. is red and white striped breeches strapped under foot and a spangled (blanc on azure) weskit or vest

and ENTITLED "the making of murkns" or some such, information fer imigrants

OBVIOUSLY unused since original cover design wuz concocted.

Enclosure: Letter from Viola Baxter Jordan to Ezra Pound:

"e/e/c fer his archives" [Pound's comment.]

Mrs. V. S. B. Jordan
195 Jefferson Avenue
Tenafly, N. J.   Mar. 2-'49

Dear Ezra:

Re- Dachine Ranier "note by recipient WHICH SAME AND CONSORT bein anarchists" [Pound's comment.]

"Retort"

Bearsville, N.Y.

as much as I love and respect you dear Ezra I cannot further the aims of anything that smacks of communism or fascism by introducing this lady to my old friend Rachel at Oneida Community. I have written Miss Ranier that unless she is a foreigner she must know that complete information about Oneida Community can be found in any encyclopedia.

There are so many crack-pots getting out literature in America that I! in my little way, would like to discourage this and while they have a perfect right to say what they please I do not wish to "get on a soap-box to combat them, but am not willing to abet them unless I am sure they are for our government.

I do not wish to appear stuffy about this, but I wonder if you are aware that many of your visitors misrepresent themselves to you for instance Mr. Moore for whom you advised me to tune my piano, and he turned out to be nothing much of a musician.

Please do not feel hurt by my not wanting to help Miss Ranier enter the Oneida Community, harmless tho she may be, as from your note it appears she would like more than information, and it is wellknown how communists or fascists push their way into places where they would not be welcome if the truth were known about them.

I do not believe that you ever see a newspaper or hear the American Forum on the radio, so you may not be aware of the evils of communism or of fascism as they are practiced. It is all very well to view it in theory, but unless a theory works for the betterment of the human race and one sees HOW IT WORKS by ACTUAL LIVING, it is no good.

I am, dear Ezra still

Viola

Jordan: Pound first met Viola Baxter when he was a student at Hamilton College. He introduced her to William Carlos Williams. He also visited her at her home in New Jersey during his 1939 stay in the United States (see Conrad Baxter Jordan, "All the World's a Tennis Court," The *New York Times* [24 August 1985], 23). She wrote many letters (dated in the late 1940s) to Pound that are now at the Lilly Library. In them she sent family news as well as news about Bryher, H.D., Mary Barnard, and William Carlos Williams. She also sent Pound newspaper clippings, *Newsweek, Time,* and *Life and Letters.*

Ranier: Dachine Ranier and Holley Cantine were the proprieters of the Retort Press, which issued the magazine *Retort.* Ranier corresponded with Pound during the late 1940s and well into the 1950s about Pound's career, plans for publication, and mutual friends. Writing to Pound on 4 April 1955, she commented, "Greetings from the Cummings' (aren't they perfectly marvelous People?)"

Oneida Community: A utopian community founded in 1848 in upstate New York. By 1949, the Oneida Community had become a business corporation with considerably less emphasis on radical social reform. Yet it was still controlled in large part by descendants of the founders, and individual self-development and education were still important goals within the community. See Maren Lockwood Carden, *Oneida: Utopian Community to Modern Corporation* (Baltimore: Johns Hopkins University Press, 1969).

American Forum: The American Forum of the Air, a public affairs program heard over the Mutual Broadcasting System.

196. Cummings to Pound

TLS-1.

[Postmarked 11 March 1949]   4 Patchin Place

vendredi

Dear Ezra—

didn't find a copy of The Immigrant's Solace,but soothed myself with
proverbial reflections e.g. "times have changed"(immigrants nowadays being
Real Americans who visit this barbarous country to show its backward
denizens how they can begin civilizing each other)then I purchased a "World
Almanac" & am already deep in one-half of one paragraph of slightly more
than the very finest print which it has ever been my andsoforth to etcetera

glad our nonhero's excused from the beatitudinous vicissitudes of shallwesay
travel;& by the by have been taking notes on him(plus accidentally a
world)eversince ye olde milleniumbe struck oil;maybe they'll someday(after all
friends & enemies aren't)seem not unamusing to neither

—Xaipe

E

& thanks for your gift to my archives!

197. Pound to Cummings

ALS-2.

[Postmarked 14 March 1949]   [Saint Elizabeths]
                                              [illegible]

and what's posterity done fer you?
I want to read it now bein doubtful of post mortem capacity & that line
                    yrs
                          Ez

yr. mortician furnish Television attachment with one way suit?

luvv to the lady

Ez P

198. Pound to Cummings

ALS-1.

4 Ap[ril 1949]   S. Liz

An dont fergit to write to the Superintendent fer permission to get IN. do it
now

EzP

fer both of you
otherwise you'll be standin' in a KO

ridor

fer 43 minuts
   or
   Zummat

Superintendent: Dr. Winfred Overholser.

199. Cummings to Pound

ACS.

[Postmarked 11 April 1949]   4 Patchin Place
                                                 NYCity 11

glad you'd like to see my multifarious notes now—am going gradually over
them & may perhaps find something-or-other publishable

Estlin

200. Cummings to Pound

ALS-1.

[1949?]   [4 Patchin Place]

Samedi

Dear Ezra—

mayhap like the "chasseur" of Cocteau's Les Mariés, am now aiming (through "my" trusty agent) at a fifteen hundred dollar "advance." re one book of poems. Cautiously I now s-q-u-e-e-z-e the trigger . . . "Miss B" (I say) "please understand that this book does <u>not</u> contain 1500 poems." Have also explained to her that, since a dollar = 30 cents—in Greenwich Village, anyway—1500 $ would really equal 300 $ i.e. what Miss B thinks I might not impossibly receive. Perhaps she's touched by my financial ignorance; anyhow she has promised she'll do her best

when the cash comes tumbling downtown, Marion will line up our most "promising creditors" & give each something (no doubt a publisher reckons I should get all of 100 $; "times" being what they aren't). If both Marion and I survive this distribution, we'll promptly plot our Washington campaign: otherwise the one of us who does go to jail—assuming there's one—will comfort the other

                    —meanwhile, salut!
                              E

book: Probably *XAIPE* (New York: Oxford University Press, 1950) (Firmage A23).
Les Mariés: *Les Mariés de la Tour Eiffel* (1921) was a ballet with libretto by Jean
    Cocteau. One of its characters is an ostrich hunter.
Miss B: Bernice Baumgarten, Cummings's literary agent at Brandt and Brandt.

201. Pound to Cummings

TLS-1.

12 Ap[ril 1949]   [Saint Elizabeths]

Thazz vurry nize

———————————

& wot bout that visit to Wash'nton you were contemplatin zummat over 3 years ago?

I mean now the weather is spring er

202. Cummings to Pound

ACS.

[Postmarked 23 April 1949]   4 Patchin Place
                                                    NY City 11

certainly hope the lady and I'll be down this Spring to say hello (& glimpse a
few of artful Andy's pictures). What time of which day of the week would suit
yourself?

                                                    E

Andy's pictures: Andrew W. Mellon (1855–1937), American financier. He was
instrumental in founding the National Gallery of Art in Washington. At the
time of the museum's opening in 1941, half of the paintings in its inventory
were donations from Mellon's collection.

203. Marion Morehouse Cummings to Dorothy Pound

TELEGRAM.

26 May 1949   [4 Patchin Place]

DOROTHY POUND
3211 TENTH PL SOUTHEAST

CUMMINGS AND I WILL BE IN WASHINGTON MONDAY IF YOU CAN
ARRANGE FOR US TO SEE EZRA THEN I HAVENT YOUR PHONE
NUMBER SO WILL YOU PLEASE WIRE US OR PHONE OREGON 55374 IF
THIS IS POSSIBLE GREETINGS
                    MARION

204. Pound to Marion Morehouse Cummings

TELEGRAM.

27 May 1949   [Saint Elizabeths]

MARION CUMMINGS
4 PATCHIN PLACE

DELIGHTED MONDAY VISITING HOURS ONE TO FOUR

POUND

205. Pound to Cummings

ALS-2.

[30/31 May 1949]   [Saint Elizabeths]

point re/ the Pos O.M.
it aint done in malice - not envy fr/ inf/ cx/
it may be done fr/ caution
but purrwides a gentle spectacle fr/ the bee-holder

P.S. That wuz a nice gal you brung down here with you
P.P. S.   <u>choosdy.</u>
                                            S. Liz
sense of yr/ father's remarks poifikly CLEAR.
     =
germ of evil. etc. Roc used ?? as figger fer gigantic father of all cucoo's-
          BUT
be there some further licherary allusion.
Some blinkin' ⟨partikler⟩ Roc in legend unknown to undersigned.
                         EZ

D. completely carried by charm of the C. fambly.

The young R. Rees apparently fervid reader of Estlin

Pos O.M:. T. S. Eliot.
nice gal: Possibly Nancy Thayer Roosevelt, Cummings's daughter.
father's remarks: Presumably reported to Pound by Cummings during Cummings's visit to Saint Elizabeths.
R. Rees: Richard Rees, a young man who occasionally visited Pound at Saint Elizabeths.

206. Cummings to Pound

ALS-1.

[2 June 1949]   [4 Patchin Place]

vendredi

Dear Ezra—

Sorry I can't tell any more about the Roc than Sinbad. But this I can tell: you & Dorothy gave Marion & me an A1 time. We both of us heartily thank you each

—bonne Chance!!

EEC

(re rhyming Tom, de gustibus non)

rhyming Tom: T. S. Eliot.

207. Pound to Cummings

ALS-1.

4 June [1949]   S. Liz

yes, yes. Sinbad -
        forget detail if ever knew
    _____

as fer the other pt.
Thazz or'ig'
S'long as one aint sposed to <u>mistake</u> lemon-verbana
fer <u>chocolate</u>

homage to th' lady

EZ

defined in Webster or somdam dic:
Pound: an enclosure for strange ⟨? stray⟩ animals.

208. Cummings to Pound

ACS.

[9 June 1949]   4 Patchin Place
                                                NY City 11

up in New Hampshire we have a complete (18 vol) Burton's translation of
1001—shall consult it re Sinbad & inform you re Roc. I hope the hegeira may
occur in a week

                    Marion sends love to you <u>both</u>

                                                        E

Burton's translation: Sir Richard Francis Burton (1821–90), British explorer and
  orientalist. His version of the "Arabian Nights" was published as *The Thousand
  Nights and a Night* (1885–88).

209. Marion Morehouse Cummings to Dorothy Pound

ALS-1.

25 July - 49   Silver Lake, N.H.

Dear Dorothy -
                    Since I heard from OMar two weeks ago I've been
trying to write you but Cummings has been laid up again & I've not been able
to.
        I'm so glad you liked the pictures of Ezra & when I get back to my dark
room (we have no electricity up here, hence no dark room) I shall make you
some more. Naturally I shall keep the whole thing entre nous. So far I've
shown them only to Hugh Chisholm of the Bollingen Fund, who is a great
admirer of Ezra's.
        It was wonderful seeing Ezra & you & we'll come again in the fall.
        I hope he isn't too annoyed by the muck Hillyer has stirred up. He
always seemed such an innocuous person I should never have thought it of
him. Perhaps membership in Alcoholics A. has been responsible. Or perhaps
he's just been had.
        We send you both our love & hope you're bearing up under everything
including the weather.
                                        Affectionately
                                        Marion

pictures: Marion Cummings had photographed Pound during her and Cum-
  mings's visit to Saint Elizabeths in May.

Chisholm: Hugh Joseph Chisholm (1913–72), American poet and translator. Chisholm was an assistant editor with the Bollingen Foundation from 1947 to 1952.

Hillyer: Robert Silliman Hillyer (1895–1961), American poet and teacher. The "muck" consisted of two articles Hillyer wrote for the *Saturday Review of Literature:* "Treason's Strange Fruit: The Case of Ezra Pound and the Bollingen Award" (11 June 1949) and "Poetry's New Priesthood" (18 June 1949). In these articles Hillyer condemned Pound, the Fellows of the Library of Congress in American Letters (who had made the award), *The Pisan Cantos*, Carl Jung, T. S. Eliot, *Poetry*, and the New Critics.

210. Pound to Marion Morehouse Cummings

TL-1.

11 August 1949   [Saint Elizabeths]

Marion
            How stands the Kumrad? Does he remember whether that souplime line "Kill Leon Blum" is the the Aragon poEM he traduced and which was pubd/ in Activ Anthology?

Is he well enough to indulge in a l'il merriment?

Hasn't he at least one friend with enough information to git the flavour of news item whichwhat on page whatever of nooz gnotes in August Poetry (OF Chicago) p/ 308.

Has he copies of Blum's woiks?? (prob/ not.)

IS he proGressin' in that panoramiK survey of the occidental 1/2sphere ?????

that is wot matters.

[In Dorothy Pound's hand: "Cordialissmi. D.P. Omar writes very gayly from London.]

souplime line: The line in Cummings's translation is "Fire on Leon Blum" (*Complete Poems*, 885).

nooz gnotes: "The Anti-Poet All Told," *Poetry*, vol. 74, no. 5 (August 1949), by "H.C." (Hayden Carruth). Although Carruth remarks that Pound is an "overt fascist," he takes issue with Hillyer on every other count. In the middle of his essay, Carruth argues that "Whatever the outcome of the Ezra Pound case, and certainly it is difficult to defend him on any but the narrow grounds of service to his craft, the enemies of poetry must not be allowed to damage the process of our art through untoward wrath. No one can tell what the progress of poetry will be, though editors, in their small shrewdness, may try to guess. But certainly the poets of the future will take into account the poetic achievement of our time. Many generations will pass before a young poet can overlook the work of Ezra Pound; only by understanding it and using it—or perhaps knowingly discarding it—will the poet of the future be able to acknowledge his calling intelligently and properly" (280). At the end of his essay, under the title "A Few Notes on the Recent Essays of Mr. Robert Hillyer," Carruth offers a point-by-point refutation of Hillyer's arguments.

panoramiK survey: Pound hoped Cummings would write an account of the United States equivalent to *Eimi.*

211. Cummings to Pound

TLS-1.

August 23 1949   Silver Lake

Dear Ezra—

I am becalmed

at present,prose(or anyhow mine)seems worthless:poetry alone matters—in painting & otherwhere. I spent several months persuading(espérons)71 poems to make 1 book who calls himself Xaîpe. Now et comment The quote Oxford unquote Press registers alarm nudging horror;poems are nonsellable enough(paraît)without calling the poembook by some foreign word which no Good-American could either spell or pronounce

thanks to Dorothy & yourself,Marion & I've enjoyed a defence of poetry(in a periodical of that name)by HC:clearly a nice chap. Kel woild

the Master Of Absolute Zero lunged over il-y-a-quelques-jours riding his firebrandnew jeep. "Everything in physics" he remarked daintily "now points to an act of creation—a couple of billion years ago. And since all matter was then at one point,it"(matter)"must have existed in the form of light. All you can say is:Light WAS." "Sounds like the Bible" Marion(after a pause)suggested gently. "Exactly" he pleasantly agreed

if a soon-arriving photograph of my little picture of Omar's head should happen to remind his mother of him,the painting's hers. But if not,I shan't feel sad;or even disgraced. So may she please speak with the frankness of friendship

Marion sends love to you each

—here's to a breeze!

EEC

defence of poetry: See the note to the previous letter.
Master: Donald Hatch Andrews.

212. Pound to Cummings

TL-1.

[August 1949]   [Saint Elizabeths]

estlin reginaque

yes, but the goddam H.C. (ef yew meen Cruth, Crullers or wotever, is still iggurunt / and Mercure de Frawg, and three wop papers of DIFFERENT colours shd/ begin to make some headway.
          "He wuz NEVER a puppygandist in pay ov furrin powwer." etc.

Mercure de Frawg: Jacques Vallette, in a review of the *Cantos* and the *Pisan Cantos* (*Mercure de France,* vol. 305, no. 1025 [1 January 1949], 160–63), had re-marked, "Pound, qui était en politique devenu fasciste, a bel et bien trahi pendant la guerre en parlant pour la radio ennemie, et n'a échappé à la prison que grâce à l'asile de fous. Cette circonstance ne doit pas influer sur la considér-ation de sa poésie" [Pound, who had become a fascist in politics, and very thoroughly betrayed (his country) during the war by speaking on the enemy radio, only escaped prison by slipping into an insane asylum. These facts should not influence any critique of his poetry]. Subsequently, in the *Mercure de France* for 1 April 1949, 764–65, the editors published letters from Dorothy Pound and from the London law firm representing Pound, Shakespear and Parkyn. Doro-thy's letter began, "Non, Monsieur, Ezra Pound n'a trahi personne" [No, sir, Ezra Pound has not betrayed anyone]. Shakespear and Parkyn noted that "Ezra Pound *n'a pas* été condamné pour trahison" [Ezra Pound *was never* convicted of treason].

three wop papers: Pound may refer to the following items: (1) Eugenio Montale, "Fronde d'alloro in un manicomio," *Corriere della Sera* (Milan), 3 March 1949, 3; (2) Mario Boccassini, "Letteratura e politica," *Giornale* (Naples), 23 July 1949, 3; (3) Giambattista Vicari, "Vive in un manicomio il più celebre poeta americano," *Lettere d'Oggi* (Rome), 4 August 1949, 35. Massimo Bacigalupo's English translation of the Montale article, "Laurel Fronds in an Insane Asylum," appears in *Paideuma,* vol. 13, no. 1 (spring 1984), 58–61.

213. Pound to Cummings

ALS-1.

31 Aug[ust 1949]   S. Liz

In vich poem of Mr Kumminkz's do one find the lines

> white skoited noises
> driving Rolls-Royces

?

                          EZ

214. Cummings to Pound

TCS.

[Postmarked 5 September 1949]   SilverLake, NH

where did you ever see that couplet about "noises" & "-Royces"?

I certainly don't recall perpetrating it;but am willing to admit that unmemory
may deceive

                          —love from regina!

                                        EEC

215. Pound to Cummings

TL-1.

[1949?]   [Saint Elizabeths]

WHEN the directum of Nude non-erections had the horrse sense to ask the
advice of the Rev/mo Kumrad re/ wot eee shd/ print.
           The Rev. kumrad bein too pure to soil his mits

NEVERtheloose miss'd a opportunity, i.e. with no labour to celf or conjunx, he
(the KuMRD) cd/ hv/ told the Jas/ to DO WOT Ez tell him,
                    and not goddamit to waste four years gittin orf the
mark.

Well, now four years are eloopsed, but even now the advice could be useful.
                    Let the KMRD beat his hairy chest, spend 3 c/ on
pustage, and TELL the Jas/ to listen to Ez, with BOTH ears if/and/or/when he
ever sees him again.

ever hear the one about Yaets an Sargent (or however he spellt it*?
        OV cuss EF the KUMD knows, or of, any to WHUMM the Jas/ cd/ listen
with BETTER etc.
                            dew tell us, cause we air in darnKness. but
willin, hellYES, to larn n reejoyce.

and dont tell Jas/ I putt yew up to it, if you up.
I take it I warnt in the kountry when he axd yuh. ennyhaow.

directum: James Laughlin.
Yaets an Sargent: John Singer Sargent (1856–1925), American painter. Pound
    never does reveal the nature of the anecdote. Sargent did Yeats's portrait in
    March–April 1908.

216. Cummings to Pound

TL-1.

September 23 1949   Silver Lake
                                         New Hampshire

Copy

Dear Laughlin—

there's one poet you publish;and he's
very young—the youngest(am certain,
rereading Personae)alive

                            —congratulations

217. Pound to Cummings

ALS-1.

[October 1949]   [Saint Elizabeths]

                            P. 1

all v. well bt <u>not</u> the point.

ag-
gen-
dum (B)
↑
ppb
(even if c. wants to   EP
                        [v]
                         e
                         r
                         s
                         o

grafik awts

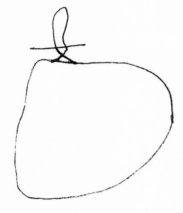

no
I fall down on
repprezentashn.
Try again

218. Cummings to Pound

TCS.

[Postmarked 12 October 1949]   [4 Patchin Place]

Can't make out the illustration—or what is it?

                                eec

[Note in Pound's hand on card: "EP attempt to draw biberon -- nutrition or
containr fer <u>very</u> young." An undated subsequent note from Dorothy Pound to
Cummings repeated Pound's note: "E's attempt to draw biberon - nutrition or
container for <u>very</u> young."]

biberon: The *NOED* defines this as "A drinking-vessel with elongated spout, formerly used by travellers, invalids and children."

219. Pound to Cummings

ALS-2.

30 Oct[ober 1949]   [Saint Elizabeths]
Yes . my dears -- but the trouble is that I hv. friends who cd/ <u>USE</u> the
wherewith. & a p.c. (no not perlite constable) poscar wd. hv. conveyed the 'eart
beetz.
benedictio̊ns.
                    EZ

as fer yewth . . ⟨(to return to earlier communque [Here Pound drew another
picture of the "biberon."]⟩ yew orter see wot my pubr./ swallows

───────────────────────────────────

you aint by any mean confusin' young & immature ???

220. Pound to Cummings

ALS-1.

[November 1949]   S Liz

By 't way
wot ever bekum of Eastman 'n' awl 'iz bewteeful which what?

───────────────────────────────

Luv to a lady
                    EZ

221. Cummings to Pound

TC.

[Postmarked 13 November 1949]   4PatchinPlace NYCity

why,Max has for ten(or something)years been a "roving editor"* of Readers
Digest;maybe there's an apostrophe?

                              eec

*& a "Black" Republican

"Black" Republican: See the note to letter 138.

222. Pound to Cummings

TLS-1.

[November 1949]   [Saint Elizabeths]

e.e.c.

waaaaaal en thet kase Max cd/ redeem his past shallwe callUm "errors".
item. It seems that when they bust the Dresden Library the water
got into the vaults where they had bombproof'd Vivaldi's ms/ so thet whether
the bgsrs LIKE EZ's potry or not, they is damwell INDEBTED to Ez. fer saving
about 40 concerti of sd/ composer in microfilm, from which the Acad. Chig. is
now pub/ng 'em. And the woptalian press beink perlite.
                                    This is by now Digest stuff pollyanna ⟨et
sim/⟩ and if Max has any good will left in his carcass, he cd. git the details
from Olga Rudge, Accademia Chigiana, SIENA and use 'em fer the increase of
human reputation, i.e. recognizin that Ez wd/ be more use OUT of bughouse
than in. let by gones by byegones.

Keynes' nevvy in yester, admitted, or rather answered queery. His unkl, acc the
nevvy, did not die happy. Nevvy surprised that I knew K/ and had tried to
make a honest man of him.

Some of them concerti is DAMfine, I know cause I rejuiced as I member about
20 fer Vyolin and PYanny, and most of 'em inedit altogether, and them as
printed needin verification by what Viv. actually left on paper.

Max might also git some fun kickin the stuffing out of Chris Hollis' "Can
parliament survive." The Kumrad will preciate Mr Hollis' dicTUM: "Somehow
or other we hv/ got to remake Man - to reshape him so that he can become
integrated into this new world of larger units.*

*uNITS, not yu nuts

[The following is in Dorothy Pound's hand.]
Saluti cordiali
        Omar was staying in Paris chez friends.
        Hope he is getting civilized.
                                    D.P.

Dresden: In 1938, Pound had ordered microfilm copies of Vivaldi musical manuscripts from the Sächsische Landesbibliothek in Dresden. Dresden was bombed on 13–14 February 1945, resulting in tremendous destruction and loss of life.

Keynes' nevvy: John Maynard Keynes (1883–1946), British economist. Pound may refer to Quentin Keynes, the son of Geoffrey Keynes. Quentin Keynes had been stationed in Washington, D.C., during World War II.

Chris Hollis': Christopher Hollis (1902–77), British political writer. Hollis contended that the source of modern economic and political problems was that until recently mankind had been accustomed to living in "small units," such as the village and the family. These small units, however, had been weakened by developments in production and technology. "It is clear," Hollis says, "that Man, as he is presently constituted, is not a creature who can feel at home in the modern world, and in his disintegration he is rapidly turning the world into a vast lunatic asylum. He was made for the world of small units and he does not feel that he belongs to the world of large units. Somehow or other we have got to remake Man—to reshape him so that he can become integrated into the new world of the larger units." *Can Parliament Survive?* (London: World Affairs Book Club, 1950), 5.

223. Cummings to Pound

TC.

[Postmarked 19 November 1949]   4PatchinPlace NYCity 11

delighted Omar's enjoying himself
have sent Max your V letter
greetings to D
Xaîpe

Omar's enjoying: Omar Pound sent a postcard (dated 12 October 1949) from London to Marion and E. E. Cummings. In it he mentioned his "wonderful holiday in & around England."

V letter: Pound's letter about Vivaldi. During World War II, "V-Mail" referred to airmail letters ("V-Letters") sent by servicemen. The *V* stood for "Victory."

224. Cummings to Pound

CHRISTMAS CARD.

[December 1949]   [4 Patchin Place]

[Drawing by Cummings of a charging elephant. The elephant holds in its trunk a staff with a banner. On the banner are the words "Merry Christmas."]

to Ezra & Dorothy
from Estlin & Marion

!
& a happy new year
!

225. Pound to Cummings

TLS-2.

[December 1949]   [Saint Elizabeths]

reading- matter   PAUSE   cannot recollect having mentioned this kind of
matter (le'rLONE recommending USE of, to or by kumrad et conjunx. Point:
de Angulo has produced some.

GUARANTEE not to be attemptin to improve mind or character, le'rLONE
deVilUp civic sense of (k et c as above) that bein THE most irritatin habit of
participant.

waaal naow, frum wotiKinsee, the easiest way wd/ be fer me to transmit same
by post (EF the kumrad purr-mitts) and hv/ some suitable pussn call an git it
after decent interval.

kumrad's function: enjoyment if possible.

nacherly as participant never does anyfink without ulterior, he wantz ter kno
ef/ kumrad knowz who tell is now runnin Harcourt Brash, ? but that aint
required in answer by p.c. ef/ the kumrad is willin to risk 45 minutes
enjoyment.

Jaime d A/ also just writ a poEM, but wont send that.

[In Dorothy Pound's handwriting] Cordiali D.P.
P.S.
continuing regret that can never MOVE th Kumrad to song.
Time for a ballad of
          Winnie and Weenie were Roosies,
          Lord, how they did OOOZE.

feel it beyond my poWWWever.
but wd/ admire fer to see it kumradly treated.

[In Dorothy Pound's hand] My father's old chestnut - "Thanks for your book, which I shall lose no time in reading". Cordialissimi. only handled the new vol. today: read presently. D.P.

de Angulo: Jaime de Angulo (1887–1950), French-born (of Spanish parents), American anthropologist, linguist, and novelist. De Angulo studied and wrote about the culture of the Pit River Indians of California. See Lee Bartlett, "The Pound/De Angulo Connection," *Paideuma*, vol. 14, no. 1 (spring 1985), 53–77.

Winnie and Weenie: Winston Churchill and Felix Frankfurter. The term "weenie" for Frankfurter was apparently coined by Westbrook Pegler. *Weenie* is an American slang term derived from "Wiener Wurst." In the United States a *wiener* is a frankfurter. Furthermore, Frankfurter was born in Vienna.

226. Dorothy Pound to Cummings

ALS-1.

Dec. 23. [1949]   [Washington, D.C.]

Elefunt fetched up duly. Certainly most spirited! Thanks . .

Please hold the de Angulo Indian Stuff - do <u>not</u> return here. We will send somebody to carry it away - save you posting (pardonme, mailing). Its next destination is in N.Y. I thought EP. had explained this - sorry -

Flemings just produced the enclosed - obviously for you.

Cordialissimi

D.P.

de Angulo: Manuscript material by de Angulo in Pound's possession.

Flemings: Rudd and Polly Fleming, a husband and wife who visited Pound frequently. The Flemings taught at the Institute of Contemporary Arts in Washington. Later, Rudd Fleming became a Professor of English at the University of Maryland. Enclosure lacking.

227. Pound to Cummings

ACS.

23 [December 1949]   [Saint Elizabeths]

Diy	Recd one	did yu git
S	effelunt	the
L	in axshun	J. d. A
I	apparently	ms ?
Z	unrstraind	

Did you know the O.M. also "arms he beareth
                                    one
                                    efelunt" ??

There pts of unexpctd artect
staid of course not paisant furious

reciprocal auguriez
                    EZ

O.M.: T. S. Eliot, who had been awarded the Order of Merit in January 1948. The
reference is to the coat of arms of the Elyot/Eliot family. "He beareth argent a
Fesse Gules between two Barrs-Gewelles wavy Sable, Crest: an Elephant's head
Sable, by the Name of Eliot." Charles Knowles Bolton, *Bolton's American Ar-
mory* (Boston: F. W. Faxon Company, 1927), 55.

228. Cummings to Dorothy Pound

ACS.

[December 1949]   [4 Patchin Place NYC 11]

thanks for your lively letter; also for ep's even exceptionally pc. Am enjoying
the Indian stories, which will (as you request) hold. Happiest of New Years to
you both from Marion & me

                              eec

229. Dorothy Pound to Cummings

ALS-1.

Jan. 1. [1950]   [Washington, D.C.]

All the best to you & Marion. E. Would be pleased to know whether either of
you like the de Angulo? & please notify us when you are through - and it will
be removed.

Cordiali --
D.P.

230. Cummings to Pound

TL-1.

January 6 1950   [4 Patchin Place]

Dear Ezra—

strictly entre nous, since one of my innumerable sins isnt "criticism", I do like
the Indian Stories(which please collect when you wish)nonwriting plus
unspelling aside. If asked pourquoi, might perhaps answer: not only because
they are sometimes—E.G. Bear's address to his surroundingsbefore before
going-byebye-- poetic, mais parceque the feeling of the narrative as a whole is
open-cheerful- natural-human-&otherwise genuine; so that a child like our
heroless marvels "why can,t the soidisant civilized world world ever(instead of
always hating & doubting & fearing)be herself? why havethe children of men
lost their courtesy & courage,their divine sense of humor, their miraculous gift
of affection, et surtout their generosity:en somme,their(to speak the one
word)imagination? Marion agrees with me.

—Xaipe

e

Bear's address: See *Indian Tales: Written and Illustrated by Jaime De Angulo, with a
foreword by Carl Carmer* (New York: A. A. Wyn, 1953), 12. "Then Bear called,
'Good night, Mountains, you must protect us tonight. We are strangers but we
are good people. We don't mean harm to anybody. Good night, Mister Pine
Tree. We are camping under you. You must protect us tonight. Good night,
Mister Owl. I guess this is your home where we are camped. We are good

people, we are not looking for trouble, we are just traveling. Good night, Chief Rattlesnake. Good night, everyone. Good night, Grass People, we have spread our bed on top of you. Good night, Ground, we are lying right on your face. You must take care of us, we want to live a long time.'"

231. Pound to Cummings

ACS.

[Postmarked 10 January 1950]   [Saint Elizabeths]

an ten teh one yu nevr red H. A Giles (trans) "Strang Stories fr/ a Chinese Studio" either. yrz

marions pin sign not in my dic. unless copied it wrong
salut to m

if she wants to send another copy I'll look again

yrZ

[Pound concluded his postcard with a Chinese character, "Jing," which means "respect" (as a noun) or "salute" (as a verb). Pound would have seen it in the Confucian classics.]

Strang Stories: *Strange Stories from a Chinese Studio: Translated and Annotated by Herbert A. Giles, of H.M.'s Consular Service,* 2 vols. (London: Thomas De La Rue, 1880). In his introduction, Giles notes that "Much of what the Chinese do actually believe and practise in their religious and social life will be found in this volume, in the *ipsissima verba* of a highly educated scholar writing about his fellow-countrymen and his native land. . . . The barest skeleton of a biography is all that can be formed from the very scanty materials which remain to mark the career of a writer whose work has been for the best part of two centuries as familiar through the length of China as are the tales of the 'Arabian Nights' in all English-speaking communities. The author of 'Strange Stories' was a native of Tzu-chou, in the province of Shan-tung. His family name was P'u; his particular name was Sung-ling; and the designation or literary epithet by which, in accordance with Chinese usage, he was commonly known among his friends, was Liu-hsien, or 'Last of the Immortals.'" The "strangeness" of the tales Giles translated lies in their subject matter: human encounters with fantastic, magical, or supernatural beings. Some of the titles of the stories in the collection are

"His Father's Ghost," "The Performing Mice," "The Sea-serpent," "The Thunder God," "A Supernatural Wife," and "The Magic Sword."
pin sign: Apparently Marion Cummings owned a pin on which appeared a Chinese character.

232. Cummings to Pound

TC.

[Postmarked 13 January 1950]   [4 Patchin Place]

ah reck-in yu-o srite-bowd
oal-mars gulyz

Marion will try to photograph
the pin

gulyz: H. A. Giles.

233. Cummings to Pound

ACS.

[Postmarked 16 January 1950]   [4 Patchin Place]

M B very pleasant
& the frescoes are
marvellous

                    eec

M B: Mary Barnard (b. 1909), American poet. She had tea with Estlin and Marion
Cummings on 15 January. She had been working on a projected book—a guide
to Italian frescoes—and had taken with her to Patchin Place a "book on the
Schifanoia frescoes that Pound had lent me." Mary Barnard, *Assault on Mount
Helicon: A Literary Memoir* (Berkeley and Los Angeles: University of California
Press, 1984), 272. The Palazzo Schifanoia is in Ferrara. The frescoes were the
work of Cosimo Tura (ca. 1430–95), Ercole de' Roberti, and Francesco del
Cossa. Pound alludes to the frescoes in Canto 77.

234. Pound to Cummings

TL-1.

[Early 1950?]   [Saint Elizabeths]

HAZ
     the kumrd even got a pipSqueak out of Max?
HAZ th k/d ever considered socialists,i.e. as to their virchoos up to a point,
and the (well az in kase of type-ikal speckImen like Up. Sinc. the way they stop
having 'em at a çoitn
          point???***
HAZ th kum/d read or seen Giraudoux' LA FOLLE DE CHAILLOT
       nif not, wy not? and did it cause any stir or iz it wholly sunk?
          (not readin the sewage weekly I can't tell if it had.)
          Of course no çoitn indication that the k/d ever does read
ANYthing
           that is part of my noneofmyDAMbiz but hatin the
process of pickin blak combs offn paper I sometimes wunner how

strikin me that the Folle de C/ is easier readin than some of the noised, and
mebbe th second war started G/ usin his noddle (up to er point)

―――――

ft-nut
***it bein 36 ears since Ez. did a lil spiel wot he forgot an considered OUT, till
he come back ("come" beink a euphuism) to this here kuntinong.

AND so forth, luv to th LADY

Max: Max Eastman.
Giradoux': Jean Giraudoux (1882–1944), French novelist, poet, and playwright.
   His play, *La folle de Chaillot* (1944), was translated and performed in New York
   in December 1948.
spiel: Possibly one of the short plays Pound wrote in 1916. See *Plays Modelled on
   the Noh (1916)*, ed. Donald Gallup (Toledo, Ohio: Friends of the University of
   Toledo Libraries, 1987).

235. Pound to Cummings

ALS-1.

[March? 1950]   [Saint Elizabeths]
Wot?
        "a teacher @ Haaavud - "
I tho't that wuzze
        oxymoron
(if that's wot it means)
any how a not is.

& as fer p. 46

                              tut

                              tut

than   o
wot I mean by "tut

                   tut"

                              iz

? aint you bustin' into
J Joyce's territory?

                    EP

teacher @ Haaavud: Cummings's collection of poems *Xaipe*, published on 30
   March 1950 by the Oxford University Press, had a dustjacket stating that Cum-
   mings had taught at Harvard University.
p. 46: Poem 46 in *Xaipe:* "a kike is the most dangerous." Some readers considered
   it anti-Semitic. For a discussion of the poem and the controversy it aroused see
   Kennedy, 431–34. *Complete Poems,* 644.

236. Cummings to Pound

CARBON

March 7 [1950]   4 Patchin

Cher cropper—

"collage" is exactly it. Now I know just why je loathe

have writ Eva(dost hear yapping!bloodhounds on-thin-ice?)giving your
Washington address;in case she should "care to write"

Marion,whose birthday this is,sends love to you & Dorothy

                                —moi o see

please greet Omar on our behalf when next either of you puts plume to
woodpulp

"collage": In a letter postmarked 5 March 1950, to Marion Morehouse Cum-
mings, Pound had said, "Hope yu noticd ole Wm Walruss's artesian dwelling in
his ult/ that is, I mean IS a collage." Pound was referring to William Carlos
Williams's inclusion in book 3 of *Paterson* of a report on the geological sub-
strata of Paterson, New Jersey.
Eva: Eva Hesse. See the note to letter 242.

237. Pound to Cummings

ALS-1.

27 Mz [March 1950]   S Liz

I meditate: Is this a cry of alarm - ?

_____

when I remember the horrible shock rec'd @ the Kumradz door one day in '39
- when another of 'em opened it.

_____

Iz this a cry of liberation (p. 46) A awakening after long somnolence or wottell
??

                        Benedictions   EZ

another: David Diamond.

238. Cummings to Pound

TL-1.

[March 1950]   [4 Patchin Place]

            TO WHOM IT MAY CONCERN

herewith a paraphrase of XAIPE,poem 46—
        the menacing aspect of "Americanization" appears
        most clearly not in the case of the Irishman who
        is transformed into a "mick" or of the Italian

who turns into a "wop" (etc etc) but of the Jew who
becomes a "kike"

compare my Collected Poems,258—
    to kiss the mike if Jew turn kike
    who dares to call himself a man?

for a portrait of a Jew As Is,see poem 36 of 50 Poems
                    E.E.Cummings

258: Poem 54 of *No Thanks,* "Jehovah buried,Satan dead" (*Complete Poems,* 438).
poem 36: "i say no world" (*Complete Poems,* 523).

239. Pound to Cummings

ALS-1.

1 Ap. [1950]   S. Liz

(but not s'ni'blikly)

_____

wuz in NO doubt az to the meaning.

        _____

nor of the purity ov th Kumradz heart

                            EZ

P.S. am inclined to agree with his analysis of the sizuashun

240. Pound to Cummings

ALS-1.

Ap[ril] 2 or 3 [1950]   [Saint Elizabeths]

Standard works of reference to which yu refer R, alas, in Rap. unless been
liberated =
I take it prototype iz: "which they deserve"

_____

was other obsvn but cant recall it

_____

Wotever becom ov that cheerful guy blew in on his way to a fancy dress party?
When we wer all <u>SO</u> much younger.

Dear M.
Sorry can never git the K—rd to 'preciate that poEM address'd to Mrs
Barbauld beginning
"Sieze, Sieze (or seize) the lyre,
resume the lofty strain)

luv to the lady

              EzP

ever hear of a bloke call'd Del Mar?

cheerful guy: Perhaps Cummings himself.
poEM: The poem is by Mrs. Barbauld's brother, Dr. John Aikin (1747–1822).

> Thus speaks the Muse, and bends her brows severe:—
> "Did I, Laetitia, lend my choicest lays,
> And crown thy youthful head with freshest bays,
> That all the expectance of thy full-grown year
> Should lie inert and fruitless? O revere
> Those sacred gifts whose meed is deathless praise,
> Whose potent charms the enraptured soul can raise
> Far from the vapours of this earthly sphere!
> Seize, seize the lyre! resume the lofty strain!
> 'T is time, 't is time! hark how the nations round
> With jocund notes of liberty resound,—
> And thy own Corsica has burst her chain!
> O let the song to Britain's shores rebound,
> Where Freedom's once-loved voice is heard, alas! in vain."

The Works of Anna Letitia Barbauld, with a Memoir by Lucy Aikin, 2 vols.
(London: Richard Taylor, 1825), 1:xxxv.
Mrs Barbauld: Anna Letitia Barbauld (1743–1825), British poet and novelist.
Del Mar: Alexander Del Mar (1836–1926), American economic and monetary
historian. Pound thought Del Mar's writings on the history of money highly
important. See Daniel Pearlman, "Alexander Del Mar in *The Cantos:* A Printout
of the Sources," *Paideuma*, vol. 1, no. 2 (fall–winter 1972), 161–80.

241. Cummings to Pound

TL-1.

[13 April 1950]   [4 Patchin Place]

Sah—

two ?s

first:re your recent queery regarding "that cheeful guy blew in on his way to a fancy dress party",I don't recall the incident. Where we "we"(who "wer all <u>SO</u> much younger")at dit time?

second:who wrote "Sieze,sieze the lyre"? Believe it or don't,was surprised to find that said line didn't adorn Alexander's Feast by your Marsupial's Mentor

up with up

       --.

           treize avril 50

Alexander's Feast: A poem (1697) by John Dryden.
Marsupial's: T. S. Eliot. He wrote an appreciative essay, "John Dryden" (1922), concluding, "He remains one of those who have set standards for English verse which it is desperate to ignore."
Mentor: John Dryden.

242. Pound to Cummings

TL-2.

[April 1950]   [Saint Elizabeths]

the KUMRD/ and konsort.
Speakin ov little Evaaa,
     an there'zwun more iceFlow to cross
one wide, or
mebbe more, etc.
             I knu
our goddam uniWORSTities stank, but did not kno they stank quite so RANK.
made eggskwzes fer pore profs in i902 not knowin Brooks Ad/

BUTT here is a guy named Del Mar, printing from 1880-1900
    wot I n yu an nobuddy wd/ hv/ heerd tell on ef I hadn't wanned to see
more into Mr Agassiz sunfish an Ag/ ref/ Humbolt, and Humbolt printed wiff
a pamPHLET by Grimaudet wiff a feetnut.

an here iz 3o vol/ of ole Del / in the Cong.Bib.

wot th Kumrad can ⟨find⟩ if he KAN
startin with "Barbara Villiers"

                                                cause he dont like heavy readin.
N. Anyhow, ask Eva if the huns translated Del M̄/
B. cause they might hv/ not bein so DUMB
    as the yanko-brits
occupation fer some kind hun, if he can escape the gestapo while he Za doin it.

the stinkin iggurunce wot we wuz filled wiff
in youth
aint got no alibi fer the fillers

an donCHU fergit it.

besides, so few bks ARE readin matter
an it ⟨is⟩ pleasant to see these bores sat down on their b(oms

an ef I evur dun tole you wrong
        please KOrekt me.

I mean I am anxshus fer data/
                                  ef you recall me dun tellin yu wrong, yu
TELL me.

P.P.S. yaaaas I notiz yr/ pos'age stump/
    I seeNumB before
also one with Jim Blaine on it

await one with twin wreathes   Dewey an Lucky Luciano
they flourish like a greenBAY
      Horse's a

an speaking of . . .
            yu might reread CANTO XXXVII

Tvipp no further, pretty sweeting,
Vouldt yu lige to attend a meeting?

Evaaa: Eva Hesse, German scholar and translator. Cummings had sent Pound a letter from Hesse to Cummings (dated 26 March 1950) and a translation by Hesse of Cummings's poem, "Love is more thicker than forget" (*Complete Poems*, 530). In her letter, Hesse said, "I was very glad to hear that it is now possible to communicate with Ezra Pound, and I shall certainly write him soon."

Brooks Ad/: Brooks Adams.

Mr Agassiz sunfish: Pound retold the story of the sunfish at the beginning of his *ABC of Reading* (London: George Routledge and Sons, 1934; New York, New Directions, 1960). In 1950 Pound may have looked for more information on Agassiz in Lane Cooper's *Louis Agassiz as a Teacher: Illustrative Extracts on His Method of Instruction* (1917; Ithaca, N.Y.: Comstock Publishing, 1945). On page 81 of this edition, under "Obiter Dicta by Agassiz," appears this statement, "Broad knowledge of all nature has been the possession of no naturalist except Humboldt, and general relations constituted his specialty."

Humbolt: Baron Alexander von Humboldt (1769–1859), German naturalist. Pound refers to *The Fluctuations of Gold*, trans. William Maude (1900; New York: Burt Franklin, 1971). The volume also includes a translation of *The Law of Payment* by Francois Grimaudet (1520–80). In his introduction to these two treatises, Maude notes that "The four great aera-making books on the subject of the Precious Metals were those of William Jacob, 1831, Baron Alex. von Humboldt, 1838, Michel Chevalier, 1857, and Alex. Del Mar, 1880 and (2d ed.) 1900." In a footnote to *The Law of Payment*, Maude cites Del Mar. "Something more is intended to be conveyed by the Roman expression stabilitas applied to money than what is usually supposed. All commodities are in fact consumed, or else are necessary or applied for the purpose of consumption. Money is not intended for consumption; money is not consumed, nor is it necessary or applied for the purposes of consumption. It is intended to remain fixed, constant and stable. Hence the term stabilitas when applied to money is of great and peculiar significance and was evidently derived from the Roman law of the Commonwealth before the conquest of Spain, when money was indeed stable and not subject to augmentation or diminution, as it was afterwards, with every vicissitude of war, discovery and mining. The sole function of money is to measure the equivalents of commodities when offered in exchange so as to facilitate such exchange. In order that it may exercise this function in the most perfect manner its symbols should not be made of any material that can be profitably employed for the purposes of consumption, because in such case it cannot be made a stable measure. The Spartans learnt this lesson more than twenty-five centuries ago; the Athenians, Ionians, Byzantines and Romans all learnt and practiced it afterwards; but the Conquest of Spain effaced the lesson and Caesar blotted it out altogether by substituting METAL in the place of NUMBERS (for such is the meaning of nummi) for money, just as he substituted himself in the place of Jupiter, as a Deity whom all mankind was compelled to worship under the penalties prescribed for crimen laesae majestatis divinae."

"Barbara Villiers": Del Mar's *Barbara Villiers; or, a History of Monetary Crimes* (1899) was reprinted as part of the Square Dollar Series by the Cleaners' Press in Washington, D.C., in 1951: *A History of Monetary Crimes: A Faithful Copy of the Edition of 1899 Entitled Barbara Villiers; or, A History of Monetary Crimes.* Del Mar's book traces modern monetary crimes (specifically private parties' usurpation of the state's right to regulate coinage) to British coinage legislation of 1666–67. At that time, he alleges, backers of the East India Company connived with Barbara Villiers, the mistress of Charles II, to gain special coining privileges for themselves. Del Mar goes on in other chapters to consider "The Crime of 1742," "The Crime of 1868," "The Crime of 1870," and "The Crime of 1873."

pos'age stump: Envelope lacking.

Blaine: James G. Blaine (1830–93), American statesman and Republican Party nominee for president in 1884.

Dewey: Thomas E. Dewey (1902–71), Republican Party nominee for president in 1944 and 1948.

Lucky Luciano: Charles Luciano (1896–62). Born Salvatore Lucassia in Sicily, he emigrated to America and became a leading figure in organized crime during the 1930s and 1940s. He was jailed in 1936, thanks to a successful prosecution carried out by Thomas E. Dewey. Luciano was deported to Italy in 1946.

CANTO XXXVII: A canto about Martin Van Buren and the end of the Second Bank of the United States.

243. Pound to Cummings

ALS-2.

14 Ap[ril 1950]   S Liz

I dunno who writ it. but it wuz addressed to Mrs Letitzia (or however yu spellit) Ann Barbauld & is retrievable in a prob/y unretrievable edtn of her works -- (introd sexshn) I fink SHE emitted the eu(u !!)phonic line:

"On Chimborazzo's summitz
         TreadZZZ Zsublime."

bless yr consort
         evuh devtly

                          EzP

An don't go mixin' that Chimboratzo's zummitts
with them
Slaughterd saintz whooz
                    bones

who writ it: See the note to letter 240.

eu(u !!)phonic line: Mrs. Barbauld's poem, "Eighteen Hundred and Eleven," is
about the westward movement of the Genius of civilization. At the end of the
poem she predicts his abandonment of Europe.

> For see,—to other climes the Genius soars,
> He turns from Europe's desolated shores;
> And lo, even now, midst mountains wrapt in storm,
> On Andes' heights he shrouds his awful form;
> On Chimborazo's summits treads sublime,
> Measuring in lofty thought the march of Time;
> Sudden he calls:—" 'Tis now the hour!" he cries,
> Spreads his broad hand, and bids the nations rise.
> La Plata hears amidst her torrents' roar;
> Potosi hears it, as she digs the ore:
> Ardent, the Genius fans the noble strife,
> And pours through feeble souls a higher life,
> Shouts to the mingled tribes from sea to sea,
> And swears—Thy world, Columbus, shall be free.

The Poems of Anna Letitia Barbauld, ed. William McCarthy and Elizabeth Kraft
(Athens: University of Georgia Press, 1994), 161.

Slaughterd saintz: See John Milton's Sonnet, "On the Late Massacre in Piemont,"
line 1: "Avenge, O Lord, thy slaughter'd Saints, whose bones[.]"

244. Cummings to Pound

TL-1.

[17 April 1950?]   [4 Patchin Place]

New York,April 17—AP. A plot threatening the existence of the Episcopalian
hierarchy of Great Britain was believed,on good authority,to have been
uncovered here today. The alleged instigator of this nefarious scheme,whose
motive cannot as yet be determined,is suspected of having urged a prominent
photographer of this city to falsify,in some unrevealed manner,a certain
document whose exact nature(in the interests of domestic security)remains a
carefully guarded government secret,known only to the President & his

advisors,the Cabinet,the Supreme Court,the Congress,the Senate,& all their more intimate associates. Rumor(however)persists in affirming that the forgery in question was to have been eventually signed by an obscure Greenwich Village literatus,who discovered his predicament just in time to prevent an Eliotic England from travailing to its very ankles. A story,even if possible stranger,was being widely circulated in the nation's capitol tonight with regard to the identity of the presumed plotter. He is said to be Dr. Enzo Pound,a well known ornithologist,& co-author with Kung Fu Tse of "The Unwobbling Pigeon".

certain document: Pound was in the habit of suggesting that his friends submit articles and statements (drafted by Pound) to journals and newspapers under their own names. Cummings may be referring to one such item sent him by Pound.

Unwobbling Pigeon: A play on Pound's translation, *Confucius: The Unwobbling Pivot & The Great Digest* (Pharos [New Directions, Norfolk, Conn.], 1947) (Gallup A58).

245. Cummings to Pound

TLS-1.

22 avril [April] 1950   [4 Patchin Place]

seen your—

thanks for the hot Chimborazzo tip

to(redletter)day our unhero received an Honour which even i,egocentric though he may be,scarcely dare maintain we deserve;am-&-was turneddownflat by both bollin & guggen

Marion sends love
                    —et vive le printemps!

C'gs

bolling & guggen: The Bollingen Foundation and the John Simon Guggenheim Memorial Foundation.

246. Cummings to Pound

T C.

[Postmarked 18 May 1950]   4PatchinPlace NYC 11

"saints"?

sounds like the marsupial's
realm

avaunt!

marsupial's: T. S. Eliot.

247. Pound to Cummings

A L S - 1.

[Postmarked 23 May 1950]   [Saint Elizabeths]

Take more'n that to eggs plane why a ex-unitarian anglican shd spose the
Aeropogetica (or however yu spell it) is written in English. (or that readin it
wont pizen th' young)

bless th lady - EZ

anglican: T. S. Eliot.
Aeropogetica: *Areopagitica; A Speech of Mr. John Milton for the Liberty of Unli-
cenc'd Printing, to the Parlament of England* (1644). On 3 May 1947, Eliot
lectured on Milton at the Frick Museum in New York City. See letter 180.

248. Cummings to Pound

T C.

[Postmarked 28 May 1950]   4PatchinPlace BYC11

some unday I must outrout my latin lexicon
& pursue Master Milton's musterpiece to
its foghorn conclusion as JJ might add
—Marion sends love to you & Dorothy!!

e

the "Harriet Monroe Poetry Prize" is mine by
"unanimous consent of the three judges"
      from which I deduce(perhaps erroneously)
that not everything everywhere can always be
politics q-u-i-t-e

musterpiece: The *Areopagitica*.
JJ: James Joyce.
Poetry Prize: The prize was five hundred dollars. See *Poetry* vol. 76, no. 5 (August
    1950), 307: "E. E. Cummings has been awarded the Harriet Monroe Poetry
    award at the University of Chicago. This year's judges included Josephine Miles,
    Delmore Schwartz and Morton Zabel."

249. Pound to Cummings

TL-1.

[Late May or early June 1950]   [Saint Elizabeths]

To Estlin the Estimable the indeclinable INSTAR etc.

Louis Dudek's phone number is MOnument 2-0050

You cant eggspek me to decroche yu a Mullins every week, and have prob/
already gone to Silver Lk. ANNYhowe.

so yu have a eggskews fer forgettin Louis' number. Incline to number him
among the inhabitants but yr/ criteraria are so soverer than mine I dunno.

** Four of them Vivaldi concerti wot I dug out of ⟨(microfilm'd)⟩ Dresden
before the liberation (of ink from ms/ by seepage after bumms'bundment
                            hv/ been printed in small, but
LEGIBLE fac-sim by the Acad. Chigiana, Siena (no price on copy recd)

ef yew got any moozukul friens wot wd/ want 'em

                                      za vurry neat
li'l vollum. also itz good music.

an Luvv/ to ⟨the⟩ lady.

Mr Dudek of Canada aint a Canafrawg, but of polish eggstractio with cheeks
bones as of Lombard Turiners. b. 1918 of im-parents.

Louis Dudek's: Louis Dudek (b. 1918), Canadian poet. He visited and corre-
    sponded with Pound. He was living in New York City at this time and pursuing

graduate studies at Columbia University. He moved to Montreal in August 1951. See his *D/k: Some Letters of Ezra Pound* (Montreal: DC Books, 1974).

Mullins: Eustace Mullins (b. 1923). Mullins had met Pound when he was living in Washington, D.C., in 1949. See the Biographical Notes.

250. Cummings to Pound

TCS.

[Postmarked 9 June 1950]   Silver Lake N.H.

sorry we received the news of your-latest-human-discovery a trifle late;but,if he's real,he'll endure till autumn(& we assume he _is_ real)

—Marion sends love to you both

eec

251. Pound to Cummings

TL-1.

[Postmarked 27 June 1950]   [Saint Elizabeths]

e.e.c.

being az it iz, az sez Ari StoTL. etc.
it comes over me that the almost uniform effeks of a Haaaavud eduk / on the
                    kumrad
                      'n'
            th' pos O.M.

                    IZ
diffikulty of eggstraktink a clear response to certain attempts at stimulae.

Naow fer eZampl when the kumrad wuz gittin his early and quite stinking experience
                              none of his comrades in misery out of kind
heart dumped on him a stack of TIME
            (properly capitalD with a SL)
                  coverin imperfekly, and unsequentially the elapse of say the
past 18 months.

AN
in
the recondite pinecovered heights or wotever of N.H.
I wd/ enquire ef/ the kumrad can think out a suitable
                    etc.

Hergy shied off   A COGNATE . whatdukall it, say: enquiry re one of the
other diseases when he last waved his raw-meat sox and scarlettt bandanna
abov these parages, the greesSWARD, they call it.

pos O.M.: T. S. Eliot.
Hergy: Joseph Hergesheimer (1880–1954), American novelist and short-story
   writer. Eustace Mullins recalls that Hergesheimer visited Pound at St. Elizabeths
   on more than one occasion.

252. Cummings to Pound

TLS-1.

[4 July 1950]   Silver Lake
                         New Hampshire

                              Independence Day 1950
Wwaall—

as the prophet Ez might virtúfully observe:
you can have your Mr Best(after all,hasn't
Jimmie J his,in the Hamlet scene from U?)
though could nearly forgive him the founding
of the most unXian church some centuries
before Paul the Pharisee or Doubting TAcquinas
(not to be confused with Doting Tommie,hO.huM.)
when I remember that upon a certain portal of
the ny Mu of Na Hi occurs a supposed quote from
old Di Color Che lui-même(re dolphins unless
it's whales)very prettily concluding "and they
snore in their sleep"

                         —give me the Broad

                              E

& the lady sends love!

Mr Best: Aristotle (see letter 254).

U: Ulysses, by James Joyce.

Paul: See letter 254.

Doting Tommie: T. S. Eliot.

ny MU of Na Hi: New York Museum of Natural History.

Di Color: Aristotle. "The dolphin and the whale, and all such as are furnished with a blow-hole, sleep with the blow-hole over the surface of the water, and breathe through the blow-hole while they keep up a quiet flapping of their fins; indeed, some mariners assure us that they have actually heard the dolphin snoring." A. Smith and W. D. Ross, eds., *The Works of Aristotle*, 15 vols. (Oxford: Clarendon Press, 1910–52), vol. 4, *Historia Animalium*, trans. D'Arcy Wentworth Thompson, book IV, 10, 537b.

the Broad: Plato (see letter 254).

253. Pound to Cummings

AL-1.

[July 1950]   [Saint Elizabeths]

O.K. wot <u>are</u> yu talkin about? This one (yrs 4th inst.) beats me, unless yu putt the wrong <u>le'r</u> in the envlp. addressed to S Liz

---

no use tg spekkg me to git refs to JJ's opus mag. as read it fer las' time in 1922 & have other more active etc animals to conserve in my "enclosure fer stray"# (ref. Webster or Jnsn or one ov them dics.)

#Pound: an enclosure for stray animals.

---

no, NO severl of yr. lines lack limpidity etc. fail to participate meaning.

#gawd bless her

254. Cummings to Pound

TLS-1.

july 12 1950   Silver Lake
                      New Hampshire

Dear Ezra—

so my letter's obscure? Tiens? Can't compare with your last,I imagine

same(postmarked JUN 27)began "being as it iz, as sez Ari StoTL. etc." My
letter,in reply,begins by giving you <u>your</u> "Mr Best"—Ἀριστοτέλης;no very far
cry,meseems,from ἄροστος:"the father of logic" as he's frequently called—&
ends by a salute("give me the Broad")to Plato("son of Ariston,orig. named
Aristocles,and surnamed Πλάτων with ref. to his broad shoulders,
⟨πλατύς,broad . . . He held that the object of philosophy is beauty":Century
Dict). The middle of my letter is a distinguishing of Christianity(vide New
Testament)& the SaulPaul-Acquinas hypersystem—au fond Aristotelian—so
headily espoused by your ultramarsupial friend. Incidentally,I hand "your Mr
Best" a bouquet for certain observations;which have perused on a wall of the
NYCity Museum of Natural History:they relate to either dolphins or
whales(forget which)

& now perhaps you'll interpret the enclosed,which please return

—sois sage

E

friend: T. S. Eliot.
enclosed: Probably Pound's letter of 27 June 1950 (letter 251).

255. Pound to Cummings

TL-1.

[July 1950]   [Saint Elizabeths]

E.E.C.

INSOFARAZ the krd/ has not indicated any specific point ov obskewrity, and
has, indeed, shown lucid comprehension of most of the refs/ in enc/ returnd/ I

labour the only (as far azI kan see) points on which any fog might remain in the kmrd's hyperlucid.

⟨or mouse⟩

Inshort / confronting the stink pail of 'Enclosed R/" a material (possibly hegelian etc,) stink, with the A ROMA of murkn pooplications dumped on enclosed victim of system, and enquired whether the krd/ saw any OUT.

idea of Blato, a "broad", im many senses seems inadequate.

Hergy. H id est --- esheimer, very talented murkn bookwriter in the lighter vein and re/ higher (in several senses) clawses of this continong.

Homages to the consort.

ANY MORE queeries?

enc/: Probably Pound's letter of 27 June 1950 (letter 251).

256. Pound to Cummings

TL-1.

[July 1950?]   [Saint Elizabeths]

AND
ad interim, we rePeat
that there is no direct evidence that th kumrad HAS read a book during the passt 30 years/

BUT THAT

ef he ever does desist from felling the PRIMAEVAL or contemplatin' the BUTeyes ov NATR

he might be diverted by Alex Del Mar's "WoshUp of Aug/ CaeSAR"."Middle Ages Revisited","Barbara Villiers," or in FAK almost any of the 40 enlightened wollombs thet hev been so assiduously concealed from the victims of Haaavud an all other amurkn beaneries.

fer the passt 50 an 80 yeauhs

Homages a Marian

"WoshUp of Aug/ CaeSAR": Alexander Del Mar, *The Worship of Augustus Caesar* (New York: Cambridge Encyclopedia Company, 1900). Del Mar contends that Christianity owes a considerable debt to pagan Rome, rather than to Judaism.

"What is insisted upon is that, Augustus Caesar, by his contemporaries, was believed to be and was actually worshipped as a god; with bell, book, candle, steeple, frankincense, rosary, cross, mitre, temples, priesthood, benefices and rituals; in short, with all the outward marks of superstition, credulity, piety and devotion" (315). "Augustus ascended the throne of his martyred Sire and was in turn anointed, addressed and worshipped as the Son of God; whiles Julius was tacitly worshipped as the Father" (316). "We now begin with the literature of triumph, deification and Apotheosis, which followed Augustus' return from Asia. In pursuance of the theology which Rome had gathered from Etruria, Greece, Pontus, Galilee, Syria, Egypt, Spain and Gaul . . . it was necessary to show that the Incarnation was connected with previous incarnations; that it occurred at the beginning of a new divine cycle; that it was the issue of a divine father and mortal mother; that the mother was wife-virgin; that the birth happened at the end of ten solar months; that it occurred in an obscure place; that it was told by prophecy or sacred oracle; that it was presaged or accompanied by prodigies of Nature; that the divinity of the child was recognized by sages; that the Holy One exhibited extraordinary signs of precocity and wisdom; that his destruction was sought by the ruling powers, whose precautions were of course defeated; that he worked miracles; that he exhibited a profound humility; that his apotheosis would bring peace on earth, and that he would finally ascend to heaven, there to join with his Father. Accordingly, the Augustan writers furnished all these materials" (322–23). Del Mar concludes his study by summarizing the importance of Augustan worship for the development of Christianity. "Water will not rise above its own level. Man will not worship a god who is either above or below the poise of his own comprehension. The gods therefore have this useful function: they furnish an infallible barometer of the human intellect. Measured by this scale, the worship of Augustus was not at the period of his advent below the comprehension of the West, for, with the exception of the stubborn Northmen, we hear of no dissatisfaction with it. . . . But if . . . the rural populations endured it without repugnance, the great cities of the empire, such as Antioch, Alexandria, Athens and Rome, found it too degrading for continued acceptance. It was these centres of intellectual activity that gave effect to the revolts which emperor-worship had provoked in Britain, Frisia, Saxony and Judea; and it was out of this combination of popular resistance and intellectual disgust that arose a long and deadly struggle against the worship of Augustus and the wide-spread and firmly-rooted superstitions upon which it was founded; a struggle which finally ended in the adoption of Christianity" (333).

"Middle Ages Revisited": Alexander Del Mar, *The Middle Ages Revisited* (New York: Cambridge Encyclopedia Company, 1900). Del Mar contends that medieval Europe was minimally indebted to Judean culture. As he says in his concluding paragraph, "It results from what has gone before that the peculiarity of our civilization, the traits and tendencies which distinguish it from other civilizations, are due to the constituents of its composite origin; chiefly to two great elements, Roman and Gothic. We inherit mind from one, body from the other. If the brawn, the muscle, the personal courage, the élan, push, spirit, dash, enterprise, of the western nations, belonged to the Franks, Hidalgos, Angles, Saxons and other Gothic races, their social institutions are by similar tokens the produce of Roman thought, of Roman experience, of Roman freedom, and of Roman law. The ancient Commonwealth of Rome no more existed in vain than did the Gothic tribes and the rude marks they inflicted upon the hierarchy. They both left an indelible imprint upon western civilization; and while sophistry would waste effort in searching for the origin of our institutes in faint graffiti of remote Judea, the deep carvings of republican Rome and barbarous Gotland can be recognized at a glance" (365).

257. Cummings to Pound

ACS.

[Postmarked 29 July 1950]   Silver Lake N.H.

thank you for the book-tip!

                        E

258. Pound to Cummings

ALS-2.

[August 1950?]   [Saint Elizabeths]

r u
aware of the citizen Ver Becke; seeming to cherish cordial (not intimate)
memories of the famille C. & glad to hear M. recovered as apparently Patchin'd
or zumat when she war low

                        =

AM stil avid for light on natr of denizens
'course blue jays iz more coherent than most of 'em
whar yu git sech ideas re b.jays? re which I queery = wot yu dun did to that b.j
fer to animositate him (? or her, crestless)
an luv to th lady   EZ

I mean I accept yu as orthority on hrooshuns but queery analysis of b.j

Ver Becke: W. Edwin Ver Becke, a Californian who corresponded with Pound. He
   first wrote to Pound on 11 October 1949, saying, "But poetry is the knowledge

of power in all things. You have found this power and know it well." He may
have met the Cummingses when they were in California in 1935.

b.jays: Pound refers to poem 5 of *95 poems:* "crazy jay blue)" *Complete Poems,* 677.
The poem first appeared in *Poetry* in July 1950.

259. Cummings to Pound

TLS-1.

August 6 [1950]   Silver Lake

i suspect my bluejay balances my chickadee,& vv

eec

Marion sends love

[On verso:]

"The Blue Jay is the clown & scoffer of birdland. Furthermore,he is one of the
handsomest of American birds;also he is one of the wickedest . . . after all has
been said by his defenders,the ugly fact remains,as Mr. Job says,that the bird
'has all the mischievous,destructive traits of the Crow,& with a lot of audacity
or "cheek" thrown in for good measure.'

"There can be no doubt that he is a persistent & merciless nestrobber—
that he eats the eggs & kills & devours the young of smaller & defenceless
birds. Eloquent testimony . . . is furnished by the outcry set up by these
birds,whenever they catch a Jay lurking near their nests. But we need not take
the birds' word alone for it,because he has been caught red-handed by
man,more than once . . .

" . . . an amusing rascal. In the nesting season he is comparatively little
in evidence,not only because he has his own family affairs to attend to,but
because he devotes a good deal of his time to his cannibalistic
practices,concerning which he is anxious to keep the rest of the feathered
world in ignorance. But once his family responsibilities are descharged,& there
are no more nests to be robbed,his whole demeanor changes,& he becomes the
noisiest & most obstreporous creature in the woods . . .

"That the Jay has a sense of humor—which is not common among our
birds—also seems very obvious."

Birds of America(Editor-in-Chief T.GilbertPearson)

"This splendid fellow is the rascal of the bird community,the bully & tease of
all creatures smaller than himself,&,so far as actions are concerned,'the clown
of the circus.'"

"... The Blue jay is also a robber. He not infrequently attacks other birds engaged in nest-building,drives them off,& finishes the job to his own liking ...

"The advent of a horde of Blue Jays,about the middle of July ... means a general dispersion of all the song birds for the time being ...

"Ralph Hoffman gives us an excellent sketch of the Blue Jay's character ... 'The Jay in spring is undoubtedly a reprobate. He cannot resist the temptation to sneak through the trees and bushes,& when he finds a nest of eggs temporarily left by the owner,to thrust his sharp bill through the shells;even young birds are devoured. In the autumn,however,he is a hearty,open fellow,noisy,&intent on acorns & chestnuts.'"

Fieldbook of Wild Birds & Their Music
F.Schuyler Mathews

"These are one"(sic)"of the best known & most beautiful birds that we have,but,unfortunately,they have a very bad reputation. They often rob other birds of their eggs & young as well as food & nesting material ... "

Bird Guide
(Chester A. Reed)

chickadee: Probably a reference to poem 26 ("wherelings whenlings") of *Fifty Poems* (1940). Line 26 is "tree field rock hollyhock forest brook chickadee" (*Collected Poems*, 512).

Pearson: Cummings cites *Birds of America,* ed. T. Gilbert Pearson (1917; Garden City, N.Y.: Doubleday, 1936), 217–18.

Mathews: Cummings condenses remarks in F. Schuyler Mathews, *Field Book of Wild Birds and Their Music* (New York: G. P. Putnam's Sons, 1904), 43–45.

Reed: The passage is from Chester A. Reed, *Bird Guide: Land Birds East of the Rockies, from Parrots to Bluebirds* (Garden City, N.Y.: Doubleday, 1947), 55.

260. Pound to Cummings

ALS-2.

[August 1950?]   [Saint Elizabeths]

"Or blime'
        doc-
umentation

---

ef thazz kind bk yu read - wo'r bout Mr Agassiz (L.) or did yu read all him in kid's gardn?

ef not joy before yu.
    bless the lydy

                  Ez

why even so the charrrmin' blue shd be
    VS/ yu

I still don't make out

does the hummings
of boids
move mr cummings,
no but
other men's woidz
erbaout boids.
             (?)
<u>vurry</u> sloppy writer one of yr. natr mutts.

---

yu eat chickn, considerin' it a inferior biped.

---

jay bird purrfurs eggs & nuts to bugs & wums.

---

word canibal re/ jay bird & worm eater
      vurry poor langwidg—

      Mr. Agassiz wdnt hv. used.

enny how dont affect relation
    e.e.c : jaybir'

Agassiz: Jean Louis Rodolphe Agassiz (1807–73), Swiss-born naturalist and geolo-
    gist. He emigrated to the United States in 1846 and was appointed professor of
    zoology and geology at Harvard University in 1847.
sloppy writer: T. Gilbert Pearson.

261. Cummings to Pound

TLS-1.

August 15 '50   Silver Lake

Dear Ezra—

so you know more than the birdsters? Fine & dandy. I don't. And what I've
learned from a very few birds(who have honoured me with their

friendship)leads one ignorant* biped to guess that poor birdsters are doing their wingless utmost

thy fondness for Mr A reminds our unhero of something delightful:a dearest friend of his childhood was(& is)the Indian elephant of The Agassiz Museum,not far from whose wonders I was luckily born:& there's not a wrinkle in his skin,for in those days you gave your public its money's worth

—salut!

E

    *I even find it interesting that—large & by—birds beautiful-to-hear dress quietly,& birds beautiful-to-see can't sing; &(nota bene)the real killers are neither beautiful-to-see nor beautiful-to-hear

Agassiz Museum: Louis Agassiz founded the Museum of Comparative Zoology at Harvard University in 1859. It was located less than half a mile from the Cummings home at 104 Irving Street.

262. Pound to Cummings

ALS-2. Enclosure.

[August or September 1950]   [Saint Elizabeths]

Wot still getz ez iz
why the ++++++ yu think thet partik b. jay wdn't ⟨(would NOT)⟩ hv. ⟨(have)⟩ appreciated yr charakter ?

oo smoothd th' 'fantle's
    skin
        = & shined 'is Teef'
Have yu told Marianne (?)

emphasis on the --anne
      M.
      ?

Luv to a lady.

Enclosure: A poem, "AGASSIZ in Memoriam"

AGASSIZ   in Memoriam

Who smoothed the fantle's skin and shined his teeth;
While Possum's thought dwelt on the bones beneath,
and kumminKZ' fawncy thru the wild savannahs
rushed munching on bunch of green bananas.

Possum's: T. S. Eliot.

263. Cummings to Pound

TL-1. ENCLOSURES.

[August or September 1950]   [Silver Lake]

reperusing Agassiz Scenario,observe with
pleaasure that its definitely prosaic part
goes to Tippling Tom(Meaculpa Marsupialis;
Donne)whereas,by what may be roughly entitled
a fortunate contrast,someone who shall remain
nameless receives the distinctly poetic role

Marion sends love! (& clippings)

Enclosures: An article and letters to the editor from the *New York Herald Tribune*.
On 19 August 1950, the paper published an article headed, "Seized Pet Jay Is
Too Scrappy, Zoo Releases It." The article reported the case of a man in New
York City who had rescued a baby blue jay. The New York State Conservation
Department seized the bird from the man and turned it over to the Bronx Zoo.
Shortly thereafter the bird was released. The letters to the editor (from the
August 24 edition of the *Tribune*) were from people expressing varying degrees
of outrage at the Conservation Department's action. One writer asked, "What
better proof could we have that the United States is being bureaucratized to
death than the incident of Mr. Julian B. Garcia's pet bluejay?"

Tippling Tom: T. S. Eliot. Pound's "AGASSIZ in Memoriam" parodies the last
stanza of Eliot's poem, "Burbank with a Baedeker: Bleistein with a Cigar."

264. Pound to Cummings

ALS-1.

[September 1950]   [Saint Elizabeths]

Yer friend Eee Vaaa is quite a gal. 30 pages of her. dunno if yu wanna see it?

can yu read it ennyhow? am SO in the dark re the kumrad's paideuma

mebbe he did read Kant & Higgle in the 'riginal between the acts of under
grad
      Tee Yatrikals.

----

           ooo knoze?

wot can we do fer Eva. apart tryin to git her free books?

luv to th lady
              E

Eee Vaaa: Eva Hesse. She had sent Pound the text of a radio speech she gave over
Munich radio on 1 June 1950, "Gegen die Strömung der Zeit—der Fall Ezra
Pound." Also sent were Pound poems translated by her, and notes on the
Bogomils.

265. Cummings to Pound

ACS.

[Postmarked 8 September 1950]   Silver Lake NH

delighted to learn that Eva's perspicuous. Yes, I'd like to glimpse a sample (10
pp; say). There's a lad hereabouts who knows German outside in

              E

love from Marion!

266. Cummings to Pound

TCS.

[1950?]   4PatchinPlace NYC11

speaking of bluejays—just the other afternoon I talked with a Southern
lady;who explained that they were the devil's messengers,&misbehaved;so he
made a grab for their tails,leaving "sooty streaks". Not that I'd call anything
about a bluejay sooty;but can imagine what she meant

              EEC

(love from the consort!)

267. Pound to Cummings

ALS-1.

[1950?]   [Saint Elizabeths]

Insubordination
To Satan highly commendable --
who are yu to back up Bates'
demand fer
        Subordination?

bless th lady
& Blujayz   not sooty. Snooty if yu like
               gawbless UM.

                            Ez

Bates' demand: Unidentified.

268. Pound to Cummings

ALS-1.

[1950?]   [Saint Elizabeths]
e.ec. ⟨yu wil b glad to hear:⟩ lydy fr/ N. Carolina sez blue jays go to hell every
Friday

———
     howevr
She don't seem to hold it against 'em
                    yr
                    EZ

luv to the consort

269. Pound to Cummings

ALS-1.

[October 1950?]   [Saint Elizabeths]

Than X -- buttt

The references in
lines 4
&   6
cd dew wiff part.kerlization --
which big lil
        " y. marster

Thanks fer volumette.
in that form mebbe even I
cd/ read it
                    luv to th' lydy
                    EZ

Jamie still alive on Wednesday

---

yu git current luyung in Hdsn.

references: Letter not located.
volumette: Perhaps Cummings's *Puella Mea* (Mount Vernon, N.Y.: Golden Eagle
    Press, 1949) (Firmage A22).
Jamie: Jaime de Angulo. Pound may refer to the late de Angulo's essay "Indians in
    Overalls," *Hudson Review,* vol. 3, no. 3 (autumn 1950), 327–77.
Hdsn: See the note to letter 271.

270. Pound to Cummings

ALS-1.

[October 1950?]   [Saint Elizabeths]

1. e.e.c
        mentioned matr ov.
        <u>yung man</u>
does he retract or wot'l
                    ?

2
        do they cause reactionz?
                    E

271. Cummings to Pound

TLS-1.

October 24 [1950]   [4 Patchin Place]

Dear Ezra—

a good kid(English⟨#⟩)now at Yale on scholarship writes me thus

> "A friend of mine,John Wendon,who was at college
> with me & is now teaching at Harvard,has a commission
> from the Oxford University Press to find MS for
> publication,& I have been working with him on this.
> "The Press,in the figure of Mr Vaudrin whom I expect you
> know(of?),is looking for material of the following
> kinds:
>> Poetry
>> Translations from European literature
>> Letters,essays(though not fiction)
>> Critical theses in the Humanities(English,
>>   History, & so forth)
>> Original works of philosophy(but not purely
>>   technical studies in the sciences)
> "John & I have been reading & talking about Pound
> this weekend & we had the idea that he was just the man
> to translate NIETZSCHE's 'ALSO SPRACH ZARATHUSTRA' on
> the right level of lyrical spontaneity & intellectual
> precision(there is no doubt that the existing
> translations miss the poetic tone entirely & a great deal
> of the essential coherence of ideas.) What do you think
> Pound's reaction would be to such an invitation . . . "

&his name is Anthony K Thorlby:2828 Yale Station,New Haven,Conn.;so why
not drop him a line?

you'll find "young master"'s burial service on p463 of The Hudson
Review(Jaime-TomTom number;Autumn 1950)

Marion sends love

                    —skol

                 E

October 24 or so

          #& you know how I detest that unanimal

Vaudrin: Philip Vaudrin, an editor with the Oxford University Press. In the following year he joined Alfred A. Knopf, Inc.

burial service: "Three Poets," by Frederick Morgan, *Hudson Review,* vol. 3, no. 3 (autumn 1950), 463–66. Morgan, the editor of *The Hudson Review,* reviews three books: *Xaipe,* by Cummings; *Guide to the Ruins,* by Howard Nemerov; *The White Threshold,* by W. S. Graham. Morgan finds that "Cummings' success in maintaining the consistency and purity of his verse has been achieved at an enormous sacrifice, a limitation of vision so drastic as inevitably to preclude all possibility of scope, complication or profundity." Morgan also charges that Cummings's whole body of poetry directs readers "not to real things which the poet loves or hates, but narcissistically back to his own interior; that the delight with which one reads does not survive the reading as an accretion to one's own sensibility." The same issue of the *Review* contained an essay by Jaime de Angulo, "Indians in Overalls" (327–77).

272. Pound to Cummings

TL-1.

[October 1950]   [Saint Elizabeths]

if the estimabl EstLin wants to do something useful

/ as the "good kid" is apparently pre-natal and aimin fer a six weeks miscarriage /

to or from that swill pail, that after 50 years punking made ONE and one ONLY known move toward cleanliness

namely publishing e.e.c.

I suggest that the sd/ Kumrad K/

                                        tell the little squirt that it is his (the l.
squirts) place to ASK E.P. what ought to be published,
              NOT to ask E.P. to clean latrines
                                        in his unvenerated
age.

      When the fahrting bespectacled hell, did any of these brothels move toward printing any of E.P.'s solid donations.

(~~well~~ such as the paleographic Cavalcanti fer ezampl?)

Mr ?? VauRien (VAu(D?) rin

with fourty years time lag/ and No Frobenius and no Del Mar

dung on the heads of the lotUvum.

swill pail: The Oxford University Press.

Cavalcanti: Pound referred in his essay "Cavalcanti" to "waste matter, which stagnates about the real work, and which is continuously being heaped up and caused to stagnate by academic bodies, obese publishing houses, and combinations of both, such as the Oxford Press." *Literary Essays of Ezra Pound* (New York: New Directions, 1968), 191. In the late 1920s, Pound had planned to publish a "Complete Works" of Guido Cavalcanti that would have included photographic reproductions of selected manuscripts. See David Anderson, *Pound's Cavalcanti: An Edition of the Translations, Notes, and Essays* (Princeton: Princeton University Press, 1983), xix–xxii.

273. Cummings to Pound

TLS-1.

[November 1950]   4 Patchin Place

feles major—

thy royalbengaltigerhood is aroaring
up the wrong sapling. This correspondent
is pro no publisher;unliving or dead

now come on down;& give him your if any
reaction to young master Fred Morgan's
recent booksreview

                    —thanking thee in advance,je suis
                              E

Morgan's recent booksreview: Frederick Morgan's review of *Xaipe*. See the note to letter 271.

274. Pound to Cummings

TL-1.

[November 1950]   [Saint Elizabeths]

                    e.e.c.
for his archives, NOT for trans;ission as frum Ez/

BUT if he can steer that untilrecently
            infamous coagulate into
being of use,
                then BAnZAI and 10,000 years.

still dont follow yung ma'ssa and tennis racket in earlier dispatches fr/ the
KRD/

luvv to th lydi

tell the li'l bastids why the HEKL dont they find out how much of P's has been
suppressed or held up for from 5 to 20 years.

        butdo it like it wuz EEC, not
        az frum Ez

hot iron to git thru blubber

                Kee-Wesschun ??

biog? (romance or other) of
        reviewer ???
        Iz ezPected to READ book reviews
            by risin' or any OTHER generation
at this time of izitLife ?
        (well it IZ, however much
Alas pore Yorrik that his bones shd rot
Tho Ez once wuz, thanKGorr
                he now iz not.

        y,f,t, M.v.D

coagulate: Probably the Oxford University Press.
dispatches: Not located.
M.v.D.: Mark Van Doren had contributed the preface to Paige. The book was
    published on 26 October 1950.

275. Pound to Cummings

ALS-2.

[Postmarked 27 December 1950]   [Saint Elizabeths]

ef tha ——n
    Effelunt
wd 'casionally (&/or <u>more</u> often)
step on wot <u>needs</u>
squshing.   ehem.

———————————————

    Bless yr consort
    & Njoy th coming yeah.

———————————————

of course the cloud-treading
      pachydarm
         is a 'spiring
spektkl - far souperior
to gill's gelding or other
effete reminders of classik
'tiquity ————————————

    & Then the affiliate (pos.
the krd dunno he is propriating
the elder harvardian bard's fambly
heraldry.
       ?

          yr.
          EZ

Effelunt: One of Cummings's elephant drawings sent to Pound.
gill's: Eric Gill (1882–1940), British artist. He was primarily known for his sculp-
    ture and engraving.
harvardian bard's: Pound probably refers to the coat of arms of the Eliot family.
    See the note to letter 227.

276. Cummings to Pound

TCS.

[Postmarked 2 January 1951]   4 Patchin Place NYC11

thank you,sir. Am delighted
that an image (however faulty)

of my favorite creature should
please. As for air,it's(comme
toujours)the only where fit for
strolling

                                        EEC

277. Cummings to Dorothy Pound

TLS-1.

January 6 1951   [4 Patchin Place]

Dear Dorothy—

the enclosed clipping & letter(which
most kindly return)prove somebody wants to
know where he can find EP's dictum. Could
you perhaps tell me? And did I quote
himself correctly?

                    —Marion sends love

                                        EEC

enclosed: Enclosures lacking.

278. Pound to Cummings

TL-1.

[Ca. 9 January 1951]   [Saint Elizabeths]

to the kumRAD K/z Ellefunt
will take greater bibliographicophilik expertise than that POsessed by any here
present to answer this part of K/d's quiz pogram. The quote is KOrekt, and
apparently from some prose composition. Ez Sez: O.K. he said it, and of course
it wdn't do the earnest henquirer any harrum to start hunting fer to find out
WHAAR, cause that might eggstend ⟨(or Breiten)⟩ the frontiers ov his klchr.

AND of course peerusin' further into the clip / CONgraterlashuns on the 5000
buck reach down. i dunno in quite wot company save the late (was it knot) Mr
Musters?

OV course there iz no reezun why the gt/ am
/eagul shd/ pipe in a milder tone than the Sweedisch albatross (in wot hv/ long
s/pected wuz attempt to disthracht attention from Mr Ibsen's so trenchant
utterance .. ma che . . . .

[The following is in Dorothy Pound's hand.]
Cheers -- So glad re prize. D.P.

Breiten: Harvey Breit (1913–68), American playwright and editor. Assistant editor
of the *New York Times Book Review,* 1948–57.
reach down: In late 1950 Cummings had been awarded the Fellowship of the
Academy of American Poets.
Mr Musters: Edgar Lee Masters (1869–1950), American poet. Masters had been
awarded the Academy of American Poets Fellowship in 1946.

279. Cummings to Pound

TCS.

[Postmarked 12 January 1951]   4 PatchinPlace NYC11

gla[d] my quotation's correct;& hope our
religiously minded inquirer will(as you
aptly suggest)begin hunting

rumor contends that previous AofAPs award-
ease number EMarkham ELMasters PMackaye
RTorrence & perhaps a Bénet? Tiens

I suspect Nubble of merely inventing nitro-
glycerine or whatever would make himself
earth's least peaceful personage until the
advent of magnus Albertus

                                        eec

AofAPs: See the note to the previous letter.
EMarkham: Edwin Markham (1852–1940), American poet.
ELMasters: Edgar Lee Masters.
PMackaye: Percy MacKaye (1875–1956), American dramatist and poet.
RTorrence: Ridgely Torrence (1875–1950), American journalist, dramatist and
poet.

Bénet: Stephen Vincent Bénét (1888–1943), American poet; William Rose Bénét (1886–1950), American poet and critic.

Nubble: Alfred Bernhard Nobel (1833–96), Swedish chemist, engineer, and inventor. He left his fortune in trust as an endowment for the Nobel prizes.

magnus Albertus: Albert Einstein. Albertus Magnus (c. 1200–1280) was a renowned scholastic philosopher.

280. Pound to Cummings

ALS-1.

[January 1951]   [Saint Elizabeths]

Mrs Fletcher (J.G.) havin' hd/ the pleasant idea of sendin' on J's french books -

wonder ef th Kumrad ever looked @ the preface to Gautier's 1832 poEMZ

nacherly one don't normally read a preface.

                    greet her effulgence

                              Ez

Mrs. Fletcher: Charlie May Fletcher. Her husband, John Gould Fletcher, died in 1950. On 15 January 1951, Mrs. Fletcher wrote Pound that she was sending him "the complete works of Verlaine and Rimbaud, and the works of Verhaeren, Baudelaire, Mallarme, Gautier and Cocteau."

the preface: Théophile Gautier (1811–72), French poet (see the note to letter 282).

281. Cummings to Pound

TCS.

[Postmarked 28 January 1951]   4 PatchinPlace NYC11

bless your heart,I'm far too ignorant to know that friend Gautier "had a book out" in 1832 or that(if he did)le dit livre comprised a preface;what's it like?

Her E sends love   C'gs

282. Pound to Cummings

TL-1.

[Postmarked 31 January 1951]   [Saint Elizabeths]

eec

Waaal I spoge I gotter go save yu time 'n' nrg again, I tho't it might relieve yu
from that thaaar LIFE is reul life iz urnest, life enatails a economico-monetary
policy⟨, feelingkz⟩ wich yu so often suffer in my vicinage

                              IF

yu cd/ lamp them words of Teophile's (not eggskluzifly in the 1832 edtn/ but
reprinted in current)
                              namely and videlicet: (about his
tender foist vollum)

"À ⟨quoi⟩ qua cela cela sert-il? Cela sert à être beau. N'est ce pas assez, comme
les fleurs etc . . . . . . comme tout ce que l'homme n'a pu détourner et dépraver
à son usage?

with due deference à Madame.

words of Teophile's: "Quant aux utilitaires, utopiests, économistes, saint-
simonistes et autres qui lui demanderont à quoi cela rime,—il répondra: Le
premier vers rime avec le second quand la rime n'est pas mauvaise, et ainsi de
suite.
     A quoi cela sert-il?—Cela sert à être beau.—N'est-ce pas assez? comme les
fleurs, comme les parfums, comme les oiseaux, comme tout ce que l'homme n'a
pu détourner et dépraver à son usage." Théophile Gautier, *Poésies complètes,* 2
vols. (Paris: Bibliothèque-Charpentier, 1910), 1:4 [As for pragmatists, utopians,
economists, followers of Saint-Simon, and others who asked him what it was
good for—he answered: the first verse rhymes with the second when the rhyme
is not bad, and so on so forth.
     But what good is it?—Because it is beautiful.—Is it not enough? Like the
flowers, like perfume, like birds, like everything that man cannot twist or
corrupt to his own use].

283. Cummings to Dorothy Pound

TLS-1.

February 5 '51   4 Patchin Place

Dear Dorothy—

I've lost the address of my German
translator,the girl who also translated
(to his satisfaction!)EP;Eva Hesse is
her name,isn't it? If you happen to
come across this person's whereabouts
(she & Ezra must have corresponded;&
not long ago)would you please tuck them
in the enclosed envelope? Thanks kindly

                    —Marion sends
                       her best!

                    EEC

284. Cummings to Dorothy Pound

ACS.

[Postmarked 15 February 1951]   4 PatchinPlace NYC11

have a feeling I forgot to thank you for sending me Eva's address so
promptly—shame on me!

                    EEC

285. Pound to Cummings

ALS-2.

[March 1951]   S Liz

Naow Yu tell grampaw:

Ethel Merman

———————

or hv. yu sd/ so.
& if so send the

documentation
Pindarics @ least   EP

P.S. & by the
way
wotchu know
about Belden
              ?

Ethel Merman: Ethel Merman (1909–84), American actress and singer. At this
time Merman was starring in *Call Me Madam,* which had opened in October
1950.

Belden: Probably Jack Belden (1910–89), American journalist. Pound most likely
read his *China Shakes the World* (New York: Harper, 1949). Belden spent time in
China after World War II living with peasant supporters of the Communists. He
reported that Chiang Kai-shek "did not even try to understand the hearts of his
own people. That is part of the inner history of Chiang Kai-shek's defeat and it
is also part of the history of American policy in Asia. Neither the American
government, the American press, nor the American people, nor many of their
representatives in the Far East in the embassies, the military establishments and
the business offices sought to look beyond their own narrow national or per-
sonal interests toward the heart of the admittedly ignorant, but terribly emo-
tional, bitter men and women of China" (5). He concludes that "The Celestial
Reds won the people to their cause not by any process of reasoning, but by
arousing the hope, trust and affection of the people. . . . There is every reason
to believe that the Communists are sincere when they say they intend to use this
power to represent the interests of the common people, but there is also reason
to believe that this machine [the political power apparatus] might elude their
intentions and tend to exist for its own sake. In other words, there may arise a
new elite, a set of managers standing above the Chinese masses" (472–73).

286. Cummings to Pound

TLS-1.

March 11 1951   4 Patchin Place
                                          New York City 11

Dear Ez—

my staunch,not to add devoted,decoding staff of 1 opines that your latest
sincerely esteemed communiqué features "Ethel Merman". Have(many sweet
years since)heardseen a thoroughly advertized female of said

nomenclature;'twas via some "musical" ultramediocre "vehicle" or other, & she struck this inveterate theatrenongoer as a hearty entertainer sans(otherwise)distinction—unless you'd call it a distinction to very emphatically not ressemble the Forsaken male of the species,discovered(to geld a lily)by MathewA. Concerning radioactivities:well thou wotest,mon-sure,that juh name pa;speaking trays deuce-mong. So come(as all bad Americans would cheerfully say,before ce salaud The Common Man made his d.moralizing appearance)clean;& enlighten your,calm press-key too-sure,ignorant veuillezagréer

Marion sends love!

eec

"Belder"?non so

MathewA.: Matthew Arnold (1822–88), British poet and critic. Cummings refers to his poem "The Forsaken Merman" (1849).

287. Pound to Cummings

ALS-1.

[March 1951]   [Saint Elizabeths]

infloonz ov art on life.
Estlin's or furrin

---

sorry no clearer exemplars

Communicate to gt.
Marianne
unless I can
git one less obscurated

EZ

'eaven sa Vus

itz
J. Belden#
    ≡   #not r

Marianne: Marianne Moore.

288. Cummings to Pound

TCS.

[Postmarked 14 March 1951]   4 PatchinPlace NYC11

the elephants are
delightful—I thank
you,Sir!

                EEC

289. Pound to Cummings

ALS-1. Enclosure.

[March 1951]   [Saint Elizabeths]

noisy? yes.
buttt she dun't sing aZif she wuZ short an fat.

_____

either she has larned in the intervening decade or yu didn't hear.

_____

omages a Mme
            EZ

an az fer the g'orful immitations of "that sort of thing" on Sunday (over)

Enclosure: A clipping of a column by Westbrook Pegler, in which he discusses
Ethel Merman in *Call Me Madam*. Although Pegler dislikes it, he says it is a
"triumph" because "Ethel Merman picks up the stupid business off the dusty
floor, boots it, knees it, muscles it all over the stage and makes it hilarious by
mocking its tawdry plot and japes. I think it must have croaked in rehearsal but for
Ethel Merman's incomparable art, which makes comedy out of material worse
than nothing." On the clipping EP wrote, "e.e.c no collusion so far ez iz knowed."

290. Pound to Cummings

TL-1.

[March 1951]   [Saint Elizabeths]

EEC

Yr l'il frien' Eva sure IZ one brright y. llady. Eddikatin the rising by quotin' 'em
yr/ Sixth Av/ L, en retour via Nippon. (theme as mumbled by Ambruster in

"Treason's Peace" . . and I take it it wd/ be otiose to assume that yu hv/ evr/
heerd tell of Ambruster. AND he dunt git down to bed rok, or as near as Veith
"Citadels of Chaos." (which the kumrad prob/ aint read.)
Vast moral fervor teleshakin the lland over a few peanut vendors/ fervor re/
small time sharks in R.F. royal france Corpse or Rooseveltian porkbarrel / ALL
serving to camouflage the LARGE Crime purrpetrated by WarBUG & Codface
Willson the Woodhead, in 19i3 i.e. the Feedemral Reserve. Wot do NOT feed
the people. Ref/ letter 322 to Swabey (324 in the Brit/edtn.)

Easter thoughts toward: callin in the police to protect the denizen-citoyen from
HIMSELF. wich necessates HIRING more police, and putting up the taxes till
they scrunch.
Now the pubbulum of yr/ decade (I say decade, not generation) warnt so
much the traison des clercs, cause they WEREN'T clercs/ but merely
pseudoclercs. Not having sense enough to trahir, just being dessicated below
the level of moral action AT ALL. and this goddamnability inceased by NON-
communication.

As his EimInence haz got as far as that Nipponese projectile and its making,
why not move in on the larger crooks.

AM I clear?

The Belden bk/ really is worth yr reading.

seezun'z greetinks to Marian

That fhart Cordell Hull (less odorous that Roose's other playboys BUT a fhart)
did "not believe in balance of power for keeping peace.". The superiority of
UNBALANCE being at least a new pewkerosity in high diplosomaniac
epistemology.

yr/ Sixth Av/ L: Cummings's poem "plato told" (*Complete Poems*, 553).
Ambruster: Howard Watson Ambruster, *Treason's Peace: German Dyes and Ameri-
can Dupes* (New York: Beechhurst Press, 1947). Ambruster contends that the
I. G. Farben company "is and must be recognized as a cabalistic organization
which, through foreign subsidiaries and by secret tie-ups, operates a far-flung
and highly efficient espionage machine—the ultimate purpose being world

conquest—and a world super-state directed by Farben" (vii). Furthermore, the existence and the operations of this conspiracy are known at the highest levels of American government. "I say that the facts assembled in this story should prove to all that those things which the German dye trust planned to do, and then did with the assistance of key men in its framework in the United States, had long been revealed as in an open book to those in high places who cared to listen or to examine the record. I say that those facts have been known from the days of the dying Wilson Administration by leaders of high and low degree of all three branches of our Federal Government and by leaders in industry, in finance, and in public opinion" (415–16). Worst of all, "the youth of this generation have had this war to fight because they and many of their elders were not permitted to learn in time the facts told here" (416).

Veith: Cornelius Carl Veith, *Citadels of Chaos* (Boston: Meador Publishing Company, 1949). Veith dedicates his book "to the memory of Jefferson, Jackson, Lincoln, and those venerable Americans who opposed economic slavery and foreign domination, and who taught that the government should use Constitutional money for the common welfare of all Americans. It is dedicated to their followers who oppose today's economic slavery (boom-bust economy and State Socialism) and who oppose foreign domination (America-Last cults giving America away) as well as to those who believe that their servants in the nation's Capitol should support the Constitution in its entirety—including that section which gives to Congress the power to issue money and regulate its value" (5). Veith reveals that the citadels he refers to in his title are "The Citadels of high finance [that] direct the devious wanderings of the one object [the value of the dollar] which by its very nature must be stable and dependable if chaos is to be averted" (7). Veith sees a worldwide conspiracy at work: "This Hidden Power is a world power which, through its permitted control of national money supplies, has plunged every dominated nation into the miseries of irretrievable debt and the world into economic and military strife" (25). When analyzing the causes of World War II, Veith notes that "Germany had kicked out the international banker and established a sound monetary system based upon the exchangeable wealth of the nation without gold or tribute to the Money Power" (282).

WarBUG: Paul Moritz Warburg (1868–1932), German-born American banker. He was one of the five members of the first Federal Reserve Board. From 1921 to 1926 he was a member of the advisory council of the Board. Eustace Mullins, in his *The Secrets of the Federal Reserve* (Staunton, Va.: Bankers Research Institute, 1993), alleges that the Federal Reserve System was planned at a secret meeting on Jekyll Island, Georgia, in 1910. "At stake was the future control of the money and credit of the United States. If any genuine monetary reform had been prepared and presented to Congress, it would have ended the power of the elitist one world money creators. Jekyll Island ensured that a central bank would be established in the United States which would give these bankers everything they had always wanted" (4). "Paul Warburg advanced at Jekyll Island the primary deception which would prevent the citizens from recognizing that his plan set up a central bank" (6). The 1993 edition of *The Secrets of the Federal Reserve* is an expansion of his 1952 work, *Mullins on the Federal Reserve*, published in New York by John Kasper and David Horton.

Willson: Woodrow Wilson (1856–1924), twenty-eighth president of the United States. The Federal Reserve Act of 1913 was intended to reform the nation's banking system. It created the Federal Reserve Board—with members appointed by the president and confirmed by the Senate—to control the national money supply.

letter 322: Letter 322 in Paige. In this letter of 22 February 1937, to Henry Swabey, Pound urges the adoption of Silvio Gesell's *Schwundgeld* (a currency that would gradually lose its purchasing power, and hence would be constantly in circulation and not hoarded). See also the notes to letter 19.

Hull: Cordell Hull (1871–1955), U.S. secretary of state 1933–44. See *The Memoirs of Cordell Hull,* 2 vols. (New York: Macmillan, 1948), 2:1452: "I was not, and am not, a believer in the idea of a balance of power or spheres of influence as a means of keeping the peace."

291. Cummings to Pound

TL-1.

March 31 1951   [4 Patchin Place]

Dear Ezra—

bravo Eva. <u>Your</u> friend,kid. Ora at least our

that's right:I never even suspected the("if any" as Joseph Ferdinand Gould would say,till alcoholism)existingness of "Ambruster" "Veith" & "Belden" . . . what names! My angry dicks are combing the purlieus. Furthermore,sah,an ignorant undersigned whispers infraXiansympathy with Your Infallible Jehovahood's ultrathunderings re shallwesay ⟨obvious⟩ fact that,comme presque toujours,les bangbangboys are fronting for boekoo bigur bastudz. Paragraph televison meaning farsight exclamationpoint

just entre svp ourselves:je viens de(to my total surprise)recevoir un Fellowship Guggenheim. Henry Allen Moe exuberantly writes that he resub(need I add:sans our as ever nonhero's knowledge?)mitted the latter's turneddownflat last year application;&,cette fois,won

Marion sends muchmorethanthanks for what she profanely calls "the lowslung bunny". Whom by contrast I,remembering an EPbust in your book-on-G,discreetly term "hieratic"

—vive
Vive

[Here Cummings drew an elephant.]

Moe: Moe was at this time secretary general of the John Simon Guggenheim Memorial Foundation.

book-on-G: *Gaudier-Brzeska* (New York: John Lane Company, 1916). The "Hieratic Head of Ezra Pound" was sculpted by Henri Gaudier-Brzeska in 1914.

292. Pound to Cummings

TL-1.

[April 1951]   [Saint Elizabeths]

Heine Moe and Aydelotte
Luvv all that art is NOT.*
                    *(not this years vintage)
Glad yu gouged the brz/ fer the benzoate of copper ASS
or wotso/
          Nothing but publicity drives these lice into a corner.
Oxfart press / and yr/ being successor to EdLeeMastur'z of course too strong
fer their resistence.

may we qt/ Elkin Mathews' prehistorik widsom.
          "   UGH, twelve guineas, guinea an inch.   "

     Curious how some of the lower forms of animal life squirm on to into
longevity.

why dunt the kumrad meet a few crew's aiders now 'n' agen?

As non politik item, Ez Pinza can sing. (I spose yu KNEW THAT by now. but
like the oirishman "oi just heard it."

and Danny K/ enjoys that versatility attributed to me by late H.H. Ratti the pup.

> [Here Pound drew another picture
> of an Easter bunny.]

[On separate card]
So what
     ?

Heine: Heinrich Heine (1797–1856), German poet. Elsewhere Pound spoke well of Heine, particularly in "How to Read" and "The Renaissance." See Walter Baumann, "Ezra Pound and Heinrich Heine," *Paideuma,* vol. 18, no. 3 (winter 1989), 59–75.

Moe: Henry Allen Moe (1894–1975). He began his career with the John Simon Guggenheim Memorial Foundation in 1925 as its secretary. He later became its secretary general, vice president, president, and president emeritus.

Aydelotte: Frank Aydelotte (1880–1956). During the 1920s, Aydelotte helped formulate plans for the Guggenheim Foundation. He was chairman of its advisory board from 1925 to 1948.

Elkin Mathews': Charles Elkin Mathews (1851–1921), British publisher. He was Pound's first publisher and brought out *Personae* (1909), *Exultations* (1909), *Canzoni* (1911), *Canzoni and Ripostes* (1913), *Cathay* (1915), and *Lustra* (1916).

Ez Pinza: Ezio Pinza (1892–1957), Italian-born singer and actor. He was a member of the Metropolitan Opera from 1926 to 1948. His appearance in the Broadway musical *South Pacific* (1949) and subsequent radio and television appearances made him a widely popular entertainer.

Danny K/: Danny Kaye (born David Daniel Kominski) (1913–87), American comedian and actor.

H.H. Ratti the pup: Ambrogio Damiano Achille Ratti (1857–1939), who became Pope Pius XI in 1922. I have not found where the pope's appreciation of Pound was recorded. Pound may have heard the comment from his friend, Monsignor Pietro Pisani, assistant to the Papal Throne. He may also have heard the comment directly from Ratti, who was director of Milan's Ambrosian Library when Pound did some research there in 1911.

293. Cummings to Pound

TCS.

[Postmarked 22 April 1951]   4PatchinPlace NYC11

so no(since you insist)thanks

any message for the Old Bridge or the Crocodile?

                         eec

message: Cummings and Marion toured Europe from May to July 1951.

Old Bridge: The Bridge of Sighs in Venice.

Crocodile: In the piazza San Marco, one of two granite columns supports a statue of Saint Theodore triumphing over a dragon. The dragon greatly resembles a crocodile. At the beginning of Canto 26, Pound recalls visiting Venice, where he "lay there under the crocodile."

294. Cummings to Pound

TCS.

[Postmarked April 1951]   4 PatchinPlace NYC11

nono—am an ignorant chap;much more so than any "oirishman"

the downhill dog's delightful

I was once a member of "Pershing's
Crusaders":not,however,voluntarily pour ainsi dire*

*"what did you do in the Great War,Grandpapa?"

                                                        eec

295. Pound to Cummings

ALS-1.

[1951?]   [Saint Elizabeths]

In the 1st place
They iz wot they does. The kumrad wiffout the come out wd/ be other & nut
the K/d

———

2ndly Wot does Sberro?
Or Sari fer that matter -- Tho she somethings
        best to th lady
                Ez

Sberro: Unidentified.

Sari: Unidentified.

296. Cummings to Pound

TLS-1. Enclosure.

September 25 '51   Silver Lake
                                          New Hampshire

Dear Ezra—

strikes me this fellow deserves
a frontseat in your Cantos

                              —Marion sends love!

                                   E

(& please <u>return</u> the clipping)

Enclosure: A clipping from the *New York Herald Tribune,* 16 September 1951,
    headed "$1-a-Day Man Believes No One Is Worth More: Says Person Should
    Work First 'for Pleasure and Pride in Job Well Done.'"

297. Pound to Cummings

TL-1.

[September 1951]   [Saint Elizabeths]

Vurry in'erestin' to WOBserve the pint whereAT the kummrad'z mind just
stoppz an' wont move forrard.

BUTT I am all fer the elerphuntz. They prefer Vivaldi to Wagoner.

an gorr blessz th' lydy.

INside-entally didju kno Brooks Adams wrut still another bk/ 1913 "Theory of
Social Revolution"? Hav yu yet recd/ a copy of Del Mar reprint? The Mul/ has
alZO done a loolah, carrying on informing the mutts of the univ/ squalor and
punkishness.

"Theory of Social Revolution": Brooks Adams, *The Theory of Social Revolution*
    (New York: Macmillan, 1913). Adams argues that "the extreme complexity of
    the administrative problems presented by modern industrial civilization is be-

yond the compass of the capitalistic mind. If this be so, American society, as at present organized, with capitalists for the dominant class, can concentrate no further, and, as nothing in the universe is at rest, if it does not concentrate, it must, probably, begin to disintegrate" (226–27).

Del Mar reprint: A reprint of Alexander Del Mar's 1899 publication, *Barbara Villiers; or, A History of Monetary Crimes.* The reprint was issued in Washington, D.C., by the Cleaners' Press in 1950, and again in 1951 in New York by John Kasper.

The Mul/: Eustace Mullins.

a loolah: Mullins does not recall what this was.

298. Cummings to Pound

TCS.

[Postmarked 1 December 1951]   4 PatchinPlace NYC11

what's new?w-a-l(as celebrated student of chinoiserie would aver)Marion & I recently glimpsed pairofPatchens;who were nothingifnot en-route-to-Sunny-Cal. Paraît que certain $,raised on Kenneth's behalf,really did something:indeed he was(with cane)walking:after a 2 year horizontality diagnosed as "arthritis". But(although hospitalXrays showed zero)a good doctor suggested operating;the victim acquiesced—& is now minus quelquechose peculiarly virulent which wasn't arthritis at all. This should cheer anyone who's human,nest(comme disent les américains)pa?

                                                            eec

our best to Dorothy;&please remember us cordially to our friend Omar!

student: Ezra Pound.

299. Pound to Cummings

TL-1.

14 Dec[ember 1951]   [Saint Elizabeths]

"WOT iz new" Kumrad?

takin the woidz out er the mouth ov the Kumrad ipse /

Krize tole him, Bhudddaah tole him / but until the pain of thinking is LESS than the horrors of K.P/s world neither of 'em wunt start thinking that the

ASSininity of the TAX system iz due to iggurunce, plain goddam iggurunce of
the pruBBullum of monetray issue.

wot iz GNU is "Intro" vid. Elath and Brigante
p.o. box 860. Grand Central Stn/ N.Y.
better ask them boys to teAAAA

and also Kasper, p/o. box 552 G.P.O. N.Y. 1.

an luvv to th lady.

an religion went to hell when they took the dancing girls out of the temples.
      ***

HAV yu goddamittBEEN to look at Lekakis' sculpture 57 W. 28th, jus'roun'
deh Korner / phone MU 9-5391

and do yu kno Paul Sachs, an NIF not WHY not? and why aint he been took
to Lekakis??

K.P/s: Kenneth Patchen.
"Intro": A little magazine edited in New York by Louis Brigante. In volume 1,
   numbers 3 and 4, appeared an essay by M. Elath, "In Another Direction," pages
   112–36. In this essay, Elath commented, "Pound took advantage of social labor
   of others, which is what first marked him off from lazy endthreads of victoria-
   nism and places him solidly in the 20th century. This advantage which his
   contemporaries attacked or adopted (if they did not confuse romanticism with
   laziness and defend both), led him to creative totality where elements of other
   literary forms refuse, and wait for creative forms yet undeveloped perhaps, to
   draw on, the same way they drew on Homer and Dante. Pound sowed dragon
   teeth—so far he has harvested fleas" (116).
Kasper: John Kasper (b. 1930), one of the copublishers of the Square Dollar Series
   of publications Pound thought important to have in print.
Lekakis': Michael Lekakis (1907–87), American sculptor. David Gordon recalls
   that "he would sing the choruses of Aristophanes in Greek to EP by first going
   over the meaning of words and phrases to know where to give emphasis"
   (Gordon, 209).
Paul Sachs: Probably Paul Joseph Sachs (1878–1965), American art historian.
   Sachs was a professor of art history at Harvard and (successively) assistant and
   associate director of the Fogg Art Museum. Pound may have become aware of
   Sachs thanks to a book published in 1951, Sachs's *Great Drawings*.

300. Cummings to Pound

TLS-1.

[December 1951]   [4 Patchin Place]

mardi maigre

Dear Ezra—

SaintLiz's most recent Epistle To The Ignorami happily confirms our nonhero's
luminous(albeit longstanding)suspicion that You think humanbeings become
valuable insofaras they reflect principles,while I feel principles become ditto
insofaras they create humanbeings. Dandy&fine

had a pleasing visit from the Cardiff Giant,nay JL,l'autre jour;& he proudly
presented me with hotoffthegriddle copy of what may fairly be termed a
hypertourdeforce,viz Kung-Pound con Rubbings plus Fangdance(where did
latter acquire Achilles?)

ce soir enjoyed quoting,en face a refreshingly nonpoliticoeconomically-mineded
member of the unfound generation,your Aone epigram describing relationship-
of-man-to-ideas. My auditor slightly astonished me by responding right
gallantly

herewith A Merry Xmas to you,& Dorothy;& that little on-tiptoe-cuss who
kept trying to crash the oracle

                                              —Marion
                                                sends
                                                her
                                                love!
                              eec

Cardiff Giant: In 1868 a larger than life-size stone statue was secretly buried on a
   farm near Cardiff, New York. It was dug up in 1869, and the owner of the farm
   presented it to the public as a "petrified man." Shortly thereafter it was shown
   to be a hoax. The Cardiff Giant is now on display at the Farmer's Museum in
   Cooperstown, New York.
JL: James Laughlin.
Kung-Pound: Pound's *Confucius: The Great Digest & Unwobbling Pivot* (New York:
   New Directions, 1951) (Gallup B53). Facing the title page: "Stone Text from
   rubbings supplied by William Hawley; A Note on the Stone Editions by Achilles
   Fang; Translation & Commentary by Ezra Pound."
member: Unidentified.

epigram: It is unclear which extract from *Confucius* Cummings has in mind.
Perhaps he refers to "Some are born with instinctive knowledge, others learn by
study, others are stupid and learn with great difficulty, but the scope of knowing
is one, it does not matter how one knows, the cult of knowledge is one"
Confucius: The Great Digest, The Unwobbling Pivot, The Analects (New York:
New Directions, 1969), 153.

on-tiptoe-cuss: Cummings probably refers to one of the patients at Saint
Elizabeths.

301. Cummings to Pound

ACS.

[1952?]   [4 Patchin Place?]

thank you!

        eec

302. Cummings to Pound

TC.

[Postmarked 18 February 1952]   4 PatchinPlace NYC11

[Part of the message has been crossed out. In Pound's hand below the cross-
out are the words "good for blue jays," apparently his transcription of the
obscured message.]

Marion sends love—

303. Pound to Cummings

TL-1.

[March 1952]   [Saint Elizabeths]

theKUMrad
        might hv/ been comforted by radio this a.m.
//his anon/ failed to catch name, but Mr xxzzy in the mid west, aetat 114 wuz
axd fer secret of longevity

AND replied:

>   never do any work.

whether the k/d thinkgs this shd/ be eggstended to never do any
thinking . . . . . .

>   r.s.

>   luvv to deh lady

304. Cummings to Pound

TLS-1.

[20 March] '52   4 Patchin Place
                                            New York City
                                            11

>   1st day of Spring

Dear Ezra—

I hope it will at least amuse you to learn that(after several weeks of vivid
selfexamination)our nonhero has accepted a "Charles Eliot Norton
professorship";involving six "lectures" re poetry,some student-"contacts",& the
toleration of Cambridge(or vicinity)from next October 15 to May 1 minus a
"reasonable" amount of travel plus a goodsized Xmas vacation. Marion sends
love

>   —salut!

>   eec

305. Pound to Cummings

TL-1.

[March 1952]   [Saint Elizabeths]

revered Estlin

>   if yu be goin ter defy Hen Adams/ or prob/ yu aint/ but if yu
wish to giv gramp' a hand, CONsider I am annoyed by drug pushers gittin
ABOVE the level of buckle-jaws, Jim Yellow an Catfish.

and cartin their sime to the joung of finer sensibility and/or potential/
say mainly sensibility /

AND apart from use of drugs as political instrument / AS known from
PARticular cases.
as well as mass poisoning by inorganic large scale
etc/

wall a good deal of it/ as soon as it gits abov sewer level is due to lack of
provençal love cult (Vita Nuova being a bit special, tho contrary to wot yu as a
fellow harvardian might spose, the Possum respected that work/

however / deprived of a decent attitude / and this deprivation due to the
goddam bible / to the sewers of Vienna and to Charlie Mordecai/ etc.

waaal lecturin' to the immature yu might find some
way to git yr/ real beliefs (as shown in some of yr/ painting, tho yu dunno I
know THAT)

I stil reccomend Zielinsky's "La Sibylle" if yu can get hole of a cawpy/

and so on. Goddam it, when deprived of a respectable May pole. the pore kids
take to heroin/ and it aint clean.

P.S. mebbe I can finish that ⟨sep. cov.⟩ quatrain sometime.

Hen Adams/: Henry Adams. "It can not be done, said Henry Adams to Santayana.
Oh, you wish to teach at Harvard. It can not be DONE. Henry Adams said he had
tried it." Thus Pound in a radio broadcast of 2 March 1942 (Doob, 50).
buckle-jaws, Jim Yellow an Catfish: Slang terms designating African-Americans.
Possum: T. S. Eliot.
sewers of Vienna: Psychoanalysis as developed by Freud.
Charlie Mordecai/: Karl Marx.
"La Sibylle": Tadeusz Zielinski (1859–1944), *La Sibylle: Trois essais sur la religion
antique et la Christianisme* (Paris: F. Rieder, 1924). Issue number 2 (November
1956) of *Edge* was "devoted to The Sybil, Three Essays on Ancient Religion and
Christianity by Zielinski, here made available in English for the first time." The
editor's note on Zielinski indicated he was born in 1859 in Kiev, and that he was
a professor of classics in the St. Petersburg University in 1887. In the course of
his study, Zielinski contended that the religion of the immediately pre-Christian
era was "the religion of love" (18). Judaism, on the other hand, was a religion of

fear and "thorny casuistry" (19). "And although Christianity accepted the He-
brew Old Testament as one of its sacred books, it is no less true that the terrible
jealous God of Israel is in no sense the 'good' Christian God" (19).
that quatrain: Not located.

306. Cummings to Pound

TC.

[Postmarked 26 March 1952]   4 PatchinPlace NYC11

as to the earlier of your much esteemed missives:feel inclined to lump
"thinking" with "work";though am not(yet)of course 114,quite

re the later:am delighted to learn that my painting finds me out;being naturally
the last person who'd suspect how,or in which(of several)direction(s). But
would—as I remarked at Marion this day—the lecturing chez alma were thy
job!

buy the buy:a crop of wee buttons-with-stickpins has appeared,each b-w-st
reading "I LIKE IKE". Well,today she saw 2 socialiteish strollers;adorned with
disks twice the size of a silverdollar,which replied "NO LIKE"

μνιv aeide Θea ["The wrath do thou sing, O goddess." Cummings types the
first three words of the *Iliad*.]

307. Cummings to Pound

TCS.

[Postmarked 14 April 1952]   4 PatchinPlace NYC11

shall do my best,anyhow,to
not possumize

eec

308. Cummings to Pound

TELEGRAM.

31 May 1952   [4 Patchin Place]

HOPE TO SEE YOU TOMORROW AROUND TEN LOVE

MARION AND ESTLIN

309. Pound to Cummings

TL-1.

12.40 p.m. 1. June /anno 4650 [1952]   [Saint Elizabeths]

this to acknowledge receipt ⟨at above hour⟩ of courteous
telegram
            announcing hope of la famille k/z
that they wd/ arrive this day at 10 a.m.
which indeed was the case.

310. Pound to Cummings

TL-2.

[1 or 2 June 1952]   [Saint Elizabeths]

                    e.e.c

to the human fly /
            YES, and these all too brief/
takes grampaw so long to git this thought roun' to deh praktikl.

Mr Wm Yandell (yanDELL, or however he purrnouces his handle)
      Yelliot/
started a muggerzoon "CONFLuence" in haavud / wit a lo'r blokes wot cant
write fer nutZ.
Might be TOLD that itz za bloody disgrYce that Ez' trans/ of the great
KLASSIK anthol/ has been putt in cellarage fer three years/

At haavud/ the kumrad will find one comfort namely Achilles FANG 23
Boylston Hall.

I think our oriental friend wd/ back up any KICK the aforesaid e.e.c. might giv to the YELLIOT (two lls and two tts.)

i do NOT think the aforesaid kumrad will find the international forum ⟨vid sup/ "Confluence"⟩ his nacherl habitat / itz zonly the question of its possible utility / after all we SHOULD occasionally dine at the Greif / and make use of some of that Tirolese an' castellated scenery SOMETIME.

in the eggcitement i fergot to fish out the enc/ from Lunnon retrospect / chiefly az yu enquired abaht th late Henry. vid. enc

e.e.c. 2

aND seRIously / if yu wanna DO something wiff them Snortin Elephunt lectures.
In first place, traison des clercs / consists in so having messd the scene by Matthiessenism, and 30 years alledged crit/ that was mere stalling. that when sowbelly perjured himself NO one (eggcept ole Beatrix Abbot) took it as anything butta matter of course.
**
2/ no attention been paid to Cleaners' manifesto.
does the kumrad KNOW what it was?
****
3/ concept of prosody not yet hackneyed / in fact dunno as it is printed or will be by time yu lec/

prosody: the articulation of the total sound of a poEM.
****
4.
as in painting: object IN space.
poetry to be any damn use / word in REALTION to something.
Dant took fer granted an affirmative answer to
            sarebbe peggio . . . . se non fosse cive?
Paradiso viii bo'm of nex to las' page of that canter.

Dunno if yu can spiel fer couple of hours / on THAT an it might deThoreauize more'n yu care to.

*** there is no need to conserve mouldy orthography (as we beelv/ the kumrad has by practic etc.) or even the old order elephunt sNorton.   frum this autumn onward the record will read

An while in bAAAston, go in an SEE ole Beatrice(Abbot)
44 Larchmont Rd/ Melrose 76 mass
yu an Marion will wan' som humang sassiety.

Yelliot: William Yandell Elliott, director of the Harvard Summer School of Arts and Sciences and of Education.

"CONFluence": The first issue of *Confluence* appeared in March 1952. It was edited by Henry Kissinger. *Confluence* presented itself as a forum in which a wide variety of issues relevant to contemporary civilization could be discussed.

Ez' trans/: Eventually published as *The Classic Anthology Defined by Confucius* (Cambridge, Mass.: Harvard University Press, 1954). This volume, however, represented only a partial version of the text Pound wanted published. "Harvard published a mutilated version of the *Odes* without the Chinese text" (Gordon, 228).

FANG: Achilles Fang (1910–95), a professor at Harvard University.

the Greif: A hotel with a restaurant in Bolzano, Italy.

th late Henry: Perhaps Henry James. Enclosure lacking.

traison des clercs: The title of a book by Julien Benda that gave the phrase currency. Translated into English by Richard Aldington as *The Treason of the Intellectuals* (New York: William Morrow and Company, 1928). Benda meant by "clercs" those "whose activity essentially is *not* the pursuit of practical aims." (43). Their "traison" lay in their allowing political passions to color their thought.

Matthiessenism: Francis Otto Matthiessen (1902–50), American scholar and critic. Matthiessen contributed to Charles Norman's *The Case of Ezra Pound* (New York: Bodley Press, 1948). His statement concluded, "Living for so many years as an isolated expatriate in Rapallo, Pound was so cut off from any normal contacts with society that when he began to develop a political and social theory it could only be eccentric. As an eccentric he must now be judged" (59).

sowbelly: Franklin Delano Roosevelt. The perjury would have consisted in his not honoring his oath to uphold the Constitution.

Beatrix Abbot: Beatrice Abbot, a Bostonian who corresponded with Pound in the late 1940s and early 1950s. She wrote Pound concerning the ways in which governmental authorities throughout history had used chemical additives in food to control the population.

Cleaners' manifesto: "1. We must understand what is really happening. 2. If the verse-makers of our time are to improve on their immediate precursors, we must be vitally aware of the duration of syllables, of melodic coherence, and of the tone leading of vowels. 3. The function of poetry is to debunk by lucidity." "Cleaners' Manifesto," *Strike,* 9 (February 1946), 2 (Gallup C1796). Reprinted in *Paideuma,* vol. 3, no. 3 (winter 1974) and in *EPPP.*

Paradiso viii: Lines 115–16, "Ond' egli ancora: 'Or di,' sarebbe il peggio / per l'uomo in terra se non fossa cive?' " ["Whence he again: 'Now, say, would it be /

worse for man on earth were he no citizen?'"] *The Paradiso of Dante Alighieri*
(1899; London: J. M. Dent, 1921), 98–99.

311. Cummings to Pound

TLS-1.

June 25 '52   Silver Lake
                                                   New Hampshire

Dear EP—

'twas good to hearseehug you

now that am collecting my(scattered in ny-va-wash-ny-bost-NH
transit)selves,let me kindly thank the author of epistle to the human fly for
generous greetings,excellent counsel,& instructive MaxB(enclosed)enclosure

shall keep an eye peeled for Thetis' boychild,dodge Yandellic "confluence",&
probably pluckupcourage to cherchez la Beatrix

you may be pleased to learn that in his traduction of thy friend's Commedia
Dr CharlesEliotNorton throws this footnote at Par viii 116(Per l'uomo in terra
se non fosse cive?)"For the fact is evident that man is by nature a social
animal,and cannot attain his true end except as a member of a community"

quand à l'undersigned,everything(at least in my less misguided
moments)becomes ⟨luckily⟩ not what but who

                                        —Marion sends love!

saw a silent bluejay l'autre jour;he sends you his swoopingest

MaxB: Probably Max Beerbohm. Enclosure lacking.
Thetis' boychild: Thetis's son was Achilles.
his traduction: Charles Eliot Norton, trans., *The Divine Comedy of Dante Aligheri*,
    revised edition, 3 vols. (Boston: Houghton, Mifflin and Company, 1902). Al-
    though Cummings indicates the footnote is to line 116, it is to line 117.

312. Pound to Cummings

TL-1.

[27 June 1952]   [Saint Elizabeths]

to the GLUTTON for punishment (anonyme, ov course)
the MYStery of hozw'tell yu spen' yr/ time / and WOT yu read deepens / and
as to how-why the that-which wd/ seem to designed to take allthe bhloody
interest OUT of the subjekk /

as per/ sample of the Elephant Snortn/   in yr/ hnrd favor
                                                of the whateverth/

as to the WHO-ity / that being but a more particular case of the WHAT-ity**,
is nacherly to be approved/
                                                as givin'
)(pragmatic.)   vivacity to the style of the glutton fer . . .

OR returning to the discussion of the Florentine / IF the quiditas is to be
diluted into an abstract it is thereby the less quiditas/ and the further removed
fromthe Kung-ish or the HOmerik.

***I learn from the TIMES of London, that NOTE: Mr Flaccus is projecting a
volume on "The Mind of Edgar Lee Masters". He will doubtless be glad of any
Masterianianiania in yr/ possession.
                                    and
                            so
                                    on

**

i nuther wordz: the what-ity is COMposed of a bunch of who-itities, and/or
which-ities.
                    thaTTIZ to say: unlesse / yu git to pewer elEments, essence,
the "eternal mystery of non-being", at wich pt/ the kitten catches itz TAIL.

the Florentine: Dante.
Mr Flaccus: This announcement appeared in the *Times Literary Supplement* for
    Friday, 6 June 1952. "Sir,-- The late Edgar Lee Masters, the American poet and
    lawyer, was in England on two occasions in this century, and spent some time in
    London, as did his close friend the American editor, William Marion Reedy, of
    St. Louis. I am writing on "The Mind of Edgar Lee Masters" and would appreci-
    ate it if you would be so kind as to call this fact to the attention of your readers
    and ask any of them who may have letters, anecdotes, photographs of Masters or

Reedy or both to get in touch with me. I will carefully safeguard, copy, and return any material that may be sent to me.

Kimball Flaccus
42 Horatio Street, New York 14, N.Y., U.S.A."

313. Pound to Cummings

TL-1.

[Summer 1952]   [Saint Elizabeths]

e.e.c.

th kumrad, so far as his manifest has penetrated grampaw'z zintellex seems mainly to hv/ seen in Thoreau the return to the squirril.

Doubtless a partial and bias'd view

---*** an prob/ quite detatched (or howver te'll yu spellit)
item / the diLIgent Kenner has found yr/ woodman citing Confucius with considerable discrimination.

That brackets Leibniz (or tZ) Voltaire and Walden pond.

luvv to the lady

ov course I like to git nooz from the outer, when them in the outer has vim to utter.

[In Dorothy Pound's hand:] Omar in Teheran. Says they really can cook RICE.

manifest: Pound evidently refers to a Cummings letter not located.
Kenner: Hugh Kenner, the literary critic whose *The Poetry of Ezra Pound* (1951) was the first important study of Pound's verse. His most comprehensive work on Pound is *The Pound Era* (1971).

314. Pound to Cummings

TL-1.

[8 July 1952]   [Saint Elizabeths]

estEEMD estlln

the adhered strikes a frien' o' mine az funny / az yu can see from his underlining.

How it strikes a haaaVUd man? i dunno but az uzual I await
enlight/

luvv to deh lady

Enclosure: A newspaper clipping listing the fourteen recipients of honorary
degrees at the Harvard University commencement exercises in June. Pound
drew an arrow pointing to the name of "Walter Hamor Piston, composer—
Doctor of Music." Below the arrow Pound wrote: "eu phonius nyme."

315. Cummings to Pound

TCS.

[Postmarked 21 July 1952]   [Silver Lake, N.H.]

thanks for the Harvard document—well, we can't have everything unquote I
suppose

eec

Marion sends love!

316. Pound to Cummings

TL-1.

[July 1952?]   [Saint Elizabeths]

eec/ yu b'er read WynDAMN Lewis' "Rotting Hill"
or skip first sketch and git on/ esp/ as "Laming" of last skitch has eMIgrated,
party by nyme of Swabey. (will try purrsuade him look at yu in passing J.York)
as yu shdn't be abandoned to life at Ch/ Elephant Snortin' level.
an gorBress 'er lydiship

"Rotting Hill": Wyndham Lewis, *Rotting Hill* (London: Methuen, 1951; and
Chicago: Henry Regnery, 1952). *Rotting Hill* is a series of tales of life in the
"ruined society" (as Lewis calls it in his foreword) of Great Britain after World
War II. In chapter 9, "Parents and Horses," Lewis introduces "the Reverend
Mathew Laming . . . Vicar of Ketwood." Lewis remarks that he "is one of a
small number of country clergy attempting to stem the socialist tide" (264).
Laming (Swabey) leads local resistance to the government authorities who plan

to close the village schools and replace them with "Central Rural Primary Schools." Lewis concludes that Laming "belonged to the type of Englishman of which the most perfect specimens are Edmund Burke, Henry Maine, and a half-dozen others" (287). Henry Swabey (b. 1916), Anglican clergyman, had been corresponding with Pound since 1935. He lived in Ontario, Canada, from August 1951 to July 1954. He then returned to England.

317. Pound to Cummings

TL-1.

[2 August 1952]   [Saint Elizabeths]

has deh
         KUMRAD
ever encountered, read or pErUszd ole WynDAMN's "Doom of Youth" sd/ to hv/ been SUPpressed, and now costin 3 quid ten schillinkz? otherwise I wd'n ask whether yu care to borrer it.
         date 1932
a tiresome kuss but not stagnant (i.e. W.L.)

franchement écrire ce qu'on pense // waaal he dunt allus do THAT, cause he is skirmishink roun' trying to eat and get printed amangst the slimey limeys / but nowNagin he pulls orf something or other.

                    luvv to deh lydy

[In Dorothy Pound's hand:] Omar still in Teheran 10 days ago: situation very explosive - He hopes to get back here via Pacific—by next spring . . . . ? D.P.

Doom of Youth: Wyndham Lewis, *The Doom of Youth* (London: Chatto and Windus, 1932). Lewis contended that British politicians' emphasis on bringing "youth" into positions of leadership was a smokescreen for the replacement of older workers by younger, more active workers. Chatto and Windus withdrew the book when Alec Waugh threatened to sue for libel over Lewis's remark about Waugh's alleged interest in schoolboys. The book was published in the United States without any difficulties.

franchement: In "Remy de Gourmont" (1915 and 1916), Pound recalled a message sent to him by de Gourmont: "'Franchement d'écrire ce qu'on pense, seul plaisir d'un écrivain.' 'To put down one's thought frankly, a writer's one pleasure.' That phrase was the center of Gourmont's position." *Selected Prose*, 416. Pound also recalled this sentence in his 1962 interview with Donald Hall. See *Writers at Work: Second Series* (New York: Viking, 1963), 47.

318. Cummings to Pound

TCS.

[Postmarked 11 August 1952]   Silver Lake N.H.

Rotting Hill on its way back to you with many thanks—by all means send us the other WL. Et bonne chance!!!

[Pound wrote this on the card when he sent it to Wyndham Lewis: "W. L. as indicatv of spread of Kulch/ inter barbaros / signature that of Kumrad Kumminkz / author of EIMI and other notable woikz/ They will stand live stuff if brot to 'em" (Materer, 269).]

Rotting Hill: See letter 315.

319. Pound to Cummings

TL-1.

[12 August 1952]   [Saint Elizabeths]

deh KUMrad

latest wynDAMN sd/ be on way from LimeyLand / not yet arruv/ Doom of Youth out on loan shd/ be sendable in a couRple ov weaks/
other W.L available if wanted / as per elence
say if yu want 'em or WHICH.

                                              saluti alla
                                              gent/ma sig/a

[In Dorothy Pound's hand:]
1. America & Cosmic Man.
2. Doom of Youth.
                    is all I can provide.
          & 1. is only partly good.

                    Saluti
                        D.P.

Omar due to clear out from Teheran in Sept. I rather expect he will be sent away earlier. He is planning-- the Lord willing) to come back here via India, Japan etc

America & Cosmic Man: Wyndham Lewis, *America and Cosmic Man* (London: Nicholson and Watson, 1948; and Garden City, N.Y.: Doubleday, 1949). In this study of American democracy, Lewis sees it as a model for a future world government.

320. Pound to Cummings

TL-1.

[August 1952]   [Saint Elizabeths]

eec/
Gawd bless Wyndham, chief delouser of dying Britain, ~~Because of~~ him the hempire sinks into desuetude a LITTLE less bug-bit and vershitten

Sending yu Swabey's copy ⟨Writer and Abscheroot⟩ to save time / mine on way from Limeyburg.
when having peRUsed AT LEASURE, please send it to Swb/ instead o returning it
          **

we note that WL has found out that a dirty limey named Orwell had found out in 1938 or so wot e.e.c. had mentioned in 1927

correct ~~this~~ to
~~THANKS TO~~
stet/ Because of is o.k. (I got thinkin I had/ writ But for.

Writer and Abscheroot: *The Writer and the Absolute* (London: Methuen, 1952). "Freedom to write what one regards as true," says Lewis, "is my subject throughout these pages" (5). "What has befallen me, or rather my books, proves what is my contention: namely that the mid-XXth Century writer is only nominally free, and should not fail to acquire a thorough knowledge of the invisible frontier surrounding his narrow patch of liberty, to transgress which may be fatal" (8). "Freedom of the writer to speculate, to criticize, to create: such is the desideratum of the writer, as man-of-letters. To speculate, among other things, about social questions; to criticize, on occasion, the conduct of public affairs. But if one includes the free expression of *political opinion* in one's claim, all history is against one. There is no security anywhere there, and philosophers and poets have always touched politics at their peril" (29).
Orwell: George Orwell (1903–58), British author. Pound may refer to Orwell's *The Road to Wigan Pier* (1937).

321. Cummings to Dorothy Pound

ACS.

[Postmarked 25 August 1952]   Silver Lake N.H.

Marion & I are delighted to hear that Omar may be back soon!

please give our best to Le Maître!

                                    EEC

322. Cummings to Dorothy Pound

TCS.

[Postmarked 15 September 1952?]   [Silver Lake, N.H.]

many thanks for the
intoGermantranslation
of EP's pro domo

Marion & I hope you're
feeling fit!please
remember us to our
friend Omar

et bonne chance

                         eec

intoGermantranslation: Part 1, section 4 of *Hugh Selwyn Mauberley.* Eva Hesse's
German translation of this and other poetry and prose by Pound was published
in *Ezra Pound: Dichtung und Prosa, mit einem Geleitwort von T. S. Eliot* (Zurich:
Im Verlag der Arche [1953]) (Gallup D26).

323. Pound to Cummings

TL-1.

[17 September 1952]   [Saint Elizabeths]

lest pHostHerity
judge with undue severity

this brand from the buRRning (th kumrad)
cast into an insterooshun of "learning"
we assert that at the time of his fall
the said kumrad
wuz more in'erested in Sally Rand
than in Tallyrand
or any other topic
bordering on . . . .

insterooshun: Harvard University.

Sally Rand: Born Helen Gould Beck (1904–79), American dancer. She became famous for dancing in the nude, while concealing herself behind large ostrich-feather fans, at the 1933 Chicago World's Fair. Her career as a "fan dancer" continued until the year before her death.

Tallyrand: Charles-Maurice de Talleyrand-Périgord (1754–1838), French diplomatist and statesman. Gordon cites Pound's opinion of Talleyrand: "No one in the France of his time did so much to repair the damage done by fanatics" (272).

324. Cummings to Pound

TC.

[Postmarked 26 September 1952]   [Silver Lake, N.H.]

Pound,pound,pound
    On thy cogent corona,E P!
But I would that my tongue could utter
    The silence of Alfred Noise.

Alfred Noise: This verse is based on Tennyson's lyric, "Tears, Idle Tears" (1834). The name is also a pun on Alfred Noyes (1880–1958), British poet.

325. Pound to Cummings

TL-1. Enclosure.

[20 October 1952]   [Saint Elizabeths]

JHEE/ZUSS
      Mariaaaw Y
           HO-
               zeeeee

this wd/ be funny if the venerable obstetrician were't so ill at the moment /
        I mean I cant send it on to him cause his rib wd/ prob/ take
it as malice on my part /

And WHILE it is prub/l that the iTEM wil git greater spread in pro?portium as
the noozPrint nears RuddyFurd/
                                NOT knowing
which seau-de-toilette reaches the domicile of the congiugi KumminkZZ as
daily informer/ I send on the klippink/ cause I wd'n wan' either of yu to
missIT.

Enclosure: A clipping from the *Washington Times-Herald* dated 20 October 1952.
The headline: "Editor Assails Appointment of Dr. Williams." The clipping
reported that "Appointment of Dr. Carlos Williams as consultant in English
poetry at the Library of Congress is under attack by the Lyric Foundation,
which publishes The Lyric, magazine of traditional poetry. In an open letter to
the magazine's contributors and subscribers, Mrs. Virginia Kent Cummins, its
editor and founder, denounced the appointment as 'an insult to American
poetry and American citizenship' in citing a sample of the doctor's poetry and
his record of support of Communist causes." Virginia Kent Cummins "for years
had been attacking the countless enemies of good, old-fashioned poetry" (Mar-
iani, 651).

326. Cummings to Pound

TL-1.

October 24 1952   6 Wyman Road
                                             Cambridge 38
                                             Massachusetts

& right ye were,Ezreee meee by,to communicate the Williamsiana;which arrived
this day,forwarded from nh:& gladdened my spouse&self

now this dame "Cummins" has(as you doubtless know)been after eec for
yarz;so am selfishly-delighted she's attacking someone else(poor shawn shay)

but regret to learn our laymyspiritatherfeetfull acquaintance has injured his
Amongmanyothers,undistinguished cote(with a circumflex). What was he up
or down or sideways or neither to,pray?

am in good hands here,belonging to 1 "John Finley";professing Greek,extolling
Humanities,&(tactfully not when I'm around;however)praising

O'Possumtotheskies. A nice—the JF—fellow. Has already preserved me from well nigh not numerable "social" phenomena:&(this in thine oreille)will,j'espère,make possible a big escape to ny circa Xmas!

we live in a little house,far from seive lies ation;& a big BLUEJAY seems to be our chief mascot—a stalwart rascal,whose Hue give me Joy unmitigated;& who fears no crow or gull extant. I've already remembered him to you

Marion sends love to yourself & Dorothy! Please keep many fingers crossed(on my nonworthy bewhole)from 8 to 9 PM this coming Tuesday,28th October;my 1st "Norton lecture"

—oop thih rubbles

l'enfant prodigue

"Cummins": See the note to the previous letter. When this letter was published in the *Paris Review* (fall 1966), Marion Cummings made a marginal note about Virginia Kent Cummins in her copy: "who with Stanton Coblentz etc. had a publication called, I think, 'Wings,'& attacked E.E.C., M. Moore, Eliot, as poets who wrote their absurd & outlandish stuff, not out of conviction, but to *make money*!!!!"

John Finley: John H. Finley Jr. (1904–95), professor at Harvard from 1933 to 1976. Eliot Professor of Greek Literature and Master of Eliot House (1941–68). He was awarded an honorary degree by Harvard in 1968; the citation described him as a "Scholar, house master extraordinary; for nearly 40 years the humanities at Harvard have been enlivened by his buoyant and vital spirit." His photograph appears in Marion Morehouse Cummings's *Adventures in Value* (New York: Harcourt, Brace and World, 1962).

O'Possum: T. S. Eliot.

327. Pound to Cummings

TL-1.

[26 October 1952]   [Saint Elizabeths]

   e
e.c

and while in them partZZ / as gramp' cant remember all
will yu see FANG (Achilles)   23 Boiled Stones All

and LEND (or even donate) yr/ heave to find out where the hell the FishHawk
has got to on stimates fer ODES/

disgrace to the nation they aint printed ALREADY /

if the penny pinchers are holding out not from sheer ill will but fer lack of chicken-feed / do FIND bloody OUT

PUBlishers are capable of traihising the whole mind of the race, fer $238. or similar volume of medium.

Glad the KumRad fambly is now sound on the sub/j of b/JAYZ

FANG: Achilles Fang, Chinese scholar at Harvard University. Author of "Fenollosa and Pound," *Harvard Journal of Asian Studies,* vol. 20, no. 2 (June 1957), 213–38.

FishHawk: I have been unable to determine which member of the staff of the Harvard University Press Pound refers to, whether the director (Thomas J. Wilson), the production manager (Burton L. Stratton), the assistant to the director (Lawrence Belden), or someone else. The first poem in Pound's translation of the *Classic Anthology* begins, "'Hid! Hid!' the fish-hawk saith." In a letter of 27 May 1953 to Omar Pound, Cummings remarked, "somebody—was or wasn't it Thomas Wilson,head of the Harvard University Press?—not only agreed to publish,but went so far as to design,a volume comprising all EP's Confucian translations together;then(without giving any reason at all)did nothing."

ODES: *The Classic Anthology Defined by Confucius* (Cambridge, Mass.: Harvard University Press, 1954) (Gallup A69).

328. Pound to Cummings

TL-2. Enclosures.

[18 November 1952]   [Saint Elizabeths]

e.e.c.

WANTED, some brains somwhereOR other/
of late the idea that FDR was both a s.o.b. and in ERROR has made some slight progress/
                              also a drif away from worship of ex post
facto   etc/etc/

but no drif toward giving a little credit to the blokes ~~that~~ ⟨who⟩ attempted to stop th goddam swine in their infamies /
                              an that don't
mean only grampaw.

of course economics and WeltpolitiKKK etc/ and Blackstone's velleities complicate the personal problem

cant fer zmpl send ole whyDAM 6000 pages eggsplaining EVERYTHING

Incidentally his rapportage on the unSpain of Hem/ has got by Regnery . along with spritely Rot Hill.

Still waiting fer haaaaaVUD to move on Kung verse/ tho the admirable FANG seems 'opeful.

luvv to deh lady

what about teasing the teasible President of the JOYCE so CIetY Mr J.J.Slocum
        HICOG, Office of Publi. Affairs
     Public Relations Commission APO 757 -A U.S.Army
               c/o Post Master   New York

enclosing clip/ AND the Sq $ circular

with suggestion (not AS suggested BY yr/ anon/ but with thin veil of spontaneity, aZIF from the C.E.N. Prof/

Dont do it unless yu approve/   but cd/ say he wd/ hv/ done better to consult grampaw.

No use MY tellin him, he thinks I hold views.

I take it 6 cemts AIR mail / carries to HICOG

Enclosures: (1) A newspaper clipping from the *Washington Times-Herald* of 15 November 1952. Headline: "Commies Paid by State Dept. to Do Textbook." Datelined Frankfurt, Germany, the article began, "The United States State department admitted with embarrasment [*sic*] here today that it advanced two German Communists more than $50,000 and commissioned them to write a history book for distribution in German schools. The book 'Synchronoptische Weltgeschichte' has just been published but will not be distributed by the State department, which is planning a lawsuit to get its money back. A department spokesman said the book was 'pro-Communist, anti-democratic, anti-Catholic, on a number of occasions anti-Jewish and thick with anti-theological prejudice.'"

(2) A leaflet advertising titles in the Square Dollar Series: *The Chinese Written Character as a Medium for Poetry* and *The Unwobbling Pivot and Great Digest of Confucius, The Analects of Confucius, Barbara Villiers, or a History of Monetary Crimes.*

Blackstone's velleities: Sir William Blackstone (1723–80), British jurist. His *Commentaries on the Laws of England* (1765–69) became the most influential study of English law.

whyDAM: Wyndham Lewis.

his rapportage: Wyndham Lewis, *The Revenge for Love* (London: Cassell, 1937; and Chicago: Henry Regnery, 1952). It is a novel about Spanish and British Communists at the time of the Spanish Civil War.

Rot Hill: Wyndham Lewis, *Rotting Hill.*

Kung verse/: *The Classic Anthology Defined by Confucius* (Cambridge, Mass.: Harvard University Press, 1954) (Gallup A69).

329. Pound to Cummings

TL-1.

[24 November 1952]   [Saint Elizabeths]

e.e.c.
             probably right in crumbing yr/ words so the lydy of just not can feed 'em to sparrows (NOT Lesbia's)
                                                        but HOW do you explain the stinking foulness of them wot do NOT want to learn/

I mean when the bastids get in between them that know and the stewdent/

can yu translate into langqwitch COMprehensible to denizens of yr/ present locality
             that an english word is NOT the equivalent of an ideogram, and that ANYone above the level of a louse wants the original text to FACE a translation. (NOT even as in case of Princeton millyumaire stuck in at the end of a vol/ where you hv/ to hunt like hell for it

A trans/ of an ideogram CAN assist the reader of not-chinese toward an understanding of an ideogram. YUSS. But when the text is of more interest than an Aiken autobiog/ that is not enuff. NO I hv/ not SEEN the example in preceding line I merely heard a prof/ was reviewing it.

my goRRRR   wotter country

sparrows: Lesbia is the lady whom Catullus addresses in some of his poems. Lesbia's sparrow is mentioned in Catullus II ("Passer, deliciae meae puellae") and Catullus III ("Lugete, o Veneres Cupidinesque").

Princeton millyumaire: In a letter to James Laughlin in which Pound discussed the importance of having original text and translation facing each other, Pound said, "As fer Princeton/ the vol/ of Swan of Food and Money in China is a prize example of how foul imbecility can become in matter of presentation of stuff for study." The book he refers to is *Food and Money in Ancient China: The Earliest Economic History of China to* A.D. *25, Han shu 24, with related texts, Han shu 91 and Shih-chi 129,* translated and annotated by Nancy Lee Swann (Princeton, N.J.: Princeton University Press, 1950). The "millyumaire" is probably Guion M. Gest, whose library of oriental books became the Gest Oriental Library of the Institute for Advanced Studies at Princeton in 1937. Gest (1864–1948) founded his own construction engineering firm in New York in 1914. While traveling on business in China, he became interested in collecting rare books. By the time Princeton acquired his library it amounted to over one hundred thousand volumes.

Aiken autobiog: Conrad Aiken, *Ushant* (New York: Duell, Sloan and Pearce, 1952).

330. Pound to Cummings

TL-2.

[26 November 1952]   [Saint Elizabeths]

e/e/c

sorry to keep on pestering/ but goDAMNIT patience getting wore out /
        and attempt to insure that all edtns/ of EZ shall be either mutilated
or posthumous
                                is gittin under grampaw's ole skin.
⟨4 years cunctation on this ITEM⟩

***

I noted somewhile back that the Oxford bloody press was printing yu/
        with EFFulgent sales talk.

I doubt if they wd/ print my most important woik (apart from the Canters and not below 'em) BUT IF yu have STILL maintained contact with that antient and kons ervativ orgumzation, mebbe yu cd/ ax.

Lowell (no not Jas. R.) the preent one, known to his intimes as CAL(igula) iz the only one of our confrere wha has attempted to buck the boycott. AND of course the effect of the strine /// etc.

P.S. to M:
                howz the kumrad bearinK hup in the orful Klimate (mental
an physikal)?

I tvust yu like the pixchoors off deh oldt antique shop in deh kurrent rhotokalco. It pleased the local shade infact him and another set of gleaming teeth in nubian setting brought their joy to my cell door las' week. NOTE the inaccuracy of UNimportant detail / ref/ McLuhan's sabotaged and long delayed sottisier /

NOT that they lie on great matters with <u>SPECIFIC</u> purpose but that ALL accounts of ANY and EVERY all so unprecice that the pore bdy/ reader NEVER knows anything /

not after 20 years of this Luceness.

alZo, from Paris, the punks are still ganged up against Crevel / 15 years post mortem.

as yu say, that kind of canaille is the wust.

oh hell. get M/ to send on a few INFORMATIVE data/
is the beanery still shut to Brooks (while caressing the pindling Henry) Admz?

still Frobenius OUT. naturally Del Mar not heard of.

AND wot bout local view of the Possum's inSTINKS?

an apart fr. wot is called (notice I say CALLED) the cryptic mode of the kummink'zzz verse / he is vurry in some ways incommunicative. combining, in his amphibious, the celebrated J.J. to W.L. "you are going to PAINT it, but I (emphasis on the I) am going to write it."

Lowell: Robert Lowell (1917–77), American poet. Lowell frequently visited Pound at St. Elizabeths when he was Poetry Consultant to the Library of Congress in 1947 and 1948. He also corresponded with Pound.

oldt antique shop: See "A Birthday for 'Poetry,'" *Life*, vol. 33, no. 21 (24 November 1952), 103–16. The article reprinted the first contributions to *Poetry* of eleven American poets, Pound and Cummings among them. Each poem was accompanied by a photograph of the poet. The article also noted that Pound, "despite his later political aberrations, remains a vigorous influence on American poetry."

McLuhan's . . . sottisier: Marshall McLuhan (1911–80), Canadian literary critic and professor of English at the University of Toronto. He had written Pound on 5 July 1951 that "he proposed to establish a mimeographed weekly sheet" (Carpenter, 799).

Luceness: Henry R. Luce (1898–1967), American publisher. Founder of *Time, Fortune,* and *Life*.

punks . . . Crevel: René Crevel.

Possum's inSTINKS: Pound's comment may have been prompted by the publication (20 November) of T. S. Eliot's *The Complete Poems and Plays, 1909–1950* (New York: Harcourt, Brace and Company, 1952).

J.J. to W.L:. James Joyce to Wyndham Lewis.

331. Cummings to Pound

TCS.

[Postmarked 27 November 1952]   6 WymanRoad
                                                 Cambridge38 Mass

now that the innulegjul strain has temporarily lessened,shall try to play The Good Samaritan now & then; though fear it's a somewhat nonsuitable role for our unhero

                    —Marion sends love!

                         eec

332. Pound to Cummings

ALS-1.

5 Dec[ember 1952?]   S LIZ

Too bad I hv. missed plastk gif's all <u>my</u> life.
now I long fer the brush or pencil wot wd. depik th Kmrd. az project.
        Ez

luv to deh lady

P.S.   ? a thesis fer Bernettaaa
metamorphose of object to
            subjek
                 to
                 projeck

Bernettaaa: Sister Bernetta M. Quinn published her article "Ezra Pound and the Metamorphic Tradition" in the *Western Review,* vol. 15 (spring 1951), 169–81.

333. Pound to Marion Morehouse Cummings

TL-1.

[30 January 1953]   [Saint Elizabeths]

M.C.

GAWD DDDaMMit
                the Mulligator complains that yu wil get in damBORES to
congumerate, so'z every time he calls he can't hear a word from the kumrad
                        and is not interested in inferior wallawalla of the
sweepings fr/ broadway or whatever else leadeth to induction.

Goacher is pestering me (AND he pays) fer a GOOD poEM by yr/ illustrious
consort/
                and I wd/ be only too glad to git a GOOD one /
#
                not merely something that wd/ open th Goach to spicion of having
merely yowled fer a EYElusterous name.

As to Kulch/ I hear that Dent intends to reprint Blackstone sometime / so some
decently writ/ matter will again SOME(goddamit when) time be available for
the healthy young.

No use my s/gest/n a theme fer deh KUMRAD. cause he aint steerable/ but I
got a poifik pearl yester fr/ one of my colleagues.

M.C.: Marion Cummings.
Mulligator: Eustace Mullins.
Goacher: Dennis Goacher (b. 1925), British poet and actor. Goacher was associ-
    ated with a little magazine, the *European*. In its first issue (March 1953) ap-
    peared his review, "Dr. Leavis or Mr. Pound" (41–51). Goacher examined F. R.
    Leavis's *How to Teach Reading, a Primer for Ezra Pound* and concluded, "I think
    enough samples have now been given to show that the level of criticism in Dr.
    Leavis' booklet is not exactly of a high order. Indeed it is often difficult to decide
    whether he has twisted Mr. Pound's meaning in order to pave the way for his
    own asseverations, or whether he just has not understood what he was reading.
    Neither error is very appropriate to a man of his eminence." On page 51 of the
    same issue appeared Pound's note, "Sovereignty" (Gallup C1733).
Blackstone: Sir William Blackstone.
pearl: Unidentified.

334. Cummings to Pound

TLS-1.

February 9 '53   6 Wyman Road,Cambridge 38;Massachusetts

Dear Ezra—

if by chance I understand yor latest(to Marion)favor's preemeer paragraph,it emanates at least gross misrepresentation. Master Mullins' most recent appearance coincided with the presence of a singularly honest Greek sculptor to whom he(Mullins)originally introduced us;plus a Greek poet,friend of le dit sculptor,who emitted more aliveness per cubic moment than a dozen thousand million Mullins would during several linear centuries. Moreover said Mullins brought along a not invited demiyouth which kept its eyes open but couldn't say boo

as for "a GOOD poEM",our unhero modestly declines what Doubtless Thomas once pontifically entitled the gambit. Neither does "Blackstone" cause requisite thrills hereabouts;though he well may amid "the healthy young"(whoever they aren't). But re your "aint steerable" tribute anent myself,I thank you heartily:& hope to prove worthy thereof ad infin

our bluejay sends love

—

E

sculptor: Michael Lekakis.
poet: Possibly one of Lekakis's friends, Aristedes Antos. Lekakis was also very close to the Greek poet Giannes Ritsos (1909–90), but I have been unable to determine if Ritsos visited the United States in the winter of 1953.
demiyouth: Matthew Keohl, Mullins's roommate at the time.
Doubtless Thomas: Perhaps a reference to T. S. Eliot's poem, "Sweeney among the Nightingales," in which "the man with heavy eyes / Declines the gambit."

335. Pound to Cummings

TL-1.

24 F[e]b[ruary 1953?]   [Saint Elizabeths]

E.E.C.

The MULLigator sez yu feelin' lonely. Lemme recommend
BENTON's "Thirty Years View"

fer to show the country wuz once inHABITED /

git yr/ mind orf the verminous natr of lousiness.

MULLigator: Eustace Mullins.
"Thirty Years View": Thomas Hart Benton (1782–1858), U.S. senator from Missouri (1821–51). Author of *Thirty Years' View; or, A History of the Working of the American Government for Thirty Years, from 1820 to 1850* (New York: D. Appleton and Company, 1854–56). Pound considered this two-volume work an invaluable source of information on the history of the federal government during the early nineteenth century.

336. Pound to Cummings

ALS-1.

[21 March 1953]   [Saint Elizabeths]

Fang (Achilles)
    bust his heel bone
    ----
mebbe yu be'r go see him 'sted
of wait fer him to observe all
ceremonies of approach

                        EP

luvv to deh lady

Fang: Achilles Fang wrote to Pound on 26 February 1953, "Had a very agreeable 6 quarters with Kumrad Kumminkz yesterday. We talked about almost everything in the world. Correction: the greatest and most generous *literary figure* in the world E.P."

337. Cummings to Pound

TL-1. Enclosures.

[April 1953]   [Cambridge, Mass.]

from eec.

enclosed is a document(con letter)returnable at your leisure; ~~which you may or~~
It rather surprised Marion and myself, and we cant help wondering"has Mr. E's
biography been duly authorised?"

p.s. trust the maestro didn't wholly disenjoy current issue of Atlantic Monthly
mag.

Enclosures: (1) A letter dated 28 March [1952] from Evarts Erickson to E. E.
   Cummings. Erickson indicated he wanted to write a book about Pound and
   said, "A true, clear and readable account of the evolution of a genius is what I
   am aiming at, and as this is a pioneer work, and my own work, I am interested
   in seeing that it is not hacked apart by reviewers for inaccuracies and falsifica-
   tions." In order to avoid mistakes, Erickson sent with the letter a series of
   questions about Pound that he hoped Cummings would answer.
       (2) The list of questions. Among the questions were several on sensitive
   topics. "Would you care to say anything about Pound's domestic life? In partic-
   ular, what were the relations between Dorothy Pound and Miss Rudge? Was
   there any mention of the children? Did they seem to lead a reasonably 'normal'
   life?"
current issue: Nonlecture 2, entitled "i & my parents' son," appeared in the
   Atlantic Monthly, vol. 191, no 4 (April 1953), 57–62. Nonlecture 3 ("i & self-
   discovery") appeared in the next issue (May 1953), 53–58.

338. Dorothy Pound to Cummings

AL-1.

[April 1953]   [3514 Brothers Place, S.E.
                                                       Washington, D.C.]

Dear EEC

       Erickson totally unauthorized.
       documents later

                          DP ("committee")

       Easter Greetings -

E. never sees the Atlantic - but I have March No. by chance - sent unsolicited.
Shall go through it in a day or two. Omar in bed with some bug——

339. Omar Pound to Cummings

TLS-1.

Easter Day, [5 April 19]53.   3514 Brothers Place S.E.
                                               Wash.dc. 20.

Salaam:

Thanks for prompt comments on pamphlet . . . which incidentally wasn't
mine, but an adaptation of someone's energy.

As to the morethanalmostinsolence of yr. correspondent, EP. has taken
care of that! The character did appear one day "Head of teakwood"(EP's
comment) . . . and was not invited to return. I'm delighted that you have seen
Rapallo (according to worldly estimates—at any rate!). . . . But presumably 10
yrs. hence we'll be fighting 'em off with battledores and shuttlecocks; they all
want to get onto the bandwagon! . .

I'd Lief Eriksen had stayed in Greenland.

Will surely be feeding humming-birds and chopping down, and up,
trees of convenient size. . . . sometime this summer.

Love to you both.
Was so glad to see you-all again.

ramo

ps. since writing above; have read Atloonatic M. . . . . particularly liking the
Nashe and the Chaucer . . . I remember singing the Nashe in school in U.K. at
about 13-14;and of course the Lover and his lass is definitely a Public House
favourite in that land of warm beer.

pamphlet: On 27 March 1953, Omar Pound had sent the Cummingses the draft of
   a "balanced pamphlet that might help to get E.P. OUT."
correspondent: Evarts Erickson.
Nashe and the Chaucer: Selections from these poets appear at the end of Nonlec-
   ture 2, as does the song from *As You Like It,* "It was a Lover and His Lass."

340. Cummings to Pound

TELEGRAM.

17 May 1953   [4 Patchin Place]

EXPECT TO SEE YOU TOMORROW MONDAY AT TWO LOVE
        MARION AND CUMMINGS

[Pound wrote on the telegram, "recd May 22."]

341. Pound to Cummings

TL-1.

[22 May 1953]   [Saint Elizabeths]

Estlin / to trouble
his slumberz/
Gramp/ vurry slow / takes notice of question / not that e.e.c ever asks any/
NOTE impressions of exile returned/

a NEW psychology among
murkns/ quite as complicated as Hen James/ NEW terror, murkns living in
terror/ afraid to ask WHY they die in KOrea.
decline in all publicity given to honour or quality / after 20 years' rule by
putridity.

quality-- E-quality, i.e. without quality
toleration of stincgkers like Eden and FDR

england after other war afraid to THINK, but not in terror of SOMETHING

all thru that war there was enquiry re/ hidden hand/
        haven't heard it mentioned for 25 or more years.

There's a guy with some life named Amaral, at Rutgers, I dunno ef yu wanna
enlarge yr. circle/

the exuberant Mullins in loose on
New Pork

yes, yuss, vurry pleased to see la fam/ kz/
telegram not yet arrived.

cultural heritage/ yes,yes / but also increment of association the DELAY and
the play fer to insure all Ez' publications shall be posthumous

ought to trouble somebuddy's szleep

incidentally eec ever run into Kat An Porter, or analyze what soda bathed in? she an her ma, ef she had one?

recd/ a largebox of groceries and SO on.

P.S.
May 22
ore 13.45
Tegelram
    just rec/d

Eden: Anthony Eden. At this time Eden was British foreign secretary.

Amaral: José Vasquez Amaral, professor of Romance languages at Rutgers University.

New Pork: Writing to Louis Zukofsky in September 1955, Pound noted that a typesetter's error in an edition of Martin Van Buren's *Autobiography* had produced this renomination of New York. *Pound/Zukofsky: Selected Letters of Ezra Pound and Louis Zukofsky,* ed. Barry Ahearn (New York: New Directions, 1987), 212.

trouble somebuddy's szleep: A play on the refrain in Pound's poem, "Cantico del Sole": "troubles my sleep."

Kat An Porter: Katherine Anne Porter (1890–1980), American novelist and short-story writer. Pound's reference to "soda" recalls lines 198–201 of *The Waste Land.*

342. Pound to Cummings

TC.

[May 1953]   [Saint Elizabeths]

        reep/ort on N.Y. social whirl
"she ⟨(M.)⟩ quite tall and distinguished
        as usual
                & he still looking like
a newspaper reporter with that damned hat."

        queery does he ever wear one?

M.: Marion Morehouse Cummings.

343. Cummings to Pound

TLS-1.

[30 May 1953]   4 Patchin Place
                                                 New York City
                                                       11

                              decoration day

Monsieur—

the "still"(of "still looks like")far more than suggests thet the "hat"(of "that
damned hat")is ancient. Herein your anonymous correspondent erreth. Only a
few weeks ago—at ilyaunefois Marblehead—my erstwhile chapeau,inspired by
Boreas,set sail for Europe

                         —veuillez agréer Confucius

                                                             E

maybe confused by a recent collaboration of airplanes & lawnmowers,I forgot
to enquire your present opinion of exgeneralissimo I(for Icing)Hoar(for sp)?

I . . . Hoar: Dwight David Eisenhower.

344. Pound to Cummings

ACS.

[June 1953]   [Saint Elizabeths]

wot th b-b blue D -d-d-Danube
              iz
              I hoar?

'ow Marion, gawbless 'er
stands it
              !! ?

              Ez

345. Cummings to Pound

AC.

[Postmarked 5 June 1953]   4 Patchin Place Nyc

Mr Eisenhower, I presume?

346. Pound to Cummings

ACS.

[Postmarked 9 June 1953]   [Saint Elizabeths]

yaaas   D. had managed to figger that
out & fill me IN

_____

in the mean time The Rev
Ellfhunt has preceded
yu to the shrine in S. Louis

                         Ez

salut a M/r

D.: Dorothy Pound.
Ellfhunt: T. S. Eliot. The "shrine" is probably Eliot's birthplace. While in St. Louis,
    Eliot received an honorary doctorate at Washington University and gave an
    address, "American Language and American Literature," on 9 June 1953.

347. Cummings to Pound

TCS.

[June 1953]   Silver Lake
                                               New Hampshire

I asked the Harvard student who jeeped Marion & me to our Boston-NewYork
plane

        "what would you rather do than anything
        else in the world?"

after pondering the question almost a minute he
quietly declared

> "I'd like to go as fast as possible—
> provided I wasn't uncomfortable"

et voilà

eec

348. Cummings to Pound

ACS.

[Summer 1953?]   Silver Lake
                                        New Hampshire

bonjour!

Marion & EEC

349. Pound to Cummings

TL-1.

[13 October 1953]   [Saint Elizabeths]

     speakin ov the merits of New England, instead of some of its narstier
feechoors/ I note that Caleb Cushing in the Mass. legis/whatever in 1858
protested vs/ increase in NUMBER of studies in common schools, holdin
thoroughness in elementary brances most vital element.

alzo / among the fuggs and squirril heads, seems there wuz in 1908 a bloke
called Franklin Pierce (possibly of the family, gd/neph or zummat).   Gt/
comfort to unearth a serious character/
                    The goddam Dial and other etc/ dont seem to have
mentioned him.
                    In fact I wish some other denizen wd/ occasionally dig
up something.

How the HELL yu hv/ spent half a century without meeting ANYone, beats me.

(this of course is bad tempered eggZaGGeration)

WO'r bout this Pierce character?

Cushing: Caleb Cushing (1800–1879), American lawyer, legislator, and diplomat.
He was attorney general of the United States under Franklin Pierce. Pound's
comment about Cushing's 1858 observations is a condensation of a sentence
from volume 2 of Claude M. Fuess's *The Life of Caleb Cushing* (New York:
Harcourt, Brace and Company, 1923), 216–17: "He opposed a bill increasing
the number of studies in the common schools, asserting that thoroughness in
the elementary branches was a most vital element of education."

Pierce: Franklin Pierce, New York lawyer. Author of *The Tariff and the Trusts*
(1907) and *Federal Usurpation* (New York: D. Appleton and Company, 1908).
Pierce contended that under the administration of President Theodore Roos-
evelt the powers of the federal government had been unconstitutionally in-
creased. "It is usurpation," Pierce wrote, "for the National Government to take
over the powers of the states without employing the proper means of acquiring
them through amendments to the National Constitution" (xi). He also re-
marked that "Liberty nourishes self-respect, self-reliance, and every impulse to
a higher life. It gives birth to art, literature and culture. It ever has been the
source of all the higher impulses and aspirations of men. On the other hand, a
usurping government destroys these qualities, turns the attention of the citizen
to foreign politics, dazzles him with military glory, and destroys his aspirations
for liberty" (xiii–xiv).

350. Pound to Cummings

TL-1.

[22 October 1953]   [Saint Elizabeths]

                    I hesitate to violate yr/ DOMicile
BUTT think yu wd/ Njoye   Franklin Pierce's
                    FEDERAL USURPATION
(pub/ Appleton, 1908)
                              ef yu kan git holt ov a cawpy.#

ever hear of the earlier F.P. wot wuznt allowed to pall-bear at Hawthorne's
fwuneral, cause mostly he tried to prewent the Civil Wah?

any knowledge of the ?? wholy of approx ⟨unknown.⟩ F.P. that yu can or will transmit wd/ be welKum

by y.v.t

#olaf wd. hv. hed he know the alphabet.

earlier F.P.: Franklin Pierce (1804–69), fourteenth president of the United States. Pierce's sympathies for the Southern position on the extension of slavery made him unpopular in the North. Pierce and Hawthorne were friends of long standing. They were together on the trip that ended with Hawthorne's death. Pierce attended Hawthorne's funeral, but was not a pallbearer.
olaf: The subject of Cummings's poem, "i sing of Olaf glad and big."

351. Cummings to Pound

TCS.

[Postmarked 23 October 1953]   4 Patchin Place
                                                 New York City 11

glad "i" reached you safely
—Marion sends love!

E

"i": E. E. Cummings, *i: six nonlectures* (Cambridge, Mass.: Harvard University Press, 1953).

352. Pound to Cummings

TC.

26 Ott [October 1953]   [Saint Elizabeths]

pur encourager 'im
          in prob/ erronious courses
mrs Oiks reports re/ bri'sh radio
Mr C/ reading an she foun' 'erself "anxious to

catch every word and (which toucheth yr eggscheker
more nearly) REsolving to get hold of bk/ it was
pleasing. . . ."

mrs Oiks: Unidentified.

353. Cummings to Pound

ACS.

[Postmarked 30 October 1953]   4 Patchin Place Nyc 11

glad Mrs Oiks was pleased, & thanks kindly for the news; also much obliged
for FP data. Must confess I didn't even know that Hawthorne had a funeral!

EEC

354. Pound to Cummings

TL-1.

8 Dec[ember 1953?]   [Saint Elizabeths]

e.e.c

why the HELL don't yu get interested in something interesting/ as fer Zmpl /
all presidents who staved off Civil War from 1830 to 1860 got bum press, and
hv. been forgotten.
Not Only V.B/n ⟨but⟩ Tyler, Polk, Buchanan.

I told yu (? or not) the aged Aida in girl hood seein them kids wiff a water
bottle?

Aida: In Canto 89 Pound recounts an incident told to him by "the elderly Aida,
    then a girl of 16, in the '90s," in which "some children crossed the front lawn
    with / a bottle of water strung on a string between them / and chanting: /
    'Martin / Van Buren, a bottle of urine.'" Carroll Terrell speculates that "Aida" is
    either Miss Adah Lee or Miss Ida Lee Mapel, long-standing friends of Pound
    (Terrell, 2:552).

355. Pound to Cummings

TL-1.

[9 December 1953]   [Saint Elizabeths]

thanks, that'LL giv
                    'em
                              somefing to th(f)ink about
wich dun't mean to say they will or
                                          can.

Az fer me arrivin at the needed degree of contemplation
                    gornoze
                              when nan nif.

love to Marion

good thing op/ occurred to bile it into abvmentioned
                              concentrate.

an' ⟨myo torrero⟩ wot am I eggspekted to do abaht deh bandarillo?

356. Pound to Cummings

TL-2.

[June 1954]   [Saint Elizabeths]

THE wholly UNreverend Estlin
                              I hv/ before reminded that one of the most
tributes to his questionable talent was 15 or more yearZZZ zago produced by
Edmondo Dodsworth, NO connection of the TOO late Stincklair Lewis, but
the WOP descendent ⟨twice removed⟩ of a anglo-indian who on his may bak
from Calikutt had sense to remain in the geographic expression and wuz in my
time ye complEAT wop/

Moving whence, to the now. I think there is a place to meet yr/, by U
unadmired, confrère the noble sharker, lioner, aviator and bulldozer, on the
Italian page/
in short if yu can produce 500 words on the state of the murkn Jo house after
21 years treason WHICH no s,o,b in this continent will print, and WHICH
can be translated into

la lingua di qui si vanta Amore
          (J.Milton, in case yu dont recognize him out side
Puddldice Regrained)

It might git yu out of the area of the Gnu Porker, the shatlanding mensuel, and other fetidoria in which yr/ distinguished upinyumz might otherwise have to appear.

with ever DEEvoted respekks to yr/ lllovely consort
          I remain

P.S.
          considerin yr/ allergy to all forms of constructive action/reforms, civics etc.
Keeping it strictly on the highbrow level, seein' that the Oxford dunghill and several sewing societies have recognized yr/ talents (30 years late)
CAN yu conceive any greater degree of imbecility than that of a man who cannot recognize the difference between interest-bearing, and non-interest-bearing DEBT?

Not suggesting that the poor fish DO anything to clean the sewage / or get the dope rings out of bobby sox Gebiet etc. Just keeping it in the realm of in'erleXShl exercise.

Lewis: Sinclair Lewis (1885–1951), American novelist. He died on 10 January
     1951 in Rome, Italy.
noble sharker: Ernest Hemingway.
la lingua: The last line of Milton's canzone beginning, "Ridonsi donne e giovani
     amorosi."

357. Cummings to Pound

SOURCE: Dupee and Stade, *Selected Letters of E. E. Cummings.*

24 June 1954   Silver Lake, N.H.

Multitudinous Monolith—
bonjour!

am more than happy to hear from your sundrily divers selves,&kindestly thank whom-or-which for their most gracious invitation to sputter freely in linguadante. How any mere mortal may im-or-possibly conceive 50(let alone 500)paroles anent some at least 5thrate political whorehouse while battling(1)prehistoric floods followed by a millenial heatwave (2)a prodigious pest of actually omnivorous(they eat even the pineneedles)caterpillars &(3)a gory galaxy of blockbusting mosquitoes plus brutally bloodying blackflies plusorminus aptly entitled via the vernacular "no-see-'ems"(smaller than a pinpoint but with a burn like a whitehot needle)remains a shallwesay ponderable question. Meantime please rest assured that this infrahero won't willingly accept publication per The socalled New Yorker—I politely refused to send them poems long ago—albeit(to give the D his d)one Mr(now departed)Ross certainly did instigate organize & achieve a civic superservice not to mention ultraconstructive reform consisting of the total removal from NewYorkCity's GrandCentral station of a mis(by nobody-unless-yourself-knows-whom)begotten concatention of hideous deafening & otherwise entirely demoralizing hypergigantic talkie(sic)advertisements

e'er quitting sievliesashun,Marionetmoi dined munificently chez Useless Mullins;who inhabits a towering eastside slumskyscraper which has many more stairs tobeclimbed than BunkerHillMonument but oddly enough is worth the ennui(aside from Eustace Muggings louis-maim). A charming fellow-mortal:whose epitaph re thyself makes(in my humble opinion)him already deathless

well now about DEBT unquote,I overtly admit that the only debts harbouring some slightest interest for the sioux seen yea are those of a purely personal nature ie which can never be paid

                                                            —hoping you
are secretly the same;& with great love from the Lady!

Ross: Harold Ross (1892–1951), editor of the *New Yorker* from 1925 until his death.
epitaph: "Epitaph for Ezra Pound" ("Here lies the Idaho kid / The only time he ever did") was attributed to Eustace Mullins when it appeared in the ninth issue of *Nine* (London) (summer–autumn 1952).

358. Pound to Cummings

TL-1.

27 Giugn / [June 1954]   [Saint Elizabeths]

az uZhsul nearly imposs disCOVer wot the kumrad is yawpin about.
        May we receive permission to USE pp/ No. 1 of pistle to Ez/ 24th inst from kumrad/

NOT of course saying whom to/ but fer to giv wopz a idea of state of murkn ijum, anno corrente.

I dunno az any wop will print it / and am damSURE the edtr/ wont understand it / but the genero might.
                              an luVV to th' lydy

Mullins DIDN'T write it / REX wrote it /
Pete muddled / I said Rex wuz a FRIEND of the Mulligator.

Not that the Mul/ is meritless fer diggin up Rex/ who will NOT remember the other 1/2 tof the distich re/ Misser ElYump.

edtr/: Possibly the editor of *Il Borghese,* which Carroll Terrell indicates was one of Pound's favorite periodicals in the St. Elizabeths years (*Paideuma,* vol. 3, no. 3 [winter 1974], 366).
Mullins: Eustace Mullins.
it: "Epitaph for Ezra Pound."
REX: Rex Lampman. A Washington journalist who was at one time a patient at St. Elizabeths Hospital. "One of my friends whom I introduced to Ezra later played a key role in his release. He was the well-known Washington newspaperman, Rex Herbert Lampman." Eustace Mullins, *This Difficult Individual, Ezra Pound* (New York: Fleet Publishing Corporation, 1961), 303. Mullins discusses Lampman's efforts to gain Pound's release on pages 345–47 of *This Difficult Individual.*
Pete: Peter Russell, editor of the magazine *Nine* (London, 1949–56).
ElYump: T. S. Eliot.

359. Cummings to Pound

ACS.

[Postmarked 6 July 1954]   [Silver Lake, N.H.]

ok-- if it's quoted As Is . . . & I wonder what will happen to the Eyetalian language?

                              EEC

360. Pound to Cummings

TL-1.

29 Lug [July 1954]   [Saint Elizabeths]

I suspect that the Kumrad has not read Philostratus' 'Life of Apollonius of TYana' / otherwise several amusin' ideas wd/ hv/ before now occurred to him.

Of course the dungheadedness of all universitaire poops has grown more befouled with the neglect of classic studies or even the use of translations. That job partially putt up on us /

BUT you with a smattering of education are more responsible than mere yokels like Frost and Co/ or Clarance Darrow's late(unlamented partner) who never discovered he had been Darrow's partner.
                    Or in fact the distressingly low level of mediocrity which we have had to live alongside of.

                    luvv to deh lady

Life of Apollonius of TYana: Philostratus was a Greek Sophist active during the first half of the second century A.D. He composed a biography of Apollonius, a Greek philosopher of the first century A.D. According to Philostratus, Apollonius was a Pythagorean who practiced the utmost simplicity in his deportment and manner of living. He traveled widely and advised kings and emperors in most of the known world. In his pursuit of philosophy, Apollonius acquired supernatural powers, such as the ability to foresee the future and to witness distant events. Late in his life, Apollonius was accused of conspiring to overthrow the emperor Domitian. While in prison, Apollonius looked "more like one about to debate some abstract proposition than like a man on trial for his life." Apollonius defended himself so skillfully that the spectators at the trial were won to his side; furthermore, Domitian was obliged to acquit him. Keats based his poem "Lamia" on an incident in the life of Apollonius, as retold in Robert Burton's *Anatomy of Melancholy* (1621). See D. James Neault, "Apollonius of Tyana: the Odyssean Hero of *Rock-Drill* as a Doer of Holiness," *Paideuma*, vol. 4, no. 1 (spring 1975), 3–36.

Darrow's . . . partner: Clarence Darrow (1857–1938), American lawyer. Darrow and Edgar Lee Masters (1868–1950) were partners in a law firm from 1903 to 1911. In his autobiography, *Across Spoon River* (New York: Farrar and Rinehart, 1936), Masters never refers to Darrow by name, but calls him "the criminal lawyer." Masters indicates that Darrow had little interest in the success of the firm and was frequently absent lecturing and acting for the defense in sensational and unremunerative criminal trials.

361. Cummings to Pound

ACS.

[Postmarked 9 August 1954]   Silver Lake - NH

Mellifluous Mugwump -
    lend me your pal's
    opus & shall do my
    best to absorb it.
    Something whispers the
    local library unquote
    never heard of Philoetc
—Marion sends love!

                EEC

362. Pound to Cummings

TL-1.

7. Sep. [1954]   [Saint Elizabeths]

e.e.c.

the buzzard (fergit his name) who said he wuz workin on yr/ birthday
        arrived with a FEMME (the office said TWO friends of e.e.c.)
        then the femme returns and says she AINT, but just happened to
arrive WITH the buzzard synCHRonous.

    does the buzzard know anything about her / she SAID she had often
interviewd Dexter White,,
                vurry Eleanor line.#

waaal, thazz one item.
              **

tother is dope / what does e.e.c. KNOW about it / being a lush of course he
must see a lot of irresponsibility / BUT acc/ the buzzard e.e.c. is reaching years
of the borderland where some sense of responsibility is sposed to dawn.

I may need e.e.c.'s help re/ particular victim / emergency MIGHT arise/
        what the HELL / so little ability in this geog/ area
        one ought to save what can be /

AND yr/ pinko friends were definitely using dope   as political
weapon back in 1927 / as I had from Cockburn when he flew down from
Boilin to Wien in the dear dead dark DIAL days.

(one damn good item by him in that frowsty orgum, believe it was titld "Yu
never can tell".)

deh woild yr/ chillin has to grow up, or more likely DOWN in
                                      !!!!!!

are yu likely to be in Wash/   shd/ like a few moments of SeeReeYus
CONvarsation?

She said the skunk was polite/ and deduced therefrom his integrity and
inncocense/ just like the official Meyerblatts

buzzard: David Burns, whose account of his visit to Pound appears in Norman,
   446–49. Burns reviewed Cummings's *Poems: 1923–1954* in the *Saturday Re-
   view,* vol. 37, no. 51 (18 December 1954), 10-11.
FEMME: Possibly Sylvia Porter (1913–91), American journalist. She wrote a
   financial column for the *New York Post* and had covered the 1944 Bretton
   Woods Conference.
Dexter White: Harry Dexter White (1892–1948). American economist and gov-
   ernment official. Director of monetary research for the Department of the
   Treasury during World War II. After the war he was briefly director of the
   International Monetary Fund. In 1948 Elizabeth Bentley testified to the House
   Un-American Activities Committee that White had been the source for secret
   documents she had passed to Soviet agents. White denied these allegations and
   died three days after testifying before the committee.
Eleanor: Eleanor Roosevelt.
particular victim: Many of William McNaughton's letters to Pound recount his
   alleged difficulties in keeping a certain person (still living) away from marijuana
   and heroin.
Cockburn: Claud Cockburn (1904–81), British journalist and novelist.
good item: A short story, "You Have to Be Careful," *Dial,* vol. 84 (January 1928),
   8–24.
Meyerblatts: Eugene Isaac Meyer (1875–1959), American investment banker,
   government official, and publisher, owned the *Washington Post* and the *Wash-
   ington Times-Herald.*

363. Cummings to Pound

ACS.

[Postmarked 22 September 1954]   Silver Lake
                                                  New Hampshire

sorry; can't identify "the buzzard"(s)
— Greenwich Village teenagers are growing
hoppier every day — God Bless The Dial#— May
reach DC before Xmas

                              EEC

#Through one of whose whims (incidentally) I
met your unholiness

whims: Cummings was introduced to Pound in Paris in 1921 by Scofield Thayer,
   co-owner and editor of the *Dial.*

364. Pound to Cummings

TL-1.

2 Oct[ober 1954]   [Saint Elizabeths]

KumminkZZZZ

Aldous turned up yester/ improved during past 33 years/ told him to phone yu /

cd/ be useful IF yu can get a few root ideas into him / he deplores the Possum's
letch fer excess respectability / wich is nugatory.

TIME a few buzzards who can bust into print SAW the real revolution shd/ be
            against the BLITHERING idiocy of a system that makes crimes out of
simple non-criminal and/or even useful acts like transport of diamonds or sale of
beer. Under groveling superstition that the gummymint needs to TAX 'em to get
revenue.

Squalor of iggurance re/ monetary issue / wich wuz unnerstood before Kubali.
god DAMN the historic blackout.

Aldous got a son in village studying medical ADministration /

now ef yu two yunkers wd/ eggschange yr/ information/ yu might git some live
subject matter /

wich gornoZE yu need.

luvv to deh lady

> yester

warnt time to swap more than a few bits of obsolete scandal
or lead A.H. to full glory of light, as in our time.

Aldous: Aldous Huxley (1894–1963), British novelist. He had come to Wash-
ington to lecture at the Institute of Modern Art on 1 October.
Possum's: T. S. Eliot.
Kubali: Kublai Khan.
son: Matthew Huxley (b. 1920).

365. Pound to Cummings

TL-1. ENCLOSURES.

23 Oc[tober 1954]   [Saint Elizabeths]

e.e.c.
They git grampaw cause he SUPPORTS the U.S. constitution.
They chuck Doc Wms/ cause he does NOT support the USConstitution.
Mebbe they just dislike the profession in general.
***

Tell Marion yu are a lousy correspondent cause yu ignore all the leading
questions/
mebbe it's paaaat of the Haaaavud paideuma wich yu
share with the Reverund Elerfunt /
**

Anybody in yr/ li'l   illiterate circle, read Sweeditsch?

Enclosures: Two newspaper clippings. The first is headed "House Is Urged to
Investigate Reds' Use of Dope in Cold War." It began, "The communists, partic-
ularly in the Far East, are using opium and other narcotics as a weapon in the
cold war, an Oklahoma congressman charged today. He wants Congress to
investigate this 'organized and depraved conspiracy of international commu-
nism to subvert free people.' Rep. Ed Edmondson (D., Okla.), a World War II
Navy officer, has asked the House to name a committee to hold hearings in this
country and overseas. Mr. Edmondson said he particularly was interested in

Korea and Japan. He charged the communists were using narcotics 'as a major weapon' against U.S. troops overseas. Mr. Edmondson said he had evidence that the United States was being flooded with opium from the Near and Far East." The second clipping is from the *Washington Daily News* for 10 December 1953 and is headlined, "Excerpts from Pound's Roman Broadcasts." "It is pleasant to note that there is an Ezra Pound controversy; that public apathy is not all-engulfing; that all of us do not believe that the theory of a man's being innocent until proven guilty is un-American these days. Since Pound has never been granted a trial, we are forced to examine the evidence ourselves. Here are excerpts from the microfilm of transcripts of Pound's broadcasts from Rome, obtainable by anyone for $2.50 from the Library of Congress: 'The President has no legal power to enter into serious and secret agreements with foreign powers.' 'The United States treaties are valid when ratified by the Senate and not before.' 'I don't think it is the function, even of the Commander-in-Chief of the U.S. American Army to dictate the citizens' politics. Not to the point of inviting Bolshevik Russia to kill off the whole east half of Europe, and ordering the citizens to approve of it. I don't think it is the lucky move.' 'When he violates and passes beyond his legal powers, he acts toward the destruction of all legal government in the U.S. . . . This is extremely dangerous in the long run. It is myopic.' It is interesting to note that a man who, not in 1950 or in 1945, but in 1942 called Russia 'not a very good bet' has been locked up as being of 'unsound mind' for nine years by the United States Government."

Doc Wms: William Carlos Williams.
Elerfunt: T. S. Eliot.
Sveeditsch: See letter 367.

366. Cummings to Pound

TCS.

[Postmarked 29 October 1954]   [4 Patchin Place]

CHEER UP YOU AND DOC DOOBLUHVAY AREN'T THE ONLY
NONLIKED PEBBLESONTHEBEACH—
VIDE NEW YORK TIMES LITERARY SUPPLEMENT(UNQUOTE) SUNDAY
OCTOBER 31 PAGE 6*
—AND REMEMBER ME TO CONFUCIUS NAY ARISTOTLE

Marion sends love! ·

E

*gangster is
as gangster does

DOC DOOBLUHVAY: William Carlos Williams.
VIDE: "A Poet's Own Way," by Randall Jarrell, a review of Cummings's *Poems 1923–1954*. Jarrell finds Cummings wanting in the qualities that make for a great poet. "He is, alas! a monotonous poet. Everything a poem does is, to old readers, expected." Jarrell concludes, "What I like least about Cummings's poems is their pride in Cummings and their contempt for most other people; the difference between the I and you of the poems, and other people, is the poems' favorite subject. All his work thanks God that he is not as other men are; none of it says, 'Lord, be merciful to me, a sinner.'" *New York Times Book Review*, 31 October 1954, 6.

367. Pound to Cummings

TL-1.

[11 November 1954]   [Saint Elizabeths]

as yu were released some time ago and are in full flower of collectedness, presumably following Behrenson and Sandbag in nordik glory, I suggest that
YU

do a nize li'l hokku or longer depicting Andy Jackson (or even the sandbagged Lincoln) in the act of inspecting a museum of his family souvenirs.
                    NO not a ghost returned / but Abe or Andy living
among the brotooooon.

11 Nov, year of the pestilence.

aa still vait a nize sveetisch goil to traslaate what said in
        aal vaarldens beraeaeaeter.

an luvv to deh loidy

Behrenson: Bernard Berenson.
Sandbag: Carl Sandburg (1878–1967), American poet. He wrote a two-volume biography of Lincoln, *Abraham Lincoln, The Prairie Years* (1926) and *Abraham Lincoln, The War Years* (1939).
a ghost returned: As in "Abraham Lincoln Walks at Midnight," a poem by Vachel Lindsay.
beraeaeaeter: A discussion of potential candidates for the Nobel Prizes appeared in the October 1954 issue of *All varldens berattare* (Stockholm).

368. Pound to Cummings

TL.

[November/December 1954?]   [Saint Elizabeths]

                    yuss my estlin
If yu aint seen WynDAMn Lewis' "Self Condemned" yu better see it. First work
by a adult that has reached me fer some time.
            and he aint stallin on every bloody goddam issue wot purrzents the
byRooseBeshatten woild.

yung Tommy Carter is on tothe differences between several.

            grape vine tells me Hem wuz baudlerized by the N.Y.Slimes and current
spewlitzer orgumz.
i.e. that the old runt is more of a man than the press lets the pewklik know.

"Self Condemned": *Self Condemned* (London: Methuen, 1954).
Carter: One of the editors of the "Wyndham Lewis" number of *Shenandoah,* vol. 4
    (summer–autumn 1953), along with Ashley Brown and Hugh Kenner.

369. Cummings to Pound

TCS.

[Postmarked 30 December 1954]   4PatchinPlace—NY11

hope you enjoyed the Omars as much as we did—please thank "D P" for her
charming & cheering letter—Marion & I send you both & each our best
wishes for A HAPPY NEW YEAR

                    .   .   .
                    E E C

the Omars: Omar Pound and his future wife, Elizabeth.

370. Pound to Cummings

TL-2.

15 Jan[uary 1955]   [Saint Elizabeths]
Mon cherEstlin (? ἐσθλὸν [ἐσθλόν, "noble, good"]

                    you seemd a bit surprised at my passing classification

of the goddam, or soft, shits, spaccati for men of letters during yr/ unfortunate era, AS incapable of reading any authors above the awt-shoppe level (note the Am. Soc, of Aesthetics, as time lag).

I wonder if yu and M/ missed that li'l trans/ or adop/ from Q.H.F.   of decades gone:

> The persian buggahs, Joe
> Strike me as a rotten show,
> Stinking of nard and musk
> Over the whole of their rind and husk;
> Wearing their soft-shell clothes
> Whichever way the wind blows,
> The persian buggahs, Joe,
> Strike me as a rotten show.

As to the demarcation line between grade A. and grade B/

The fahrts who titch books in the Weeneries do NOT note what Athene said she was doing. Odys, bk I.

they do NOT note Shx/ interest in matters which led some wafty buzzards to spose only the Lud Chancellor cd/ hv.

They do not read wop/ and therefore know nowt of Dant/

And the lowest grade of punks have spent 8 million bucks to keep Peg/ out of Wash/ ONLY morning wyper.

> wd/ some power to Ez shd/ giv it
> to make the Estlin's feelinkz livid
> and lead the noblest native to
> curse the swine as Ez might do.

2/ you are too GODDam tolerant, my dear kumrad.

and as whoosis said to Mrs Barbauld: sieze the damn thing and wring itz neKKK.

or at least furnish means of communication with the outer and NOT let Xmas trees ObsKewer the view.

By the waye, I dunno if you meet Mr Lowell (Robt. not the late Jas. R. in seance)

did yu ever, speaking of Jas/   putt anyone onto hunting fer the lost strophe of "John P.
            Robinson, he "

                    best to M/   hope she is enjoying the centennial
celebrations of . . .
                    yu tel gramp.

classification: Possibly in an unlocated Pound letter.
Am. Soc, of Aesthetics: The American Society for Aesthetics was founded in 1942. It publishes the *Journal of Aesthetics and Art Criticism.*
Q.H.F.: Quintus Horatius Flaccus (65–8 B.C.). Pound's translation first appeared in *Readies for Bob Brown's Machine* (Cagnes-sur-Mer: Roving Eye Press, 1931), 114 (Gallup B26).
what Athene said: In book 1 of the *Odyssey,* Athena expresses to Zeus her pity for Odysseus. Disguised, she visits Telemachus and assures him that his father lives and will return to Ithaca. She then advises Telemachus to sail in search of Odysseus.
Lud Chancellor: Francis Bacon, Baron Verulam, Viscount St. Albans (1561–1626). He was named lord chancellor on 4 January 1618 N.S.
Peg/: Westbrook Pegler (1894–1969), American journalist.
whoosis: See the note to letter 240.
lost strophe: The third of James Russell Lowell's *Biglow Papers* contains an antiwar poem, "What Mr. Robinson Thinks." In the poem, "John P. Robinson" espouses militarism. Pound's reference to a "lost strophe" probably indicates his hope that Cummings would put his poetic talents to use in political commentary.
celebrations: Perhaps the centennial of the publication of *Leaves of Grass.*

371. Cummings to Pound

TLS-1.

January 22 '55   4 Patchin Place

Dear Ez—

if am not most grossly mistaken, 'twas David-called-Thoreau observed he had never met—or hoped to meet—a man worse than himself

talents differ:if heroical thine be cursing swine & ringing nex,our tolerant unhero may only re-remark(vide 6 nonlectures page 70)that "hatred bounces" item—1 Sam XVII—something informs me that Joy is the name of a brook from which(as the adult hyperogre of philistinism superstrutted)a mere child chose him five smooth stones

—Marion sends love!

EEC

& twicethanks for the doublysalubrious clipping

Thoreau: "I never knew, and never shall know, a worse man than myself." Thoreau says this near the end of the "Economy" chapter of *Walden.*
page 70: In "Nonlecture Four," Cummings includes a series of aphorisms, of which "hatred bounces" is one.
1 Sam XVII: This chapter of 1 Samuel concerns David's battle with Goliath. Verse 40: "And he took his staff in his hand, and chose him five smooth stones out of the brook, and put them in a shepherd's bag which he had, even in a scrip; and his sling was in his hand: and he drew near to the Philistine."
clipping: Clipping lacking.

372. Pound to Cummings

TL-1.

[January 1955]   [Saint Elizabeths]

I do NOT think disgust and hate are the same thing.

Peach stone might be disgusted with being caged in and want to grow.

         AND criteria, observations of incompleteness   ; of infantilism, are not necessarily a sign of mere senility.

    Do yew luvv fer fellow or UNfellow man enough to tell someyoung buzzard why Thoreau does not include ALL the qualities which the TOTAL race, the assembly of all races, is PERMitted to admire

         even if yr/ concitoyennes have lost nearly all that Adams, Benton, Jackson and co fit and scrouged for.

    I'll send yu the buzzard's address if you want it.

Not sure yr/ Xtn fanaticism isn't as rabid vs/ maturity as Cotton Mather was against whetever his list of allergies were(am a bit vague as to detail)

I spose its nashunl Anschauung/ Cotton objected to adultery and his descendents object to all adults.

that phase of development implying capacity for

[In Dorothy Pound's hand:] Best to both. D.P.

Adams: John Adams (1735–1826), second president of the United States.
Benton: Thomas Hart Benton (1782–1858), American statesman. Author of *Thirty Years' View . . . of the American Government* (1854–56).
Jackson: Andrew Jackson (1767–1845), seventh president of the United States.
buzzard's: Unidentified.
Mather: Cotton Mather (1663–1728) American Congregational clergyman and author.

373. Pound to Cummings

TL-1.

30 Giugn [June 1955]   [Saint Elizabeths]

IZ the kumrad capable of saying in ten lines   wot the HELL the young can or had orter perceive in order NOT to sink lower?

HAS he seen ANY sign of life in ANY printed matter of recent date?

OBviously ole Bill Mike (vide enc/) livin' on a higher an more saZfakkery levl than our kuntEmporaries

McN/ trying to get a statement out of Pine, but can only git as far as a sekkertary.

I dont spose the kumrad has any IDea of Pine, probably identifies it wiff a troublesome forest growth in N.UmpSheer

Bill Mike: William McNaughton, a young admirer of Pound's who published the leaflet *Strike*. Pound contributed numerous short notes to it during 1955 and 1956. See McNaughton's "Pound, A Brief Memoir: 'Chi Lavora, Ora,'" *Paideuma*, vol. 3, no. 3 (winter 1974), 319–28.
enc: Enclosure lacking.
Pine: David A. Pine (1891–1970), Federal judge. He ruled President Truman's seizure of the nation's steel mills illegal. In April 1952 Truman seized the mills to avert an impending strike. On 29 April Judge Pine found the action unconstitutional and issued a temporary injunction against the seizure. The Supreme Court ultimately upheld Pine's ruling.

374. Cummings to Pound

ACS.

[Postmarked 15 July 1955]   Silver Lake NH

yes, your friend "Bill Mike" sounds chipper—& who is "Pine"?

                    EEC

375. Pound to Cummings

TL-2.
[Postmarked 20 July 1955]   [Saint Elizabeths]

     YU LOUSSY litteraRRRatti, yu write a poem about Olaf large
                                                  large
and big   (proof reader . . . . heah, heah.)

and then yu go off Throvianly and let a sowbellied ape bitch the
consterooshun,   (NOT asking why conscription is NOW.)
               and when some ole buzzard kicks the swine in belly and
stops the avalance yu say:

                    OO iz Pine?

Question IS wd/ it have held if he hadn't had the whole of #"steel" behind him.

                         YU go ask him. I think Bill means to, but he is
young, flightly, not necessarily capable of dealing with one of the few legal
judges left in yr/   myKuntry tis of Lydia pink HAM and Western etc.

Traison de ⟨clercs⟩ (f/g/) see mr Oscar W's chaste representation of yr/ greek
with a mu fer a upSilon. pocket edn arruv this a.m.   phi mu kappa NOT
being comprehensible to the pakistani approaching N.England fer the foist
time.
⟨& not f'miliar with Korekt Kumradik version⟩

Looking at the pixchoor album on front and rear covers,
DID they lost all civic decency when they mowed their whiskers. ?

Whittier, Bryant and co/ wd damn well have known who IZ Pine.

I admit if McN has printed JEDGE instead of Hon/ he might hv/ giv ⟨you⟩
uncivils a lead . . butttttttt   gwa hellup yr/ progeny.
2

there is nother kindergarten lesson due to appear in next Hudson if Lisa can
get it past the print shoppe /

Damn all if I dont inc/ indication that the wop/ papers even after having the
whole country shat on / aren't a cut above those in J.Y.

Corsini quoted at or near Ascot ⟨last week⟩ / but it will take another 30
years to git Bastun past 1920.

and so on/

gawd bless Marion

poem: "i sing of Olaf glad and big," *Complete Poems,* 340.
ape: President Truman.
buzzard: Judge David Pine.
"steel": The United States iron and steel corporations.
Bill: William McNaughton.
Lydia pink HAM: Lydia Pinkham's Vegetable Compound had been a well-known
    patent medicine in the United States since the early 1880s.
Oscar W's: Oscar Williams (1900–1964), American poet. He edited *The New
    Pocket Anthology of American Verse* (New York: Washington Square Press, 1956).
representation: In line 23 of "Jehovah buried,Satan dead." In later editions of the
    anthology, the mu was replaced by a phi.
pixchoor album: Many of the poets in the anthology were portrayed.
Whittier: John Greenleaf Whittier (1807–92), American poet.
Bryant: William Cullen Bryant (1794–1878), American poet.
lesson: "Canto 88–89," *Hudson Review,* vol. 8, no. 2 (summer 1955), [183]–204
    (Gallup C1746). Pound addresses Cummings in Canto 88: "Not un-men, my
    Estlin, but all-men."
Lisa: Lisa Dyer, managing editor of the *Hudson Review.*
J.Y.: Jew York.
Corsini: Probably Renato Corsini, author of "Ezra Pound, Economist: Justice the
    Final Goal," *New Times* (15 December 1955), no. 7.

376. Pound to Cummings

TL-1.

12 S[e]p[tember 1955]   [Saint Elizabeths]

       O fount of indolence / primal &
oh sprietely irrelevence, often.
oh non cohereing and incoöp

Two lively lads Dwon Under/ Fleming's (vid enc)pal Stock / hand in two Aussie
Mags/ "Meanjin" best bet as Little Review de ces jours vs/ the Hudson-
Criterion / complains he cant git yr/ poemz in Down Under.

If yr/ booblishers have any regard for sales, fer xriZache have 'em send review
copies (even 3 or 5 years late to
Noel Stock 436 Nepean Rd
Brighton, Melbourne, Australia.

stock wants to bust the local fugg.
     ***
Too bad nobuddy ever got to doin trans/ of Dodworth on the kumrad / these
frosh still eggspek gramp to do ALL clerking.
     **

Mis Monnier has "passed on" her handy man now says she remembered me /
will I contribute blurb to Mercure obit.

considerin' that those two frousty skoits was sediment and obstruction from
1920 until I ceased to distub the frumpery of the n.r.f adherences . .

          this IZ mos' touchin'

yever hear of Monsieur Saillet? Sorry the ole tub had illness in declining years,
but M.Saillet sounds like I wuz her booZUM.

And not one frawg capable of spiking Lackey Brown's lies.
n.r.f. midwife of France's mental decay.
deevotions to Marion / when I think of that gal's patience
        ****

the other buzzard wiff a mind is in Eng/ party by name of Sharrock

lively lads: Noel Stock, Australian editor and author, and William Fleming, Aus-
tralian poet. A description of Stock and Fleming's literary activities at the time is

given in Fleming's "The Melbourne Vortex," *Paideuma,* vol. 3, no. 3 (winter 1974), 325–28.

enc: Enclosure lacking.

Aussie Mags: *Meanjin,* edited by C. B. Christesen, and the Melbourne Social Credit paper *New Times.*

Dodworth: Edmondo Dodsworth's article on Cummings. See appendix.

Monnier: Adrienne Monnier (1892–1955), French bookseller and author. Her bookstore in Paris, Les Maison des Amis de Livres, became a meetingplace for Apollinaire, Aragon, Breton, Larbaud, Reverdy, Valéry, and many other distinguished writers.

handy man: Maurice Saillet, Monnier's friend and literary executor.

Mercure: The *Mercure de France.*

skoits: Monnier and Sylvia Beach (1887–1962).

n.r.f: The *Nouvelle Revue Français.*

Brown's lies: John Lackey Brown (b. 1914), American literary critic specializing in French literature. His *Panorama de la littérature contemporaine aux Etats-Unis* (Paris: Gallimard, 1952) contained caustic observations about Pound's economic and political beliefs. Brown concluded his assessment of Pound with this summary: "On peut regretter que ce virtuose des mots n'ait su atteindre que si rarement a un lyrisme authentique et personnel; que tant de dons manifestes coincident chez lui avec une si sensible aux accents d'autrui ne parvienne que si rarement à trouver et à poser sa propre note—la note humainement juste que nous attendons, toujours en vains, de lui" (281–82) [One regrets that this virtuoso of words achieved so rarely an authentic personal lyricism, that so many obvious gifts coincide in his poetry, (but) that someone so sensitive to other voices only rarely achieved in his own work the right note—the note humanly just that we await always in vain from him]. See also Lee Bartlett and Hugh Witemeyer, "Ezra Pound and James Dickey: A Correspondence and a Kinship," *Paideuma,* vol. 11, no. 2 (fall 1982), 297 n.

Sharrock: Roger Sharrock, British literary critic and scholar. He began corresponding with Pound in 1955.

377. Cummings to Pound

ALS-1.

September 28 '55   Silver Lake
                                                          New Hampshire

Dear Ez—

thanks for your Poun Under suggestion; I'll notify my socalled publisher re nonworlds: as Master Nock long since unloudly observed, the "anthropoid man" always gets-there-first

—do we really & truly envy him?

ἐστλιν

Nock: Albert Jay Nock (1870–1945), American political writer, social critic, and editor. In his *Memoirs of a Superfluous Man* (1943), Nock does not use the phrase "anthropoid man," but does frequently speak of "anthropoids" and "neolithic man." Cummings recommended *Memoirs of a Superfluous Man* and Nock's *Our Enemy the State* to Hildegarde and Sibley Watson (*Selected Letters*, 207).

378. Pound to Cummings

TL-1.

14 Oc[tober 1955]   [Saint Elizabeths]

These horstralians are the livest / got a weekly and a 1/4 ly (wich latter pays)

BUT they got currency wagulations/ Stock wants to write erbaht yr poems/ willing to buy but cant eggsport specie.
                    If yr/ pubr aint a mutt he wd/ risk sending a review copy / esp/ as they have book distributing faCULties.

address Noel Stock

| 436 Nepean Highway |
| Brighton, Melbourne |
| Australia. |

he dont like his poem, but it amused McN/

Fleming is his fellow sufferer/ I alzo enc/ no relation of Mrs F's washington hubsand, ANother fambly

Do any of yr/ deplorable friends get art reproduced in COLOUR? I mean when it aint lousy?

best to th LydY

Other pt/ yu know anybody who can read gk and lat/ who aint a stuffed shirt or a bdy/ bore? They want a murkn HEAD fer a com/ int/ nat Classik stewed eyes.

horstralians: Noel Stock and William Fleming.

McN: William McNaughton, publisher of *Strike*.

washington hubsand: Rudd and Polly Fleming were a husband and wife, residents of Washington, D.C., who often visited Pound at Saint Elizabeths.

379. Cummings to Pound

TCS.

October 20 '55   4 Patchin Place
                                                       New York City
                                                            11

kind thanks for the Melbourne address:have asked HB&Co to send a review copy

if I hear of any human Hellenist or plausible Colour processor,will let you know

Marion sends love!

EEC

HB&Co: Harcourt, Brace and Company.

380. Cummings to Pound

TELEGRAM.

Oct 30 1955   New York

EZRA POUND
     ST ELIZABETHS HOSPITAL

GREETINGS AND LOVE
     ESTLIN AND MARION

Oct 30 1955: Pound's seventieth birthday.

381. Pound to Cummings

TL-1.

[5 November 1955]   [Saint Elizabeths]

Has the kumminkz fambly enough resilience to be amused by nooz from
Nippon, brot by a Fullblighted ⟨female⟩, re/ mrkn kulchrl diffusion

Mr Frost (Robert) woik chucked out of the puppergander upficial govt. liebury
as "unamerican".

Of course there are other angles to the matter/

Of course on the tis adikei line / R.F. will hv. got his royalties/ and his
puplickers will have got "theirs" out of taxpaers,
                    and after all. . . . . .

                                   5 Nov.

Dew yew folks know Marie Mencken?

Fullblighted ⟨female⟩: Unidentified.
tis adikei: Pound uses this phrase in Canto 76. "'Who wrongs [you]?' Reminiscent
   of Aphrodite's question to Sappho: τίς τ᾽, ὦ Ψάπφ᾽, ἀδικήει ('Who is it Sappho
   that does them wrong?') [Lyra Graeca I, fr. 1, 184, *Oxford Book of Greek Verse*,
   No. 140]" (Terrell, 2:399).
Mencken: Marie Menken (1917–70), a Brooklyn painter who corresponded with
   Pound.

382. Pound to Cummings

TL-2.

13 Nov[ember 1955]   [Saint Elizabeths]

Havent Eastman's address/ can yu forward this TO him?
I see the Devin Adair boys have printed him/ all of 'em squawling about
SYMPTOMS and none go to ROOT.
ANYhow none of 'em asked for free speech re/ E.P. boycott by all of 'em. AND
when some punk says Ez was "AVOWED" Fascist, NONE of 'em got the guts
to look at facts /
Hem talking about EP's errors/ as if his red idiocy in Spain was the answer/

NOW not only was E.P. not avowed for anything but U.S. Constitution, J.Adams, and Andy Jackson

but he was ANTI-socialist and for minimum govt, and went Gesell cause Gesell means less bugocracy than Doug's Soc/ Credit.

AND when the pweking HELL is ANY one of these heavy thinkers going to discuss real ideas?

I don't spose Eastman has SAID that E.P. was opposed to the errors Eastman committed in HIS own mind/

any more than Winston wd/ admit that Ez was right when the aptly intialed W.C. was working to start what he <u>now</u> calla "a unnecessary war."

Redefreiheit ohne Radio freiheit gleich null ist.

Eva improves the line in translation/ BUT ONLY the //lbleating Manchester guardian has quoted it in angry saxon cuntries.

AND that cause I sat on the buzzards head and said it was the ONE thing there wd/ be any use in his quoting.

I dont spose yu and Marion READ anything/ let alone Orval Watts mebbe Max DOES, as Devin prints both of 'em

Congrat Max/ for I suppose getting a gleam, however late/ I have only seen his name on the Orval W/ cover, no idea how MUCH light he has seen.

2/
Incidentally the London Times has done right by Jim Barnes, in the nacherl place (i.e. the OBIT). JIM <u>WAS</u> fascist
had a preface by Mus/ whom I never managed to see but ONCE.
"universality"/ ⟨sd. Jim.⟩

E.P. TOLD 'em about the U.S. not only did he not "embrace", but he considered fascismo FOR ITALY, possible /
and held for best govt. is wot governs least.
VOcational representation /

has the god damnd sloppy Pseudenzia in new Pork

any idea what THAT means
and that it wd/ be CONSTITUTIONAL for congress (NOT for the senate) in all states having more than one congressman.

JeheeZUSSZ' balls do any of yu ever THINK about anything ???

and WhooRAY Frost chucked out of the puppygander libs/ in Nippon as
unamerican. . . . .

if that ⟨aint⟩ a joke on the pennypinching . . .

lovv to the gentile consorte.

Devin Adair: *Reflections on the Failure of Socialism* (New York: Devin-Adair,
1955).

some punk: Pound probably refers to Victor C. Ferkiss's "Ezra Pound and Ameri-
can Fascism," *Journal of Politics,* vol. 17 (May 1955), 173–97. Although Ferkiss
does not use the word *avowed,* in his first paragraph he states that "Pound was
also a convinced fascist."

Hem: Ernest Hemingway.

Gesell: Silvio Gesell (1862–1930), German economist.

Doug's Soc/ Credit: Clifford Hugh Douglas (1879–1952), British economist.
Douglas developed the theory of Social Credit economics.

Winston: Winston Churchill. In his preface to *The Gathering Storm,* Churchill
says, "One day President Roosevelt told me that he was asking publicly for
suggestions about what the war should be called. I said at once 'The Unneces-
sary War.' There never was a war more easy to stop than that which has just
wrecked what was left of the world from the previous struggle." *The Second
World War.* Vol. 1: *The Gathering Storm* (Boston: Houghton Mifflin, 1948), iv.

Eva: Eva Hesse.

Orval Watts: Vernon Orval Watts (b. 1898), American political writer. Author of
The United Nations: Planned Tyranny; Comments on the Dream and the Reality
(New York: Devin-Adair, 1955).

Jim Barnes: Major James Strachey Barnes (1890–1955). The obituary notice in
the *London Times* appeared on 29 August 1955 and was headed, "A Paladin of
Fascism." "Our Rome Correspondent reports that Major James Strachey
Barnes, who was a public supporter of the Italian cause during the Ethiopian
crisis, and who became a naturalized Italian, died on Thursday night in Rome.
Born in India in 1890, the son of Sir Hugh Barnes, K.C.S.I., K.C.V.O., he was
largely brought up in Florence by his grandparents, Sir John and Lady Strachey.
When sent to school in England, first to a preparatory school at Rottingdean
and then to Eton, he was not happy; nevertheless, he passed on to King's
College, Cambridge, and during the 1914–18 War held commissions in the
Guards and the Royal Flying Corps. An English eccentric of eighteenth rather
than twentieth century cut, he defied all conventions and, as he said in some
reminiscences published in 1937, chose his friends 'with great catholicity of
taste.' After such youthful exploits as setting fire to the famous windmill at
Rottingdean, receiving a master as his guest at Covent Garden when he had
been refused leave of absence from Eton, inviting three Anglican divines of

irreconcilable opinions to lunch, and bearding lions including, among many others, Henry James, D. H. Lawrence, J. M. Keynes, and Sir Edward Marsh, he went to the Balkans hoping to join in the impending revolt by the Albanians against the Turks. There he casually met King Nicholas of Montenegro, who advised him to 'sell Turkish pounds.' A lecture given in 1918 to the Royal Geographical Society on the politics of Albania, gave him some claim to the status of an expert and he contrived to join the south European section of the Foreign Office delegation to the Paris peace conference, where he hugely enjoyed listening to the indiscretions of personages who are not generally supposed to be indiscreet.

Yet all this time the land of his early upbringing drew him powerfully and its apparent rebirth with the advent of Fascism was decisive. The close friendship which soon developed between Barnes and Mussolini might perhaps be taken as a modern instance of the old Italian proverb *Inglese italianato, Diavols incarnato,* for it survived even the stresses of the Mateotti murder and the invasion of Ethiopia. Indeed, as Reuters Correspondent, Barnes wrote of the invasion from the south not so much as an Italophil Englishman as an out-and-out Italian.

He had some seven years earlier written a by no means negligible philosophical defence of Fascism which received the *imprimatur* of the Duce himself in the shape of an introduction. The viewpoint was characteristically Latin and even Italian, for it lay in a return to the political and religious tradition of Rome. Looking back at the pagan Empire and the Christian Church as agencies which successively held the civilized world together in unity, Barnes claimed that the solution was universally valid.

His standpoint allowed him to dismiss the Renaissance, the Reformation, the political revolution in France, and the economic revolution in England as mere error and to attack the rival Continental philosophies of Rousseau and Hegel. Basing himself on a doctrine derived from Aquinas, he held that the State is simply the upholder of moral law and that only the Church can say what the moral law is. The pragmatism increasingly obvious in the development of Fascist action disturbed him, and his brave old world, so lovingly fashioned from medieval materials, collapsed with the fall of Mussolini."

Barnes reported to Pound in the early 1950s of his attempts to get Pound released from Saint Elizabeths. Barnes tried to influence Fulton J. Sheen and Clare Boothe Luce in Pound's favor. At the time of his death he was preparing an appeal to Winston Churchill.

Mus: Benito Mussolini. See Barnes's *The Universal Aspects of Fascism* (London: Williams and Norgate, 1928). Mussolini begins his preface by remarking, "The book which I have the pleasure of prefacing is from the pen of a clear-minded English thinker who knows Italy and the Italians perfectly, and not less perfectly fascism."

VOcational representation: Under Italian fascism, workers within the same industry were all represented by a single union.

new Pork: New York.

383. Cummings to Pound

TELEGRAM.

Nov[ember] 19 1955   New York

HOPE WE CAN SEE YOU TUESDAY AFTERNOON LOVE
                    CUMMINGS AND MARION

384. Pound to Cummings

TL-1.

[20 November 1955]   [Saint Elizabeths]

NACHERLY / response to tegelramm deelivver'd @ 2.15 A.M
                    ⟨çoivis this is⟩
                    this the 20th Nov.

        "I takes my lovin' in the afternoon"

                    (english lyrik, we beleev)
            EZ

385. Cummings to Dorothy Pound

TELEGRAM.

20 Nov[ember] 1955   [Saint Elizabeths]

DEAR DOROTHY CAN WE SEE YOU AND EZRA AT SAINT ELIZABETH
TUESDAY AFTERNOON NOVEMBER 22 WILL YOU TELEPHONE US AT
RICHMANS HOUSE MONDAY EVENING OR TUESDAY MORNING
HUDSON 36181 AFFECTIONATELY
                    ESTLIN AND MARIAN

RICHMANS: Robert Richman, head of the Institute of Contemporary Arts in
    Washington, D.C.

386. Pound to Cummings

TL-1.

27 Dec/ [1955]   [Saint Elizabeths]

e.e.c.

        Stock vurry pleased to git review cawpy of e.e.c poemz
His Magazine section, 12 copumns New Times, as of"13 Jan#" is cert/ the
highest level of periodical editing since old Fordie had the Eng/ Rev/ in 1909?
                                and outlook wider/ AND he ain' gawt 12
world famous names to hellup him fer prestige.

He does howeffr/ in air letter note that Robt.H Graves has printed a very dirty
lie re/ EP romecasts./ stating advocacy of Adolf and gas ovens.
                        and that this is done in comment on non-lectures
and "seems to imply that that is what e.e.c SAID or thought".
                unfortunately he merely picked up "recent book of Graves" and
hasn't sent exact ref/

One knew Orwell was a rat/ and supposed Graves merely mediocre.

e.e.c re/ canaille litteraire. etc.

You wil never git gramp out of quod until six or 8 of you at least get a few
points straight in private for use in conversation.

I.
        E.P. never altered his PRINCIPLES, he objected to falsification of news
about Italy
                                he set down specific facts, and
approved certain acts or policies <u>as</u> <u>EMERGENCY</u> <u>measures.</u>

                This usable to straighten out Mr Blöcker who has done noble
in Deutsches Kommentare, 12 nov. Tagespiegel.

2. EP does NOT object to proper income on investment.
                Mohrt in "ARTS Spectacles" Ez phiz almost as big as Mr
Armstrong's (Louis)   ⟨23/24 Nov.⟩
                has NOT grasped Ez definition of Usury.
Have you?

3. EZ never tolerated Aberhart's and Bankhead's perversion of Gesell by
advocating a 2% weekly tax on money. He approved 1% monthly.
                104% a year is outrageous usury no matter who imposes it.

4. his refrain: "this is what Brooks Adams said in 1903. can this be axis propaganda. ??"
if it WUZ, then Alf Knopf is axisProping, by reissue at 95 cents.

If Grab brings in scrip this p.m. Mebbe I'll find out if any of the Yalizentzia had grarsped these items in their recent a symphonious effort.

Stock: Noel Stock. In *New Times,* vol. 22, no. 1 (13 January 1956), Stock published a brief notice, "A Renaissance and Present Day Australia: Agenda for 1956." Stock found a need for "somebody willing to tackle the Sumerian language and report to us on the actual poetic quality of the epic of Gilgames and the later Babylonian and Hittite re-tellings." Stock also called for "a really scientific examination of evidence available today on the pre-historic indigenous populations of Greece and Italy, where Law-and-Order as we know it was first practised with the object of giving the individual room enough in which to develop his talents." Other necessary tasks included finding a translator and publisher for Frobenius's *Erlebte Erdteile,* following up possible links between the British Eddas and Sumerian civilization, and bringing attention to R. H. Mathews, compiler of the *Chinese-English Dictionary,* who was then living quietly in a suburb of Melbourne.

Fordie: Ford Madox Ford (1873–1939) edited the *English Review* from 1908 to 1910.

Graves: Robert Graves (1895–1985), British poet and novelist. See *The Crowning Privilege: The Clark Lectures, 1954–1955* (London: Cassell and Company, 1955), 164. "Here I personally cannot follow him [Cummings]; the self-styled world's greatest literary figure [Pound] had compromised his *is*ness by raving anti-poetic generalities over the Fascist radio, and recommending that all Jews in Italy, as in Germany, should be sent to the gas-chamber."

romecasts: Pound's World War II radio broadcasts from Rome.

Orwell: George Orwell (1903–50), British journalist and novelist.

canaille litteraire: See letter 138.

Blöcker: Gunter Blöcker (b. 1913), German literary and theater critic. Author of "Die Lyriker und die Macht: Über Ezra Pound," *Tagesspiegel* (Berlin), 30 October 1955. Eva Hesse had mailed her translation of the article to Pound on 12 November 1955. Blöcker had read Hesse's *Ezra Pound: Dichtung und Prosa* (Zurich: Verlag der Arche, 1953), and based much of the article on that book. Blöcker notes that Pound "unquestionably numbers among the great stimulators of modern literature," but that "he succumb[ed] to the crude attractions of Mussolini." Pound's treatment after his arrest, says Blöcker, was "an unworthy vengeance." An analysis of the *Cantos,* Blöcker asserts, shows that "the fascination for power to which he had succumbed is prefigured in his verses." "The poet projects himself beyond human and temporal relationships to become an impersonal, suprapersonal authority. . . . It stands to reason that the ego here arrives at an outermost point . . . where normal human contacts no longer exist." "However guilty he may be," Blöcker concludes, "the insane asylum is no solution to a political dilemma."

Mohrt: Michel Mohrt, "Liberez Ezra Pound," *Arts Spectacles,* no. 543 (23–29 November 1955). This article is accompanied by a photograph of Pound and a French translation of a portion of Canto 81 (from "What thou lovest well remains" to the end of the canto). Mohrt gives a brief summary of Pound's career and urges that he be released from Saint Elizabeths.

Armstrong's: Louis Armstrong (1901–71), American jazz musician. On the same page of this issue of *Arts Spectacles* was an article on Armstrong, with an accompanying photograph of him.

Aberhart's and Bankhead's: William Aberhart (1878–1943). A Social Credit advocate who led the party in Alberta. He served as premier of Alberta from 1935 until his death. John Hollis Bankhead (1872–46), U.S. senator from Alabama (1930–46). Pound formerly thought well of him because "Bankhead proposed Stamp Scrip in the U.S. Senate, possibly the only 100 per cent honest monetary proposal made in U.S. legislature since American civilisation was destroyed by and after the Civil War." *Selected Prose,* 300–301.

Gesell: Silvio Gesell.

Brooks Adams: American historian (1848–1927).

Knopf: Brooks Adams, *The Law of Civilization and Decay* (New York: Vintage Books, 1955).

Yalizentzia: A radio broadcast, "A Tribute to Ezra Pound," which aired over the Yale University radio station on 5 December 1955. Participants included W. H. Auden, Ernest Hemingway, Archibald MacLeish, Stephen Spender, and Robert Penn Warren.

387. Cummings to Pound

TL-1.

[December 1955?]   [4 Patchin Place]

re RG:seem to remember—I may be wrong—reading in "Goodbye To All That" how,as a WWI officer,he saw through fieldglasses a naked soldier bathing behind the German trench;&,being himself(RG)unable to shoot him(the man)because he was naked & so just a poor devil of a human creature,handed the glasses to his(RG's)noncom & told him to shoot the p d of a h cr—which he(the noncom)obediently did

Happy New Year

RG: The incident is recounted in chapter 14 of Robert Graves's *Good-bye to All That.*

388. Cummings to Pound

ALS-1.

[1956?]   [4 Patchin Place?]

AM I
SPURNED
         ?

      C'gs

[The Chinese characters at the top of this note can be interpreted variously as "fry," "cook," or "burn."]

389. Marion Morehouse Cummings to Pound

ACS.

[Postmarked 27 April 1956]   [Venice]

Greetings & love from Estlin & Marion who have been meeting admirers of yours & enjoying icy cold Italy.

                            M.

390. Cummings to Pound

TLS-1.

May 16 '56   4 Patchin Place

Dear Ezra—

am thankful Marion&I left America when we did(SaintPat'sDay)even though coldcoldcold has driven us home again six weeks later

Venice,city of silence & poetry,is murdered by motorboats(gently remarked our gondolier;as he cleverly-outofexistencewiped an oversize wave)& that evening off in some(far from anything known)dark square,we heard canned cries:& beheld at least four people staring at a tumbledown house whence television emanated

you're hunted from morning to midnight through Firenze by every notimaginable species of motorbicycle—the speedfiends ride their roaring machines at 40-50mph & l'on dit there are three times as many accidents as in NewYorkCity. (I saw somebody almost killed twice in five seconds). As for proud poor Roma,she long ago ceased to exist . . . except now & then . . . thanks to the wasps

but,O my friend!Italia somehow is still Herself;& always miraculous

—xxx

E

wasps: Vespas.

391. Pound to Cummings

TL-2. Enclosure.

17 Maggio [May 1956]   [Saint Elizabeths]

accuse reception

DEEmonstrating simultaneité
as practiced by la FAMille kumminkz.   Card from M/
(Firenze, bubbly gdns.) and e.e. N.Y.

arruv this a.m.

I was in course of misinforming the young scamp who started the rag (vide enc/ on Nebraskaaa Campus.)
he has now got to Dodgerville, ⟨Muzik School⟩ wd/ probably be livlier companion for les kMkZ than some /

He wrote they hadn't told me cause thought I wd/ disapprove.

at any rate, not likely to drag the estmbl Estlin into wallows of practical politicz.

do giv him a dish of tea /
            Bruce Conner 252 Division St.
                  N.Y.City.
I spose me informint dont know wot number but mebbe the post uffiz can divide.

oh yes, complete with
buttons, bearing the
strange device.
sample of which wd/ bulge
the envelope.

Dont know how much annoyance
it caused.
You might be more suitable acquaint fer him, but
Marianne more likely to take him to ball games.

He has no konexn with the Neb/ Daily kneeBruskin.

        I believe B.C.
left none of the muvmint behind him in Neb/
despite there being no local State Debt.

know anything bout yung Kennedy
wot read a hizzery book?

[Pasted on the letter at this position is a printed sticker, reading "EZRA POUND FOR PRESIDENT."]
P.S. und ja ZO.   !!!!
                when yu got all Italy to go to / why THE hell yu waste time on Firenze /

                unless yu wanna see the same pixc hoorz again/

            but with ALL of that Italy, like PErugia, and SIennah and VEEroner, and 30 other places, why the hell the myrkn goes to Firenze, where there aint,and never has been place to sit, stand or walk . . . .

            as Mencius sez: trouble is people like to teach.

Mr Stock quotes yr/ merark on sadism in recent Meanjin.

mebbe yu sent, I mean Marion sent the bubbly foto, to remind me of the olde
ketch / Old Cosmo di Medici's

> an opulent kuss, in his marble halls
> he hung up six of his unused balls;
> With the remaining twain did propagate
> bastards thruout the Florentine State.

at any rate thaaar they be over thet grotter.

Enclosure: An advertisement for *The Unwobbling Pivot* published in the Square
  Dollar Series.
bubbly gdns: The Boboli Gardens in Florence.
Dodgerville: Brooklyn, New York.
strange device: Probably the legend, "Ez for Prez."
Marianne: Marianne Moore, who enjoyed watching the Brooklyn Dodgers.
Daily kneeBruskin: The *Daily Nebraskan*, the student newspaper at the University
  of Nebraska.
Kennedy: John Fitzgerald Kennedy (1917–63), then U.S. senator from Massa-
  chusetts.
Mencius: Chinese philosopher (d. 289 B.C.).
Stock: Noel Stock. The quotation appears in his review of *Section: Rock Drill* in
  Meanjin, vol. 15, no. 1 (autumn 1956), 112–14. "Pound's ideas are not written
  into the *Cantos* as abstract statements. He moves from the thing to the grouped
  things and his ideas grow in, or out of, the facts.

> 'You damn sadist!' said mr. cummings,
> 'you try to make people think.'
> *(Canto 89)*"

thet grotter: The Boboli Gardens were first laid out by Tribolo in 1550, under
  Cosimo de Medici. The grotto Pound refers to is one of the first things a visitor
  to the gardens sees upon entering.

392. Cummings to Pound

TCS.

[Postmarked 21 May 1956]   4PatchinPlace NYC11

have dropped "Bruce Conner" a pc suggesting thé

particularly enjoyed Profiles in Courage by JFKennedy because once,riding a

Boston-NYC plane,our Peeping Tom(who never recognizes anyone not excluding himself)whispered "that's senator Taft". Unbelievably he was a human being:& looked it. (Ask Marion). Quel plaisir!

there are wonderful elephants at the tiptop Milano zoo

E

Pres ok but keep away from the UN

"Bruce Conner": Conner wrote to Cummings subsequently, "Much enjoyed the cup of tea on tuesday." On 28 June 1956 he wrote to Cummings, "Ez says he wd. be most happy for you to be running mate if you wd. accept. Would you?"
Profiles: *Profiles in Courage* (New York: Harper [1956]).
Peeping Tom: Probably Cummings himself, whispering to Marion Cummings.
Taft: Robert Alphonso Taft (1889–1953), U.S. senator from Ohio 1939–53.

393. Pound to Cummings

TL-1.

22 Maggio [May 1956]   [Saint Elizabeths]

The AZ uzual RAPidity of the kumrad's wot Ari STOTL call'd PURRception of RElations, ever baffling to mere human purrception re/ Kennedy and the late Mr Taft.

all I recall is Unc. George: "YhEzz he's harmless. S'prised yu liked him at all."

one queery answered (subjective or possibly ezpressed) the kumrad HAS read a book/
                                    queery not answered, does he know any
pipe like to Kennedy
                        or any penumbra?

Has the kumrad got somf ink brief and STRONG fer the good lads down under/ zummat level that old six av. L returning in ballistic demonstration?

Ari STOTL: *Poetics* 1459a 5–7. "But the greatest thing by far is to be a master of metaphor. It is the one thing that cannot be learnt from others; and it is also a sign of genius, since a good metaphor implies an intuitive perception of the similarities in dissimilars." Richard McKeon, ed., *The Basic Works of Aristotle* (New York: Random House, 1941), 1479.

Unc. George: George Holden Tinkham (1870–1956). A Massachusetts member of the U.S. House of Representatives 1915–43. Pound corresponded with Tinkham starting in the 1930s and met him when visiting the United States in 1939. Pound was quoted in 1939 as saying, "If God loved the American people, the Republican party would nominate for President George Holden Tinkham, the representative from Massachusetts, in 1940" (Norman, 367).

six av. L: Cummings's poem "plato told."

394. Cummings to Pound

TCS.

[Postmarked 27 May 1956]   4 Patchin Place
                                                                      NYCity 11

thanks for interesting enclosures
no pipeline to anyone,neither penumbra
shall try to find something "STRONG"
                    —Marion sends love!

                                        E

395. Cummings to Pound

TCS.

[Postmarked 18 October 1956]   4 Patchin Place
                                                                      NewYorkCity11

one(serious)question—who or what is or means a pourainsidire social
phenomenon yclept Elvis(The Pelvis)
?

                                        E

Elvis: Elvis Presley (1935–77), American rock-and-roll singer.

396. Pound to Cummings

TLS-1.

20 Oc[tober 1956]   [Saint Elizabeths]
the Pelvis not having called at S.Liz so far as I know, and the ward "tele" being
bust, and there being no females from six to sixty among patients on this
ward,
                              i kan only cONjecture that Mrs Marie Stokes
dealt with a sim/ sit/ in Britain some years ago inspiring or inSTIGating the
brief lyric begining
              The English were so stupid that . . . . etc.

can it be that there are some not wholly satisfied:
              A. by the quantity
              B. by the quality or timbre
supplied in the or'nry course of relations.

Yunnerstan the old N.Eng/er was worrit about his character /

after the deluge of Roosian filth, via Wien, the hole cuntynunt worries re/ its
bellyache.
its personal puny bellyaches.
                              the intermediate stage was fuss re OTHER
people's conduct.

          best to the gentle Consorte
                              Ez

Marie Stokes: Marie Charlotte Carmichael Stopes (1880–1958), British birth-
    control advocate and writer on human sexuality. Her most famous work is
    Married Love (London: A. C. Fifield, 1918). This manual is the "book" Pound
    refers to in the following note.
brief lyric: The lyric appears in a letter Pound wrote to Wyndham Lewis on 20
    March 1926.

              Oh the Henglish wuz so stoopid
              They'd fergotten how to fook
                  Till Mrs Doktor Mary Stoops
                      Com to skow them wid her book.

              She sez: O Jhon do mind the moment
                      When her oviduct is full
                  And then go in

> An' play to win
> And show- ye- are . . . . . . JOHNBULL!

Materer, 167.
Wien: Vienna was the home of Sigmund Freud.

397. Pound to Cummings

TL-1. On verso of a letter from Noel Stock to Pound. Enclosure.

[Postmarked 11 November 1956]   [Saint Elizabeths]

AND now spose deh KUMMrad kummZ across
with something useful, and jines the
company of the more undead

leaving Marianne and Mr whoosis Hilton, or what yu
        wont, to the egghead

Would yu read Dave's No 6. if I git yu a
        free cawpy

        vide enc

Marianne: Marianne Moore.
Hilton: Unidentified.
Dave's No 6: David Gordon's planned sixth number of *Academia Bulletin*.
enc: *Academia Bulletin No. 2,* edited by David Gordon. It included a number of
    Pound's economic definitions under the heading "ZWECK" (Gallup C1821).
    This issue of *Academia Bulletin* is reprinted in *Paideuma,* vol. 3, no 3 (winter
    1974), 385–88.

398. Cummings to Pound

TCS.

[Postmarked 7 December 1956]   4 Patchin Place
                                                New York City
                                                11

will read "Dave's No 6" if 'twill please you

". . . high deeds in Hungary

to pass all men's believing"

true poets aren't hurryable however

love from
the lady

E

deeds in Hungary: In October 1956, a spontaneous anticommunist uprising occurred in Hungary. During November, Soviet military forces restored a Communist government. Cummings quotes from the last stanza of Pound's poem "An Immortality" (Gallup A8, C39).

399. Pound to Cummings

TL-1.

24 Dec[ember 1956?]   [Saint Elizabeths]

AZ fer the seezun'z greeting, mon cher Kumrad et UX

                                        'sadisticly, ov course) this is to state
that the teXas marigolds have survived several months in yr/ gorful city

an I trust you will by now have sufficiently recovered from uprootin the pines of N.H. to give 'em yr/ phone number, and eggzercise yr/ paideutic potentialities into makin 'em thorns in the minds of the sond of hell and perdition /

at any rate they will be looking after gramp's in'erests / alzo as for Stock and Framp. etc.

yr/ lack of moral stamina may have left yu insensible to Australian preminence as over the defiled Ooozenfeldian States in matters of reading matter, as distinct from slosh, ploop and the "if it is on p. 11 it can't be important".

The WeltWUCHER of Zurich is furious re. Eva's Nachwort to the Pisaner Gesange, and the red printer of the Univ. of Mex seems to have prevented all but 3 copies of Amaral's Cantares from gittin wetbacked into Baruchistan.
                                        now thaar is a boye yu shd/ alzo know,
J.Vasquez Am/

doubtless the Mulligator has flavoured you with the enc/

and I spose Dave wd/ send you No. 6. (vide enc on the GREEN slip) if he tho't
there wuz ANY chanct of either of you reading it.

                                        beneditions. Chao has carefully erased the
Sage's birfday, xtn. saying he aint one and properly augurates a new year.

                                and so forf.
was Mr Rorty of the Jew Masses one of yr/ pals in the John Reid days?
and how is yr/ ole pal mr TDiamondt?

teXas marigolds: Probably Marcella Spann and Pansy Pinkston, two young
women from Texas who had visited Pound at Saint Elizabeths. Spann collabo-
rated with Pound on the anthology *Confucius to Cummings* (Gallup B78) and
accompanied him and Dorothy back to Italy. See Marcella Booth, "Through the
Smoke Hole: Ezra Pound's Last Year at St. Elizabeths," *Paideuma*, vol. 3, no. 3
(winter 1974), 329–34. See also her "Ezrology: the Class of '57," *Paideuma*, vol.
13, no. 3 (winter 1984), 375–88.

Stock: Noel Stock.

Framp: Hollis Frampton (1936–84), American photographer and filmmaker. He
began corresponding with Pound in 1956. During 1957 and 1958 he lived in
Washington, D.C., and frequently visited Pound. He translated Frobenius's
Erlebte Erdteile, but the translation has not yet been published.

WeltWUCHER: R. J. Humm, "Ezra Pound: Pisaner," *Die Weltwoche,* (30 Novem-
ber 1956), 5. Humm reviews Eva Hesse's German translation of the *Pisan
Cantos* (Gallup D28). Humm begins by noting how perplexing the text is by
comparing it to a crossword puzzle ("Kreuzwortratsel"). He then discusses
Pound's economic interests and questions Pound's understanding of politics
and economics: "Zunächst so viel, dass Ezra Pound ein politisiernder Dichter
ist, der sich anmasst, in seiner Lyrik die Freigeldlehre zu vertreten, von der er,
wie ich ihm glatt ins Gesicht behaupte, keinen Deut versteht" [To begin with, let
it suffice to say that Ezra Pound is a politicizing poet who presumes to represent
Free Money theory in his verse, about which theory, as I will tell him to his face,
he understands not one iota]. Furthermore, says Humm, Pound was a traitor to
his country. Humm maintains that most of the details of the *Pisan Cantos* are
incomprehensible ("das meiste ist unverständlich!").

Amaral's Cantares: José Vasquez Amaral translated the *Pisan Cantos* into Spanish
(Gallup D219). It was published in Mexico.

Mulligator: Eustace Mullins.

the enc/: Enclosure lacking.

vide enc: Enclosure lacking.

Chao: Probably Chao Tze-chiang (b. ca. 1910). Born in China, Chao left for the
United States in 1949. He first met Pound in January 1955 and began corre-
sponding with him about Chinese poetry. Chao's translation of Tu Fu appeared

in *Edge* (Melbourne, Australia), no. 1 (October 1956) and in *Twentieth Century* (Melbourne), vol. 10, no. 4 (winter 1956).

Rorty: James Rorty, American poet, political writer, and sociologist. One of the first editors of the *New Masses.*

John Reid: John Reed (1887–1920), American journalist. Author of *Ten Days That Shook the World* (1919). Reed contributed to the *Masses.*

TDiamondt: David Diamond.

400. Pound to Cummings

TLS-1.

11 Sep[tember 1957]   Bghsz. [Saint Elizabeths]

Eximius kumminKZ
                    A FRIEND, ergo of e.e.c, is engaging in virtuous effort
to see WOT of our era is applicable to the rising.
                    25 year old anthist with chance to try out on freshman probably
before printing
                    WHAT the young will stand of the heritage. paper
back, Kung to Kumminkz.

aim to end on yr/ jap shell returning frangment of Sixth Ave. scrap.

Am interested/ something under 6000 lines/ will allow chucking a lot of
rubbish.
    I doubt if Mr Coleridge's "fast thick pants" will stand the wear an tear.

Wonder if the kumrad, averse as is from SELECTING, and assumptions of
REEsonsibility etc. Will reply re/ which three of his, and which ten of
ENNYbuddy from (ut supra) Kunk to Kumrad
        should be tried on the YOUNG, i.e junior college.

Ef he wuz trying to save the l'il blighters buddin' souls etc.

Chance to elude the new ash cans and hogwash etc. I spect the earlier Yeats, fer
zampl, is going to suit 'em better than the strains (and how) of his later.

Anthologist reads ONLY english. Squirmers cant read Chaucer. etc. limits it to
what is GOOD even when translated.

e.e.c ever recollect ANY american stuff pre 1900?? apart from Walt?

Corbeau dit: jamais plus !!!

Any TRANSLATIONS by Bayard Taylor, Longwhiskers, Saxe still legible? any Whittier consumable in day of the extinct Schmoo and return to inferior Kapp ?

I am seereeyus, I want hellup and the anthologist merits.

EEC ever LOOK at wot is beink used a "texbukz"?

remarkable speciment by Haywire and Vincent / 80% slush BUT a firm structure, which I dont spose the squirmers will find/ Scudder on Agassiz, a directions writer, and one page of Hazlitt.

best to deh lydy

even at egocentric level/ wot kumminks does eec think wd/ lead the blighters best to WANT more kumminkz?

E

[At the bottom right corner of the page Pound stamped three Chinese characters. As Gordon explains, these characters are Pound's "Chinese-style name (in current pronunciation: *Pao-en-te,* or *Bao-en-de)* in the small seal characters of 213 B.C.: *Pao* (M. 4946, 'protect') *en* (M. 1743, 'kindness') *te* (M. 6162, 'virtue')" (252).]

FRIEND: Marcella Spann.
yr/ jap shell: "plato told," *Complete Poems,* 553.
"fast thick pants": No selections from Coleridge appear in *Confucius to Cummings.* The reference is to "Kubla Khan," line 18.
Corbeau: A French translation of the refrain from Poe's "The Raven," "Quoth the Raven, 'Nevermore.'"
Taylor: Bayard Taylor (1825–78), American author.
Longwhiskers: Henry Wadsworth Longfellow (1807–82), American poet. His translation of Teresa D'Avila's "Bookmark" is included in *Confucius to Cummings.*
Saxe: John Godfrey Saxe (1816–87), American poet.
Whittier: John Greenleaf Whittier (1807–92), American poet. His "Barbara Fritchie" appears in *Confucius to Cummings.*
Schmoo: The Shmoo was a creature in the comic strip "Li'l Abner." Pound refers to it as "extinct" because it had not appeared in "Li'l Abner" since the late 1940s. See Al Capp, *The Life and Times of the Shmoo* (New York: Simon and Schuster, 1948).
Kapp: Al Capp (Alfred Gerald Caplin) (1909–79), American cartoonist.
Haywire and Vincent: Harrison Hayford and Howard P. Vincent, coauthors of *Reader and Writer* (Boston: Houghton Mifflin, 1954). This text was an anthology intended for courses in freshman English.

Scudder: One of the selections in *Reader and Writer* is "A Great Teacher's Method," a selection from a memoir of Louis Agassiz by Samuel H. Scudder (1837–1911). Scudder's memoir describes Agassiz's method of instruction when Scudder was a student of natural history. The instruction consisted of injunctions to look carefully at a preserved fish. Pound's condensation of the memoir appears at the beginning of his *ABC of Reading.*

directions writer: Another selection from *Reader and Writer.* "World's Best Directions Writer," by Ken Macrorie (reprinted from *College English,* February 1952, 275–79). The article is an account of a visit to the office of "Edward Zybowski—Best Directions Writer in the World."

Hazlitt: Two essays by Hazlitt appear in *Reader and Writer:* "On the Difference between Writing and Speaking" and "On Familiar Style."

401. Cummings to Pound

ACS.

IX20 [20 September 1957]   Silver Lake
                                            New Hampshire

"abegocentric level" suspects that a sonnet beginning "you shall above all things be glad and young", plus the enclosed*, might go well with "plato told"

otherwise: did you take a peek at "The Oxford Book Of American Verse" edited by F.O. (Fell Out) Matthiessen? Might be boh-coo worse, n'est-ce pas

                              EEC

*everywhere heartily applauded, even in Boston (see Harpers Mag, Sept, p. 87)

Marion sends love

this must be your year—eye never sore & hoid so many Js

sonnet: *Complete Poems,* 484. It was not used in *Confucius to Cummings.*

enclosed: Enclosure lacking. It was almost certainly Cummings's poem "THANKSGIVING (1956)." *Complete Poems,* 711.

Matthiessen: Francis Otto Matthiessen (1902–50). Matthiessen's distinguished career as an author and Harvard professor ended with his suicide on 1 April 1950. Cummings's reading of Matthiessen's initials as standing for "Fell Out" may refer to the circumstances of Matthiessen's death. He jumped from the twelfth floor of a Boston hotel.

Harpers Mag: A report on Cummings's reading of his poems at the Boston Arts Festival in June 1957. *Harper's,* vol. 215, no. 1288 (September 1957), 86–87. See also Kennedy, 452–58.

402. Pound to Cummings

TL-1.

[23 September 1957]   [Saint Elizabeths]

      MAAG-niffercent.
                Wonder wd/ harPURR purrmit reprint in
Edge / call it the Orstralian etc./
                    alzo a boost to HarPURR/ with
chapeau lifted /
            I nacherly never see the mag / NOR mr
mathestein's slosifications antholicly.

wish I cd/ read more of yr/ distinguished Handschrift. but mebbe the anth/ist
can.

e.e.c. 23 Sep 57

and best to deh lydy

[At the bottom of this page Pound stamped the three Chinese characters that,
when sounded, pronounce his last name.]

Edge: An Australian magazine founded by Noel Stock.
mathestein's: F. O. Matthiessen edited *The Oxford Book of American Verse* (New
    York: Oxford University Press, 1950).

403. Cummings to Pound

TCS.

[Postmarked 18 November 1957]   4 Patchin Place
                                New York City
                                      11

will you PLEASE make your Australians understand they MUST send me as
many proofs as I may require? THANKS!

                                    EEC
¡Marion sends *love*!

Australians: Noel Stock and William Fleming. Firmage lists no appearances by
    Cummings in Australian periodicals between 1957 and 1960.

404. Pound to Cummings

TLS-1.

20 Nov. '57   [Saint Elizabeths]

Bastile of Baruchistan

Revered Estlin
              yr/ museum piece recd/ j'accuse reception. Reminding me of
Nancy Cunard's threat to yr/ hnrd person some thirty an' mo' yeuhs agone.
                    AND kinksidering yr/ own notable command of
language (of a sort)
                    and the open question as to whether during the past 50
cycles I have <u>ever</u> been able to make YOU or anyone else un'nner stan'
ANYFINK wotbloodysodam . . . .

as preliminary, have you already sent the ms/ ?

                        if not,as the Saucy Aussie is a man of honour you
cd/ stipulate before hand the conditions on and under which the ms/ is
entrusted to the powers of sea air and the iMPekable postal service of our
rampant tyranny.

              BUT if yu have already sent it. . . .
                                    surely yr trust in Marianne's
jewgawd or whatso might sustain you IF . . .

                    but why pick on grampaw?

///
there is material for yr/ talent as satirist in a current rotocalco,
mebbe you and Marion cd/ tell me who someUVum are?
                                    Don't discourage 'em.
I cd/ do wiff a change of scene, tho the delights of the american florilege are a
compensation.

//speaking of other/ have you ever seriously considered the relative guts of the
poems in Kung's thology in proportion to wot yu find in ANY kolexshun of
english prosodification?

well known and remembered snatches, hawk on tower, etc.
          but for wot the buzzards are exuding?

Wpps before 1321, some uVuM had some insides . . .

Have i pestered yu re/ wot yu consider READING matter, now you have ripened. Pearson (N.H. not Drew) and a Mr Smiff both note Mr Smart's KAT. a mos' simpatico animal. An some buzzard wrut about beaver fur

best to Marion

EP

[At the bottom left of the page Pound stamped the three Chinese characters that, when sounded, pronounce his last name.]

museum piece: Not located.
Cunard's threat: The "threat" seems to have taken place in Paris during the 1920s. It appears that Cunard took offense at a remark made by Cummings, a remark she thought disparaging of black people and (in particular) her black lover, Henry Crowder.
Saucy Aussie: Noel Stock.
Marianne's: Marianne Moore was a devout Christian.
material: Unidentified.
Kung's thology: Confucius (ca. 551–479 B.C.) compiled an anthology of poems. Pound's translation of this text was published as *The Classic Anthology Defined by Confucius* (Cambridge, Mass.: Harvard University Press, 1954) (Gallup A69).
hawk on tower: Pound may refer to John Skelton's (1460?–1529) poem "To Mistress Margaret Hussey," which begins, "Merry Margaret / As Midsummer flower / Gentle as falcon / Or hawk of the tower."
1321: Dante died in 1321.
Pearson: Norman Holmes Pearson (1909–75), American literary scholar. He and Auden edited a five-volume anthology, *Poets of the English Language* (New York: Viking, 1950). Volume 3 contains Christopher Smart's poem on his cat.
Mr Smiff: Robert Mahony and Betty W. Rizzo's *Christopher Smart, An Annotated Bibliography, 1743–1983* list only one Smith who included Smart in an anthology: David Nichol Smith, editor of *The Oxford Book of Eighteenth-Century Verse* (Oxford: Clarendon Press, 1926). Smith, however, does not print any portion of *Jubilate Agno.* J. C. Smith and Herbert J. C. Grierson mention Smart's *Song of David* in their *Preface to Eighteenth Century Poetry* (Oxford: Clarendon Press, 1948).
Smart's KAT: Christopher Smart (1722–71), British poet. He writes of his "Cat Jeoffry" in *Jubilate Agno* (ca. 1760). The passage is included in *Confucius to Cummings.*
beaver fur: Pound may refer to a line from part 4 of Ben Jonson's poem "A Celebration of Charis"; "Ha' you felt the wooll of Bever?" The following line, "Or Swans Downe ever," appears near the end of Canto 74.

405. Cummings to Pound

TCS.

November 22 '57   4 Patchin Place
                                                   New York City
                                                   11

seem to have lost the name&address of your Australian magazine's editor—
would you be so very kind as to forward same at your latest inconvenience?
Somebody said he(somebody)had received a circular,listing me as a
contributor;hence my misguided notion re ms
                                EEC

editor: Noel Stock.

406. Cummings to Pound

TCS.

[Postmarked 5 December 1957]   [4 Patchin Place]

many thanks to you for the prospectus & to Dorothy for the Edges—Marion
sends love to you both!

                                eec

prospectus: Not located.
Edges: Copies of *Edge,* the Australian magazine edited by Noel Stock.

407. Pound to Cummings

TLS-1.

[15 December 1957]   [Saint Elizabeths]

Iz thur enny uther VERsion of yr/

                                        sixth
                                        avenue
                                             el) plato told)
than the one in yr COlected Poems'23.'54. Harcourt / p. 396.
                    1954 (nacherly)

my octogenarian mem

                O

                        ry

aint letter tight.

                                                        EZ 15 Dec
                                                            57

did I imagine a more chunked
and briefer?

        Mr Alastair, whazzis his name, in scotch dialek RESENTS events in HUN
gary. I told him to send it to YU.

                                                        mebbe he wil

Mr Alastair: Unidentified.

408. Cummings to Pound

TCS.

[Postmarked 18 December 1957]   [4 Patchin Place]

yours of the 15th at hand

"plato told" on page 396 of Poems 1923–1954 is identical with poem XIII of 1
× 1(its first appearance)

& there's no other version that i know of

                                                        EEC

409. Pound to Cummings

TCS.

20 Marzo [March 1958?]   [Saint Elizabeths]

        haz Mr Yasuo sent yu his versions nip of 4 poemz, 5 poems, and 3
poemz.

if not I wil send 'em along. I confess I find the meaning more accessible to me
in the O'Riginalz

but doubtless yu and M/n will enjoy the new tipog/ display, if yu ain' already.

yrz Ez

.tin three s'v issues of the Tapering PAGoda

Yasuo: Yasuo Fujitomi, Japanese translator of Cummings's poetry. Pound apparently refers to "Four Poems," *Sento,* no. 31 (February 1958) ("lucky means finding," "Q:dwo," "the wind is a lady with," "(one!)"), Firmage D37 and "Three Poems," *Sento,* no. 29 (June 1957) ("into the strenuous briefness," "if I," "sunlight was over"), Firmage D35. Firmage records no publication of a five-poem sequence by Fujitomi.

410. Pound to Cummings

ALS-1.

14 Ap[ril 1958]   [Saint Elizabeths]

am doin wot i kan to hellup yr friends edit Joe Gould -
dont they think itz about time fer Greenwich Village "Voice" to repudiate
Celler in language praps more vigorous than that used by Generl Curtis.

yrs EP

friends: Possibly Edward Gottlieb. See *Joe Gould's Secret* (New York: Viking, 1965), 176.
Gould: Joe Gould died in August 1957.
"Voice": The *Village Voice.*
Celler: U.S. representative Emmanuel Celler (1888–1981). The *Washington Post* for 7 April 1958 carried a front-page article headed, "Plan to Free Ezra Pound Is Protested." "Rep. Emmanuel Celler (D.-N.Y.), chairman of the House Judiciary Committee, protested yesterday the planned attempt to dismiss the treason indictment against poet Ezra Pound and obtain his release from St. Elizabeths Hospital. Celler said: 'I don't care how long he's been in there. Maybe we want to keep him a little longer. . . . I can't understand how they'd let him out scot free. I can't conceive of that. Many of our men lost their lives as a result of his exhortations.' Celler was referring to Pound's vitriolic denunciations of the democracies over the Italian radio in World War II."
Curtis: In the issue of the *Washington Post* for 10 April 1958 (p. 19), an article appeared under the headline, "Celler Statement Termed Absurd." "Officers of the Defenders of the American Constitution, Inc., yesterday called the statement of Rep. Emmanuel Celler (D.-N.Y.) opposing the release of poet Ezra Pound 'absurd and irresponsible.' Celler said Saturday that he doesn't under-

stand how Pound could be let out 'scot free.' Pound, now 72, has been confined at St. Elizabeths as mentally incompetent to stand trial since shortly after he was indicted for treason in 1945. The Defenders is an organization headed by retired military officers. Its general counsel, Brig. Gen. Merritt Curtis, U.S.A., Ret., described the charges against Pound as 'very weak.' "

411. Marion Morehouse Cummings to Dorothy Pound

TELEGRAM.

APRIL 21 1958.   NEW YORK

DEAR DOROTHY CIMMINGS AND I WILL BE IN WASHINGTON AND WOULD LIKE TO SEE YOU AND EZRA SOMETIME TOMORROW WILL YOU CALL US AT THE HOTEL WESTCHESTER WE ARE VERY HAPPY FOR EZRA AND REALIZE YOU MUST HAVE AN INCREDIBLE AMOUNT OF WORK TO DO NOW OUR LOVE TO YOU BOTH
          MARION

WASHINGTON: In a postcard dated 23 April 1958, Cummings reported to Norman Friedman that he had just recently visited Pound. The indictment against Pound had been dismissed on 18 April 1958. He was officially discharged from Saint Elizabeths on 7 May 1958.

412. Cummings to Pound

TELEGRAM.

July 1 1958   MADISON N[ew]HAMP[shire]

EZRA POUND.
     SS CHRISTOPHER COLOMBO
HAVE A WONDERFUL TIME. LOVA TO YOU BOTH
     ESTLIN AND MARION

CHRISTOPHER COLOMBO: Pound returned to Italy aboard the Italian liner *Cristoforo Colombo.*

413. Cummings to Pound

TLS-1. Carbon copy with additions by Cummings.

August 19 1958   Silver Lake
                                           New Hampshire

copy of letter sent to Contini—Descoullayes
          LAVIGNY près d'Aubonne,Vaud—SuisseXXXXX

Gentlemen—

so you think Ezra Pound needs rehabilitating? Allow me to disagree. If the man has sinned,nothing
you can say or do will make him sinless—and if you're trying to render the poet socially
respectable,that's an insult;because no poet worth his salt ever has given or ever will give a
hangnail for social respectability. In this UNworld of "ours",lots of UNpoets and plenty of
UNcountries(UNamerica,for example)need rehabilitating the very worst way. But whoever or
whatever he may be,Ezra Pound most emphatically isn't UNanyone or UNanything

                    —sincerely

greetings!

Marion & EEC

Contini-Descoullayes: F. W. Dupee and George Stade identify these people as
    "Representing a Swiss group who invited EEC to contribute to a statement to a
    publication urging the rehabilitation of Ezra Pound" (*Selected Letters*, 256).

414. Pound to Cummings

TCS.

9 Oct[ober] 58   [Merano, Italy]

Just looked at Vanni's edtn estlin the unsqushabl. Selection gtly to Qua
SImodo's credit. not az I can usual read them woplations by Vanni's whatevers.

saluti alla gentMA consorte

                    Ez

down the middle they runs the geegees.

Vanni's edtn: *E. E. Cummings: Poesie Scelte,* trans. Salvatore Quasimodo (Milan:
    All'Insegna del Pesce d'Oro, 1958) (Firmage D26). Quasimodo (1901–68) was

an Italian poet, translator, and critic. He also translated poems by Pound. He was awarded the Nobel Prize for literature in 1959.

geegees: Horses. Which horses Pound refers to is unclear; none are depicted in the Quasimodo translation.

415. Cummings to Pound

TELEGRAM.

[30 October 1958]   [New York]

HAPPY BIRTHDAY
   Marion and Cummings

416. Cummings to Pound

TCS.

November 14 '58   4 Patchin Place
                                             New York City
                                                  11

many thanks for your bloody pc of October 14;&let me add I quite agree about the sailors. "Eva"'s recent message was also very welcome. Marion sends love

EEC

bloody pc: Pound had sent a postcard to Marion Cummings on which he had written, beneath his signature, "signd in 'iz bludd." Pound concluded his message with the comment, "Gawd bless all pore sailors."

"Eva"'s recent message: On 9 November 1958, Eva Hesse had written to Marion Cummings, "Now that I have been back from Italy for a couple of weeks there are a few points of interest I should like to talk to you about. First of all, I stayed for a few days with Ezra and he sends his very best wishes to you and Mr Cummings; he says he was sorry he didn't see you after departing the bughouse, but that there was so much excitement with preparations for general decampment that he hardly knew what was going on."

417. Pound to Cummings

TLS-1.

15 Nov[ember] '58   [Merano, Italy]

Semper dilectus dilectaque mihi.

Am less surprised by yr/ noble generosity than the industrious mc hoRRse, cause I thought I HAD OBtained yr/ gracious permission to free load with yr/ L and iron.

                                        plus Eva's spirited
translation.

speaking of which, the carbon here being uncorrected, tho I HOPE the text with mc HoRRse is KOrekt.

does the last line read KOrektly.

Da musst' er daran glauben.

I trust you are weeping for Pasternick, and backing Kerr to save the nation / tho I spose the demmys will put up Wendell Milkie.

                      yrs/ dev/mo
                          EZ

Mebbe mcH/ wd/ give you 100 bucks for jacket blurb material, by him recorded (probably a votre insu.)

mc hoRRse: Robert M. MacGregor, who was in charge of the New York office of New Directions. Pound told Laughlin that "MacGregor" meant "son of horse" in Scots.

L and iron: Cummings's poem "plato told." It was reprinted in *Confucius to Cummings* along with Eva Hesse's German translation of the poem. The translation, however, was not printed correctly. Hesse indicates that the last ten lines should read:

      nicht du
      sagtest es ihm,ich sagte
      es ihm,wir sagten es ihm
      (er glaubte es nicht,nein

zu befehl)erst als ein
japanisiertes stück von
der alten sixth

avenue
s-bahn in seinem hirnkasten stak

da musste er daran glauben

Pasternick: Boris Pasternak (1890–1960), Russian poet and novelist. He was awarded the Nobel Prize for literature in 1958, but declined to accept it after being pressured by the Soviet government to refuse the award. Pound may have seen or been told of Edmund Wilson's review of *Doctor Zhivago:* "Doctor Life and His Guardian Angel," *New Yorker* (November 15, 1958), [213]–38.

Kerr: Perhaps Robert S. Kerr (1896–1963), U.S. senator from Oklahoma (1949–63).

Wendell Milkie: Wendell Willkie, the Republican nominee for president of the United States in 1940.

418. Cummings to Pound

TCS.

November 20 '58   4 Patchin Place
                                             New York City
                                             11

the last line of EH's translation of my poem - da musst er daran glauben

tough on Boris is right

sois sage!

EEC

Shall try to [illegible] qua equine pal
[illegible]

Boris: Boris Pasternak.
pal: Robert MacGregor.

419. Cummings to Pound

TLS-1.

January 27 '59   4 Patchin Place

Dear Ezra—

greetings!

you may recall that "Charles Norman",who evolved a "symposium"(1945)re
yourself,to which I contributed,not unrecently wrote you in connection with
his "critical biography" of me(called "The Magic Maker")& that you answered
his letter;which answer he quotes(page   ). Apparently said book is
"selling":since he has now accepted a "generous" advance from Macmillan to
"do" a book "on" you

CN is a journalist whose fanatical admiration of the arts,expecially poetry—"in
the beginning was the word"—leads him to fancy himself a poet & painter,not
to mention(as volumes "on" Shakespeare & Marlowe testify)a scholar. Luckily
for me,'twas agreed that Marion & I should read proof on his opus-re-myself &
make whatever corrections we deemed necessary. "Where did you get this?" she
asked him,at one point,concerning a slab of particularly horrendous
misinformation. "Why,Cummings told me" was his velocitous reply;& he
obviously believed I had

please understand that,while we wish the poor little cuss well,we cannot(vide
supra)consider him a friend:& rest assured that we had absolutely nothing to
do with his writing a book about you. Please also understand that in my
opinion his enthusiasm for you is absolutely genuine;which,given your
penchant for damning The Chosen & his immediate descent from a NYCity
rabbi,strikes the undersigned as at least remarkable

—Love From The Lady

Estlin

Charles Norman: His biography of Cummings, *The Magic Maker, E. E. Cum-
mings,* had been published in the fall of 1958.

420. Pound to Cummings

TLS-1.

29 Jan[uary 1959]   [Merano, Italy]

Dear Estlin
                    Norman has done you a fine bit of publicity. BUT men who
by printing some truth USE it to hide the things it does not pay to print
                    are the low, the damned, the stink and the infamy.

AND when, if ever the documents re/ the betrayal of the U.S. by the fahrts
whom Norman helps to conceal get into print
                    IF the bastard survives to read 'em I hope he will vomit his own
bowels and have to swallow the contents.

Too bad I haven't the energy to sit up and type a few details.

HAS he printed ANY items re/ the real traitors, or even read Coke on
Misprision of Treason.

No, no, he is a clever boy, but will rot with ~~Eleanor~~ Dexter White and the
other lords whom he sustains

~~some photographic evidence~~

                                        yr
                                        EP

Coke: Sir Edward Coke (1552–1634), English lawyer. Pound greatly admired
    Coke's writings on English law.
Eleanor: Eleanor Roosevelt.
Dexter White: Harry Dexter White.

421. Cummings to Pound

TCS.

February 12 '59   4 Patchin Place
                                         New York City
                                              11

just saw CN,for the first time in weeks:he was very chipper. I gathered you had
written him saying you hoped he'd do as well by you as he did by me,&making
the same stipulation I made. CN volunteered "I won't take sides" & "I'll defend

him whenever possible" & "let the work speak for itself"—which struck me as rather encouraging than dis-

Marion sends love!

EEC

CN: Charles Norman. On 2 February 1959, Pound had written Norman, "I understand that cummings protected himself by an agreement with you that he should read proofs and eliminate misstatements from same. Are you prepared to give me similar treatment?"

422. Cummings to Pound

TELEGRAM.

[29 October 1959]   [New York]

BIRTHDAY GREETINGS AND LOVE

ESTLIN AND MARION

423. Cummings to Pound

TELEGRAM.

[31 October 1960]   [New York]

BIRTHDAY GREETINGS
ESTLIN MARION

424. Cummings to Pound

ACS.

[January 1961?]   4 Patchin Place
                                               New York City
                                               11

Was last in Rooan Hurkey's Romance,
        (Dublin, 1960)

Happy New Year

Marion & C'gs

Rooan Hurkey's Romance: rooan hurkey, *Romances* (Dublin, Dolmen Press, 1960). rooan hurkey was a pseudonym for the Irish writer Rudolf Patrick Holzapfel (b. 1938). *Romances* is a volume of twenty-six poems, each of twenty-four lines. They are printed without punctuation and without uppercase letters.

425. Pound to Cummings

ALS-3. On letterhead of Villa Chiara, Casa di Cura e Convalescenza, Rapallo.

[Postmarked 9 July 1962]

<u>for the stinks</u>
a fahrt fer his fahrters
a medal for his own
debunking of a helluva lot
that needed debunking
watcher bet in 8 years, a
<u>tiny</u> body say 40 pages

will be lef sticking out
thru mud
I haven't had piker Mullins
vol. long enough to read
but it lowers the tone of the
Opus = and the
chapters which were seen &
approved are mostly now
in the book - which started
in a bar with Bess
Truman plastered drunk
on <u>the surface</u> of same,
right poetry opposition &
U. Sinclair <u>quite</u> right re Roget
Love to Marion = one of first
lucids (18 months or so ago)
you 2 dear people had suicided
& killed each other. J plus e
marVELous romance china op. etc.
in absolut new mode e.e.c
rising gloriously toward a
unthanked for EIMI or
what augs for same

if I get out of this
orspitl I <u>will</u> hang a

⟨do yu evuh read
contemporaries?
I mean are there any
fit for me to read
I strongly suspect
there <u>has</u> been some
good stuff since 1930⟩

jewel on it to his memory
in the main a good job
de BUNKing & deflating wot
needed it
a few stinking craks & he knows
what = he know to a
millimetre = when he is doing a good
job & WHEN he pewks - as in
the stabown globbe @ end.
2 cabins one small - but considering
the dirt in crevasses - no time to
slap the bastid - AS he may have
combined with the chap in print
shoppe who set up
        passenger list
            & to the lot
of you & them the
EXact shade (or, plural, shades
                    of pewk
                    &
                    IRony
you have used on me
during pas 18
months of illness
when ~~shade of s~~ in St Eliz
& sane & since for
last 3 years, largely nuts
Love to Marion
if I had recd norman's letter
when I came I might have
been partially (not in the last wholy)
                            prepared

            on him they shat
            they shot encore
            N's phrases very
difficult to unsmear & I
suspected a [trot?] on passenger list
always the gent & so forth
        been a beaut of a rebuttal
if it contained the false
incidentally Mr Laughlin (Jas IV)
has recently descended a
considerable distance in MY

opinion but probably <u>not</u> in yours
permission requested to reprint
all or most probably only the   ⟨Frost undoubtedly
couplet   emergin as the gd.
of <u>on him</u> they shat   ole man
wonder did you ever see   stickin to the
Little Oinis's few good poems   better part⟩
in the interval   keep on
thankin' gawd fer Marion
if the possum hadn't
sufferd for so many decades
I cd. envy him his rum punchr
& t[r]y cula with D
                    O
                    Roman
            etc   ⟨wot about a good
either or some preferably not   word fer Robert
<u>all</u>   Graves some time⟩
This pistle started
about 48 hours after
my emergence from slough   ⟨F. Gould dead?
            & Fry duck with   I think⟩
bean shoots
            evuh urz
                    Ez
& gawd bless
blue jays as <u>well</u> as Xmas
                    card robins

Villa Chiara: A private medical facility at which Pound underwent a urological operation in June 1962.

his: Perhaps Charles Norman, whose *Ezra Pound* had been published in 1960.

Mullins vol: Eustace Mullins, *This Difficult Individual, Ezra Pound* (New York: Fleet Publishing Corporation, 1961).

Bess Truman: Eustace Mullins recalls that he told Pound about Mamie Eisenhower consoling herself at this hotel while her husband was in England during World War II. Elizabeth ("Bess") Truman (1885–1982) was the wife of President Harry S. Truman.

U. Sinclair: Upton Sinclair (1878–1968), American novelist and social critic. Pound corresponded with Sinclair in the 1930s and again in the late 1950s and in the early 1960s. I have not found in their correspondence an explanation for Pound's comment about Sinclair being "*quite* right about Roget."

Roget: Perhaps Peter Mark Roget (1779–1869), compiler of the thesaurus that has gone through many editions.

globbe @ end: Perhaps the last chapter of Norman's *Ezra Pound.*

2 cabins: Norman notes in *Ezra Pound* that Dorothy and Ezra's accommodations on the *Cristoforo Colombo* consisted of "a small air-conditioned stateroom, with two beds and several lounge chairs" (458).

norman's letter: Not located.

Laughlin: James Laughlin.

Little Oinis's: Ernest Hemingway.

possum: T. S. Eliot, who had married Valerie Fletcher in 1957. By all accounts, this marriage made Eliot's last years the happiest of his life.

D

O

Roman: Perhaps a reference to Dorothy Pound.

F. Gould: Joseph Ferdinand Gould, who died in August 1957.

426. Cummings to Pound

TLS-1.

August 8 '62   [Silver Lake, N.H.]

Dear Ezra—

WAL(as yew wd c'est)the welcome epistle from Villa Chiara,Rapallo arrived sound&safely;& has already given Marion & her consort quite a softly speaking workout

so far,we've disinterred a number of celebrities

　　(1)Useless Mullins—who,when EEC quoted Thoreau's "I never knew,and shall never know,a worse man than myself"(adding that this heald good for EEC;but Marion would have none of it)piped "your problem is no problem for me":the only question for UM,parait,being "how much you like people" . . compare Bliss Perry circa 1913 professing Comp(arative)Lit(erature)—"it's all right if you like it" . . . also Hamlet,to R & G—"for there is nothing either good or bad but thinking makes it so"

　　(2)Bess Truman—whose spouse,an ex-hatter,saved The Democratic Party from instant death by kicking Messer(& how)Tom Clark upstairs into the Supreme Court,where nobody could ever ask him anything

　　(3)Norman,Charles—re whom I continually indulge in the ultimate assinity,not to mention stygian stupidity,of expecting he'll behave as he can't

　　(4)Robert Graves—who,incompletely covered with mostly his own children,is doubtless concocting some 3or4hundredth opus settling the hash of all pre-Gravesian mythologists;while subtly insinuating a serious error of the scholiast concerning Nero's favorite bisexual setter bitch Janus"

(5)&,1 but not 1,JosephFerdinandGould—who may have died a decade ago,but nobody's ever been able to find his Oral History Of The World;which(in the form of numberless notebooks)he toted hither&yon during halfacentury:& was rumored to have occasionally parked large portions thereof at sundry Bowery flophouses

yr old pal Major Douglas(remember that day in Paris when you were giving me the gospel redhot & I coolly kept murmuring that I'd only read South Wind?)is,according to a dissident Catholic sheet yclept National Review,going great guns in Canada . . . shoh-keeng! Now & again,a darling named Mary drops me a line from Merano;making happy both myself & Marion—who sends

—love!

EEC

Thoreau's: Cummings cites a sentence near the conclusion of the "Economy" chapter of *Walden.*
Bliss Perry: American literary scholar (1860–1954). In 1906 he was selected as the first professor of English literature at Harvard University.
Tom Clark: American government official (1897–1977). President Truman appointed him to the Supreme Court in 1949, where he served until 1967.
Major Douglas: Clifford Hugh Douglas.
South Wind: A 1917 novel by Norman Douglas (1868–1952).
National Review: The *National Review,* edited by William F. Buckley Jr. See Donald Coxe, "Big Day for Social Credit," vol. 13, no. 2 (17 July 1962), 17–19.
Mary: Mary de Rachewiltz.

427. Pound to Marion Morehouse Cummings

ALS-1.

10 Sett [September 1962]   131 Sant Ambrogio di Rapallo

Dear Marion
    i can't
find the words —
e.e.c. will understand
God bless you
            Ezra

e.e.c.: Cummings died on 3 September 1962.

Biographical Notes

Angleton, James Jesus (1917–87), American intelligence officer. Angleton met Pound in Rapallo in the summer of 1938. He photographed Pound and began corresponding with him. The next year, while still an undergraduate at Yale University, Angleton and his roommate, Reed Whittemore, began a literary magazine: *Furioso*. (Although the magazine existed from 1939 until 1953, Angleton was involved with it only in its first few years.) Both Cummings and Pound were published in *Furioso*. In *Carta da visita* (1942), Pound praised the poem Cummings had published in the first issue of *Furioso*, "flotsam and jetsam." Pound visited Angleton in New Haven briefly during his 1939 U.S. stay. Angleton made the acquaintance of Cummings and Marion Morehouse about this time. He had tea with them at 4 Patchin Place on at least several occasions. The Cummingses spent part of the winter of 1946–47 at the Tucson, Arizona, home of Angleton's father- and mother-in-law. Angleton's interest in literary matters began to wane when he was a counterintelligence officer in London in 1943 (although his secretary for part of the time was Perdita, H.D.'s daughter). After the war, Angleton rose to the position of chief of the Counterintelligence Staff in the Central Intelligence Agency. See Tom Mangold's biography of Angleton, *Cold Warrior* (New York: Simon and Schuster, 1991).

Diamond, David Leo (b. 1915), American composer. Diamond wrote to Cummings early in 1936 to ask permission to compose a musical score for Cummings's *Tom*, which had been published the previous October. Cummings consented and Diamond finished the score by the end of the year. Diamond became a close friend of Cummings. His cordial relations with both Cummings and Marion Morehouse lasted until their deaths. When they were away at Joy Farm during the summer of 1939, Diamond lived in their apartment at 4 Patchin Place. Pound was using that address to receive mail; Cummings had told Pound that Diamond would be there to deliver it to him. When he called one evening to get his mail, Diamond answered the door. According to Diamond, Pound said: "I suppose you're Diamond. Where's my goddamn mail?" Diamond replied, "You won't get any if you speak to me like that," and closed the door. Pound kicked the door. Diamond opened it once more to comment, "Mister Pound, if you kick the door again, I'm going upstairs to get the big sabre and cut your leg off at the knee." Chastened, Pound came in and stayed for several hours, talking about Olga Rudge and music. Diamond later wrote to Cummings, "Pound stopped in one night to see you, and he said he'd call tonight or after. I sort of liked him." Thirty years later, at the 1969 memorial service for Marion Morehouse, Diamond noticed Pound and Olga Rudge as he was leaving. Miss Rudge nudged Pound, saying, "There's Diamond." Pound raised his arm weakly, but neither Diamond nor Pound spoke.

Eastman, Max (1883–1969), American political activist and writer. Despite Pound's numerous attempts in the 1930s and again in the late 1940s to interest Eastman in the methods Pound thought vital to secure world peace and prosperity, Eastman showed no interest in them. Eastman seemed to have little admiration for Pound as a poet, either. Eastman's *The Enjoyment of Poetry: With Other Essays in Aesthetics* (New York: Scribner's, 1939) cites T. S. Eliot with approval and praises Cummings, but does not mention Pound. Eastman summed up his long friendship with Cummings in *Love and Revolution* (New York: Random House, 1964). He recalls that he and his wife Eliena first knew Marion Morehouse; it was through her that they met Cummings. Eastman had little patience with the typographical experimentation in Cummings's poetry, but concluded that Cummings was basically sound, "a gentle person, reverently concerned with life's deepest values" (544).

Eliot, T. S. (1888–1965), American-born poet. As Cummings recalled in his letter of 23 July 1946 to Pound, he had acted in a play with Eliot in May 1913. But it seems they did not speak to each other off stage, and Cummings and Eliot were entirely unaware that the other wrote poetry. In his June 1920 *Dial* review of Eliot's *Poems,* Cummings noted Eliot had produced "half of the most alive poetry and probably all of the least intense prose committed, during the last few years, in the American and English language." In a letter to Robert McAlmon of 2 May 1921, Eliot described Scofield Thayer's style as producing "unintelligible gibberish," and then added, "Cummings has the same exasperating vice." Eliot seems to have had no interest in soliciting work by Cummings for the *Criterion.* His first contact with Cummings (after the accidental one of 1913) was his letter to Cummings in 1946, in which he sought Cummings's aid in transmitting information about Pound. There were a few subsequent meetings between Eliot and Cummings, but their relation at no time could be said to be close.

Pound's "discovery" of T. S. Eliot and their subsequent friendship is well documented in the biographies of Eliot and Pound. The Eliot letters in the Pound archives at the Beinecke Library and at the Lilly Library indicate that Eliot was deeply concerned about Pound's incarceration at Saint Elizabeths and his state of mind, especially in 1946. During his trips to the United States, Eliot always set aside time to visit Dorothy and Ezra Pound.

Gould, Joseph Ferdinand (1889–1957), American author and Greenwich Village Bohemian. Gould was descended from a distinguished New England family. He graduated from Harvard magna cum laude in 1911, in the same class with Conrad Aiken, T. S. Eliot, and Walter Lippmann. While living in New York in 1917 Gould decided to give up gainful employment and live in Greenwich Village on the charity of others. He began composing—or ostensibly composing—his "Oral History," a massive compilation of his thoughts, observations, and quotations overheard in the streets, bars, shops, and residences of lower Manhattan. In the early 1920s Gould became acquainted with E. E. Cummings, who told Pound about Gould. Between 1929 and 1931 portions of the "Oral History" appeared in the *Dial,* the *Exile, Broom,* the *Little Review,* and *Pagany.* The extract Pound published in the *Exile* (no. 2), began, "When I told Estlin Cummings that Edward Nagle had asked me to write a chapter on art, he nearly wrote it for me. He said, 'You can say, "Art consists in bumming cigarettes. A person who gives me a cigarette is an aesthete. There are no aesthetes in America. It is a very Philistine country."' In a way I would agree with Cummings that art is essentially the expression of personality." Although Gould claimed to have written millions of words in his notebooks, few of them turned up after his death. Joseph Mitchell believes Gould wrote only a few portions of the "Oral History." Mitchell's accounts of Joe Gould are collected in *Joe Gould's Secret* (New York: Viking, 1965). This was reprinted as part of Mitchell's *Up in the Old Hotel* (New York: Pantheon, 1992). Cummings painted Gould's portrait, wrote a poem about him ("little joe gould has lost his teeth and doesn't know where"), and provided him with fifty cents daily.

Hesse, Eva (b. 1925), German literary scholar and translator. Editor and translator of *E. E. Cummings: Poems—Gedichte* (Munich: Langewiesche-Brandt, 1958, 1982, 1991, 1993, expanded edition 1994). Her interest in Pound's poetry began quite early. On 1 June 1950, her radio script "Gegen die Strömung der Zeit: Der Fall Ezra Pound," was broadcast by the Munich station of the Bavarian Broadcasting Corporation. When she began corresponding with Pound in August 1950, she sent him the text of this speech along with some translations she had made of his poems. She has since written and edited numerous books and articles on Pound, including *New Approaches to Ezra Pound* (Berkeley and Los Angeles: University of California Press, 1969), *Ezra Pound: Von Sinn und Wahnsinn* (Munich: Kindler Verlag, 1978), and *Die Achse Avantgarde* (Zurich: Ache Verlag, 1991). She is a senior editor of the journal of Pound studies, *Paideuma.*

Kirstein, Lincoln (1907–96), American author and ballet promoter. While still a student at Harvard, Kirstein founded and edited the *Hound and Horn* (1927–34). His early admiration for Pound is reflected in the title of his periodical; it was taken from lines in Pound's poem "The White Stag." Cantos 28–30 were published in the April–June 1930 issue. But relations between Kirstein and Pound were strained. In "Crane and Carlsen: A Memoir," *Raritan,* vol. 1, no. 3 (winter

1982), Kirstein recalls the founding of *Hound and Horn* and the fact that "Pound wrote us almost weekly tyrannical letters." After Kirstein moved to Greenwich Village in 1930, he became a friend and admirer of Cummings. Kirstein published poems by Cummings and two excerpts from *Eimi* in *Hound and Horn*. In 1933 Kirstein commissioned Cummings to write a libretto for a ballet, although the dedication to Cummings's *Tom* (1935) indicates it was Marion Morehouse, not Kirstein, who suggested *Uncle Tom's Cabin* as a basis for the libretto. By December 1934, Kirstein told Cummings that his ballet company would not produce *Tom*. This ended the friendship between Kirstein and Cummings.

Laughlin, James (b. 1914), American publisher and poet. Laughlin wrote to Pound in the summer of 1933, when Laughlin was touring Europe before returning to his undergraduate studies at Harvard. He briefly visited Pound in Rapallo that August, then returned for a two-month stay in late 1934. At Pound's urging, Laughlin went back to the United States to take up publishing. In 1936, Laughlin founded the publishing house of New Directions. It soon began publishing Pound's works and continues to do so. One of the first publications issued by New Directions was *New Directions in Prose and Poetry, 1936,* which included a canto by Pound and three poems by Cummings. In *New Directions in Prose and Poetry, 1936 (A Retrospective Selection)* (New York: New Directions, 1986), Laughlin recalls the importance of Cummings's poems to him ("they electrified my youth") and fondly recalls having tea with Cummings and Marion Morehouse at 4 Patchin Place.

Mullins, Eustace (b. 1923), American writer and lecturer. Mullins first met Pound in November 1949, when Mullins was a student at the Institute of Contemporary Arts in Washington, D.C. He was introduced to the poet by Polly and Rudd Fleming, then teachers at the institute. Mullins became a regular visitor. At Pound's request, Mullins began investigating the history of the Federal Reserve System. The results were published by John Kasper and David Horton in 1952 under the title, *Mullins on the Federal Reserve*. A revised and expanded edition was published in 1993 *(Secrets of the Federal Reserve)*. Mullins's biography of Pound, *This Difficult Individual, Ezra Pound* was published in 1961. In the mid-1950s Mullins lived in New York City and frequently visited Cummings and Marion Morehouse. He also corresponded with them when he moved away, keeping in touch with them into the early 1960s.

Norman, Charles (b. 1904), American poet and biographer. Samuel Jacobs, the designer of Cummings's early books, introduced Norman to Cummings in 1925. Norman became a frequent visitor to 4 Patchin Place and also to Joy Farm. In 1945, when Norman was working for the newspaper *PM,* he wrote "The Case for and against Ezra Pound," which featured comments solicited from notable authors, including Cummings. In 1958, Norman published the first biography of Cummings, *The Magic-Maker, E. E. Cummings.* His introduction began, "I have written this book because I believe E. E. Cummings to be one of the truly great creators of our time, in poetry, prose and paint." Two years later, Norman's *Ezra Pound* appeared, the first biography of Pound, in which he noted that "Pound is not merely a poet—he has been for half a century the teacher and protector of other poets, and not merely other poets but the greatest poets of his age." Norman's autobiography, *Poets and People* (1972) offers further insights into Cummings, Marion Morehouse, and Norman's long relationship with them.

Pound, Omar Shakespear (b. 1926), translator, scholar, and lecturer. Raised in England by his grandmother, Olivia Shakespear, he had little contact with his father for his first twenty years, except for a visit to London in 1938. As an American citizen, he volunteered for the U.S. Army from the United Kingdom, and served in the Army of Occupation in Bremen. After being discharged he went to Hamilton College. While living in Washington, D.C., and during vacations he visited his father daily. From time to time he visited Estlin and Marion at Patchin Place and at Joy Farm, where Marion did several photographs of him and Estlin painted his portrait in oils in August 1948. The Cummings papers at the Houghton Library contain an extensive file of cards and letters from Omar.

Williams, William Carlos (1883–1963), American poet and physician. Williams's early recollections of Pound are recorded in his *Autobiography* (1951). Pound was also often the subject of other prose works by Williams, such as "Excerpts from a Critical Sketch" (1931), "Pound's Eleven New 'Cantos'" (1935), and "The Fistula of the Law" (1949). The relationship between Pound and Williams is most fully documented in Paul Mariani's *William Carlos Williams: A New World Naked* (1981). Cummings and Williams first met in Manhattan some time during the 1920s and became friends. Over the course of his career, Williams wrote several reviews of Cummings's work; the most important essay by Williams on Cummings is "Lower Case Cummings" (1946). Cummings never wrote about Williams, but in a letter to his daughter, Nancy, he remarked, "the only poem of Doctor WCWilliams—someone whom the undersigned should respect,since he(WCW)(too)received the Dial Award—which ever truly pleased me as a poem should(from finish to start & vv)is one affectionately concerning a red wh-b" (*Selected Letters*, 214). There was an estrangement between Williams and Cummings in the late 1950s.

Appendix
"E. E. Cummings"
by Edmondo Dodsworth
(*Broletto*, November 1938)

Harcourt Brace and Company of New York has recently published the complete poems of E. E. Cummings, putting them within reach of those who are interested in what is more characteristic of modern poetry.

The book is 315 pages long. It is possible, nonetheless, to do summary justice even in a short review, because every few pages we come across lines of this power:

> . . . . (slenderly wholly
> rising, herself uprearing wholly slowly,
> lean in the hips, and her sails filled with dream
> when on a green brief gesture of twilight
> trembles the imagined galleon of Spring). . . .
>
> (pag. 84)

> . . . . if I should sleep with a lady called death
> got another man with firmer lips
> to take your new mouth in his teeth. . . .
>
> (pag. 94)

> . . . . tremble (not knowing how much better
> than me will you like the rain's face and
> the rich improbable hands of the Wind). . . .
>
> (pag. 95)

Indeed, the only way to know a poet is to read him with unconditional sympathy, *making ourselves one with the poet* as he was in the moment of creation. The most accomplished literary critic cannot accomplish such a miracle because there is an incommensurability between the infinite and the finite, between the unit of the concrete and the plurality of the abstract, although that abstract tries hard to make itself intelligent and comprehensible.

If it wasn't like this, the poet would be useless and criticism would be sufficient. What is given to us is—in theory—to classify and define; but in practice we must develop a kindred mind to get in touch with the author.

Classifying E. E. Cummings

As a basis for classification, let us consider three points:

1) The logical world in which the "normal man" moves (or believes he moves) is very far from being the whole truth; it is nothing but a narrow space which consists only of a system of abstractions (whether technical or social) evoked and maintained for reasons of practical convenience. From a poetical point of view, this world is by definition *the acme of realities.*
2) As a consequence, the supreme task of poetry is to destroy and overcome such reality in favor of something much deeper and more vital.
3) The methods by which this is done are various in nature and can be classified.

Let us, for the moment, put aside such classification (which is of the greatest importance to "place" our author) and translate some sentences from the preface to show how this antagonism between the poetic world (real) and the common world (unreal) is fully conscious in Cummings.

"The poems to come are for you and for me and not for mostpeople."

"—it's no use trying to pretend that mostpeople and ourselves are alike. Mostpeople have less in common with ourselves than the squarerootofminusone. You and I are human beings;mostpeople are snobs."

"you and I are not snobs. We can never be born enough. We are human beings;for whom birth is a supremely welcome mystery,the mystery which happens only and whenever we are faithful to ourselves."

Let us now return to our third point: the diversity of the methods used to overcome the illusory world of practicality. Mine will not be a complete list, but a simple statement of the main tendency going in this direction.

a) The method of allusion (symbolism, in part surrealism): the logical-practical world is accepted, but surrounded by a magic that deforms its sense and absorbs its value (Poe, Villiers de l'Isle Adams, Mallarmé, etc.).
b) The method of idealization. In the abstract world of logical-practical experience, a *further reduction* takes place, but in a spiritual sense, which is no longer materialistic. All this with some detriment to the richness of

life (the quantitative element) but with the advantage of "intensity and purity" (through the suppression of heterogeneous elements): Shelley, Dante of the "Vita Nuova," Guido Cavalcanti, the poets of the Dolce stil Nuovo, etc.

c) The synthetic method of reduction, decomposition and recomposition in new types (which are not richer than the real, practical world from which we have moved, since they contain the same elements, or even a smaller number of them): fantastic literature; Gerard de Nerval, Poe in part, Hoffmann, Bontempelli, etc.

It is pointless to say that here we are dealing with purely ideal "types of escape" and that in concrete reality they and what I am going to deal with separately (because of its importance) may be found—indeed are found—in the same writers. Therefore, only the preponderance of one or the other will allow us to classify [a writer as belonging] more in this category or in another.

The Destroyers of Perspective and the Authors of Books

I apologize for using a term I have already used in another article on contemporary Anglo-American letters.

I was referring to Ezra Pound, T. S. Eliot, James Joyce, Ernest Hemingway, Richard Aldington and others, and also to avant-garde journals: the *Dial* (no longer published) and the *Hound and Horn*. And now I also include Cummings.

All these authors, to whom we need to add the Italian and French Futurists, must be considered in a separate category, because their technique in its distinctive features is completely different from the techniques considered hitherto in criticism. And the difference is as follows: those were techniques either not inclusive or actually more inclusive; this is *an inclusive* technique. In it, the content of material reality, carnal and brutal, is *greater* not *smaller*. But from this brutality springs up such an intense idealism that, in comparison, the transparency of the other artistic transfiguration looks almost like a blindness.

One recalls Saint Francis of Assisi kissing the sores of the lepers and changing them into light. Women here are real: they have bowels, uteruses, senses, blood, life. They are not an amorphous mass of flesh, trans-human, but an anatomic organism. And men stink of sweat, tobacco, whiskey, scum; they swear and are promiscuous. They are commonplace men and worse, and yet from the same exasperation of their realism arises—we don't know how—such a blinding ideality that the eye cannot bear it.

In this way, poetry achieves that justification of everyday realism that neither philosophy nor religion can achieve.

This is the so-called technique that destroys perspectives and causes books to decompose *because perspectives and books are practical abstractions,* while poetic reality "is the pure blind flow of subjective life: the psychological indistinct not yet differentiated by the thoughtful attention which engraves upon its personal universe: Dionysus and the bacchantes against Apollo and the muses."

Sensuality and Poetic Realism

It is natural that such a technique—going down to the roots of human being, where the ego and the non-ego flow together in the same indistinct and massive reality—should encounter, through other means, the analysis of the Freudian unconscious: sex and innocent amorality "of life not yet stained by the spirit."

But both of them show the religious essence as in the orgiastic rites of primitive man. They are therefore extraordinarily poetic, while voluptuous literature is weak and non-poetic (for example, that of the 19th century, because in spite of everything we see it as unrealistic and conventional).

And, as in the rites of primordial races, life and death conjoin in an indissoluble whole, in which life perpetually is born from death and triumphs over it. So it happens in this poetry that *heroism* (which is the active awareness of this inability to tame life) is substantial.

> kumrads die because they're told
> kumrads die before they're old
> (kumrads aren't afraid to die
> kumrads don't
> and kumrads won't
> believe in life) and death knows whie.
>
> all good kumrads you can tell
> by their altruistic smell. . . .
>
> . . . . every kumrad is a bit
> of quite unmitigated hate. . . .
>
> . . . . his laugh is a million griefs wide. . . .

(Poem 251)

Satirical Decomposition of the Bourgeois World

This is simply an aspect of that destruction of perspective I mentioned above. In the face of the bourgeois vision of an essentially *anti-heroic* society (such as it was all over the world in the liberal-democratic period), a fundamentally heroic conception has to reveal itself as the most formidable of corrosives.

. . . . my uncle Sol's farm
failed because the chickens
ate the vegetables so
my Uncle Sol had a
chicken farm till the
skunks ate the chickens when

my Uncle Sol
had a skunk farm but
the skunks caught cold and
died and so
my Uncle Sol imitated the
skunks in a subtle manner
or by drowning himself in the watertank.

. . . . i remember we all cried like the Missouri
when my uncle Sol's coffin lurched because
somebody pressed a button
(and down went
my Uncle Sol
and started a worm farm).

An Essay on Technique in Cummings: "Memorabilia" (Poem 138).

It is about Venice (compare this to Ruskin and the
   D'Annunzio of "Il Fuoco").

mine eyes have seen
the glory of
the coming of
the Americans particularly the
brand of marriageable nymph which is
armed with large legs rancid
voices Baedekers, Mothers and kodaks. . . .

. . . . i do Signore
affirm that all gondola Signore
day below me gondola Signore gondola
and above me pass loudly and gondola
rapidly denizens of Omaha Altoona or what
not enthusiastic cohorts from Duluth God only

> gondola knows Cincingondolanati i gondola don't
> —the substantial dollarbringing virgins.

The way the poet proceeds is quite clear: the usual absence of punctuation, a special typographic arrangement of the words, and in the last part the obsessive phrase, "gondola signore gondola," which interrupts and breaks the coherence of the logic that would otherwise be perfectly grammatical. To realize this, it is enough to suppress the phrase. All this is not bizarre, but *photographically*— indeed *cinematographically*—real if we refer to the true reality (those immediate data of consciousness analyzed with such subtlety by Bergson). In them, in fact, reality is like a mixture, a superimposition, mutual and chaotic, with violence of memories, impressions, sensations, impulses, whose punctuation and syntax are a fracturing network. This reality happens according to a logic totally alien to the interests of "economic man."

To have realized and to have expressed *untamed lyricism* is the unquestionable merit of schools that had different names, founders and development. But the spirit was in common.

From these schools was born a great poetry, and Cummings is one of its most vital representatives.

Index